Palgrave Studies in Urban Anthropology

Series Editors
Italo Pardo
School of Anthropology and Conservation
University of Kent
Canterbury, Kent, UK

Giuliana B. Prato
School of Anthropology and Conservation
University of Kent
Canterbury, Kent, UK

Half of humanity lives in towns and cities and that proportion is expected to increase in the coming decades. Society, both Western and non-Western, is fast becoming urban and mega-urban as existing cities and a growing number of smaller towns are set on a path of demographic and spatial expansion. Given the disciplinary commitment to an empirically-based analysis, anthropology has a unique contribution to make to our understanding of our evolving urban world. It is in such a belief that we have established the Palgrave Studies in Urban Anthropology series. In the awareness of the unique contribution that ethnography offers for a better theoretical and practical grasp of our rapidly changing and increasingly complex cities, the series will seek high-quality contributions from anthropologists and other social scientists, such as geographers, political scientists, sociologists and others, engaged in empirical research in diverse ethnographic settings. Proposed topics should set the agenda concerning new debates and chart new theoretical directions, encouraging reflection on the significance of the anthropological paradigm in urban research and its centrality to mainstream academic debates and to society more broadly. The series aims to promote critical scholarship in international anthropology. Volumes published in the series should address theoretical and methodological issues, showing the relevance of ethnographic research in understanding the socio-cultural, demographic, economic and geo-political changes of contemporary society.

More information about this series at
http://www.palgrave.com/gp/series/14573

Manos Spyridakis
Editor

Market Versus Society

Anthropological Insights

Editor
Manos Spyridakis
Department of Social and Educational
  Policy
University of the Peloponnese
Corinth, Greece

Palgrave Studies in Urban Anthropology
ISBN 978-3-030-08931-3   ISBN 978-3-319-74189-5   (eBook)
https://doi.org/10.1007/978-3-319-74189-5

Cover design: Jenny Vong

Printed on acid-free paper

This Palgrave Macmillan imprint is published by the registered company Springer
International Publishing AG part of Springer Nature
The registered company address is: Gewerbestrasse 11, 6330 Cham, Switzerland

Acknowledgements

Looking back over the people who played a role in shaping this book my first and great debt is to Dr. Italo Pardo and Dr. Giuliana Prato whose permanent encouragement and assistance was and is always inestimable. I also feel indebted to the peer reviewers whose insightful remarks improved the content of the texts as well as to Dr. Michael Christodoulou for commenting critically on several versions of them. The idea of this book matured during the annual conference of the Commission on Urban Anthropology on '*Market versus Society. Human principles and economic rationale in changing times*', that was held at the University of the Peloponnese in 2011. Several chapters in this volume are revised and expanded versions of papers that were presented at that conference. I finally thank the authors for the originality of their texts and their willingness to contribute to this spiritual effort. Of course it is necessary to add the usual rider that the responsibility for the contents of this book rests entirely with the editor.

Sitia-Crete, Greece
2017

Contents

CHAPTER 1

Introduction

Manos Spyridakis

After the disastrous economic crisis in 1929, John Maynard Keynes delivered a lecture extolling optimism in the certainty that capitalism will make us all happy by meeting all our seemingly insatiable needs. Believing in the miraculous power of human will, Keynes put forward the view that the intensification and development of productivity will be the decisive factor in the satisfaction of human needs, leading to the next significant step in human development—going from meeting material toward spiritual necessities. As he describes the way the crisis was seen by pessimists neglecting to see the seeds of future prosperity it theoretically conveyed:

> For the moment the very rapidity of these changes is hurting us and bringing difficult problems to solve. Those countries are suffering relatively which are not in the vanguard of progress. We are being afflicted with a new disease of which some readers may not yet have heard the name, but of which they will hear a great deal in the years to come, namely, *technological unemployment*. This means unemployment due to our discovery of means of economising the use of labour outrunning the pace at which we can find new uses for labour. But this is only a temporary phase of

M. Spyridakis (✉)
Department of Social and Educational Policy,
University of the Peloponnese, Corinth, Greece

© The Author(s) 2018
M. Spyridakis (ed.), *Market Versus Society*, Palgrave Studies in Urban Anthropology, https://doi.org/10.1007/978-3-319-74189-5_1

1

maladjustment. All this means in the long run *that mankind is solving its economic problem*. I would predict that the standard of life in progressive countries one hundred years hence will be between four and eight times as high as it is today. There would be nothing surprising in this even in the light of our present knowledge. It would not be foolish to contemplate the possibility of afar greater progress still. (Keynes 1963)

Throughout the lecture, which appeared in literary form in 1930 titled *Economic Possibilities for our grandchildren*, Keynes argues, in essence, that after one hundred years peoples' lives will be improved. No doubt there is no more convincing counterargument to Keynes' over optimism than history itself, which is full of economic disasters, inequalities and catastrophic consequences for ordinary people, including the current crisis. The problem with Keynes' assertion is that it takes the capitalist economy as having a built-in virtue for self recovery, as if this system has an intrinsic dynamic toward welfare. Hence Keynes meets those conventional economists who falsely believe that as material prosperity increases people will search for personal satisfaction and happiness in the non-material aspects of life. Yet, this dream has not been empirically confirmed. As De Grauwe believes, capitalism keeps on shifting the critical point where people will be satisfied while at the same time it is doubtful exactly what people mean by material satisfaction. In addition, as productivity relies mainly upon technological innovations, such as the current digital one, it is worth mentioning that there is little observable effect on growth statistics especially after 1990s (De Grauwe 2017). The main reason is the dolorous combination of productivity and unemployment. The increase of the first takes place on a spatiotemporal era in which permanent low growth is marked by acute economic fragility and companies profiting from joblessness. Consider, for instance, the NAFTA agreement in 1993 between the United States, Mexico and Canada, which on paper intended to make true globalisation's bright side; that is, investment and development. As Dowd has shown, however, this agreement was but a free pass for the recreation of the dark satanic mills of the industrial revolution. Mexican workers got under two dollars wage per hour, products' prices, mainly cars, rose significantly in US and by 1999, 316,000 jobs were lost due to trade and investments effects (Dowd 2004: 203). As a matter of fact, globalisation entailed a steady tendency to uncertainty and to de-fixation of the supposed solid social and economic structures of the past along with the augmentation of inequalities and poverty. Thus, according to Bauman:

> The International Labour Organization estimates that 3 billion people are now living below the poverty line, set at US$2 per day. John Galbraith, in the preface to the Human Development Report of the United Nations in 1998, documented that 20 percent of the world's population cornered 86 percent of all goods and services produced worldwide, while the poorest 20 percent of them consumed only 1.3 percent; whereas today, after nearly 15 years, these figures have gone from bad to worse: the richest 20 percent of the population consume 90 percent of the goods produced, while the poorest 20 percent consume one percent. It is also estimated that 40 percent of the world's wealth is owned by one percent of the world population, while the 20 richest people in the world have resources equal to those of the billion poorest. (Bauman 2017: 87)

It seems then that these old sayings had accurately described the inner logic of the capitalist movement: 'Constant revolutionising of production, uninterrupted disturbance of all social conditions, everlasting uncertainty and agitation distinguish the bourgeois epoch from all earlier ones. All fixed, fast frozen relations, with their train of ancient and venerable prejudices and opinions, are swept away, all new formed ones become antiquated before they can ossify. All that is solid melts into air, all that is holy is profaned, and man is at last compelled to face with sober senses his real conditions of life, and his relations with his kind. The need of a constantly expanding market for its products chases the bourgeoisie over the entire surface of the globe. It must nestle everywhere, settle everywhere, establish connexions everywhere' (Marx and Engels 1967: 83).

As argued elsewhere (Spyridakis 2013), within a neoliberally oriented context favouring adverse social incorporation, deregulated labour relations and massive layoffs, contemporary people experience the gradual disappearance of standard aspects of life and the advent of its insecure forms as well as the emergence of vulnerable social relationships (Castel 2000), threatening both their material survival and life trajectories. Caught in a situation defined by distant economic power structures and pedagogic political technologies that advocate less social protection for the market's invisible hand, vulnerable people, being de-unionised and unable to forge a 'class in itself' solidarity, become powerless to defend themselves and are unwittingly lead to a grey area regarding their work identity and life trajectory (Spyridakis 2017b). As neoliberalism has become the dominant policy paradigm, its main philosophy being guided by a teleological faith in the assumption that unfettered markets distribute goods, services and happiness more efficiently (Durrenberger 2017), vulnerable people are not just found in the middle of the complex relation between the local and the global but they also experience its devastating effects on structural adjustment programs entailing increased poverty and restrictions on public spending. From an anthropological point of view Paul Durrenberger and Judith Martí's work has shown the negative burdens this paradigm's philosophy has brought upon the disadvantaged and the underprivileged. They make clear that the first victims of this philosophy are social services as well as the more vulnerable members of society, like women and children, to the benefit of multinational corporations looking for a flexible, docile and cheap labour supply, despite their well polished rhetoric (Durrenberger and Martí 2006: 12–16). Without doubt profit accumulation through human labour exploitation is not a new phenomenon in the history of capitalism; however, its recent expression connotes clear cut dissociations from the post-World War II social contract.

So, along with the ironic repetition of history, people today find themselves experiencing a new form of the Enclosures Act, which makes the weak weaker and even more vulnerable to unpredicted economic externalities. One such example is the mortgage lending process in the United States, which began in 2007 and which eventually led to a burst bubble, causing problems of liquidity and solvency for banks— leading either to their collapse or to the edge of it and spreading like an infectious disease to Europe. This insecure condition, which as Michel Aglietta very convincingly argues is an inherent and for this reason a permanent component of capitalism (Aglietta 2008), has been described and analysed as a financialisation crisis, producing the so-called financial expropriation of unsuspecting people.

This financialisation crisis should be read against the background of three interrelated processes. The first, according to Lapavitsas, refers to, as already mentioned, the relation between productivity and growth, which has been problematic especially from the 1970s to the 1990s. New technologies did not contribute to the improvement in this area; their role still remains unclear. The second concerns the transformation of work. Casual and flexible labour arrangements have concertedly entailed the intensification of work rhythm and the lowering of wages, both of which are associated with augmenting workers' dissatisfaction as well as with forced employment choices. The third is about global production and trade, which have been dominated by multinational enterprises. This condition has been accompanied by a movement away from the West towards the ex-capitalist periphery, mainly China (Lapavitsas 2012: 27). The combination of these processes provided the background against which financialisation blossomed on an almost global scale, particularly since the late 1970s, the most important consequence being the emergence of the financial expropriation of ordinary people. Briefly put, banks, due to the narrowing of their profit margins, began to use personal revenues of their clients as a profit-making mechanism through investment banking functions. This shift resulted in the increasing involvement of many people to the unknown world of financial mechanisms in order to face basic needs such as housing, health, education and old age security. It is in this connection that banks could extract sound amounts of profit from wages, salaries and people's savings. And, as Lapavitsas stresses, this process should be differentiated from the exploitation taking place in production process and which no doubt is the cornerstone of the contemporary capitalist economy. Financial expropriation is an additional source of profit occurring in the sphere of circulation (Lapavitsas 2012: 31). In this sphere of activity, transactions involve the exchange of promises and obligations mediated through loanable capital destined to meet basic needs in the light of limited social provisions. Individuals in one way or another have been increasingly directed to rely on financial organizations to improve their living conditions and to satisfy personal interests.

Using more anthropological terms, Gudeman notes that the contemporary market economy dominates the house economy in ideological and material terms. Irrespective of location and size—being either in the margins of small scale economies or at the center of developed market systems—the house subsidizes the markets. In this light, 'The abstraction of economic relations from the material world ascends from the house through the commercial sphere of goods and services, to the financial sphere where money is exchanged for money (over time), to the meta financial circuit that uses calculations of risk taking to secure money' (Gudeman 2016: 3–4). This arrangement is part of what Gudeman considers as being the ingredients of the contemporary market, which for him consists of three spheres: the commercial one, which is made up of goods and services; the financial one consisting of money transactions by commercial banks, insurance firms, mortgage companies, pension funds and national banks and; as mentioned, the meta-financial, which is based on the calculation of risk and exchanged as derivative (Gudeman 2016: 19).

While setting aside the phase of contemporary Viking capitalism (Durrenberger and Erem 2010: 279), it should be always remembered that we refer to a cruel system of exploitation, either in the realm of production or in circulation. From this point of view, it seems reasonable to conclude that capitalism expands itself by promoting and imposing the market logic everywhere and by all available means. However, although its decentralized character is attractive and even operational to companies, to consumers and to entrepreneurs, there is much dissatisfaction and opposition to the system and even to the culture it represents. The basis of this dissatisfaction can be traced to the core cultural condition upon which this system is founded: the priority of satisfaction of self interest as a means to meet society's primary and secondary needs, which is inherently paradoxical and irrational, as anthropologists have already revealed. As Godelier has shown, the 'visible' structure of the system has been incorporated into the theory along with the driving force of it, the maximization of capitalist profit which in turn is treated as the personification of social structures and functions. From then on any inequality in the realm of production and circulation has been legitimated and taken to express the 'just remuneration of different functions and factors' (Godelier 1972: 47). In this light, conventional supporters of this system should struggle to prove how it is possible to bring together in theoretical terms the rational maximiser or else, the winner-takes-all figure with social welfare and supposed social harmony. Efforts taken to construct theories with a social angle aroma like, human capital, game theory or even the economics of happiness, to mention but a few, are not very convincing as that they take for granted that economy is a neutral and value-free system while at the same time neglecting to understand that ordinary people cannot make any significant decisions in this system and, as Durrenberger and Erem claim, 'nothing they can say or decide or think has anything to do with how it operates' (Durrenberger and Erem 2010: 269). Besides, the notions of perfect competition, of system equilibrium, of perfect information, of perfect decision-making as well as of perfect forecasting as aspects of the rational decision-maker are still to be proved empirically. Paul De Grauwe shows very aptly that these theoretical perfectology constructions are far away from reality, as real people in real life are not value-free agents and while their decisions are rational, they are seen in social terms (De Grauwe 2017: 84).

In this connection, as I have argued (Spyridakis 2013), Jane Schneider has already shown that the anthropological enquiry regarding the relation between free-market culture and rational behaviour has been based on a set of ethnocentric principles associated with market-mediated laws and institutional adjustments such as: (1) All humans will be driven by an inherent impetus towards rational decision making in a sea of opportunities offered by markets to maximise their gains, (2) As markets stand for progress and advancement they should be allowed to exist without dysfunctional regulations and obstacles, (3) Unhampered markets will lead to human happiness for all social strata, and (4) Social inequality between the haves and the have nots is a temporary condition attributable mostly to the unworthiness of the have nots (Schneider 2002: 64). In the context of a constantly spreading marketisation, not only of Polanyi's three classics (land, labour and the money) (Kjaerluff 2015), but of knowledge as well (Burawoy 2014), some argue for a universal human capability of benefits maximizing and cost minimizing whereas others argue that market culture is a kind of capitalistic straightjacket indifferent to cultural diversity and hence to other forms of rationalities. As this issue concerns the origins of human choices in a seemingly homogenizing world (Prato 2009: 15), anthropological reflection calls for the empirical testing of those models in order to interpret and understand these choices. As with De Grauwe (2017), Richard Wilk and Lisa Cliggett argue that the extreme poles of total rationality and of total irrationality are inadequate for a satisfactory explanation of complex human motives and their consequent practical effects in the real world.

Although what seems rational in one context might seem irrational in another, there exists the possibility of understanding the variety of motives lurking behind their perpetrators by not looking upon them as given and self evident. For these writers, anthropology is in the unique position to combine interpretative models and methodological tools tested through empirical evidence to overpass trapping categorisations, such as those stemming from the rationality debate, and to bring to the fore the polysemic dimensions of human activities (Wilk and Cliggett 2007). Hence, one of the main aims of this book is to show that peoples' attitudes and conceptions are Maussian 'total facts' dialectically informed and mediated by specific social, economic, political and cultural contexts, by what Clammer called an holistic way in seeing economy as related to culture and social structure (Clammer 1985: 11). This condition informs a stasis that in many aspects is the outcome of people's definition of situations that may put their lives in high risk if not actual peril.

This takes place in a context where changes in the international economy after the 1970s—and the ensuing shift towards neoliberalism in the 1980s—brought out a rediscovery of the ideas of Friedrich Hayek. The concept of liberalism was the ideological guise of economic globalisation. The liberalisation of market forces, as an ideological and economic project, imposed a model of compliance through employment flexibility, the minimisation of social security, the fragmentation of social solidarity and the conceptualisation of the economy as money exchanged in the market rather than as an efficient management of resources. In this light, states and policy decision-making are evaluated according to criteria related to the severity of macroeconomic strategies aiming at reducing fiscal deficits and cutting welfare and social benefits. It seems as if Polanyi's claim is being confirmed, that the economy has gained an independent life. Thus, the concepts of economy and society seem to be defined in terms of conflict rather than of harmonious coexistence. As a consequence, social life has become increasingly insecure and individualistic, the natural environment is being destroyed and the markets have changed into arenas of unfair competition and opportunistic speculation, while the unrestricted movement of capital jeopardizes the economic bases of the welfare state internationally and its subsequent ability to sustain full employment policies. For the majority it has become gradually impossible to make the connection between the impersonal market institutions and the reality they experience in their daily lives. As anthropologists have shown, although people try to resist explicitly or implicitly 'self regulating' economic processes, they would appear to play no role in the calculation of economic theory and practice.

If anything, Polanyi's insight was a very sophisticated critique of the unfettered market ideology, the paradigm of utilitarian rationality in particular, as well as of the implied claim that *homo oeconomicus* is the normative prototype model to which all human behavior and action should be fitted in Beckert (1997: 9). His perspective, echoing the Marxist approach of the commodity fetishism, is of utmost importance for the present volume as he problematises the so-called economistic fallacy, the logical error of equating the human economy in general with its market form (Resta 2014: 11) and interpreting human behavior almost exclusively through an economic lens. As Polanyi says:

Economic rationalism appears to achieve both the systematic limitation of reason to scarcity situations and its systematic extension to all human ends and means, thus validating an economistic culture with all the appearances of irresistible logic. The social philosophy erected on such foundations was as radical as it was fantastic. To atomize society and make every individual atom behave according to the principles of economic rationalism would, in a sense, place the whole of human existence, with all its depth and wealth, in the frame of reference of the market, this of course, would not really do individuals have personalities and society has history. (Polanyi 1977: 13–14)

In essence, Polnayi shows that any so-called economic behavior cannot be studied separately of what is happening within society. I don't mean to imply the simple idea that of course even the people thinking in economic terms are part of the society. That would be self evident. His well-timed contribution lies in the fact that economy is a complex social institution comprising a mixture of ideology, culture and political decision-making. According to Dale, 'It is misleading to suggest that Polanyi's analysis divides social life in market society into reified spheres; his point concerns, rather, the separate institutionalization of economic and political activity' (Dale 2010: 198).

Indeed, as far as the current crisis is concerned, especially with an exemplary regard to what is going on in the European Union (EU), one could support the view that it is mainly the result of the strict division of the economic and political spheres, the first taking the priority over the latter. Although on surface political decision-making seems to play a secondary role regarding EU's economic policy, in essence austerity programmes and antisocial neoliberal measures come from countless remote Eurogroup meetings, which paradoxically enough as an administrative unit is not accountable to EU law! From another point of view, this condition sheds light on the level of democratic decision-making in the EU, a fact that, once more, has already been made by Polanyi, as he was very much concerned about the fact that, as soon as economic logic becomes an autonomous mechanism, then democracy is in danger.

Suffice it to say that in broad terms the current Eurozone crisis is seen as the result of a Union that is economically integrated but politically fragmented (Holmes 2014: 582). In this light, the economy as a separate and remote entity from society and even beyond democratic decision-making, becomes day by day so obvious and worryingly given.

Under the cloak of scientific neutrality and of deliberately complex terminology (needing to be deciphered by ordinary people), governments' decision-making is dominated by the so called experts, who construct deductive models for foreseeing the market's inner 'psychology'. However, such models do not really work because of their limited analytical penetration and their inadequacy in taking into account social conditions (Lawson 2009). At the same time this decision-making is colonized by international organizations detached from other dimensions of ordinary life at the expense of people's welfare, thus recalling Stiglitz's idea, 'That economists, like doctors, have much to learn from pathology: we see more clearly in these unusual events [crises] how the economy really functions' (Stiglitz 2009: 293). One has but to look at recent developments in the European South, where in Greece, for instance, in 2011 the ex vice president of the European Central Bank has been imposed as a prime minister without being elected. In neighboring Italy a similar story has been going on since 2011 as well, the only difference being that elections are still expected! Hence, as Earle, Moran and Ward-Perkins observe, the issue is not to argue for the preference of one or another economic route but, 'To show that citizens are unaware that decisions with political consequences are being made, decisions that directly concern themselves and society, and that they have little knowledge of these decisions and no control over them' (Earle et al. 2017: 23).

To the extent that the gaps between the rich and the poor are at an all time high because an international powerful elite amasses the wealth while more than half of humanity is left out (Ong 1999: 11; Wacquant 2009: 5), this volume aims at exploring, in both anthropological and ethnographic terms, the mechanisms of contemporary neoliberal market functioning and its insecurity derivatives as well as to bring to the fore how this condition is experienced by ordinary people. Keeping in mind that much of our lives are dependent and defined by the wider economic structure, the theoretical approaches and case studies assembled here illustrate that while a complex international form of social coordination exists (Pérez-Díaz 2009), there is a great strain between those who hold the power to manipulate the strings of the deliberately vague markets, thus accumulating wealth and sociocultural status and those who incessantly struggle while trying to make their daily living. Indeed, it seems that currently, perhaps more than ever, an impersonal market operates against society in the sense that two separate mindsets and ways of behaving are almost antithetical (Hornborg 2005: 70). In this context, rather than looking at the much criticized and indeed poor, if not super-stitious, idea of rational choice—which in times of crisis it seems doubt-ful to act in that way (Carrier 1997: 12)—contributors seek to explore the ways in which peoples' agency has the possibility (or not) to create the preconditions needed for the management of their existence (Pardo 1996) in the context of the daily duties they must accomplish.

As the logic of market regime seems to disrupt and reframe social rela-tions and values to the point that some argue about the individualisation of the social (Bezanson 2006: 32), the chapters also explore the com-plex relation between the commodification and the de-commodification of people's crucial life aspects for their social reproduction. Although this term is rather confusing, here it is understood as a dynamic pro-cess where power-laden class relations, mediated by gender aspects, the relation to the state and the labour market, reflect and define people's access to resources, income or money in order to make their lives pos-sible in material and immaterial terms; in other words, social, emotional or physical (Picchio 1992; Narotzky 1997; Bezanson 2006). As the pro-tagonists of this volume are ordinary people in the first place, contrib-utors attempt, both empirically and theoretically, to explore the extent to which they accept the unequal allocation of resources and their over-all sense of belonging in the same boat. In this light the volume seeks to make sense of contemporary peoples' double movement, understood here as a dynamic, open and progressive project of grassroots political economy encompassing daily labour routines, limits to neoliberalism's logic (Greenhouse 2010), coping strategies and struggles, either overt or hidden, against the conditions of uncertainty and risk coming from poli-cies imposed either by remote power structures or by the invisible market hand.

All the contributors of the present volume are social anthropolo-gists whose work, based on systematic and continuous ethnographic inquiry, is focused on western settings and touch upon aspects con-cerning the volatile relation between society and economy. Some of them participated in the 2011 conference of the International Union of Anthropological and Ethnological Sciences (IUAES), held in Corinth-Greece and co-organized by the Department of Social and Educational Policy of the University of the Peloponnese and the Commission on Urban Anthropology (CUA). In the following essays the tension between market and society point to a constant condition of uncer-tainty as a lived experience for the many in a post-Keynesian and de-industrialised framework, at the same time undertaking a steady course of de-standardisation, coupled with feelings of ambiguity and bewilderment for their future (Spyridakis 2017a). This book attempts to bring to the fore the way ordinary people conceive this situation through their ethnographic voices against the antisocial background of the current economic recession as well as to critically contribute to the relevant anthropologically informed analysis (Carrier 1997; Hann and Hart 2009; Greenhouse 2010; Hart 2015). As such, it holds the view that what is distinctly anthropological today is the engagement with the constant effort to reveal the suffering of the ostensibly silenced other.

Volume Presentation

The book includes an introduction and sixteen chapters focusing on the uneasy relation between market and society. James Carrier's chapter presents a framework for approaching economic deviance, activity that people take to be wrong even if it is not criminal. He does not approach deviance in terms of individuals who do wrong but in terms of social factors that can be expected to affect the likelihood that people will act in deviant ways. The social factors at issue are those associated with neoliberal reform, a widespread set of policies that reduced government spending on social services, extended market activity and reduced oversight of market actors. The chapter suggests that those reforms are likely to lead to increased petty corruption by the poor to secure social services from underfunded providers, and increased fraudulent activity by the rich and firms because of decreasing oversight. Also, by drawing a parallel between neoliberal reform and the liberalisation of the English economy late in the eighteenth century as described by E. P. Thompson, he argues that economic deviance can be seen fruitfully in terms of the distinction between economic and social values, and that neoliberal reform was a strengthening of the economic over the social.

Alf Hornborg's chapter draws on Karl Polanyi's insights on market logic and David Graeber's analyses of debt to apply a critical perspective on the very artifact of (general purpose) money. Following a momentary concession to the approach of Bruno Latour and Actor Network Theory, Hornborg suggests that the insidious trajectories of human ideas traced by Polanyi and Graeber—and more generally by Marx—are generated by the artifact of money itself. The notion that a particular form of artifact could bear responsibility for global exploitation, ecological degradation, and financial crises continues to be alien to mainstream social science, as it evidently was to Marx (his insights on fetishism notwithstanding), Polanyi, and even Graeber. Yet the structural logic following from the use of conventional money inexorably generates disastrous social and ecological consequences precisely for the three commodities that Polanyi deemed fictitious: labour, land and money. Given the apparent incapacity of society at any conceivable scale—from Robert Owen's communities to nations committed to social democracy—to remedy increasing economic inequalities, ecological degradation, and financial vulnerability, the only remaining hope hinges on our capacity to identify money itself as the source of all these evils, and consequently to critically rethink the idea of universal commensurability. Any vision of a just, sustainable, and resilient (post) capitalism that does not question the artifact of money itself is a contradiction in terms.

Italo Pardo supports the view that classical liberalism advocates the individual's entrepreneurial role in the political, cultural and economic development of the broader society, arguing for minimum state intervention to give people an opportunity to develop their potentialities and improve their social position, thus benefiting society. He argues that, to grapple with this key point, a sophisticated analysis needs to address the complex ways in which agency is capable of influencing the system. His Naples ethnography collected, in classic anthropological fashion through the study of documentary sources and an application of the tried and tested methods of participant observation (open-ended unstructured and structured interviews) and the construction of case studies of people, circumstances and events, emphasized the significance of *strong continuous interaction* between the material and the nonmaterial in people's lives. Pardo highlights significant ways in which political instrumentalism frustrates entrepreneurialism, encourages exclusion, fuels strong feeling of injustice and defines the relation between political responsibility and citizenship. His Naples ethnography strongly suggests that power which lacks authority because it lacks recognition of legitimacy at the grassroots undermines trust and seriously jeopardises the relationship between citizenship and governance and, therefore, democracy.

Giuliana B. Prato addresses the relationship between economic policies and political ideologies. Drawing on contemporary and historical evidence from anthropological fieldwork in the province of Brindisi, Italy, she looks at the influence of vested political interests on the postunification national policies for the development of the South and the post-World War II agreements on the alleged national control of the economy. She examines the effects of the modified Bretton Woods Agreement, whereby deregulation policies should have facilitated the investment of capital in less developed regions. Having addressed Italy's regional divide and the local relevance of the classical anthropological distinction between market place and market principle, she points to the significance of an ethnographically based analysis of the complex relationship between agency and the system, of policies of global restructuring that influence national decision-making and of their effects at the local level. A diachronic view of the situation shows how the new post-Fordist and postindustrial adjustments have resulted in environmental degradation, competition among southern cities and further economic downturn.

Andreas Streinzer's contribution deals with the issue of how market-oriented thinking has proven so resilient in Greece, even during the years of serious recession and austerity. Market-oriented thinking in Greece seems to provide seductive routes for personal achievement and modernist subjectivities as well to criticize Greek politics and the overlapping of friendship, kinship and business practice. The chapter is original in that it does not suggest, as much work on the Greek crisis does, that ordinary lives confront dominant capitalist relations with an Other of solidarity and mutuality. Rather, the author shows how market-oriented thinking pervades everyday interactions and guides normative evaluations of economic relations. Rather than understanding neoliberal market thinking as a coherent set of ideas, the author traces several key aspects of such thought in ethnographic cases from his doctoral fieldwork in Volos, Greece. He concludes that society and market are best understood as crucial notions informing cosmologies of capitalism rather than as sharply defined analytical tools for economic anthropology.

Manos Spyridakis' chapter addresses the issue of precarization as a way of governing those who became vulnerable due to the current economic crisis that hit the global economy and Greece in particular. He argues that these people are treated as second-class citizens since they are denied a range of rights such as equal access to forms of protection and the equal possibility to live with dignity. He describes in detail the background of how the global financial crisis and the neoliberal policies implemented by international organisations such as the International Monetary Fund (IMF) and EU negatively affected the Greek economy and the daily lives of unsuspecting citizens. By analytically using the notion of governmentality, he argues that programs like the Fund for European Aid to the Most Deprived (FEAD), coming from the EU in order to appease social gradations stemming from the vulgar economic policies implemented, are but political technologies for people's subjugation and manipulation. Based on continuing research in Athens among precarious people, he shows how they conceive such programs as well as their reaction to their conditions of existence supporting the view that understanding the precarious other presupposes understanding how it is constructed and managed.

Julia Soul discusses the relationship between the commodification of labour spurred within the neoliberal hegemony and the working class disorganization/reorganization dynamic in Argentina, pointing to changing forms of labour subsumption. Her data are based on an ethnographic study of a group of steel workers from San Nicolás de los Arroyos, the city where SOMISA, Argentina's formerly state-owned steel mill, privatized in 1992, was located. The privatization process is an historical landmark in the workers' experience that profoundly changed the relationship between labour and community. She focuses on the first microfirm that included a union delegate elected by its employees. The ethnographic approach allows for the identification of changing relationships, expectations and values, within which a new working-class generation experience is forged. She argues that, through the reassessing of organizing traditions and their integration in the union, the new working-class generation is part of an uneven and slow process of class reorganization, involving the struggle for the improvement of daily labour relationships.

Fulvia D'Aloisio takes an anthropological view in her analysis of a case of belated industrialisation in Southern Italy, the Fiat factory in Melfi (Basilicata Region). She conducted two periods of fieldwork, the second taking place when Fiat became the new corporation Fiat-Chrysler Automobiles (FCA). The important organisational turn for the Fiat Company, inspired by just-in-time production and the total quality model (the so called Japanese model), has not been able to resolve hard issues such as the weakness of the local workforce, the second-level employment contract with lower wage levels and the asymmetrical relationship between the company and the local government. The development of the factory has passed from the post-Fordist transformation to a new global productive dimension, increasing the insecurity for its workers. D'Aloisio supports the view that workers can be described as actors trying to keep together old and new strategies in order to cope with the crisis as they are engaged in new ways of transforming their employment status, which serve to accomplish productive goals but which result in increasing uncertainty and a sense that they are no longer the protagonists in the new scenario of globalisation.

Gadi Nissim discusses the reaction of labour union stewards to challenges of market fundamentalism at the heyday of neoliberalism, just before the global economic crisis. Based on an ethnographic study of twenty Israeli workers' committees in the private sector conducted from 2007 to 2008, this study reveals that the neoliberal mindset has affected these workers in three ways. First, union stewards often assumed that market rules are universal and determinist. This belief led the committees to accept recovery steps (such as privatization, laying off employees or outsourcing) when they were perceived as essential. Second, workers' committees conceived the business world as their dominant playground. Accordingly, leaders of the committees have begun educating themselves in business administration by acquiring academic degrees or other trainings in the field. Third, workers' committees have initiated alternative solutions, which can be tagged as socialist in their nature; however, they were still articulated in neoliberal terms. The hegemonic order seems dynamic in the sense that it permits opposition as long as it is not strict defiance or are articulated in the terms of the dominant cultural toolkit. It seems that the struggles of workers' committees invite a wider horizon and a new vocabulary to overcome neoliberalism. This direction may be advanced by nurturing a new strata of organic intellectuals that would revitalize the cultural and political vision for social democracy.

Iain Linsday claims that hosting sports mega-events promises unparalleled intensive urban regeneration, transformation of space and the importation of catalytic market growth. For aspiring hosts willing to play the games such legacies are powerful and attractive propositions. If successfully harnessed, the diverse benefits sporting events deliver can be articulated across a diversity of socio-economic indicators that can be used to demonstrate the vitality and image of the host. Consequently, sport has long been used to underpin and enhance diverse and significant social and economic development strategy. However, sport-driven development must be defined, measurable and contextualised appropriately to enable any meaningful projections, extrapolations or evaluations of impact to occur. To adequately quantify sport-driven growth, or legacy, more robust data are required to limit assumptions regarding the correlation between sport events and their impact. Whilst it is clear that hosting sporting mega events can bring unparalleled socio-economic growth, more needs to be done to isolate their impact. Lack of clarity in this regard will ultimately damage both confidence and trust in bidding to host events and could result in the failure to maximise post-event legacy. Indeed, in recent times the much heralded notion of sport event legacies has become increasingly questionable, particularly in relation to perceptions of return on investment and wider socio-economic beneficiation. This chapter explores these issues by drawing upon extensive ethnographic research.

Martin Büdel's chapter describes different spheres of the daily working life of cattle farmers in Massif Central in France. Farms in Cantal, as elsewhere in Europe, were forced to constantly grow and specialize during the last decades to simultaneously meet the demands of markets and society and produce enough revenue for themselves. Seen from a perspective that stresses a thorough human–animal relationship, many farmers are concerned with the difficulties of taking good care of their animals while also meeting the demands of the markets. At the least, farming individuals and families have a certain autonomy with respect to the actual performance of their work and do enjoy some freedom to perform what they regard as good work. While being relatively free in choosing their own way of organizing their work, economic factors and the organization of agricultural production by the state and the EU, respectively, are forcing them to adapt. The chapter deals with farmers' tensions between autonomy and adaptation.

Alicia Reigada, using an analysis of the intensive cultivation of strawberries in the province of Huelva (Andalusia, Southern Spain), examines some of the contradictions and dilemmas that affect the lives of small family farmers who supply global agrifood chains. By examining the changing human experience of these subjects in the context of transformations in work, production and distribution practices, the research examines how the identity of these strawberry growers is grounded in their sense of pride of being self made. By situating these smallholders' experiences in the local history of farming and the social formation of the productive model, the analysis explores the moral economy of these agricultural producers and the role that feelings of pride play in their sense of grievance, injustice and vulnerability. In taking this approach Reigada claims that it is not possible to reduce the concept of economy to monetary value. Rather, monetary value should be articulated in conjunction with the cultural and moral values that guide economic practice.

Christian Zlolniski contends that the new agriculture specialized in the production of fresh produce for international markets is characterized by deep class and ethnic inequalities in which indigenous immigrant workers from the poorest states in southern Mexico provide the bulk of the labour force. The new agriculture has also fostered a workplace regime that has led to the intensification of labour for farmworkers. This regime is based on four main components: production in sheltered environments, piece rate system, the merging of harvest and packing tasks in the field, and the use of 'good agricultural practices' to meet export certification requirements. Each of these components, Zlolniski argues, has contributed to the quantitative and qualitative intensification of the work process for farm labourers, thus heightening discipline and labour control issues in the workplace. This labour regime, he claims, embodies the neoliberal governance system that prevails in the global horticultural industry in which transnational agribusiness control the production, distribution, and commercialization of high value fresh produce. But the new labour regime has not gone uncontested, and farmworkers have developed different forms of resistance to counteract labour exploitation and the intensification of work in the fields. These forms of labour resistance speak of the tensions and class conflict between capital and labour at the heart of the global fresh produce industry.

Corine Vedrine addresses the way the contemporary policy of economic and spatial renewal of the French town Saint-Etienne is interpreted by the inhabitants of nearby Le Soleil, a former metallurgic and mining district that has been ignored by the urban local policies. Their interpretations can be seen as belonging to two imagined generational communities: the industrial one and the post-industrial one. Through this case study, she sheds light on the way the connection between economy and society is manifested in urban spaces, urban practices, urban imaginations, and therefore, in the representations of the local figures about identity and alterity. The two imagined generational communities produce two distinct stereotypical figures: the unbearable youngster and the nostalgic oldie. These stereotypes express both their values and their different relations to the history, the space and the local identity in a context of a new global environment. They stand for the difficulty of understanding both the precarious market context in general and the insecure framework of the renewal in particular as well as giving meaning to the necessity that this change takes place in an insecure post-industrial society, and finally, these stereotypes illustrate the difficulty of understanding each other.

Michel Rautenberg argues that the memory of previous social practices and manners of living take a particular place in our world to protect from what Richard Sennett called 'the culture of the new capitalism'. This new capitalism, characterized by an unpredictable time, increasing labour market flexibility, a new ideal of the self whose experiences are less valuable than the permanent adaptation to new skills, is a source of anxiety because it disempowers not the workers only but all people. In this context, the legacy of the popular culture becomes a political and societal issue that takes different forms: alter heritagisation facing metropolisation, commitment against a city centre's gentrification, symbolic reparation of the working class, renewal of previous concrete utopias. This condition is called weak heritage, defined as everything that people wish to preserve because it is supposed to stabilise the framework where they live in. Rautenberg develops his analysis by revisiting the place where he did fieldwork ten years ago, Villeneuve d'Ascq, located close to Lille, in the north of France. Villeneuve d'Ascq has been partly built according to the utopias of the 1960s and 1970s: a town in the countryside with open sociability among the neighbourhoods, friendly to strangers and new ideas. Forty years later, these great ideas have not disappeared and thanks to them people have been attracted to the town. However, these newcomers relied on the memories of some of the pioneers and on politicians' discourses, and eventually found recourse in weak heritage, not as a weapon against capitalism, but as a way to adapt to different levels of social life.

The final chapter by Paul Durrenberger looks at the relationship between market and society in the context of a neoliberal global trend in general and in the US in particular. Inspired by this volume's chapters and his own extended anthropological and teaching experience, he discusses the antithesis between the gospel of work and the gospel of wealth pointing to the fact that in order to understand contemporary capitalism one should look at the relation between class, family structure and political values, revealing at the same time the efforts made by political elites to rewrite or ignore people's oppositions. For Durrenberger, anthropology and its ethnographic methods are not only in the unique position to unveil such processes but their core role is to resist any neoliberal policy or government that puts human existence in danger.

References

Aglietta, M. 2008. *La Crise*. Paris: Édition Michalon.
Bauman, Z. 2017. *A Chronicle of Crisis: 2011–2016*. London: Social Europe Editions.
Beckert, J. 1997. *Beyond the Market. The Social Foundations of Economic Efficiency*. Princeton: Princeton University Press.
Bezanson, K. 2006. *Gender, the State, and Social Reproduction. Household Insecurity in Neo Liberal Times*. Toronto: University of Toronto Press.
Burawoy, M. 2014. Marxism After Polanyi. In *Marxisms in the 21st Century. Crisis, Critique and Struggle*, ed. M. Williams and V. Satgar, 34–52. Johannesburg: Wits University Press.
Carrier, J.G. 1997. Introduction. In *Meanings of the Market. The Free Market in Western Culture*, ed. J.G. Carrier, 1–69. Oxford: Berg.
Castel, R. 2000. The Roads to Disaffiliation: Insecure Work and Vulnerable Relationships. *International Journal of Urban and Regional Research* 24 (3): 519–535.
Clammer, J. 1985. *Anthropology and Political Economy. Theoretical and Asian Perspectives*. Basingstoke: Palgrave Macmillan.
Dale, G. 2010. *Karl Polanyi. The Limits of the Market*. Cambridge: Polity Press.
De Grauwe, P. 2017. *The Limits of the Market. The Pendulum Between Government and Market*. Oxford: Oxford University Press.
Dowd, D. 2004. *Capitalism and Its Economics. A Critical History*. London: Pluto Press.
Durrenberger, P. 2017. Introduction: Hope for Labor in a Neoliberal World. In *Uncertain Times. Anthropological Approaches to Labor in a Neoliberal World*, ed. P. Durrenberger, 3–31. Boulder: University Press of Colorado.
Durrenberger, P.E., and J. Martí. 2006. Introduction. In *Labor in Cross-Cultural Perspective*, ed. E.P. Durrenberger and J. Martí, 1–27. New York: AltaMira Press.
Durrenberger, P.E., and S. Erem. 2010. *Anthropology Unbound. A Field Guide to the 21st Century*. Boulder: Paradigm Publishers.
Earle, J., C. Moran, and Z. Ward-Perkins. 2017. *The Econocracy. The Perils of Leaving Economics to the Experts*. Manchester: Manchester University Press.
Godelier, M. 1972. *Rationality and Irrationality in Economics*. New York: Monthly Review Press.
Greenhouse, C.J. 2010. Introduction. In *Ethnographies of Neoliberalism*, ed. C.J. Greenhouse, 1–10. Philadelphia: University of Pennsylvania Press.
Gudeman, S. 2016. *Anthropology and Economy*. Cambridge: Cambridge University Press.
Hann, C., and K. Hart (eds.). 2009. *Market and Society. The Great Transformation Today*. Cambridge: Cambridge University Press.

Hart, K. 2015. Introduction. In *Economy for and Against Democracy*, ed. K. Hart, 1–15. Oxford: Berghahn.

Holmes, C. 2014. Whatever It Takes: Polanyian Perspectives on the Eurozone Crisis and the Gold Standard. *Economy and Society* 43 (4): 582–602.

Hornborg, A. 2005. Resisting the Black Hole of Neoclassical Formalism in Economic Anthropology: A Polemic. In *Peopled Economies. Conversations with Stephen Gudeman*, ed. S. Löfving, 63–83. Uppsala: Uppsala University.

Keynes, J.M. 1963. Economic Possibilities for Our Grandchildren. In *Essays in Persuasion*, ed. J.M. Keynes, 358–375. New York: W. W. Norton & Company.

Kjaerulff, J. 2015. Introduction. In *Flexible Capitalism. Exchange and Ambiguity at Work*, ed. J. Kjaerluff, 1–41. Oxford: Berghahn.

Lapavitsas, C. 2012. Financialised Capitalism: Crisis and Financial Expropriation. In *Financialisation in Crisis*, ed. C. Lapavitsas, 15–50. Boston: Brill.

Lawson, T. 2009. The Current Economic Crisis: Its Nature and the Course of Academic Economics. *Cambridge Journal of Economics* 33: 759–777.

Marx, K., and F. Engels. 1967. *The Communist Manifesto*. London: Penguin.

Narotzky, S. 1997. *New Directions in Economic Anthropology*. London: Pluto Press.

Ong, A. 1999. *Flexible Citizenship. The Cultural Logics of Transnationality*. Durham: Duke University Press.

Pardo, I. 1996. *Managing Existence in Naples: Morality, Action and Structure*. Cambridge: Cambridge University Press.

Pérez-Díaz, V. 2009. Introduction: Free Markets, Civil Societies and a Liberal Polity. In *Markets and Civil Society. The European Experience in Comparative Perspective*, ed. V. Pérez-Díaz, 1–24. Oxford: Berghahn.

Picchio, A. 1992. *Social Reproduction. The Political Economy of the Labour Market*. Cambridge: Cambridge University Press.

Polanyi, K. 1977. *The Livelihood of Man*. London: Academic Press.

Prato, G.B. 2009. Introduction-Beyond Multiculturalism: Anthropology at the Intersections Between the Local, the National and the Global. In *Beyond Multiculturalism. Views from Anthropology*, ed. G.B. Prato, 1–19. Farnham: Ashgate.

Resta, G. 2014. Introduction. In *Karl Polanyi, for a New West. Essays, 1919–1958*, ed. G. Resta and M. Catanzarini, 1–27. Cambridge: Polity.

Schneider, J. 2002. World Markets: Anthropological Perspectives. In *Exotic No More. Anthropology on the Front Lines*, ed. J. MacClancy, 64–85. Chicago: The University of Chicago Press.

Spyridakis, M. 2013. *The Liminal Worker. An Ethnography of Work, Unemployment and Precariousness in Contemporary Greece*. Farnham: Ashgate.

Spyridakis, M. 2017a. Employment Precariousness and Social Reproduction in the Shipbuilding Industry of Piraeus. In *Work and Livelihoods. History,*

Ethnography and Models in Times of Crisis, ed. S. Narotzky and V. Goddard, 109–120. London: Routledge.

Spyridakis, M. 2017b. Labor Struggles in the Shipbuilding Industry of Piraeus. In *Uncertain Times. Anthropological Approaches to Labor in a Neoliberal World*, ed. P. Durrenberger, 161–183. Boulder: University Press of Colorado.

Stiglitz, E. 2009. The Current Economic Crisis and Lessons for Economic Theory. *Eastern Economic Journal* 35: 281–296.

Wacquant, L. 2009. *Punishing the Poor. The Neoliberal Government of Social Insecurity*. Durham: Duke University Press.

Wilk, R., and L. Cliggett. 2007. *Economies and Cultures: Foundations of Economic Anthropology*. New York: Perseus Books.

CHAPTER 2

Economy and Society, Neoliberal Reform and Economic Deviance

James G. Carrier

Robbing a bank's no crime compared to owning one.
Happy End, Bertold Brecht

In this chapter, I use the distinction between economy and society to consider how we might approach economic deviance in an era of neoliberal ascendancy. I identify some of the ways that neoliberalism can affect people's economic activities, including their deviant economic activities, and how it can influence the ways they think of such activities, and do so in different ways for people in different social and economic locations.

By economic deviance I mean economic acts that violate social values, whether or not they violate the law, and I consider the fact that different sets of people can hold different values, even if they are subject to the same set of laws. I define neoliberalism as ideas and policies that became influential in many Western countries in the last quarter of the twentieth century. These vary (see, e.g., Turner 2011), but common ideas are that government should have a minimal role in the country's economy and

J. G. Carrier (✉)
Max Planck Institute for Social Anthropology, Halle (Saale), Germany

Indiana University, Bloomington, IN, USA

© The Author(s) 2018
M. Spyridakis (ed.), *Market Versus Society*, Palgrave Studies in Urban Anthropology, https://doi.org/10.1007/978-3-319-74189-5_2

that people should be independent and satisfy their needs and desires through market transactions. Common policies include a reduction in public services and government oversight and regulation of economic activities.

Like all deviance, economic deviance tends to be covert and difficult to study, and I do not analyse it empirically. Rather, I present an analytical orientation in order to pose questions about it, to therefore begin to understand it. I frame my presentation in terms of common views of economic deviance. As this might suggest, I approach economic deviance in terms of both the activities that it denotes and the ways that people think about those activities.

VIEWS OF ECONOMIC DEVIANCE

Commonly, people see economic deviance as the violation of a clear rule, by a person who is deficient in some way. In other words, both the act and the actor deviate from what is expected and proper. A story about an American economic deviant, Willie Sutton, illustrates this. He was famous for robbing banks, which is clearly against the rules. Not only are his acts deviant, so is he. It is said that when he was asked why he robbed banks, he replied: 'Because that's where the money is'. His pragmatic answer shows a self-serving indifference to the distinction between right and wrong, an inadequate moral compass.

In this view, an orderly and desirable state of affairs is threatened by the heedless deviant, and when the deviance is economic, that desirable state of affairs commonly is the orderly operation of the capitalist market. In the mid-1970s, British commentator Lord Vaizey remarked that if the free market is to operate, we need to guard against 'those who for purely selfish interests ... seek to make money for themselves and let the rest go to hell' (in Cockett 1994: 228).

This view has much to recommend it. For one thing, its individual orientation reflects the individualism that is common in Western thought, and especially in Anglo-American thought. As well, immoral, heedless individuals do exist. For instance, there is Nick Leeson, whose deceptions about his failed transactions with other people's money brought down the British merchant bank Barings in the 1990s (Stevenson 1995). Less spectacular is Mathew Martoma, a hedge fund manager convicted in 2014 of insider trading. When he was a student at Harvard Law School, he altered his university transcript to raise his grades and used the faked transcript when he applied for a clerkship with a federal judge (Stevenson and Goldstein 2014). Also, this view of deviance points to ways that we can deal with the problem. We can raise our children to have an adequate compass (e.g. Sullivan 2014), and set up programmes to encourage people to think and act in terms of that compass (e.g. Tugend 2014). More subtly, this view treats what is wrong as clear and straightforward, and so echoes the legal system, which has clear laws that define what is wrong.

Although this common view has much to recommend it, in important ways it is limited, even misleading, and the rise of neoliberalism made some of those limitations apparent. I turn now to those limitations and how they can help us to understand the relationship between neoliberalism and economic deviance. I do so by considering the two elements that I identified in that common view, that there are defective individuals and that they break clear rules.

Defective Individuals

While it is individuals who break rules, the fact remains that individuals live in a social world, one that can make it more or less likely that they will deviate. This is so in two ways. First, people's values and orientations are shaped by their socialisation. As a result, they will vary in what they value and what they expect as part of a reasonable and proper life. Second, social situations will vary in the degree to which they induce people to deviate. In some situations, it will be relatively easy to behave properly, while in others it will require substantial strength of will. We can expect more deviance in the latter situation than in the former.

In saying this, I am arguing that we need a view of economic deviance that does not see it simply as an individual fact about a single person. We need a view that sees economic deviance as taking place in the social world in which people live. This observation echoes Durkheim's approach to another deviant act, *Suicide* (1951 [1897]). He argued that different sorts of social situations make it more or less likely that people will take their own lives, and he described the relationship between the likelihood that people will kill themselves and the sorts of situations in which they live.

Robert Merton (1938) took Durkheim's approach and applied it to economic deviance. He focussed on two American values. One is oriented toward the self: it is good to make money through one's efforts. The other is oriented toward the group: it is good to play by society's rules in those efforts. Merton said that there are social situations in which the relative strength of these values differs from what is conventional. This could be because of changes that affect large parts of society, or because in some group these two values have strengths that are different from what is found more generally. This differing will influence the way people think about and act in their economic lives, and this can affect the likelihood that they will act in ways that would be considered deviant by more conventional people in more conventional times. For instance, if acquiring wealth becomes stronger relative to playing by the rules, then there is likely to be an increase in what would, in more normal circumstances, be seen as economic deviance.

Merton's two values provide a way to approach the relationship between neoliberal reform and economic deviance in terms of the distinction between economy and society. Economy is generally seen as a realm of self-serving individualism and impersonal calculation, illustrated by Willie Sutton, and society commonly is seen as a realm of social relationships and obligations (see, e.g., Carrier 2012: 3–12). In pointing to the relationship between wealth and fairness, Merton reminds us that economic activity has a moral aspect. He also reminds us that those values vary over time and across groups.

E. P. Thompson (1971) addressed that moral aspect in his description of English peasants in the second half of the eighteenth century. He said that they had expectations about proper effort and behaviour (playing by the rules) and a reasonable livelihood (acquiring wealth), manifest in a set of understandings of how people ought to act in their economic dealings with each other. In terms of common values, if not of invariable practice, this meant that people who behaved in the appropriate way in their dealings with others (playing by the rules) were entitled to receive what they needed for that reasonable life (acquiring wealth).

The economic changes occurring in England during that period, however, meant that those expectations were not met and those understandings were violated. Playing by the rules was less and less likely to be met with the wealth needed for a reasonable livelihood. Moreover, the adherents of the new order denied the basis of the old. As Adam Smith argued at the time, we are not entitled to our supper because we have behaved properly in our economic dealings. Rather, we eat only because we can give other people what they happen to want: 'Give me that which I want, and you shall have this which you want' (Smith 1976 [1776]: 18). Not surprisingly, Thompson's peasantry and their allies saw those new forms of economic practice as wrong, and they tried to impose their own rough justice to force people to behave properly. From the perspective of the adherents of the emerging liberal economic order, on the other hand, those peasants and their allies were wrong, and should be constrained or punished accordingly.

Thompson's work illustrates how there can be historical changes in the ways that different sets of people see the relationship between acquiring wealth and playing by the rules, and that these can affect the likelihood that people will engage in activities that other people see as deviant, and indeed affect what people see as deviant. I want to suggest how this sort of change might affect another form of economic deviance, gifts to minor public officials by private individuals, which count as petty bribery.

As mentioned, a common feature of neoliberal reform is a reduction in the amount of money governments spend on public services such as medical care. Like Thompson's peasants, many people facing such a situation might see this as a violation of the moral order, in which their proper effort and behaviour entitled them to medical care as part of a reasonable livelihood. Again, like those peasants, many such people may not have enough money to buy what they need at the market price. Such people would have little choice but to use the over-burdened, declining public health service, and might find the only way they can assure that care is by giving a gift to medical staff or doing favours for them. Such gifts are unfair because people would get care more quickly than they would if normal procedures were followed. However, the situation I have described would increase the likelihood that this sort of deviance will occur. Cecilia Malmstrom, the EU Commissioner for Home Affairs, noted the existence of this sort of deviance when she presented the 2014 European Union (EU) report on corruption. She pointed to corruption in the obvious places, but also noted that 'less obvious sectors also had problems, including health care, where some patients were forced to pay under the table to obtain necessary treatments' (in Jolly 2014).

Those who give gifts to secure medical care are breaking the rules, and we can investigate their deviance as individual facts. However, my example illustrates how we can approach this deviance as a social fact, the consequence of a change from a system in which individuals were entitled to a reasonable livelihood if they conformed to social expectations, to one in which entitlement comes only with having the money. Of course, not everyone in my hypothetical case would engage in that deviance, and some might see the neoliberal denial of a relationship between proper effort and livelihood as correct. In other words, people on both sides of that divide might see themselves as behaving reasonably morally, though their differing moralities would lead them to see economic acts in different ways.

In the preceding paragraphs I have suggested how seeing economic deviance as a social fact, rather than an individual one, allows us to raise questions and consider processes that are not readily apparent if one uses that more common individualist perspective.

The first concerns the relationship between neoliberal reform and economic deviance. My tale of a declining public health service is hypothetical, but not unreasonable. That is because a common element of neoliberal reform is the reduction of public money spent on public services, reflecting the assertion that such services are provided better by firms seeking a profit in a capitalist market. Such reduction increases the chance that those wanting access to those services, like those providing them, will offer and expect petty bribes for services that previously had been allocated following administrative criteria set by government. Consequently, we can expect that neoliberal reform would be associated with an increase in this sort of economic deviance among those who are relatively unable to afford to purchase those services on the market and among those who are presented with more demand for services than their public institution, with its reduced resources, can satisfy. Because richer people are likely to be able to afford to purchase those services on the market, they are less likely to engage in this kind of bribery.

The second thing that this view of economic deviance allows us to consider is the political aspect of deviance in the circumstance of neoliberal reform. I pointed to this aspect in Thompson's work, which describes a situation resembling neoliberal reform, one in which the practices and understandings of the relationship between the economic and the social realms change fairly quickly. For Thompson's crowd, those who espoused the new understandings and pursued the new practices were deviants who violated the old moral order, while the adherents of the new order saw that crowd as deviants who violated the new moral order. If the change that occurred in England in the decades around 1800 resembles the change that occurs under neoliberal reform, then we can expect similar consequences. That is, the adherents of the old and new orders each will see the other as immoral and deviant. Adherents of the old order will be cast as lacking initiative, dependent on state handouts or even of being welfare chisellers, and perhaps, if they are in the former Second World, victims of a lingering socialist mentality. On the other hand, adherents of the new order will be cast as greedy and self serving, blind to the rights of others and to their obligation to the group of which they are a part.

THE DISTRIBUTION OF DEVIANCE

I have portrayed the sort of circumstance that is associated with a particular kind of economic deviance, petty bribery. As Cris Shore (2004: 36) describes, this often is seen as 'a Third World disorder; a pathology endemic to "backward" developing countries with weak civil societies and bloated public sectors' (see also Shore and Haller 2005: 3–6), found as well in the Second World of post-socialist countries, which had what many in the First World saw as their own bloated public sectors, reduced by neoliberal reform. Those, after all, are the regions coloured deep red in Transparency International's world corruption map. Countries with sound governments, competent civil servants and proper legal structures are free of economic deviance. At least, that is what people in North America and Western Europe commonly tell themselves.

However, the economic crisis that began in 2008 revealed activities that undercut this comfortable assumption. What it revealed was not the petty bribery of individuals whose conventional livelihoods were threatened by neoliberal reform. Rather, it revealed economic deviance in the commercial world, among companies and individuals who were richer than most and who, it seems, wanted more.

As the economic crisis unfolded, we learned that companies had issued mortgages without verifying either the income of the people applying for loans or the value of the houses that they wanted to buy; companies made their money by issuing the loans and then selling them to investors, rather than by holding the loans and collecting the repayments. These were called liar loans, and Countrywide Financial was the firm best known for making them (e.g. Morgenson 2012a). We learned of financial instruments so complicated that those selling them could not understand them (e.g. Antilla 2013). We learned that the agencies that assessed the credit worthiness of those instruments, which included bundles of liar loans, were paid by the firms that issued them and, often enough, seemed happy to do what the issuers wanted, i.e., make assumptions that would justify rating them highly (e.g. Lattman 2013). And all this was only at the beginning of the mortgage process. At the other end, it could be just as bad. We learned that some firms seeking to evict people for failure to keep up their mortgage payments presented fabricated and forged documents (e.g. Henning 2010). We learned that other firms tried to evict people from their homes for failing to make their mortgage payments when, in fact, those people had not failed to make their payments, when, in fact, those people had no mortgage with the evicting firm or even had, in fact, no mortgage at all (e.g. Morgenson 2012b).

It might have been that this economic deviance was itself deviant, only a side effect of the bubble in the housing market, associated with irrational exuberance and things getting out of hand. If so, in the rest of the economy the firms people dealt with would be basically trustworthy. However, such a comforting conclusion seemed unjustified. We learned of a large American company that kept advertising and selling its artificial hip joints long after they knew that they were faulty and harmed those who got them (Meier 2013). We learned of a large drug company that bribed doctors to prescribe their products (Reuters 2013), and of drug manufacturers who published the results of trials that showed that their products were safe and effective, and suppressed the results of trials that showed that their drugs were of less use than a sugar pill and a lot more harmful (Sample 2013). We learned of a British security firm that charged the government for work that they did not do, to the tune of £24 million (Travis 2013), and of an American firm that did the same, to the tune of 650,000 security checks billed to the government but not completed (Apuzzo 2014). And, of course, we read of the electronics firm Apple, renown for its innovations that boost the company's profits. We learned that one of these innovations was the creation of a set of company divisions that are effectively nowhere, located in no tax or regulatory jurisdiction whatsoever (Schwartz and Duhigg 2013).

What I have described is very different from the petty corruption that worried Cecilia Malmstrom, but like it, this second sort of deviance can be approached as a social fact. However, we can also approach it in a different way, to consider a different sort of relationship between the rise of neoliberalism and economic deviance. I shall do so by turning to the second of the two features of the common understanding of deviance, that it involves the violation of clear rules.

CLEAR RULES

Willie Sutton robbed banks and lived in a place where that is a crime; Nick Leeson lied about his speculative trades and lived in a place where that is a crime; Martin Martoma forged his transcript and lived in a place where that is wrong. Appropriately, Sutton and Leeson went to prison and Martoma was thrown out of law school. Those people, like the people who are likely to read these words, live under the rule of law. This is not the haphazard law of simple societies, weak states and autocrats. Rather, it is the impersonal, routinised law of the statute book, the public prosecutor and the independent judiciary, the sort of law that is the ideal of organisations like Transparency International.

However, just as seeing economic deviance as an individual fact simplifies a more complex world, so too does the assumption that it involves breaking clear rules. I want to show this simplification in terms of what I call legal procedure and legal substance, and in doing so I will suggest why we can expect a distinctive sort of economic deviance to exist in the upper reaches of the economic order in a time of neoliberal ascendancy. I will begin with procedure, common legal practices.

Under the rule of law, a person is innocent until shown guilty and an act is innocent until it is shown to be wrong in a legal proceeding. However, both the US Attorney General and the future head of the UK's Prudential Regulation Authority said that some financial institutions are so important for the operation of their countries' economies that they are too big to prosecute (Scott 2012; Sorkin 2013). Not subject to legal proceedings, these institutions and their acts are innocent. So, in principle the rule may be clear, but its application may not be, which means that our assessments of rights and wrongs may be difficult.

Bringing a case to court is not, of course, the only way that governments can apply the rules to identify wrongful acts and, perhaps, deter people from doing them. There are, for instance, nonprosecution and deferred prosecution agreements (see Giudice 2011). In them, a government body with legal powers, perhaps the Securities and Exchange Commission of the United States (the SEC), has evidence that some entity over which it has jurisdiction, perhaps Citibank, has broken the rules. The SEC then approaches Citibank and comes to an agreement. According to the type of agreement, Citibank may or may not admit to any wrong act, but it is not prosecuted. It hands over money, some of which may be a fine and some of which may be used to settle civil claims against it, and it agrees not to commit such an act for a specified number of years and institutes procedures to help assure that it does not do so. The deferred prosecution agreements undertaken by the SEC are presented to a federal judge for approval, which means that if Citibank, to continue the hypothetical example, violates the agreement, the SEC can go back to that judge and ask for action.

No one is prosecuted, but a type of act is identified as wrong and the errant entity will, doubtless, be encouraged not to commit such acts in the future. Not perfect, but people probably would agree that in a world of complex regulation and large, diverse organisations, this is fairly close.

However, in practice things are not this simple. In 2011 a judge of the US District Court for the Southern District of New York, which includes Wall Street, asked the SEC whether it had ever brought legal proceedings against companies that had violated their agreements. The SEC told the judge that they had brought none in the previous ten years (for this and the remainder of this paragraph, see Wyatt 2011). The judge put his question to the SEC because they had presented to him for approval an agreement with Citibank, in which the company agreed to pay $285 million in settlement for defrauding customers in violation of a key part of US securities law and promised never to violate that law again. It seems, though, that Citibank or one of its main divisions had reached an agreement concerning a previous violation of that same part of the law in 2010, as they had in 2006, 2005 and 2000. Rather than starting legal proceedings for the previous violations of those agreements, the SEC negotiated another one. What that judge discovered shows that the rules may be clear in theory, but not in practice.

I said also that consideration of the substance of law and regulation would raise further questions about the assumption of clear rules. I turn to that now, starting with the question of whether legal penalties make a difference. If they do not, if the penalty for stealing cars were only to remain silent for 60 seconds, we would find it hard to argue that the rules are clear in a substantial, rather than trivial, way.

One could argue that their paying all that money to the SEC shows that Citibank knew that they broke the rules, which would suggest that there are clear rules. However, it need show only that Citibank officers decided that it was cheaper to pay $285 million than it would be to fight the SEC. Further, from the company's point of view, it is not clear that $285 million is really a penalty. In 2011, the year that they paid that money, Citibank's parent company, Citigroup, declared net revenues of $78.4 billion, net income of $11.1 billion and total assets of $1874 billion (Citigroup 2012). For them, in other words, it was not a lot of money.

Whether Citibank's $285 million fine actually hurt is, I have argued, a matter of substance rather than a matter of procedure. So too is the orientation of the law and of the governments that promulgate and administer it. With the rise of neoliberalism, the orientation of governments toward commercial interests changed. In the United States in the 1970s, this took the form of policies that required the federal government to become more business like. In practice, this meant cost–benefit analysis, which turned out to mean using largely commercial criteria to assess the desirability of different sorts of regulation (Maclennan 1997). In Britain in the 1980s, this took the form of encouraging government ministries to seek advice from senior officials in large companies (for the more recent form of this, see Ball and Taylor 2013). As the 1980s turned into the 1990s, in both countries this took the form of decreasing government regulation and oversight of commercial activity, justified in part by the old conventional argument that profitable companies are good for the country and in part by the rational market hypothesis, the new neoliberal argument that the market knows best (Fox 2009).

The result was that it became difficult to distinguish between governments and large companies. One sign of this is what is called 'the revolving door,' whereby governments recruit senior executives from corporations and industry groups, and corporations and industry groups recruit senior government officials (for the automobile industry in the US, see Jensen and Wald 2014). Another sign is that government departments hire corporate and industry representatives to shape policy (Press Association 2014) and that corporations and their representatives draw up legislation, rather than leaving the job to legislators (Lipton and Protess 2013).

These changes made it easier for commercial interests to shape the production and application of the rules in ways that allow them to carry out activities without legal censure, even though many people would think that those activities are wrong. With this, neoliberal reform has increased the likelihood of a distinctive sort of deviance at the upper end of the economic scale, one that complements the sort of deviance that I said we could expect at the lower end of the scale.

Moreover, what I have said in the preceding paragraphs points to a larger matter. The activities of financial firms that the economic crisis brought to light, like the activities of other firms that I have mentioned in passing, strike most people as wrong and make them unhappy (e.g. Kopicki 2013; Schmidt and Wyatt 2012). However, it is not clear that they are wrong in a legal sense, because of the nature of legal process and legal substance.

Concern for this apparent disconnection between right and wrong on the one hand, and legality on the other, is echoed in what Steven Sampson (2005: 105) said about efforts to eliminate corruption: they seek 'to restore standards that were lost, the standards of morality and responsibility which connote what we call "community"'. What Sampson said about morality and community points to another aspect of the rise of neoliberalism and its relationship to economic deviance, concerning the ethic associated with neoliberalism and its relationship to the sort of morality and responsibility he describes. That ethic contains an important set of assumptions about the relationship between economy and society.

ECONOMY AND SOCIETY

Once again, Durkheim's work is illuminating; in this case, *The Division of Labour in Society* (1984 [1893]), his sustained consideration of the relationship between the organisation of a society's economy and the nature of its moral order. If, like Sampson, people are unhappy about a loss of morality and standards, the argument Durkheim made in that book indicates that they should not be surprised by it. He said that when a society's division of labour increases, the legal system becomes more amoral. Civil and administrative law become more important and crim-inal law becomes less so, as the society's legal system becomes oriented less toward expressing a moral order and punishing those who violate it, and oriented more toward people's commercial interests, compensating them for loss arising from the failure of people to fulfil their contracts. Like the $285 million that Citibank paid as part of its agreement with the SEC, that compensation can look a lot like simply a cost of doing business.

The neoliberal ascendancy has been accompanied by the assertion of a set of arguments about the nature of economy and of people in general. These arguments embody the sort of amoralism that Sampson decried and that Durkheim described, an amoralism that suggests why certain sorts of economic deviance in the upper reaches of society might be associated with the rise of neoliberalism. However, as I argue, they are amoral only if one takes a restricted view of morality. These arguments have a long history, but they began to assume their modern form in the work of Adam Smith, and have been developed into the neoclassical economics that is their current form, which is an important part of the intellectual armoury of neoliberalism.

In *The Wealth of Nations*, Smith asserted that the basis of people's economic activity was not in their society's norms and values, people's place in the social system and the rights and duties that went with it or in the social relations in which they existed and the expectations that were part of them. Rather, it lay in their personal desires. As he (1976 [1776]: 18) observed, 'It is not from the benevolence of the butcher, the brewer, or the baker, that we expect our dinner, but from their regard to their own interest'. This left Smith with a problem: how can the collective good be helped by a system driven by individual interest? The best Smith could come up with was a *deus ex machina*, the invisible hand. That is, he postulated 'the operation of instincts planted in men by Providence. This providence was assumed to be benign and the order so established was favourable to the welfare of men' (Habakkuk 1971: 45; see also Lubasz 1992).

Smith treats people as isolated individuals to be approached only in terms of their individual desires, in terms of 'that which I want'. Marx and Engels (1948 [1848]: 11) put it more bluntly when they said that the rise of capitalism 'has drowned the most heavenly ecstasies of religious fervour, of chivalrous enthusiasm, of philistine sentimentalism, in the icy water of egotistical calculation'. On the other hand, Thompson's crowd, I have argued, rejected this individualism and its severing of the link between fairness and wealth, between society and economy. But, as Thompson observed, the crowd lost the war.

Intellectually, Smith's individualistic economism became powerful in the nineteenth century, especially with the marginalist revolution in its closing decades. Politically, as Polanyi (1957 [1944]) describes, it became powerful in the legislation of laissez faire capitalism in Britain and elsewhere. It began to weaken around 1900 in Britain and the United States, as reform movements sought to ameliorate the ill effects of its rigorous application (Turner 2011: 35–43), and it was weakened still further by Western responses to the Great Depression. After the Second World War it began to re-emerge (Cockett 1994), with 'neoclassical economics' being the common name for its re-emergence as economic thought, and 'neoliberalism' the common name for its re-emergence as political programme. They are not the same as their ancestors, but they share the old individualism, apparent in their relentless focus on the market, and within that, their elevation of the moment of choice, when individuals satisfy their desires through their transactions.

This individualism is not unprincipled. It has an ethic, for it holds that individuals pursuing their interest in the free market leads to the most rational allocation of resources and hence the greatest possible material well-being in the society (Carrier 1997: 1–3), but this assertion says nothing about who shares in that well-being and to what end. One could argue that this is only bourgeois individualism, an ideological justification for the accumulation of wealth. However, it remains a coherent and elaborated moral position that commands substantial public assent, including by those on the lower rungs of the economic ladder.

While it may have an ethic, this individualism still echoes Smith's amoralism. It takes people's desires as given, as something that they bring into the market from outside. The origin of these desires is outside the scope of neoclassical models and neoliberal policies, and are to be neither explained nor evaluated. All that is important about those desires is that people satisfy them, for that satisfaction is good and, for the more thoroughgoing, it is the only good. The effect of that satisfaction on others slips from view, and when this becomes taken for granted, it leads to things like the words of an article in *The Economist* (1995): 'Forcing consumers to pay double for ... their choice or buy something else, hardly makes them better off'.

CONCLUSION

I have used features of the common approach to deviant activity to consider deviant economic activity and to consider the relationship between it and the rise of neoliberalism. Because that rise has affected different sets of people differently, we can expect that it will be associated with different sorts of economic deviance in different parts of the population. In effect, we can expect one sort of deviance, illustrated by petty bribery, among those whose sense of reasonable livelihood was violated by neoliberalism, and another sort of deviance, illustrated by corporate wrongdoing, among those whose livelihoods were freed from constraint by neoliberalism. Saying this simplifies the complexities of neoliberal thought and reform, as well as people's lives and the ways that neoliberalism affects them, which is appropriate given that I want only to sketch the basis of an approach to neoliberalism and how it is likely to affect both those it has harmed and those it has helped.

What unites the ways it has helped and harmed different people is something that I addressed briefly in the previous section, i.e., the view of economy and society that appears central in neoliberal thought and reflected in many of its reforms. As I argued, that view is radical, for it holds that there are only individuals and their desires, and that economy is only their efforts to satisfy those desires in market transactions. Unlike Thompson's English crowd, neoliberalism speaks of no rules or expectations, or at least none beyond the sanctity of private property, and it speaks of no assumption that conformity to the rules gives anyone a claim to anything at all, much less to a reasonable livelihood.

As this view sees nothing beyond individuals, there are no criteria of good or bad, harm or benefit, beyond individual desire. There are no people who deserve our consideration, no entity or group to whom we are beholden, beyond our individual desire to be so, and no group on which we can make claims. As André Iteanu (2005) said, in his description of the intellectual heirs of the events of 1968, 'nothing stands outside the self'. In this, the world of thoroughgoing neoliberalism is one in which people are subject only to their own will and constrained only by their ability to persuade others to deal with them. This is not only the world of anarcho capitalism (see Brown 1997), but also a world that seems to attract many who protest against the power and wrongdoing of large-scale capital (see Sanneh 2013). Unfortunately, however, it gives those protestors no ground on which to stand, beyond Adam Smith's 'that which I want'.

References

Note: All articles in *The New York Times* and *The Guardian* are available on their web sites, https://www.nytimes.com and https://www.theguardian.com/uk.

Antilla, S. 2013. In Soured Investments, Brokers Emerge as Culprits and Victims. *The New York Times*, December 23.

Apuzzo, M. 2014. Security Check Firm Said to Have Defrauded U.S. *The New York Times*, January 23.

Ball, J., and H. Taylor. 2013. "Buddy" Scheme to Give More Multinationals Access to Ministers. *The Guardian*, January 18.

Brown, S.L. 1997. The Free Market as Salvation from Government: The Anarcho-Capitalist View. In *Meanings of the Market*, ed. J.G. Carrier, 99–128. Oxford: Berg.

Carrier, J.G. 1997. Introduction. In *Meanings of the Market*, ed. J.G. Carrier, 1–67. Oxford: Berg.

Carrier, J.G. 2012. Introduction. In *Ethical Consumption*, ed. J.G. Carrier and P. Luetchford, 1–35. New York: Berghahn.

Citigroup. 2012. *Annual Report 2011*. New York: Citigroup Inc.

Cockett, R. 1994. *Thinking the Unthinkable*. London: Harper Collins.

Durkheim, E. 1951 [1897]. *Suicide*. New York: The Free Press.

Durkheim, E. 1984 [1893]. *The Division of Labour in Society*. London: Routledge & Kegan Paul.

Fox, J. 2009. *Myth of the Rational Market*. New York: Harper Business.

Giudice, L. 2011. Regulating Corruption: Analyzing Uncertainty in Current Foreign Corrupt Practices Act Enforcement. *Boston University Law Review* 91 (1): 347.

Habakkuk, H.J. 1971. Population, Commerce and Economic Ideas. In *The New Cambridge Modern History VIII*, ed. A. Goodwin, 25–54. Cambridge: Cambridge University Press.

Henning, P.J. 2010. The Gathering Storm over Foreclosures. *The New York Times*, October 4.

Iteanu, A. 2005. When Nothing Stands Outside the Self. In *The Retreat of the Social*, ed. B. Kapferer, 104–113. Oxford: Berghahn.

Jensen, C., and M.L. Wald. 2014. Carmakers' Close Ties to Regulator Scrutinized. *The New York Times*, March 30.

Jolly, D. 2014. Study Details Graft in European Union. *The New York Times*, February 3.

Kopicki, A. 2013. Five Years Later, Poll Finds Disapproval of Bailout. *The New York Times*, September 26.

Lattman, P. 2013. Suit Charges 3 Credit Ratings Agencies with Fraud in Bear Stearns Case. *The New York Times*, November 11.

Lipton, E., and B. Protess. 2013. Banks' Lobbyists Help in Drafting Financial Bills. *The New York Times*, May 23.

Lubasz, H. 1992. Adam Smith and the Invisible Hand … of the Market? In *Contesting Markets*, ed. R. Dilley, 37–56. Edinburgh: Edinburgh University Press.

Maclennan, C.A. 1997. Democracy Under the Influence: Cost–Benefit Analysis in the United States. In *Meanings of the Market*, ed. J.G. Carrier, 195–224. Oxford: Berg.

Marx, K., and F. Engels. 1948 [1848]. *Manifesto of the Communist Party*. New York: International Publishers.

Meier, B. 2013. Johnson & Johnson in Deal to Settle Hip Implant Lawsuits. *The New York Times*, November 19.

Merton, R.K. 1938. Social Structure and Anomie. *American Sociological Review* 3 (5): 672–682.

Morgenson, G. 2012a. Bank Settles over Loans in Nevada. *The New York Times*, October 23.

Morgenson, G. 2012b. From East and West, Foreclosure Horror Stories. *The New York Times*, January 7.

Polanyi, K. 1957 [1944]. *The Great Transformation*. Boston: Beacon Press.

Press Association. 2014. NHS Hires Drugmaker-Funded Lobbyist. *The Guardian*, February 11.

Reuters. 2013. Medical Device Maker to Settle S.E.C. Bribery Charges. *The New York Times*, October 24.

Sample, I. 2013. Unfavourable Results from Medical Trials Are Being Withheld, MPs Warn. *The Guardian*, September 17.

Sampson, S. 2005. Integrity Warriors: Global Morality and the Anti-corruption Movement in the Balkans. In *Corruption: Anthropological Perspectives*, ed. D. Haller and C. Shore, 103–130. London: Pluto.

Sanneh, K. 2013. Paint Bombs: David Graeber's "The Democracy Project" and the Anarchist Revival. *The New Yorker*, May 13, viewed 10 August 2017, from www.newyorker.com/magazine/2013/05/13/paint-bombs.

Schmidt, M.S., and E. Wyatt. 2012. Corporate Fraud Cases Often Spare Individuals. *The New York Times*, August 7.

Schwartz, N.D., and C. Duhigg. 2013. Apple's Web of Tax Shelters Saved It Billions, Panel Finds. *The New York Times*, May 20.

Scott, M. 2012. British Regulator Says Banks "Too Big to Prosecute". *The New York Times*, December 14.

Shore, C. 2004. Corruption Scandals in America and Europe: Enron and EU Fraud in Comparative Perspective. In *Corporate Scandal*, ed. J. Gledhill, 29–39. Oxford: Berghahn.

Shore, C., and D. Haller. 2005. Introduction: Sharp Practice: Anthropology and the Study of Corruption. In *Corruption: Anthropological Perspectives*, ed. D. Haller and C. Shore, 1–26. London: Pluto.

Smith, A. 1976 [1776]. *An Inquiry into the Nature and Causes of the Wealth of Nations*. Chicago: University of Chicago Press.

Sorkin, A.R. 2013. Realities Behind Prosecuting Big Banks. *The New York Times*, March 11.

Stevenson, R.W. 1995. Breaking the Bank—A Special Report. Big Gambles, Lost Bets Sank a Venerable Firm. *The New York Times*, March 3.

Stevenson, A., and M. Goldstein. 2014. Ex-SAC Trader Convicted of Securities Fraud. *The New York Times*, February 6.

Sullivan, P. 2014. Having Enough, but Hungry for More. *The New York Times*, January 17.

The Economist. 1995. Car Wars: Mr Kanter's Outrageous Gamble. *The Economist*, May 20.

Thompson, E.P. 1971. The Moral Economy of the English Crowd in the Eighteenth Century. *Past and Present* 50: 76–136.

Travis, A. 2013. G4S Admits Overcharging MoJ £24 m on Electronic Tagging Contract. *The Guardian*, November 19.

Tugend, A. 2014. In Life and Business, Learning to Be Ethical. *The New York Times*, January 10.

Turner, R.S. 2011. *Neo-Liberal Ideology*. Edinburgh: Edinburgh University Press.

Wyatt, E. 2011. Promises Made, and Remade, by Firms in S.E.C. Fraud Cases. *The New York Times*, November 7.

CHAPTER 3

The Root of All Evil: Money, Markets, and the Prospects of Rewriting the Rules of the Game

Alf Hornborg

Anthropology is well positioned to elaborate our understanding of the financial crises which have struck several of the world's most affluent nations since the Wall Street banking collapse in 2008. At the ethnographic level, anthropologists are able to document in great detail the specific local human experiences of economic decline and the practical, symbolic, and emotional impacts of austerity measures (e.g., Knight and Stewart 2016). However, such studies rarely provide a critical perspective on the underlying cultural logic of the economic game itself. They generally do not address the macro level power structures which officially legitimize the enforcement of impoverishment, nor do they aim to defamiliarize the seemingly self-evident categories and artifacts that inexorably deprive people of formerly secure standards of living. As Knight and Stewart observe, 'austerity differs from endemic underdevelopment and poverty, in that it applies to situations where societies or individuals that formerly enjoyed a higher standard of consumption must now make do with less' (Knight and Stewart 2016: 2), yet 'the consequences

A. Hornborg (✉)
Human Ecology Division, Lund University, Lund, Sweden

M. Spyridakis (ed.), *Market Versus Society*, Palgrave Studies in Urban Anthropology, https://doi.org/10.1007/978-3-319-74189-5_3

of transnational fiscal turmoil have materialized in critical reflexion on Southern Europe's emergent proximity to the global South' (Knight and Stewart 2016: 4). In both cases—economic decline and economic marginalization—human suffering is generated by the impersonal logic of a market economy.

In this chapter, I will draw on Karl Polanyi's (1957 [1944]) analysis of the structural causes of human suffering that are immanent in the nineteenth century idea of a free and self-regulating market, particularly for commoditized labour, and on David Graeber's (2011) inquiry into the 5000-year history of such commoditization. Ultimately, however, I shall trace the structural repression illuminated by these economic anthropologists to the logic of (general purpose) money itself, viewed as a specific human artifact attributed with a particular social and ecological inertia.

THE MONEY GAME

The inertia of artifacts has been experienced by any player of a board game, and it is no coincidence that the discipline of economics has found extensive use for game theory. By 2014, eleven game theorists had won the Nobel Memorial Prize in Economic Sciences. An extensive popular literature on the activities on Wall Street and other financial markets also tends to represent investments and exchange as an obscure kind of game, in which success is more a matter of intuition than of following explicit rules (Smith 1967).

The use of specific artifacts throughout human networks generates algorithmic regularities in social behavior that can be mathematically simulated. The current author makes no pretense to proficiency in such methods, but at a general level, I will propose that the trajectories of human societies reflect the design of the artifacts that regulate their exchange relations, and that policies for transforming society thus cannot avoid considering how such artifacts are designed.

To derive trajectories of social organization from regularities emanating from the features of given artifacts is an approach that suggests affinities with Actor Network Theory (ANT) (Latour 2005), although I would reserve the anthropomorphic concept of "agency" for sentient subjects (Hornborg 2017a). The issue of how to approach the role of money artifacts in social theory inevitably relates to the perception of money in socialist and Marxist understandings of the modern economy. Some utopian socialists such as Robert Owen (1771–1858) realized that to build a society liberated from the injustices of early capitalism, it would need to abolish conventional money (North 2007: 43–50). Although profoundly aware of the repressive logic of money, Karl Marx dismissed the idea of abolishing money as idealistic, unless the capitalist relations of production were overthrown first. In Marx's worldview, money artifacts were reflections of capitalist property relations rather than their source. His insight that money is a fetishized representation of exchange relations did not prompt him to consider that the direction of influence between artifacts and relations could be reversed. A century and a half later, however, ANT has explicitly challenged Marx's understanding of fetishism (Latour 2010). Although much of what is argued in ANT is problematic or unclear, to highlight the role of artifacts as generators of particular kinds of social relations is a significant contribution to social theory. From this perspective, it is remarkable that ANT has not concerned itself with the social repercussions of the quintessential artifact of money.

Viewing the economy as a game prompted and constrained by the features attributed to the pieces employed in that game raises the issue of which rules apply, whence they derive, and how they are communicated. For most people in modern nations, the only rules a player needs to know are that money is a remuneration for labour time or products sold, and that it can be used to purchase anything available through the market. The market is the economic aspect of society, the sum of all goods and services offered in exchange for money. If the money accessible to a given market actor is not sufficient to cover the market price of a commodity desired by that actor, additional money can be borrowed from (or rather created by) a bank. Specific rules regulate the rate at which the loan is to be repaid and the cost of borrowing it. These simple rules enable billions of humans to participate in an increasingly globalized economy. They are so general as to require no formal articulation or instruction. However, beyond these minimal rules there is an incredibly complex and constantly changing mass of regulations regarding the management of money flows between individuals, households, corporations, banks, authorities, and nations. These rules are the privileged knowledge of economists, and are generally inaccessible or incomprehensible to people at large. Although the aspiration of economics is to articulate a set of regulations that would organize a perpetually viable economy, the history of recurrent financial crises clearly indicates that there are serious flaws in mainstream economic models (cf. Keen 2011 [2001]; Mirowski 2013).

KARL POLANYI'S INDICTMENT OF THE MARKET

Towards the end of the Second World War, Karl Polanyi (1957 [1944]) summarized the turbulent history since the early nineteenth century in terms of a pervasive tension between the widespread liberal ambition to organize a self-regulating market, on the one hand, and the recurrent necessity to protect society against the various deleterious consequences of market principles, on the other. In retrospect, Polanyi observed that the market system had an inherent tendency to degrade human labourers as well as land, neither of which were produced for sale but both of which were treated as commodities. At the outset of his book, he declares his thesis 'that the idea of a self adjusting market implied a stark utopia', putting faith in an institution that 'could not exist for any length of time without annihilating the human and natural substance of society' (ibid.: 3). The idea implied basing society, for the first time in history, primarily on *gain* as the explicit principle determining human relations. He shows that the wholesale subordination of society to market principles was as traumatic in early nineteenth century Europe as it has continued to be wherever the modern economy has engulfed previously nonmodern populations organized in other terms. This part of his argument builds on the classical distinction between reciprocal gift giving and the market exchange of commodities (Mauss 1990 [1925]; Gregory 1982).

Writing during the Second World War, Polanyi believed that the globalized market economy born in the nineteenth century was rapidly declining. We now know that the resurgence of world trade after the war, and more emphatically with the neoliberal creed established in the 1980s, proved him wrong in terms of the tenacity of globalization, but not in terms of the fundamental tension between market and society that runs through his book (cf. Bugra and Agartan 2007).

Polanyi cites Aristotle's misgivings, more than two thousand years earlier, about production for gain as not 'natural' to humans. Well versed in anthropology, Polanyi provides examples from different societies of how humans have traditionally distinguished between local relations of reciprocity, on the one hand, and external markets, on the other. The Industrial Revolution in England, however, encouraged a fervent faith in the extension of market organization, so as to include even what Polanyi calls the 'fictitious' commodities of labour, land, and money. Much of the social history of nineteenth century England can be understood as legislation and other initiatives for the protection of people against the pernicious consequences of transforming human lives into commodities. This countermovement aiming at the 'self protection of society' (Polanyi 1957: 130) was prompted by the fact that the unregulated market in early nineteenth century England had the same implications for labour as it had for any other commodity: it depressed the price of labour to the absolute minimum required for survival. In contrast to the inclination of any premodern society, it was only to be expected that this inexorable logic should tend to reduce early British proletarians to the verge of starvation.

But the notion of the self-regulating market was also a threat to land (i.e., nature) and even to the supply of money itself. Polanyi observes that:

> if factory legislation and social laws were required to protect industrial man from the implications of the commodity fiction in regard to labor power, if land laws and agrarian tariffs were called into being by the necessity of protecting natural resources and the culture of the countryside against the implications of the commodity fiction in respect to them, it was equally true that central banking and the management of the monetary system were needed to keep manufactures and other productive enterprises safe from the harm involved in the commodity fiction as applied to money. (Polanyi 1957: 132)

To isolate land (i.e., an element of nature) and form a market out of it, Polanyi suggests, 'was perhaps the weirdest of all undertakings of our ancestors' (Polanyi 1957: 178). Beginning with the commercialization of the soil and the production of food and raw materials for industrial populations in Europe, the division of labour between rural and urban areas was extended to the planet. 'With free trade', he writes, 'the new and tremendous hazards of planetary interdependence sprang into being' (ibid.: 181). 'Once the great investments involved in the building of steamships and railroads came to fruition, whole continents were opened up and an avalanche of grain descended upon unhappy Europe' (ibid.: 182). As Polanyi notes, the perils of relying on a global market for basic subsistence became obvious with the First World War, highlighting the necessity of protectionist measures to provide nations with some measure of agricultural self-sufficiency. European nations could protect themselves against the repercussions of free international trade (e.g., through the introduction of corn laws in Central Europe), but the revolts against imperialism in the colonies should be understood as attempts to 'shelter themselves from the social dislocations caused by European trade policies' (ibid.: 183). Even if the notion of free trade and a global self-regulating market might appear beneficial from the perspective of a European businessman, its repercussions on other continents were very far from benevolent. The market freedom celebrated by liberals to this day remains a zero sum game.

World trade, finally, could only be relied upon with a system of international commodity money, as national token (or 'artificial') money cannot circulate outside the nation. National token money, Polanyi explains, was developed to alleviate the chronic scarcity of money in relation to the domestic expansion of production and trade to avoid deflation. The gold standard was introduced in the beginning of the nineteenth century to stabilize international exchange, but the recurrent problem since then has been the utopian project of maintaining a viable calibration between national currencies and an international gold standard. Given that volumes of production and exchange in different nations tend to change quite independently of each other, and that volumes of national currencies are internally calibrated with such volumes of economic activity to avoid deflation and domestic unemployment, the relation between the two kinds of money is inevitably strained. To overproduce token money results in inflation. The incentive for nations to issue more token money than can be backed by their deposits of gold has proven pervasive, and world economic history over the past two centuries has been punctuated by national relinquishments and resumptions of the connection to gold.

These complex challenges of national monetary policy required central banking, and Polanyi observes that a nation's economic identity is 'vested in the central bank' (Polanyi 1957: 205). World trade through much of the nineteenth century was dominated by the gold standard maintained by the Bank of England. In issuing large quantities of token money to finance its military efforts during World War I, however, England disregarded the gold standard to such an extent that in 1931, after a brief attempt to resume it, the country permanently dropped the connection between its currency and its deposits of gold. The United States followed its example two years later, and France and some other countries by the mid-1930s. The global economic depression which began in 1929 had already dramatically reduced world trade, but Polanyi concludes that the 'final failure of the gold standard was the final failure of market economy' (ibid.: 200). International debts were repudiated and the principles of economic liberalism, which had been celebrated in the 1920s, were largely rejected. The mobility of money, however, in the years of the depression compensated somewhat for the protectionist barriers that reduced the flow of people and goods.

Paradoxically, to make the idea of a self-regulating market feasible, economic liberalism has required 'an enormous increase in the administrative functions of the state' (Polanyi 1957: 139). As Polanyi observes, 'there was nothing natural about *laissez-faire*; free markets could never have come into being merely by allowing things to take their course'. Internationally, the vision of a free world market required rigorous political and often military enforcement. Whereas liberal economists tend to blame the breakdown of nineteenth century globalization on imperialist rivalry gradually gathering strength and leading to World War I, Polanyi dismisses such an account as myth, arguing instead that it was the 'economic earthquake' of increasing international trade that prompted protectionist measures and nationalism. This was evident already during the depression of 1873–1886, during which Western nations protected themselves from unemployment and instability 'with the help of central banks and customs tariffs, supplemented by migration laws' (ibid.: 217). Economic imperialism was simply the concomitant struggle of these nations to extend their trade into politically unprotected markets.

Political and economic crises, Polanyi argues, are generated by the continuous tension between the utopian vision of a free market and the several policies for self-protection to which nations are compelled to resort. It is regarding the nature of this tension that Polanyi disagrees with liberal economists. While Polanyi is convinced 'that the inherent absurdity of the idea of a self-regulating market system would have eventually destroyed society', liberals accuse the various counter reactions to that idea of 'having wrecked a great initiative' (Polanyi 1957: 145). The depression of the 1930s signified the disintegration of the world economy and 'the almost unbelievable fact that a civilization was being disrupted by the blind action of soulless institutions the only purpose of which was the automatic increase of material welfare' (ibid.: 219). 'The stupendous industrial achievements of market economy had been bought at the price of great harm to the substance of society' (ibid.: 186). The bottom line of Polanyi's argument, however, is that the contradictions generated by liberal capitalism are the common denominator of various fascist movements through history, including those that ignited the Second World War. 'Fascism, like socialism',

Polanyi asserts, 'was rooted in a market society that refused to function' (ibid.: 239). Both movements are opposed to liberalism, but only the latter upholds the idea of *freedom* in a complex society.

TAMING AND UNLEASHING THE MARKET

In hindsight we know that the international gold standard and conditions for free trade were quickly restored with the agreement at Bretton Woods after World War II—the same year (1944) that Polanyi published *The Great Transformation*—and that the American dollar remained pegged to gold for a quarter of a century until 1971, when President Nixon had spent so much money on the war in Vietnam that he was compelled, again, to abandon the connection. During those two and a half postwar decades, the industrial economies of the world enjoyed unprecedented expansion, and affluent European nations such as Sweden were able to offer models of market society tempered by a mild form of socialism. In the wake of the oil crises and economic instability of the 1970s, however, leading politicians in England and the United States launched a neoliberal program that dismantled much social security and other forms of political intervention in the operation of the market. The decades following this turn have brought deepening economic inequalities between and within nations as well as alarming environmental degradation worldwide. Moreover, the major financial crisis beginning in 2008 has frequently been explained in terms of the expansion of 'financialization' following the abandonment of the gold standard 37 years previously. Although the gold standard for almost 170 years had remained the foundation of a utopian vision of a self-regulated world market, neither its maintenance nor its absence has enhanced global financial equity or sustainability. In the nineteenth century as well as during the postwar decades, free international trade, enhanced by the gold standard, has enriched some nations at the expense of others. Financial stability is not to be confused with equality.

The tension between proponents of market principles and social self-protection, which Polanyi identified in the 1940s, recurs throughout history as well as in modern times and at successive geographical scales. The formation of national markets by mercantilist European states in the fifteenth and sixteenth centuries required the subjugation of local particularism and protectionist towns and municipalities; five centuries later the European Union extended similar visions of a common market to the continental scale, reducing the autonomy of the constituent nations. In 2016, however, a majority of British voters decided that their country should leave the European common market, and it seemed possible that other nations might follow. Such movements for national protectionism continue to be viewed by liberals as regressive and a threat to world peace. Even the social democrats who for most of the twentieth century protected the population of Sweden from the worst ravages of the market economy now tend to adhere to the liberal approach to globalization. The political project of social democracy, rather than a realistic model for all nations, has been feasible in affluent nations capable of displacing market-generated poverty and inequalities to others. Modernity cannot be globalized. As David Graeber (2011: 355) observes, 'we could no more have a universal world market than we could have a system in which everyone who wasn't a capitalist was somehow able to become a respectable, regularly paid wage labourer with access to adequate dental care. A world like that has never existed and never could exist'.

Polanyi asserts that 'socialism is, essentially, the tendency inherent in an industrial civilization to transcend the self-regulating market by consciously subordinating it to a democratic society' (Polanyi 1957: 234). At the time of his writing, and up to the 1970s, it was still reasonable to believe in the prospects of an industrialized but socially domesticated market economy like that of Sweden under social democracy. He was thus able to predict, for instance, that 'industrial civilization will continue to exist when the utopian experiment of a self-regulating market will be no more than a memory' (ibid.: 250). The modified market system of the future that he advocated would not be self-regulating, he suggested, as it will not comprise labour, land, and money. But in hindsight Polanyi appears to have overlooked the extent to which national self-protection is feasible only as long as damages to people and the environment can be displaced to other nations. The issue boils down to the definition of 'society'. If the damages generated by market principles cannot be resolved but merely displaced, the question is ultimately how a *world* society shall be able to protect itself from the market.

Neoliberalism is a renewed and more relentless form of market fundamentalism provoked into existence by the failures of capital accumulation in the 1970s. The neoliberal transformations of Sweden and other European welfare states since the 1980s suggest a parallel, at the national scale, to the failure of local experiments with 'utopian socialism' such as that of Robert Owen a century and a half earlier. It is significant that

Owen's vision of socialism, generally dismissed by posterity as utopian, is treated by Polanyi with the utmost respect (Polanyi 1957: 258). Again, the contradiction between economic liberalization and societal self-protection can be identified at separate geographical scales and separate historical times. Considering the currently widening inequalities within and between nations, the escalating environmental problems generated by world capitalism, and the increasingly vulnerable global financial system, we have every reason to revisit Polanyi's indictment of the liberal idea of the self-regulating market. These three incontrovertibly unsustainable trajectories of globalization correspond to the deterioration of precisely those three factors of production which Polanyi almost eighty years ago classified as 'fictitious commodities': labour, land, and money.

Polanyi identifies many of the pernicious social consequences of market logic. He shows how untamed industrial capitalism in nineteenth century England tended to make workers 'physically dehumanized' and 'the owning classes...morally degraded' (Polanyi 1957: 102). Until the workers had been made dependent on 'the mill of the market which ground the lives of the people', popular democracy was unanimously understood as 'a danger to capitalism' (ibid.: 226). If labour is indeed supposed to find its price on the market, Polanyi observes, it should be expected 'to be almost continually on strike' (ibid.: 230–231). Such absurdities are only 'logical inference from the commodity theory of labor'.

THE LOGIC OF GLOBAL INEQUALITIES
AS EMERGENT FROM MONEY

We have every reason to agree with Polanyi that the history of the past two centuries has been dominated by a tension between a blind logic of some sort and various social forces and movements attempting to curb its most deleterious repercussions. The crucial issue, however, is how this blind logic is conceptualized. Marx framed it in terms of a 'mode of production' called capitalism. Polanyi rarely refers to 'capitalism' but prefers to identify the problem as 'the idea of the self regulating market'. Fernand Braudel, following Marx, distinguished between markets as the use of money to convert one commodity into another (C-M-C1), on the one hand, and capitalism (M-C-M1) as the use of commodities to augment one's supply of money, on the other (cf. Graeber 2011: 260). Both Marx and Polanyi are supremely aware of the inequities and human degradation that are the flip side of economic growth and technological progress since the Industrial Revolution, but both may have underplayed the root of the societal inertia that disturbs them. To be sure, it is easy to identify human advocates of this inertia, whether defined as a class of capitalists or a school of liberal economic theorists, but, given the pervasive failures to curb its destructive consequences through politics or economic discourse, we have reason to look elsewhere for its final source.

If the Actor Network theorists are correct in deriving significant aspects of human social relations from features of the artifacts that mediate those relations, we should find ourselves seriously revisiting St. Paul's observation that 'the love of money is the root of all evil'. What Marx expounded as the logic of capital and Polanyi as the idea of the market can be viewed as the societal implications of the inertia of general-purpose money. The incentives driving the behavior of capitalists and other market actors can be derived from the possibilities and imperatives that are immanent in the very artifact of conventional money. The concept of artifact as used here encompasses items manufactured by humans as well as the features attributed to them by their users. These features are ultimately ideas, but when the items with which they are invested circulate in society according to the logic determined by those ideas, they form regularities and trajectories of their own, which are external to the individual human mind and may remain largely opaque to the participants. A relevant illustration of such artifactual determinacy are the pieces in a game of chess. The potential mobility of a queen is distinctly different from that of a knight or a pawn. The possible trajectories of the game are determined by the attributes of the different pieces as defined by its rules. Transferred to the game of market capitalism, a corollary of this perspective is that its societal logic is determined by the attributes of money. Every now and then, Polanyi himself casually refers to the market economy as a game (Polanyi 1957: 160, 188, 197). From several different perspectives, it can indeed be shown to have features of a zero sum game. The market economy thus not only displaces work and environmental loads (Hornborg 2013), it also redistributes risk, freedom, mobility (Bauman 1998), and even honor (Graeber 2011: 175).

A shift in habits of thought to attribute responsibility for human social relations to features of the artifacts that are employed in mediating those relations may be what is required of us in the current global impasse. It means finally fathoming the implications of Marx's discovery of *fetishism*. We need to understand that the 'market economy', 'capitalism' and even the technological progress of the 'Industrial Revolution' are all ultimately products of our preoccupation with general-purpose money. Even in Polanyi's narrative, such insights are never far away. He is well aware that a market economy 'assumes the presence of money, which functions as purchasing power in the hands of its owners' (Polanyi 1957: 68), that eighteenth century national markets 'presupposed the almost general use of money' (ibid.: 115), and that the Owenites' attempts to transform the social logic of capitalism required 'introducing a currency of its own' (ibid.: 169).

At some level Polanyi is also aware that mechanization itself is geared to the commoditization of labour, land, and money. He writes that we cannot fully grasp the nature of the market economy unless we realize 'the impact of the machine on a commercial society' (Polanyi 1957: 40) and that 'machine production in a commercial society involves...no less a transformation than that of the natural and human substance of society into commodities' (ibid.: 42). He observes that the nineteenth century, 'whether hailing the fact as the apex of civilization or deploring it as a cancerous growth', naïvely imagined that the market economy was a 'natural outcome' rather than the 'artificial' result of policies designed 'to meet a situation which was created by the no less artificial phenomenon of the machine' (ibid.: 57). His recognition that the Industrial Revolution was inextricably interconnected with the market economy is evident in his conclusion that 'either machines had to be demolished, as the Luddites had tried to do, or a regular labour market had to be created' (ibid.: 81). According to Polanyi, the immediate self-interest of workers 'destined them to become the protectors of society against the intrinsic dangers of a machine civilization' (ibid.: 101). The Owenite movement, he asserts, represented the desire 'to discover a form of existence which would make man master of the machine' (ibid.: 167). The inextricable relation between machine technology, markets, and money to which he refers is significant but, as I shall show, widely misunderstood.

Although this is not the place to elaborate the argument in full, I have for many years tried to communicate an understanding of mechanization and technology that turns Polanyi's view of the relation between machines and markets on its head. Not only does industrialized production prompt factory owners to commoditize labour, land, and money, but industrial technology itself is a *product* of such commoditization.

The Industrial Revolution in England was made possible by the global flows of embodied labour and land. Industrial technology is an enhancement of the productivity of local labour through the appropriation, through asymmetric exchange, of commoditized human time and natural space (Hornborg 1992, 1998, 2001, 2013, 2016). Ultimately, all commoditization, and the new forms of asymmetric exchange associated with industrialization, are generated by the very idea of general-purpose money. In the same sense that a biological organism is the manifestation of its metabolic exchanges with its environment, the technological infrastructure of industrial society is the tangible manifestation of global relations of resource exchange, but orchestrated by money. Money and technology are thus recursively and inextricably intertwined. To approach 'economic growth' and 'technological progress' as separable indices of development is a pervasive illusion that continues to obstruct our grasp of contemporary concerns regarding global justice, sustainability, and financial resilience.

Polanyi recognized the *immoral* implications of market logic as a pervasive trajectory of liberal ideals of self-regulation. The history of economic thought from seventeenth century England to neoliberalism and the financial crisis of 2008 can be viewed as a succession of ideological justifications of various kinds of social injury (Ruggiero 2013). From merchant to financial capitalism, the market has served as an instrument for displacing harm to others.

The relation between economic exchange, money, and morality is complex and has been very extensively discussed by theologians, philosophers, sociologists, and anthropologists (Bloch and Parry 1989). My point here is that the establishment of neoclassical economics in the final third of the nineteenth century entailed an abandonment of moral issues. Prior schools of economic thought had applied various criteria of morality to exchange, such as thrift, land management, or justice. Their moral arguments had in various ways been connected to concerns with the material substance of exchange, whether advocating restraint in exporting precious metals, care for agricultural soils, or a labour theory of value. The turn to an exclusive preoccupation with market equilibrium in Victorian Britain implied the simultaneous and interrelated abandonment of morality and materiality as concerns of economics. The only kinds of moral assessment relevant from now on were concerns with the extent to which market mechanisms had been permitted to operate freely. To neoclassical economists the moral notion of 'unequal exchange' thus denotes market power (such as monopoly) rather than an asymmetric exchange of resources, as identified by heterodox approaches (cf. Emmanuel 1972; Dorninger and Hornborg 2015). As all other possible measures of commodity flows (such as volumes of embodied labour, land, energy, or materials) are made invisible by the exclusive concern with monetary exchange values (utility), any voluntary market transaction is, by definition, fair. Free market prices axiomatically guarantee reciprocal exchange, because concerns with reciprocity are delegated to monetary assessments. In this view, by implication, a net transfer of material resources to core sectors of world society should (incomprehensibly) be irrelevant to their prospects of accumulating technological infrastructure. It will now be evident how money and technology are intertwined. The establishment of neoclassical economics was the protection of capital accumulation from moral objections based on the asymmetry of biophysical resource flows.

Polanyi's point that the commoditization of labour and land, if left to a self-regulating market, would severely degrade both people and nature is both an analytical deduction from economic theory and an empirical inference from the history of early industrialism. Although a major theorist of money, he did not adopt the Marxian view that monetary exchange values tend to obscure the transfer of more substantial qualities. However, if he had wanted to demonstrate that unrestrained market exchange will tend to deprive both labour and land of their *physical* capacity for regeneration, it would have been completely in line with his conclusions. It is on the whole remarkable that the voluminous and profound reflections of economic anthropologists on money and exchange so very rarely go beyond the cultural semiotics of exchange to consider how these semiotics orchestrate material transfers. My guess is that anthropological training is so exclusively devoted to the 'mental' (cognitive, cultural, symbolic) aspects of human existence that 'material' aspects remain inaccessible both theoretically and methodologically. The only example of such interdisciplinarity in economic anthropology that I can think of is Maurice Godelier's (1969) identification, almost fifty years ago, of the unequal exchange of embodied labour time between two tribes of New Guinea. Regardless of Godelier's conclusions, such attempts to unearth biophysical flows veiled by cultural institutions of reciprocal exchange are unheard of among anthropologists today.

Money and Morality

David Graeber's (2011) reflections on the history of money and debt provide a significant complement to the foundational contributions to economic anthropology by Mauss (1990 [1925]) and Polanyi. He perspicaciously undermines our familiarity with monetary debt by illuminating its historical origins and contrasting it with patterns of exchange and obligation in a wide variety of cultural contexts. The argument is highly pertinent to the present discussion of destructive tendencies inherent in market exchange, its ambiguous relations to morality, and the identification of financial crisis as a manifestation of its potential for structural repression. Modern money itself, Graeber notes, is debt. Long before debt could be calculated in the unnegotiable, mathematical terms of money, interpersonal obligations were embedded in compelling moral imperatives, but Graeber's ambition is to explore how the precise, quantitative language of the market transforms our sense of morality and justice—that is, how the autonomous, mechanical rationality of cost–benefit calculation (and its frequently deadly repercussions) has emerged out of a moral sociality grounded in interpersonal relations.

This is the perennial concern of economic anthropology, epitomized in Polanyi's observations on the 'disembeddedness' of the modern market. In delegating the logic of social relations to the fetishism of money and market mechanisms, it is as if humans are able to dissociate themselves from, and relinquish responsibility for, the suffering they impose on other people and the planet. 'Any system that reduces the world to numbers', Graeber concludes, 'can only be held in place by weapons' (Graeber 2011: 386). A debt, he finally reminds us, is 'a promise corrupted by both math and violence' (ibid.: 391).

Graeber proposes that there have been historical oscillations between periods dominated by virtual or credit money, on the one hand, and commodity money made from bullion, on the other. He associates periods dominated by commodity money (800 BC–AD 600, 1450–1971) with relatively more warfare, plunder, and slavery, while periods of credit money (3500–800 BC, AD 600–1450, 1971–?) are associated with relatively more social peace and trust. The reason precious metals predominate in periods of widespread war and plunder, says Graeber, is that, unlike credit arrangements, they can be stolen. In ancient Greece, coinage made from bullion inspired the notion of a substance that could be converted into everything, which is precisely the modern concept of money. Graeber insightfully reviews the theological dimensions of money, including the denunciation of usury in Islamic and early Christian thought. The long-standing concerns over the conundrum of money are graphically reflected in Shakespeare's *The Merchant of Venice* (cf. Macfarlane 1985).

Although the empirical historical correlation between commodity money and warfare (and between credit money and peace) is not quite as neat as Graeber suggests (cf. Davies 2002; Ferguson 2008; Weatherford 1997), his argument that coins made of bullion were widely used to pay for armies and the capture of slaves (to mine more bullion) is convincing. As he himself demonstrates, however, slavery can be a consequence of credit as much as violent conquest, and the distinction between Roman slavery and feudal debt peonage is thus ultimately as equivocal as that between slavery and wage labour. The majority of slaves exported from the Bight of Biafra in the 1760s had become slaves through debt servitude, and Graeber notes that 'commercial economies had already been extracting slaves from human economies for thousands of years', finally asking if the practice is 'actually constitutive of civilization itself?' (Graeber 2011: 163). Money and markets indeed appear to be institutions for transforming persons into instruments of production. Wage labour, Graeber suggests, is 'the renting of our freedom in the same way that slavery can be conceived as its sale' (ibid.: 206).

Graeber notes that most people simultaneously hold the two contradictory convictions that to pay back one's loan is a matter of morality, while money lenders are evil. The financial crisis beginning in 2008 exposed a 'host of new, ultra sophisticated financial innovations' that had been devised by bankers but that were intentionally made impossible to fathom for the layman, as 'nothing more than very elaborate scams' (Graeber 2011: 15). Such scams are also being perpetrated at the international level. Some nations (most conspicuously the United States) can count on an indefinite extension of international credit that assumes the appearance of tribute, rather than foreign loans, while other nations are punished with austerity measures and coerced into debt repayment and poverty. 'American imperial power', Graeber says, 'is based on a debt that will never – can never – be repaid' (ibid.: 367). It is a war debt, and amounts to a tax paid to the United States by the whole world. He refers to it as 'debt imperialism'. His understanding of world capitalism is well summed up in the assertion that:

it is a gigantic financial apparatus of credit and debt that operates...to pump more and more labor out of just about everyone with whom it comes into contact, and as a result produces an endlessly expanding volume of material goods. It does so not just by moral compulsion, but above all by using moral compulsion to mobilize sheer physical force. (Graeber 2011: 346)

A significant aspect of Graeber's world history of money and debt is the recognition that an underlying tendency or inertia toward a fetishized, money-mediated repression of other people is evident over such a long period of time and in diverse cultural contexts. He notes that 'almost all elements of financial apparatus that we've come to associate with capitalism...came into being not only before the science of economics...but also before the rise of factories, and wage labor itself' (Graeber 2011: 345). This confirms the point that I made previously about money being a prerequisite of the Industrial Revolution and modern technology itself. It is striking, however, how the ontology of technology in mainstream thought—even among the most perspicacious critics of capitalism—remains sequestered from and uncontaminated by our most profound insights on social relations of exploitation. Although highly relevant to asymmetric flows of embodied labour, and although he occasionally mentions the degradation of the planet, Graeber's analysis never extends into serious consideration of material phenomena such as technology, energy, or ecology.

Another significant aspect of Graeber's study is its recurrent acknowledgement of the magical ontology of money. Money, he says, 'has no essence' (Graeber 2011: 372). Even Aristotle saw that money, even gold, is just a convention. Faust (i.e., Goethe) and Keynes were equally aware that it does not matter how much money you print, as long as people trust it. To consider it fraudulent that bankers create money out of nothing is a sign of materialism and a naïve belief in money as essence—an indication, indeed, that we have been persuaded by their magic. This is the nature of the bubble currently enveloping the world. The players of the money game know all too well that it 'can all come tumbling down' (Smith 1967: 238). Sooner or later it must. But the ontological dilemma we seem unable to digest is that what Keynes called 'organic propositions' (the truth of which depends on *beliefs*) are able to organize physical reality. The contemporary extraction of unconventional fossil fuels in North America would not be feasible without the financial fantasies of Wall Street. This means that we are allowing the human fantasy of money to magically destroy the planet (Hornborg 2016). To thus fully acknowledge the interpenetration of human fantasy and physical reality is our only chance of surviving the Anthropocene.

In conclusion, there is something profoundly emancipatory in the insight that money is ultimately an *idea* and its current form merely a convention that could, in principle, be redesigned. Many attempts to rethink what money is have been made over the years (North 2007), but all have ultimately failed, and for similar reasons. Rather than revolutionary movements challenging hegemonic power centers such as the Bank of England or Wall Street, the introduction of new forms of currency needs to be anchored in the political intentions of democratically elected authorities. It should be feasible, for instance, for a national government to issue a complementary currency for local use only, and distribute it as a basic income to all the inhabitants of a country (see Hornborg 2017b). Doing so would increase community resilience, economic diversity, and ecological sustainability, while counteracting global asymmetries and, importantly, dissolving the proletarian condition that Marx identified as a fundamental prerequisite of capitalism. It would amount precisely to a re-embedding of the market in society. The rules of the game *can* be rewritten, the pieces redesigned, and the players liberated from their delusions.

REFERENCES

Bauman, Z. 1998. *Globalization: The Human Consequences.* Cambridge: Polity Press.

Bloch, M., and J. Parry. 1989. Introduction: Money and the Morality of Exchange. In *Money and the Morality of Exchange*, ed. J. Parry and M. Bloch, 1–32. Cambridge: Cambridge University Press.

Bugra, A., and K. Agartan (eds.). 2007. *Reading Karl Polanyi for the Twenty-First Century.* New York: Palgrave Macmillan.

Davies, G. 2002. *A History of Money.* Cardiff: University of Wales Press.

Dorninger, C., and A. Hornborg. 2015. Can EEMRIO Analyses Establish the Occurrence of Ecologically Unequal Exchange? *Ecological Economics* 119: 414–418.

Emmanuel, A. 1972. *Unequal Exchange: A Study of the Imperialism of Trade.* New York: Monthly Review Press.

Ferguson, N. 2008. *The Ascent of Money: A Financial History of the World.* New York: Penguin Press.

Godelier, M. 1969. La monnaie de sel des Baruya de Nouvelle-Guinée. *L'Homme* IX (2): 5–37.

Graeber, D. 2011. *Debt: The First 5,000 Years.* Brooklyn: Melville House.

Gregory, C.A. 1982. *Gifts and Commodities*. London: Academic Press.

Hornborg, A. 1992. Machine Fetishism, Value, and the Image of Unlimited Good: Toward a Thermodynamics of Imperialism. *Man* (N.S.) 27: 1–18.

Hornborg, A. 1998. Towards an Ecological Theory of Unequal Exchange: Articulating World System Theory and Ecological Economics. *Ecological Economics* 25 (1): 127–136.

Hornborg, A. 2001. *The Power of the Machine: Global Inequalities of Economy, Technology, and Environment*. Walnut Creek: AltaMira Press.

Hornborg, A. 2013. *Global Ecology and Unequal Exchange: Fetishism in a Zero-Sum World*. London: Routledge (Revised paperback version).

Hornborg, A. 2016. *Global Magic: Technologies of Appropriation from Ancient Rome to Wall Street*. Houndmills: Palgrave Macmillan.

Hornborg, A. 2017a. Artifacts Have Consequences, Not Agency: Toward a Critical Theory of Global Environmental History. *European Journal of Social Theory* 20 (1): 95–110.

Hornborg, A. 2017b. How to Turn an Ocean Liner: A Proposal for Voluntary Degrowth by Redesigning Money for Sustainability, Justice, and Resilience. *Journal of Political Ecology* 24: 623–632.

Keen, S. 2011 [2001]. *Debunking Economics: The Naked Emperor Dethroned?* London: Zed Books.

Knight, D.M., and C. Stewart. 2016. Ethnographies of Austerity: Temporality, Crisis and Affect in Southern Europe. *History and Anthropology* 27 (1): 1–18.

Latour, B. 2005. *Reassembling the Social: An Introduction to Actor-Network-Theory*. Oxford: Oxford University Press.

Latour, B. 2010. *On the Modern Cult of the Factish Gods*. Durham: Duke University Press.

Macfarlane, A. 1985. The Root of All Evil. In *The Anthropology of Evil*, ed. D. Parkin, 57–76. Oxford: Blackwell.

Mauss, M. 1990 [1925]. *The Gift: The Form and Reason for Exchange in Archaic Societies*. London: Routledge.

Mirowski, P. 2013. *Never Let a Serious Crisis Go to Waste: How Neoliberalism Survived the Financial Meltdown*. London: Verso.

North, P. 2007. *Money and Liberation: The Micropolitics of Alternative Currency Movements*. Minneapolis: University of Minnesota Press.

Polanyi, K. 1957 [1944]. *The Great Transformation: The Political and Economic Origins of Our Time*. Boston: Beacon Press.

Ruggiero, V. 2013. *The Crimes of the Economy: A Criminological Analysis of Economic Thought*. London: Routledge.

Smith, A. [alias Goodman, G.J.W.]. 1967. *The Money Game*. New York: Vintage.

Weatherford, J. 1997. *The History of Money: From Sandstone to Cyberspace*. New York: Three Rivers.

CHAPTER 4

Managing Against the Odds: Economic Crisis, Bad Governance and Grassroots Entrepreneurialism in Naples

Italo Pardo

Classical liberalism advocates the individual's entrepreneurial role in the political, cultural, and economic fields, arguing for minimum state intervention to give individuals an opportunity to develop their potentialities and improve their social position, thus benefiting the broader society. In order to grasp the empirical magnitude of this point, a sophisticated analysis needs to address the complex ways in which agency is capable of influencing the system (Abrams 1982; Pardo 1996). With specific reference to South Italy, anthropological investigation has brought out the moral and cultural complexity of individual action, the corrupting role of politicking and, highlighting a key limit of democracy (Lukes 1991), processes of exclusion that serve the interests of those in power and their cohorts, thus compounding the perceived weak legitimacy of both governance and the law across the social spectrum (Pardo 2011, 2015, 2017).

I. Pardo (✉)
School of Anthropology and Conservation,
University of Kent, Canterbury, UK

© The Author(s) 2018
M. Spyridakis (ed.), *Market Versus Society*, Palgrave Studies in Urban Anthropology, https://doi.org/10.1007/978-3-319-74189-5_4

Sophisticated thinkers in social anthropology such as Sir Edmund Leach and Rosemary Harris (Leach 1977: xvi ff.; Harris 1986, 1988) eminently warned that abstract thinking that does not systematically rely on the in-depth knowledge of the empirical situation has little to contribute to our understanding of the individual in society. It may encourage, instead, simplistic and misleading views. If we agree that the study of human beings in society needs to account for the complexity of real life, we must also agree that it needs to responsibly take very seriously the interplay between personal morality, shared values, and action.

The Naples ethnography, I shall argue, underscores the sociological significance of people's merging social morality and personal choice into practices that observably recognize more than the self. The theoretical imperative is to ask whether individual-oriented necessarily means individualistic.[1] When it comes to abiding by the law, Italians face a triple whammy. First, the illegality and corruption of rulers and of 'the powerful' more generally regularly make the headlines but few actually serve jail sentences. Second, as prominent jurists have noted (Miller 2004; Nordio 2015), the Italian legislative system is over-complicated and often ambiguous, de facto allowing ramified injustice and distortions. Third, the democratic process is insistently circumvented through legalisms and political casuistry. Little surprise, then, that my informants should repeatedly remind me that 'a fish rots from the head down'.

NAPLES TODAY

Beyond Naples' natural beauty and historical and artistic attractions—often in disrepair or difficult to get to—the everyday reality is gloomy. Rulers' bombastic rhetoric (*Corriere del Mezzogiorno*, 16 June 2017) sounds hollow next to the stark reality of a state-led austerity and of the deepening inequality dividing a privileged few from the struggling many. Ordinary Neapolitans' life is fraught with difficulties; from the low quality of public services to the poor efficiency of the bureaucracy, from impending bust (Lo Cicero 2017) to growing local taxation; from the ever present rubbish and its pervading stench to the proliferating vermin (*Il Mattino*, 6 June 2017); from bad governance and the corresponding urban decay to official high

---

[1] The ethnography that I discuss in this chapter was originally collected in the mid-1980s in a typical *quartiere* (neighbourhood) in central Naples and has since been updated through periodic 2-to-6-month fieldtrips.

unemployment, from the strict imposition of the law onto formal business to the authorities' observable laissez-faire attitude towards illegality, particularly though not only, immigrants' (Pardo 2017).

South Italy has become known for the systematic misuse of public funds, which are used for for clientelism as opposed to investment. The Cassa del Mezzogiorno (Fund for the South, discontinued in 1984) was established in 1950 by the central government to stimulate economic growth through the development of the infrastructure, credit subsidies and tax advantages. Large companies benefited, small enterprises did not. Here, industrialization has been weak and fragmented, contributing to the prominence of nonindustrial values. Politicised prettifications multiply, including unpaid internships, apprenticeships and other fancily labelled 'qualifications' that are supposed to facilitate access to proper employment but actually do not. Formal jobs are few and permanent jobs fewer. The Italian Institute of Statistics reports that in 2016 the rate of unemployment in Italy was 11.7%; 7.2 million Italians (11.9%) lived on the poverty line. In Naples, the official unemployment rate was 23.7% of the active population, reaching 40% among the young (http://dati.istat.it/?queryid=298). The closure of large factories; the effects of small distribution being swallowed up by large retailers; cheap products from Asia flooding the market; high taxation; and the over-complicated bureaucracy that confronts anyone who runs or wants to start a business combine with great difficulties in accessing credit—therefore capital—legally (Pardo 2000). This situation is not helped by a political rhetoric that constantly shifts between naïve practical incompetence and abstract radical stances, in the process defacing the market through undue interference.

Many ordinary Neapolitans whom I have met do manage against these odds, but they do so—'depressingly', they say—with little hope of significantly improving their condition. To understand this, we need to understand the moral, normative, and practical framework that informs their relationship to the formal definition of legality and crime, and the corresponding 'coercive apparatus' (Weber 1978: 313–314). And we need to do so while steering clear of the reductive opposition of morality to interest.

Elsewhere, I have addressed the constantly re-drawn demarcations between legal and illegal work as part of the global development of the modern economy (Pardo 1996, 2012a). In this process, ordinary people's view of what is legitimate and illegitimate is key. My informants clearly differentiate between crime (and criminals) and actions which bend, sidestep or generally fall below the strictly legal line but are nevertheless ordinarily undertaken because they are seen to pose no serious challenge to the moral and socio-economic order in which they set their lives. Accordingly, their informal activities may not always be strictly legal and may not always agree with the 'laws' of market capitalism, but they cannot be misread as evidence of marginality or of an anti-market culture. Ethnographic evidence will help to address this complexity. First, let us look a little more to the odds facing the ordinary Neapolitans whom I know.

Stereotypes and Bad Governance

Notoriously, a stereotype of the South that has become predominant since the Unification of Italy (1860) is that of an amoral and ungovernable mob. In brief, bogged down by lack of trust in each other and by their amoral familism and superstitious beliefs, this stereotype goes, southerners are politically and socially backward; they are narrow individualists who lack social sense and cannot be trusted. Highlighting the pitfalls of an approach that serves vested interests, the *popolino* of Naples[2] have long been described as a *sottoproletariato* (lumpenproletariat), in dominant Marxist parlance.

I have assessed the intellectual responsibility of this stereotype (Pardo 1996: Chapter 1, 2001; see also Stewart 2001 and Schneider 2002), and its political ramifications have been the object of careful analysis (Pardo and Prato 2011). Here, suffice it to say that, riding a politically established monopoly on the 'right' intellectual credentials, generations of writers have more or less explicitly legitimated this view, fuelling at once economic exclusion and gradations of distrust *between* rulers and the ruled. I find it interesting that, despite its ugly classist and racist undertones having been amply exposed to be obnoxious to reason and observation, this view persists today,[3] as do the consequent restrictions in terms of factual citizenship. Betraying a mixture of contempt

---

[2] Traditionally, my informants thus describe themselves, rejecting the word's derogative meaning (Pardo 1996). Now, having become widely aware of their stereotype through the media, they say they proudly identify as *popolino*.

[3] Pretexts are regularly found to reiterate it. For a recent instance, see the typical remarks made in this line by the research institute CENSIS (Centro Studi Investimenti Sociali) and widely reported in the media; see, for example *la Repubblica Napoli* (13 June 2017, available at http://napoli.repubblica.it/cronaca/2017/06/13/news/il_censis_e_il_mercato_del_falso_a_napoli_deficit_di_senso_civico_e_cultura_della_legalita_-167999086/?refresh_ce).

and apprehension towards a morality that is difficult to control because it is committed to personal independence and discerning choices, local rulers of various political persuasions have practised in their own way Gramsci's idea (1966: 216–218) that popular culture—intended as a 'conception of the world'—should be taken seriously, investigated and, then, uprooted, to be replaced (ideally, with its bearers' cooperation) by a superior, enlightened conception.

With graded sophistication, informants from all walks of life reckon that this dominant approach has made them feel marginal—morally, socially and politically. Throughout the Christian Democrat-dominated second half of the twentieth century,[4] the Communist Party (PCI) was in nominal opposition at central government level *and* in power in local administrations, as well as in parliamentary commissions and other key decision-making bodies. It also combined its dominance among the intelligentsia with a belief in holding a monopoly over higher ideals and values. In its renamed version, it has enjoyed almost unchallenged power in local government. Over the past twenty-five years, leftist rulers in Naples and its region have rhetorically opposed assistance and clientelism, while practising both (Pardo 2001, 2011, 2012b) to their and their cohorts' observable advantage.

Beyond unhelpful political rhetoric, the sections that follow bring out the ethnographic ramifications of the key point that we may well be dealing with imperfect competition, constraints, and inequality. However, it cannot be reasonably argued that these conditions are culturally pre-determined and self-perpetuating, maybe with people's unwitting complicity.

THE RATIONALITY OF FULFILMENT

I maintain that moral values are crucial to purposive action—individual, associated, and collective. I have argued (Pardo 1996: esp. pp. 10–12) the importance of recognizing that such values do interact strongly and continuously with material interest but not for this they are necessarily predatory or strictly functional to utility maximization. Nor does purposive action merely (or basically) obey the 'clean' laws of economic behaviour (Parry and Bloch 1989). In managing their existence, most ordinary Neapolitans whom I have met quietly bring together personal resources of very different kinds with a commitment to action that gives satisfaction as well as producing tangible results.

---

[4]Elsewhere, I have reviewed the responsibilities of the Christian Democrats, also well-versed in using 'organic intellectuals' (Pardo 1996).

The ethnography of the *popolino* of central Naples has brought out an entrepreneurial approach that draws on community resources in defiance of attempts by the state to regulate, control and extract revenue from the production, circulation and consumption of goods. The local men and women with whose lives and moralities I have become familiar over the years are bearers of a culture of *strong continuous interaction* between material aspects (money, possessions, their own body) and nonmaterial aspects (encompassing the moral and the spiritual, the mundane and the supra-mundane) of their universes. This *interaction* distinctly qualifies the social, cultural, and political makeup of local life. It 'profoundly informs the actors' sense of the relationship between action and results in all spheres of their lives, with an emphasis on the role of the significant others (living and dead, through belief in a relationship of mutual influence) in the individual's entitlement to feeling worthy and therefore fulfilled in the broad sense—non-materially as well as materially—and in the long term' (Pardo 1996: xii).

This concept of fulfilment bears directly on the social significance of personal virtue, for it links the construction of personal well being to others' recognition of their own worthiness. It casts strong doubts on the association that is often established between personal initiative and entrepreneurialism and an inability to act disinterestedly, for it directs such construction towards society, not away from it. The *strong continuous interaction* that I have outlined is crucial to ordinary people's approach and to their representation of such an approach. Equally significant, the overwhelming majority of my *popolino* friends reject formalization and bureaucratization of their spiritual lives with the same determination they show in rejecting the formalization and bureaucratization of their economic and social lives. Relevant to mainstream social theory, their management of existence raises complex issues of moral legitimacy that invite a nonmaterialist view of the complex rationality that regulates the relationship between moral values and practical demands in the pursuit of fulfilment. This needs further attention.

BETWEEN THE FORMAL AND THE INFORMAL

A quantitative assessment of the informal 'sector' (the inverted commas are intended to stress the conceptual limitation of the word sector) is, of course, extremely difficult. Some estimates value the growing 'shadow economy' (ISTAT 2013) at about 190 billion Euros (11.9% of GDP).

In 2010, roughly six million Southerners of working age were esti-mated to be involved in informal activities. According to a Parliamentary Inquiry, the informal 'sector' is larger in the Centre-North (http://it.finance.yahoo.com/notizie/riciclaggio-bankitalia-sommerso-criminale-vale-095243438.html).

My empirical knowledge of local life has led me to reject as mislead-ing both the distinction between employment and work and the view of informal work as a separate mode of production (Pahl 1980) or, worse, as belonging to a 'casual economy' in which criminals (*Camorristi*) are power-ful employers. Expanding on an earlier point, the informality that I have doc-umented needs to be set against the background of both a general uneasiness with (and therefore distance from) organized crime and the graded relation-ships between legality and illegality that colour many local dealings.

The entrepreneurial approach of my *popolino* friends is informed by the culture of *sapé fa* (cleverness) and by the principles *aiutat' ca Dio t'aiut'* (God helps those who help themselves), *Nun voglio sta' suggett' a nisciun'* (I don't want to be subject to anyone) and *Chi pecora s' fa 'o lupo s'a magna* (If you behave like a sheep, you'll become a wolf's meal). Many officially unemployed among them aspire to a secure public sector job, believing such employment to be undemanding and to allow free time to pursue rewarding 'side activities'. The ethnographer soon realises that this approach is embodied, politically, by a disenchanted view of the powerful and of one's own relationships with them (see, for example, Pardo 1996: Chapter 6) and, economically, by small businesses rooted in the informal 'sector', at the limits or beyond the limits of the strictly legal, but gener-ally addressing the market as a whole. Many such businesses rely on work-shops that produce goods—in part or totally—illegally (evading tax on the purchase of raw materials and the sale of finished products, as well as employment tax and other welfare state contributions). A proportion of such products finds its way into the legal market.

Taking on the challenge of a normative understanding of work and entrepreneurship beyond the unlikely 'dual economy' view, I share Parry and Bloch's point (1989) on the interaction between the moral and the monetary and Wallman's (1984) on the importance of contacts, informa-tion, time, and identity. However, one further step is needed to account for the complexity of an entrepreneurialism that, profoundly informed by the aforementioned *strong continuous interaction*, thrives on the blur-ring of boundaries between the categories of the modern organization of labour.

Over the years, I have kept in touch with my socially diversified informants and their networks, in many cases reaching outside Naples. My recent case studies of small and medium businesses show people making a living, achieving an education and staying healthy in today's adverse situation. In economic terms, their *sapé fa* translates into establishing or expanding *independent* enterprises through mobilization of personal information and networks.

As I have indicated, they are often excluded from formal access to credit—therefore, after Marshall (1950), from a fundamental right of citizenship in Western society. Here, the relationship between credit and entrepreneurship is distorted by exceeding difficulties in gaining formal access to capital, by overpriced banking, arbitrary but legal hidden costs and overheads, bureaucratic complication and inefficiency, arbitrary procedural demands and sometimes dubious dealings.[5] Perhaps above all, here interest rates are between 2.5 and 5% higher than in the Centre-North; this gap varies in keeping with the state of the economy, as does the legal limit on interest rates. Perfectly legal, though highly questionable, hidden costs increase the *actual* rates and the gap. For instance, in the late 1990s the legal limit was 8.5% but the *real* gap between interest rates in the North and the South was 11%. These restrictions combine with the more ordinary difficulties that generally characterize the process of starting or expanding a business, encouraging informal ways to raise capital. People cope as best as they can. When they cannot buy money officially, they borrow at low or no interest from friends and family. Only as a last resort do they risk borrowing from usurious moneylenders (Pardo 2000).

My field notes bring out a classical theme in economic anthropology (Smith 1989: 309ff.), as they show many entrepreneurs finding it desirable—though not always doable—to operate *mainly* 'in the sunlight' because, they reckon, operating informally is too costly monetarily (bribery was recurrently mentioned as a considerable drawback), as well as in time and worry. In some cases, the informal aspect is limited to fiscal matters; in others, it extends to the purchase of part of the merchandise; still in others it may involve a proportion of employees, including foreigners. The case of Peppe and his family, that of Pietro and his staff, those of Elvira and Grazia, of the young Enzo, Rosa and Carmela and of foreign

---

[5] Some bank officials refer unsuccessful applicants to private credit agencies that grant credit easily and at high interest.

workers exemplify the complexity of local entrepreneurialism, the nature and processes of employed and unemployed work, and the ramified relationships between the formal and the informal, the legal, and the illegal.

Peppe runs a stall in a popular street market in central Naples. When I met him several years ago, he was a council employee and ran the stall on the side. Being formally employed, Peppe could not register the stall in his own name, so he registered it in that of an unemployed uncle, who worked there under him. Peppe's wife, who rarely tended the stall, was registered as a helper to accrue a small pension. Later, Peppe registered the stall in his elder son's name, Carmine, who had just finished school. Now, having retired from his formal employment, Peppe runs the stall full time. Like his brother and sisters, Carmine helps occasionally, to give Peppe time to purchase supplies and 'deal with the authorities'. The latter is a sore point with Peppe, as with the other informants who run stalls and shops in Naples.

Throughout central Naples, examples abound of officials' contradictory behaviour regarding not-strictly-legal aspects of trade and enterprise. 'On paper', Peppe says, 'licensing and trading rules are just too strict to be followed'. As examples, he mentioned the over complicated bureaucracy and health and safety regulations, and the 'way too small space allocated to stalls. In practice, no one follows such impossibly strict rules. Otherwise, there'd be no point in running a stall'. Over the years, I have collected examples of what Peppe and other informants describe as 'harassment by officials'. According to Peppe, 'most times they get a bribe in cash or in kind and go away for a few weeks'. However, he continued, 'occasionally, they get new orders. Then, younger faces turn up to raid the place and impose fines on everyone for the smallest infraction of rules and regulations'. One day in 2016, I found that his stall had shrunk to half the normal size. A white line on the pavement now delimitated the small area where the stall must be set. That morning, Peppe and his fellow traders reported, 'municipal police had appeared out of the blue' and while council workers painted the white lines, they went on to 'fine everyone for having exceeded their allocated space'. Shopkeepers were fined, too. Claudio, a business neighbour of Peppe in his mid thirties, sells household goods from a tiny shop for which he pays 'a constantly increasing rent'. Like other shopkeepers, he has been repeatedly fined for 'unlawful occupation of public land and for posing a hazard to pedestrians'. As the shop is tiny, he says, he is 'forced to display the merchandise outside', for which he has failed to get a licence. On this last occasion, the municipal police found him in breach of the law and fined him, again. Mirroring Peppe's argument, Claudio says, in desperation, 'It'd be hopeless if I didn't display goods outside, on the pavement. My family's livelihood depends on this shop. I'll just have to risk being fined again'. Then in a bitter aside, he added, 'I'll have to keep paying the fines, unlike the illegal (foreign) peddlers who operate here, run from the police just to reappear when it is safe, and if caught cannot be made to pay because officially they've no income and often no IDs'.

Peppe's son Carmine is, of course, legally—therefore fiscally—responsible for the business. This is his formal employment. Most of his income comes, however, from working informally as a waiter in various establishments. His younger brother Gennaro is an exceptionally good cook who works full time as a sous chef for a top restaurant in Naples and a luxury hotel on the coast. These activities have produced good contacts in the catering business, which Gennaro has used to help his older brother to get 'informal' occasional work. Gennaro's wife, Elvira, is a skilled unlicensed accountant. She works informally for several licensed accountants who administer blocks of flats, shops and other businesses in Naples and the province. She de facto does the accounts for most of these businesses and is paid in cash by her employers, the registered accountants. Recently, as she could no longer cope with the amount of work coming her way, she trained her sister, Grazia, who has recently completed her studies in accounting. For the time being, Grazia works under Elvira, who is trusted by the official accountants. Soon, however, Elvira says, Grazia will be able to take off on her own because she is both very good and reliable. Of course, Grazia, too, works informally and is paid in cash. When I spoke to her, Grazia said she felt lucky to get such a lucrative job so early after finishing school. She plans to marry her boyfriend soon, who has a formal job as a courier for a local company.

Peppe's children's statements fully agree with other informants' when they say that they prefer to work informally. They have managed to enter niches of the market where—although a degree of uncertainty is of course ever present—dependent informal work is available and a willingness to work informally is more than welcome. Their informal activities might not be as financially rewarding as those of my informants who run independent informal businesses but they do not carry the weight of worry experienced by the latter and the complications of corruption, including the need to bribe officials; certainly, they are less exposed to the risk of legal prosecution. They, as Carmine said, 'acknowledge that independent enterprising may be more rewarding in terms of job satisfaction and self esteem, but it also carries perhaps more risks than those involved in dependent informal work'. When I asked about insurance and pension, they replied that the jobs they do are not sufficiently dangerous to warrant a strong need for insurance. Only Carmine's job involves some physical risk, as he deals with fire, knives, etc. But, he says. 'In the many years that I have worked as a chef, I have never had a serious accident. A few minor cuts and burns, but that's part and parcel of what I do. I'll be fine'. When I remarked that this seemed fatalistic, he replied, 'No, I just know to be careful and not over worry'. As for pension, they, like many other officially unemployed with whom I have spoken in Naples and elsewhere in Italy, remarked that formal work no longer gives guarantees, given the recent radical changes in pension rights, and the promise of more such changes to come. The young Grazia pointedly said, 'one better looks after oneself, don't you think?'

From early December to early January, the month including Christmas and the Epiphany, seasonal street markets mushroom across Naples to cater for customers from the city and beyond. There, temporary stalls are licensed to sell gifts, Christmas decorations, fireworks, and toys. Street performers join in. Carmine, his siblings and their partners run a second stall in one of these markets. Like others, their temporary stall operates 18 hours a day and needs to be manned by two people at all times, 'to look after customers who turn up in great numbers', Carmine explains, 'and look out for thieves who work the crowds, and us'. Peppe helps but mostly he continues to manage the 'ordinary stall'. This seasonal Christmas trading accounts for a large part of their yearly income, which both vindicates the point that the formal and the informal are part of the same market and invites reflection on its ramifications.

Small- and medium-sized companies informally use workshops that produce goods evading tax on the purchase of raw materials and on the sale of finished products, as well as employment tax and other welfare state contributions. Many such products find their way into the legal market (Pardo 2012a). Pietro's firm exemplifies important aspects of this situation. Now in his thirties, he belongs to a family rooted in the Neapolitan sartorial tradition. His grandfather was a bespoke tailor who ran a small workshop in central Naples. His sons worked under him. Following his death, they expanded the business and started a shop selling good quality clothes. As major fashion firms began to subcontract some of their work to smaller business, Pietro's father saw an opportunity to branch out. He sold his share in the communal business and used that capital and a small bank loan to start a workshop working for high fashion firms. As Pietro's new business expanded, so did the work force, only a proportion of whom operated in the workshop's premises. There, skilled tailors made the cut. Some workers assembled parts of the clothes in the workshop. Others did this job informally in their own homes, were paid in cash and did not enjoy the benefits of formal employment or trade union protection. Pietro's father, his informal employees and many of his customers evaded taxes. Still a young boy, Pietro spent his free time in the workshop, learning the ropes, and on graduation became fully involved in the business.

Practicing his *sapé fa*, Pietro planned a strategy to expand the business and almost entirely phase out the informal element. With the help of three contacts—one is a local politician, the second is an accountant, the third is a solicitor who specializes in business law—he obtained the necessary information and support to buy the large premises auctioned by a local authority just outside Naples. Having failed to obtain a bank loan because he did not have sufficient 'patrimonial guarantees', Pietro used his savings and loans from family members. Later, the politician helped him obtain EU funding aimed at encouraging local development and secure grants from the regional authority to employ immigrants and train local young people. He has recently decided to take additional commissions.

Most of Pietro's workers are formally employed full time, including legal immigrants. A minority works part time. Pietro is particularly happy with two long-term Indian employees. One has recently married and is waiting for his Indian wife's work permit to be processed; she will then join him in Italy and will be employed full time in Pietro's workshop. The other is engaged to an Italian woman who works as a secretary for a local accountant. 'They', he says, 'are highly skilled, loyal and, like all my employees, never miss a day work and get on very well with the rest of the workforce'. Aniello, a part-time employee, has started a small informal workshop in his home. He has trained family members and neighbours to operate the machines that he has purchased using savings and money borrowed from his social network. He also employs three part-time immigrants. Meeting the approach of other formally employed informants who do informal work 'on the side', two are the skilled tailors of Indian origin who, like Aniello, work there in the evenings and over the weekends; the third is Anton, a young Ukrainian who delivers to Pietro's clients. When Anton, who is engaged to an Italian woman, started delivering 'on the side' for informal workshops like Aniello's, he used Pietro's lorry but, in line with similar entrepreneurial strategies employed by other local informants, he has recently purchased a van and is considering hiring the help of a fellow Ukrainian to expand his own business.

Aniello produces clothes for the informal market copying the original designs given to Pietro by the high-end fashion designers and using similar fabrics. He says he is not interested in the low-end of the market. A forty-seven-year-old seamstress who works for him typically remarked, 'the market for cheap, low quality clothes has been taken over by Chinese products. Moreover, I am proud of my craftsmanship and of the quality of what I make'. The first part of her remarks tallies with what I have been told repeatedly during the fieldwork. Regardless of the kind of merchandise that they produce or distribute, most informants say with obvious, if grudging, admiration that Chinese entrepreneurs have successfully forced a radical change in the dynamics and nature of the local economy. The cheap, low-quality goods that used to be made in Naples have almost completely been replaced by much cheaper Chinese merchandise. Local entrepreneurs with the necessary funds, skills, and contacts have specialized in better quality products, benefiting from a tradition of skilled work, fashionable design and good quality materials. As in the case of Aniello's production, these goods—which cannot be appropriately called 'fake' because they are not branded—sell in Naples and beyond at a fraction of the price charged by the high street brands.

The work activities of Enzo, Rosa, and Carmela stand on the borderline, half in and half out the formal market. Their case will help to clarify key dynamics at the sales end of the relationship between the formal and the informal in the economic field. Enzo, now thirty-two years old, was sixteen when he left school and started contributing to the meagre family income by working (illegally) as a delivery boy for grocery shops in the neighbourhood. Later, he found regular employment in a large supermarket chain. When he married his neighbour sweetheart Rosa, they went to live rent free in a large *basso* (ground floor premises accessed directly from the street) owned by Rosa's father in a narrow back alley in their *quartiere* and previously used for storage. Over the years, Enzo had saved money, part of which he and Rosa used to convert the *basso*, splitting the space in two: a small front room, a tiny bathroom and a largish living room cum kitchen in the back. The premises' high ceiling allowed a mezzanine where they have their bedroom. Part of the money was used to furnish their living quarters. The rest went into starting an informal all purpose shop that operates 18 hours a day 7 days a week.

Enzo and Rosa look forward to having 'much desired' babies and becoming, in their own words, 'a proper family', once things are settled financially. The twenty-four-year old Rosa works the shop mornings and afternoons. Her younger sister, Carmela, takes the shift after school and homework, from 17:00 to midnight, for pocket money. In the morning, they also sell at lower prices than usual homemade espresso coffee, cappuccino, and pastries. On Saturdays, they sell—mostly to order from individuals and shop keepers—homemade pasta and seasonal dishes, like *pastiera* (Neapolitan Easter cake) and *casatiello* (savoury bread). In this, they also benefit from the relationships Enzo has established with many shopkeepers, who are happy to sell these products for a percentage on the profits. I can testify to the high quality of Rosa's absolutely delicious homemade products. I often took my breakfast there and never failed to buy her seasonal products. From what I could see, the trio's regular customers are often joined by passers-by. Most of the profit from this activity falls in the category of 'black economy', as they deal in cash and do not pay taxes on most transactions. This business is sufficiently small to escape the attention of the law. On top of his formal job, Enzo does informal deliveries for several establishments. For lack of time, he does not help directly in running the shop; however, he uses the contacts he makes through his deliveries to recruit buyers for their homemade products.

Meeting a strategy employed by other informants (Pardo 2000), Enzo and Rosa are considering expanding their business. They are looking to market their products further through shops across Naples and the province. The combination of Enzo's steady salary, contacts and knowledge of the market and Rosa's culinary skills (she is helped by Carmela and their mother) and sound business sense promises well for their future. In developing the family business, they have encouraged the 'internet wizard' Carmela to devise a business platform, which she intends to pursue with their help once she finishes school. She plans to use her and her friends' self-taught internet skills 'to exploit new online markets'. When I asked how, she explained that she would not register as self-employed (a move that in Italy would be costly and would involve complicated bureaucratic procedures); instead, she will get involved in schemes typical of what is now called a 'sharing economy'. Carmela notes, 'these "new" schemes may be popular and accepted in today's times of crisis, but they're no different from what traditionally goes on here, in the *quartiere*. Annoyingly, when we do it, the authorities say it's illegal, therefore punishable under the Law—certainly "reproachable". Yet, now those same authorities say that these schemes are good to help the country recover from the economic recession, therefore it's honourable. How disgustingly hypocritical!'

MATTERS OF TRUST

Trust is a rational construct that may or may not include an emotional element. In the long run, trust—of any kind—stands on reciprocity (Pardo 1996, 2001, 2012b); as Lino, one of my primary informants (Pardo 1996: 6ff.), once said, 'if I trust you but find out that you don't trust me, all bets are off'. Trust between citizens and their rulers is a founding principle of democracy.

By means of a convenient conflation—from above—of individuality and individualism, the *popolino* are misrepresented, we know, as an untrustworthy mob—a fact of which they are sorely aware. Empirical analysis shows them to be, instead, citizens who ordinarily defy, in practice, such a conflation. They exercise in their own wisely pragmatic way their membership in society and their right to distrust, and defy, élites who may belong to different domains and may be differently located in such domains but share a distrust of what they call populace or, more offensively, *lazzari*. I have collected many examples of how the Naples *popolino* pool together personal resources of different kinds (contacts among bureaucrats, professionals and trade unionists; the help of kin, friends and neighbours; informal financial sources, etc.) in coping with crises or in pursuing such goals as a bed in hospital, specialist care, housing, a degree, recovery from drug addiction or in coping with the failure of local governance to guarantee public health (Pardo 2011). They assess risks carefully, and when they have sufficient information they may choose to engage in potentially profitable alliances and associative forms of action knowing that, from experience, within limits they can trust each other.[6] Apparently untroubled by the moral stigma put on those who do not belong to the 'legitimate order', they tend to do so in accordance with their own judgment and usually in ways that effectively neutralize their domestication, from above. Accordingly, trust and relations of trust take a specific outlook.

In the economic field, to say it with Karl Polanyi (1944), the informal activities that we have examined benefit from their socially 'embedded' character. Clearly, a great deal of trust is involved in these informal transactions.

[6] More ethnographic details on this issue can be found in Pardo (1996).

In the absence of contracts and legal procedures, the relationships between employers and employees rely on trust, as do the market exchanges between suppliers and workshops. Different but equally important elements of trust colour the relationships between sellers and buyers, which is especially the case when food and other products that come in contact with the human body (for example, cosmetics and toiletries) are involved.

On the other hand, more or less openly committed to the stereotypical view that we have studied, the powerful élite who have ruled Naples in the 1990s and their worthy successors have set a morally problematic and politically worrying precedent in the relationships between public powers and ordinary citizens, as they have failed to fulfil their administrative obligations while systematically pursuing selective policies and double standards.[7] To stay with Polanyi's terminology (1944), their policies respond to socially 'disembedded' economic interests. To cite one telling example, they have largely failed to repay debts contracted by their predecessors with local (mainly small) entrepreneurs who contracted work for what they thought was a financially reliable public body (Pardo 2000). Claiming that these entrepreneurs must have known that they were dealing with corrupt rulers, they have employed a combination of strong-arm tactics, soothing language, red tape, bureaucratic buck-passing and legal wrangling that illustrates what can go wrong in the relationship between bureaucracy and politics in contemporary democratic society (Smith 1989; Pardo 1996: Chapter 6; Prato 2000: 79). They, however, have gone further. Testing the very limits of citizens' tolerance, they have lobbied central government into passing ad hoc legislation that emphasizes the moral relativism of law (Fuller 1964) as a coercive apparatus that regulates the partial control of a partial order (Starr and Collier 1989). This legislation weakens ordinary people's right to justice, including economic justice (Marshall 1950; Rees 1996), as it makes rulers not responsible for the debts contracted by past administrators. It substantially restricts the definition of punishable abuse of office and transfers much legal responsibility from politicians to special committees of nonelected experts (Miller 2004). At the same time, public contracts are allocated to 'trusted' Northern companies, which then subcontract the actual work to local companies (Pardo 2001, 2011).

---

[7]Field research among local élite groups has helped to clarify this problem. Started in 1991, this research is continuing. Elsewhere (see, for example, Pardo 2000, 2012b, 2015, 2017), I have discussed some of my findings in key domains, such as the judiciary, politics, bureaucracy, banking, enterprise, the health sector, trade unions and academia.

These distortions of the relationship between legal responsibility and moral and political responsibility in the exercise of power widen the existing gap between the actual distribution of rights and their ideal distribution. The attendant exclusion factually determines a weak membership of society. It appears to be particularly problematic because, here, far from being caught in a culture of short-term moves and immediate goals, the ruled are actively engaged in negotiating the redefinition of their citizenship. Their entrepreneurialism radically challenges rulers' distrust of citizenship and their mismanagement of power and responsibility in government.

CONCLUSION

To summarize roughly, opposing representations of value and interest from above and from below have raised interesting questions on how citizenship and political responsibility are defined and work in contemporary Naples. Case material has highlighted ordinary people's entrepreneurialism in a context where the imperfect competition that generally characterizes the market is made more problematic by rulers' politicking and double standards. Distrustful and intolerant of unaligned moralities and actions—including economic actions—that escape their control, local rulers have long appeared to be unwilling to address constructively ordinary Neapolitans' instances and approach, while ruling according to their own particular interests. This fundamental limit to democracy (Lukes 1991) has serious consequences.

In a democracy, rulers' recognition—in policy and legislation—of the structural value of (all) citizens' culture and actions qualifies the relationship between the individual and the system. The Naples case discussed here tallies with recent events across Europe and gives rise to a stark warning. The democratic covenant is not undermined, it shows, by citizens' failure to be drawn to the dominant élites' visions of what is best for them; it is undermined by these élites' failure to trust and link to ordinary people, effectively alienating the legitimacy of their rule. Empirical knowledge soberly points to the need to meet the challenge of an open-minded view of the individual—including the undomesticated, entrepreneurial individual—as an intrinsically social being operating in the messiness of an increasingly complex system. Crucially, this approach requires a nonideological reading of personal initiative and of the attendant choices.

REFERENCES

Abrams, P. 1982. *Historical Sociology*. Shepton Mallet: Open Books.

Fuller, L.L. 1964. *The Rationality of Law*. New Haven: Yale University Press.

Gramsci, A. 1966. *Letteratura e Vita Nazionale*. Einaudi, Turin (English trans. In *Antonio Gramsci: Selection from Cultural Writings*, ed. D. Forgacs and G. Nowell. London: Lawrence and Wishart).

Harris, R. 1986. *Power and Powerlessness in Industry*. London: Tavistock.

Harris, R. 1988. Theory and Evidence: The 'Irish Stem Family' and Field Data. *Man* 23: 417–434.

Leach, E.R. 1977. *Rethinking Anthropology*. London: Athlone Press.

Lo Cicero, M. 2017. Conti in rosso al commune di Napoli. *Il Mattino*, July 14. Available at http://www.ilmattino.it/napoli/politica/conti_in_rosso_al_comune_di_napoli_il_purgatorio_del_predissesto_e_l_inferno_che_si_e_spalancato-2561960.html.

Lukes, S. 1991. *Moral Conflict and Politics*. Oxford: Clarendon Press.

Marshall, T.H. 1950. *Citizenship and Social Class and Other Essays*. Cambridge: Cambridge University Press.

Miller, A. 2004. Corruption Between Morality and Legitimacy in the Context of Globalization. In *Between Morality and the Law: Corruption, Anthropology and Comparative Society*, ed. I. Pardo, 53–67. London: Routledge.

Nordio, C. 2015. Leggi confuse producono tangenti. Interview by Goffredo Pistelli. *Italia Oggi*, 18 February: 5. http://www.italiaoggi.it/giornali/dettaglio_giornali.asp?preview=false&accessMode=FA&id=1963131&codiciTestate=1.

Pahl, R. 1980. Employment, Work, and Domestic Division of Labour. *International Journal of Urban and Regional Research* 4 (1): 1–20.

Pardo, I. 1996. *Managing Existence in Naples: Morality, Action and Structure*. Cambridge: Cambridge University Press.

Pardo, I. 2000. Credit, Entrepreneurship and the Repayment of Debt: Mismatched Conceptions of Legitimacy in Italy. *Self, Agency and Society* 2 (2): 51–87.

Pardo, Italo. 2001. *Élite senza fiducia: Ideologie, Etiche di Potere, Legittimità*. Catanzaro: Rubbettino.

Pardo, Italo. 2011. Italian Rubbish: Elemental Issues of Citizenship and Governance. In *Citizenship and the Legitimacy of Governance in the Mediterranean Region: A Comparative Anthropology*, ed. I. Pardo and G.B. Prato, 25–45. London: Routledge.

Pardo, I. 2012a. Entrepreneurialism in Naples: Formality and Informality. *Urbanities* 2 (1): 30–45.

Pardo, I. 2012b. Exercising Power Without Authority: Elite Groups Implode in Urban Italy. In *Anthropology in the City: Methodology and Theory*, ed. I. Pardo and G.B. Prato, 53–78. London: Routledge.

Pardo, I. 2015. Les élites italiennes au travail: un regard à partir de la base urbaine. In *Le positionnement de l'anthropologie urbaine*, ed. I. Pardo, G.B. Prato, and W. Kaltenbacher, 57–73. Special Issue of *Diogène*. Paris: Presses Universitaires de France.

Pardo, I. 2017. Between Stereotype and Bad Governance: An Italian Ethnography. In *The Palgrave Handbook of Urban Ethnography*, ed. I. Pardo and G.B. Prato, 35–52. New York: Palgrave Macmillan.

Pardo, I., and G.B. Prato. 2011. Introduction: Disconnected Governance and the Crisis of Legitimacy. In *Citizenship and the Legitimacy of Governance in the Mediterranean Region: A Comparative Anthropology*, ed. I. Pardo and G.B. Prato, 1–23. London: Routledge.

Parry, J., and M. Bloch. 1989. Introduction: Money and the Morality of Exchange. In *Money and the Morality of Exchange*, ed. M. Bloch and J. Parry, 1–32. Cambridge: Cambridge University Press.

Polanyi, K. 1944. *The Great Transformation*. New York: Reinehart.

Prato, G.B. 2000. The Cherries of the Mayor: Degrees of Morality and Responsibility in Local Italian Administration. In *Morals of Legitimacy: Between Agency and System*, ed. I. Pardo, 57–82. Oxford: Berghahn Books.

Rees, A.M. 1996. T. H. Marshall and the Progress of Citizenship. In *Citizenship Today: The Contemporary Relevance of T. H. Marshall*, ed. M. Bulmer and A.M. Rees, 1–24. London: University College London Press.

Schneider, J. 2002. World Markets: Anthropological Perspectives. In *Exotic No More*, ed. J. MacClancy, 64–85. Chicago: The University of Chicago Press.

Smith, E.M. 1989. Informal Economy. In *Economic Anthropology*, ed. S. Platner, 292–317. Stanford: Stanford University Press.

Starr, J., and J.F. Collier (eds.). 1989. *History and Power in the Study of Law: New Directions in Legal Anthropology*. New York: Cornell University Press.

Stewart, M. 2001. Conclusions: Spectres of the Underclass. In *Poverty, Ethnicity and Gender in Eastern Europe During the Market Transition*, ed. R.J. Emigh and I. Szelenyi, 191–204. Westport: Praeger Publishers.

Wallman, S. 1984. *Eight London Households*. London: Tavistock.

Weber, M. 1978. *Economy and Society*, ed. G. Roth and C. Wittich. Los Angeles, CA: University of California Press.

CHAPTER 5

From Nationalization to Neoliberalism: Territorial Development and City Marketing in Brindisi

Giuliana B. Prato

Italy's Economic Divide: A Tale of Two Regions

Since Italy's political Unification (1860–1870), several economic policies have been implemented to solve the country's regional economic disparities. Particular attention has been paid to the North–South divide and to what has become known as the Southern Question. Brindisi, in southeast Italy, has been one of the cities targeted by the national development plans. A major asset of the city is its port and the attendant activities; traditionally military, commercial, and to some extent touristic (transit tourism), and, in modern times, industrial. Apart from the port industry, the economy of the Brindisi province has traditionally been rurally based. Thus, in an attempt to bring economic development to the area, since the late 1950s national economic policies have aimed at turning local peasants into industrial workers.

The debate on the North–South divide has been at the centre of a vast array of research on the economic and social history of contemporary

G. B. Prato (✉)
School of Anthropology and Conservation,
University of Kent, Canterbury, UK

© The Author(s) 2018
M. Spyridakis (ed.), *Market Versus Society*, Palgrave Studies in Urban Anthropology, https://doi.org/10.1007/978-3-319-74189-5_5

Italy and on the role of the country in international politics. It is argued that Italy's political influence internationally is hindered by the drag factor of the less prosperous South and the political weakness of its government. At the same time, observers point out that, despite the ongoing economic recession and the continuing instability of national governments, Italy remains one of Europe's four largest economies, a member of the G8 council of leading economic powers and a key member of the European Union (EU). What economists call the 'phenomenon of clustering' (Porter 1998) has often been used to explain Italy's economic success. This has allowed local companies, especially small and medium enterprises (SMEs), to organize themselves as complementary enterprises in clusters that address each other's needs locally. For a long time, such clustering has offered the advantages normally associated with large companies while been free of their 'rigidity'; a rigidity that has often hampered the necessary flexible responses to changes in customers' demand. In spite of the pessimistic forecast on the negative impact that economic globalization would have on the competitive advantages of clustering, the Organisation for Economic Co-operation and Development (OECD 2000, 2004) has promoted this kind of economic territorial organization as part of its Local Economic and Employment Development Programme (LEED). However, given the nature of industrial development in the Brindisi area, here a strong commitment and synergy among different actors and institutions would be needed in order to promote successful clusters of SMEs. Equally important, as we shall see, the programme of industrialization has failed to boost significantly the Brindisi economy.

Mainstream sociological analyses have explained the underdevelopment of South Italy and the failure of development programmes with endemic clientelism, cultural backwardness, people's amorality and lack of civil engagement. Because of these drawbacks, it is argued, the South has been incapable of capitalizing on the opportunities offered by the industrial markets. Anthropologists, too, have adopted an orientalist approach casting South Italian society as not entirely part of the modern, industrial West.[1] Reflecting on his thirty years of ethnographic enquiry, Pardo (2017) has recently shown how this kind of stereotyping is once again playing a twisted role, serving the interest of certain dominant

---

[1] For a critical review of the literature see Pardo (1996, 2012) and Pardo and Prato (2011).

groups with adverse consequences for a large part of ordinary Italians and for Italian democracy.

I suggest that to understand fully the 'failure', or limited success, of development programmes, we need to look at the relationship between economic policies and the political ideologies that have influenced such polices, and at that between micro- and macro-processes. An analysis of the relevant political ideologies will help to shed light on the afore-mentioned 'orientalist' approach to South Italy and other Southern European regions; for a long time, critical issues brought out by the anthropological study of economic systems have been ignored.

The West and the Rest

It is generally accepted that anthropologists are methodologically well equipped to study social phenomena in their broader context; that is, analyse the specific phenomenon under observation in relation to other significant sociocultural institutions. With particular reference to the relationship between market and society, it is worth stressing that the disciplinary debate in this field has been significantly influenced by the work of the economic historian Karl Polanyi (1944), particularly by his distinction between formal and substantive aspects of the economy. Notably, Polanyi outlined three major ways in which society integrated the economy—reciprocity, redistribution and exchange. He argued that combinations of the three are found in all societies, but in each society one would be dominant. In modern capitalism, he added, the economy is embedded in the institutions of the market and is regulated by a sys-tem of market exchange based on 'rational' choices for the maximization of material profit.

Polanyi's argument that the market logic of 'rational choice' is peculiar to the sociocultural and political systems of capitalist societies prompted the anthropological distinction between 'market place' and 'market princi-ple', and the attendant argument on the relevance of social relations and noneconomic activities in the market place. In contrast, 'market exchange', intended in formalistic economic terms as the buying and selling of goods and services according to prices set by the power of supply and demand, may happen without a physical market place. For a long time, this distinc-tion has informed an almost rigid opposition between the 'West' and the 'rest'. However, as Schneider (2002) points out, classical and contemporary ethnographic analyses (e.g., Malinowski 1922; Mauss 1954; Pardo 1996) bring out the misleading nature of the opposition between 'free market culture' and 'anti-market mentality', between 'rational choices' and 'moral conduct'. As Pardo (1996, p. 11) has shown, rationality is not simply defined by maximization of material profit; instead, people engage in rational choices based on a 'strong continuous interaction' between moral values and clever practices, drawing on a combination of the material and non-material resources available to them.

Influenced by anthropology's methodological paradigm, contemporary sociologists and economists have analysed emerging economic phenomena against the neoliberal trends of global markets, looking at markets as networks and at the relevance of relations of trust in such networks (e.g., Chavdarova et al. 2010). This line of analysis has been useful in understanding phenomena such as 'innovative networks' and the 'conscious economy' in connection with SMEs, global brands and informal activities. In spite of this new field of study and of increased anthropological attention to the effects of global markets on traditional economies in the 'Global South', there are significant aspects of economic life in the western 'Global North' that continue to either be overlooked or seen as markers of socio-economic realities that can only blame themselves for their disadvantaged condition. In contrast with this approach, in-depth ethnographic studies of European urban settings have offered an articulated analysis of the complex relationship between agency and the system (see, e.g., Pardo 1996, 2012, 2017), of policies of global restructuring that influence national decision making, and of their effects at the local level (see, e.g., Spyridakis 2012, 2013).

In what follows, I draw on historical and ethnographic material collected in Brindisi and its province to offer a diachronic analysis of the policies aimed at solving the Southern Question. I look at the relationship between economic policies and the relevant political ideologies addressing the links between the local dimension and processes at regional, national, and the EU level. A diachronic view of the situation shows how the new post-Fordist and post-industrial adjustments not only have contributed to worsening the local economy but, most significant, have determined a situation of urban competition among southern cities aimed at attracting investments *mainly* through EU funds and regional programmes. For instance, in view of potential EU investment, Brindisi's Chamber of Commerce prepared a territorial plan known as the *Brindisi System*, 'marketing' the city and its territory as *the bridge* between western and eastern Europe. As we shall see, despite a promising start, the contemporary reality is not so rosy. The empirical evidence suggests that in Brindisi as elsewhere in the South the adoption of EU structural funding did bring about important improvements in local life and economic conditions, but southern Italian regions continue nonetheless to lag behind their northern counterparts. So, after the end of the EU special intervention scheme in 2006, the Southern Italian Question remains an unresolved problem.

The question is, how far will the South be affected by global restructuring and, within the specific EU context, by the shift in the decision-making process from the national to the European level? Advocates of the free market and of the values of economic liberalism argue that, overall, the Italian economy has benefited enormously from membership in the EU and particularly from the fiscal policy imposed by the Maastricht Treaty for the transition to the European Economic and Monetary Unit (EMU), for this policy has forced a competitive approach upon a productive system prone to protectionist practices (Anderson and Talani 2000, p. 141).

Anthropological analysis has brought out the complexity of the situation, highlighting the significance of the interaction between economic, political, and social institutions in the reformulation of local strategies aimed at attracting development funding in a context marked by shifting and conflictual administrative and political power. When I started my fieldwork in Brindisi in the late 1980s, I was interested in political change; in particular, I was intrigued by the new political alliances that brought together traditionally opposing parties, anticipating by decades the pattern of political coalitions in present day Italy (see Prato 1993, 2000, 2017). A most interesting case was a political coalition that formed in opposition to the construction of a new coal power station on the periphery of the city. One of the arguments in favour of building this power station was that it would boost the local economy and provide job opportunities for the many industrial workers who had been made redundant following the crisis of the major industries in the area, especially the petrochemical sector. I soon realized that a proper understanding of the economic and political dynamics around the construction of the power station could not be separated from a study of the way in which economic policies had developed over time. Here, I shall first look at the political ideologies and economic policies implemented after Unification and at the post-World War II development programmes, then I will focus on the programme of industrialization of Brindisi and on the contemporary situation.

POLITICAL IDEOLOGIES AND THE HISTORICAL EMERGENCE OF THE SOUTHERN QUESTION

The economic policies implemented after Unification aimed not only at promoting economic development, but also at addressing the cultural backwardness and clientlistic practices that allegedly bogged Southern society down.

The ideologies that in various degrees influenced such policies were the racially-based positivism of the criminal anthropologist Lombroso,[2] Liberalism, and leftist ideologies—specifically, the Republican and the Socialist. Liberalism was promoted by the so called historical Right, while the Republicans (who followed Mazzini's political doctrine) represented the historical Left; the Italian Socialist party was officially founded in 1892. There were interesting contradictions. In different ways, both the Right and the Left were concerned with the role that the State should have in economic matters.[3] Post-Unitarian governments were fully aware of the positive impact that the Bourbon policy of state's intervention had had on the economy of the Kingdom of Naples; since the 1830s, the Kingdom's commercial activities and industry had flourished as Bourbon protectionism facilitated foreign trade and encouraged foreign (especially Swiss and German) investment. However, both the Right and the Left officially advocated a strong state control of the economy as a means to fight clientelism, which they regarded as *the* major obstacle to a proper distribution of resources and, thus, to economic development. The Left, especially in the form of the newly formed Socialist party, believed that only a centralized state would weaken dyadic clientelistic relations. Although the Right believed that a Liberal State—with its ideology of minimal intervention—would be better suited to achieve economic growth, they opted for a Jacobean centralized style of government.

[2] The legacy of Lombroso's doctrine has continued to influence twentieth-century sociological and anthropological studies on South Italy. For a recent overview of these studies, see Pardo and Prato (2011, pp. 3–9).

[3] Interestingly, this kind of debate has resurfaced as particularly relevant after the fall of the Communist regimes in Eastern Europe. Gellner (1993: XIII–XIV) summarized this dilemma when he pondered about 'What kind of political control there is to be' and 'how political and economic institutions should, and actually, interact.'

Most important, these parliamentary groups had to deal with internal divisions and, often, conflicting approaches. The liberals were split between Moderates and Conservatives. In his analysis of the post-Unification government's fiscal policy Nitti (1958), a moderate, pointed out that the South's fiscal contribution was far greater than the government's investment for public work in the area. He argued that a new policy of bureaucratic decentralization and a programme of industrialization would be *the* solution to the Southern Question. Giolitti, a conservative Liberal, argued, instead, that the solution was emigration of Southern peasants to the new Italian colonies in Africa. The Socialists, too, were incapable of bringing the various intellectual streams of the party into a unified political strategy. A major role was played by Revolutionary Syndicalism, which represented the Maximalist faction and opposed decentralization. Dissatisfaction with the party Minimalist's commitment to gradual structural reforms prompted some Maximalists to leave the movement, which led to the formation of two splinter parties: the Fascist in 1919 and the Communist in 1921. However, up to the 1920s, economic policy was mainly influenced by the Liberals, encouraging migration and sporadic attempts to re-develop the Southern industries that had flourished before Unification.

The post-Unification imposition of the Piedmontese system of heavy taxation on the country has been identified as the major cause of the crisis of the southern industries. As it replaced the lighter Bourbon fiscal regime, it accelerated the decline of the domestic agrarian industry—on which the peasantry mainly depended—and the crisis of larger local industries (e.g., textile and mechanic factories, dockyards, sulphur mines). Furthermore, as Nitti (1958) pointed out, the South experienced a constant draining of capital—presented as a 'legitimate compensation for war expenses'—which was used to finance industrial development in the North. Meanwhile, contracts for public works in the South were allocated to northern companies (a practice that continues today, see, e.g., Pardo 2017). Commenting on the condition of the southern peasantry, Nitti argued that emigration or brigandage were people's responses to their unfulfilled expectations. Recent studies have shown that, before Unification, there was no real economic gap between the North and the South. Daniele and Malanima (2011) report that in 1861 the gross domestic product (GDP) in the South was higher than in the North and that until 1881 the per capita income difference between North and South was no more than 5%, raising to about 7% in 1891 and increasing to 20% in 1913. Similarly, Federico (2007) reports that agricultural production was significantly higher in the South before Unification and was still higher by one third at the end of the nineteenth century. By 1951 this picture had been reversed, as agricultural production was 40% higher in the North.

State interventionism was strengthened during the two decades of Fascist government. Significantly, Fascist social and economic policies were influenced in part by Revolutionary Syndicalism—including its opposition to administrative decentralization—and in part by a liberal version of the welfare state. On the one hand, this double influence concretized in improving workers' conditions through the expansion of trade unionism, the introduction of a 40-hour work week and the establishment of a national health service (*Ente mutalità fascista*, renamed INAM after World War II) and of the national pension scheme for public and private workers.[4] On the other hand, believing that the national economy would benefit from the country's agricultural potential, the government adopted a populist approach to 'empowering' the peasants to become 'their own masters' and, in so doing, improve their livelihood and contribute to the country's economic growth. In this perspective, the agrarian reform included the reclamation of unproductive marshlands, which were then partitioned and distributed as small holdings. While supported by the Syndicalist movement, this agricultural policy was strongly opposed by the Communists who, influenced by Gramsci (1973), argued that this land distribution would not empower the individual peasants; instead, it would impoverish them further, while raising their aspiration for embourgeoisement and, as a consequence, turn them into a reactionary force against the class struggle.

POLITICAL IDEOLOGIES AND ECONOMIC POLICIES IN POST WORLD WAR II ITALY

After World War II, the emphasis was on 'national' reconstruction, which included finding a solution to the Southern Question. Alongside economic issues, a pressing priority for the new political parties was to achieve electoral power and influence in national government. Political

---

[4] This scheme was at the basis of Italy's National Social Security Institute (the modern-day INPS, *Istituto Nazionale Previdenza Sociale*).

competition soon led to the weakening of the Liberal Party[5] and the strengthening of the Christian Democrat and the Communist parties. Significantly, in 1945–1947 both the Socialist and the Communist parties joined the Christian Democrats in the national government.

The Constitution of the Italian Republic (1946) was drafted by the *Assemblea Costituente*, a committee formed by representatives of several antifascist parties but in fact dominated by two main groupings: the Marxist-oriented and Soviet-inspired Socialists and Communists, and the Vatican-influenced Christian Democrats. They shared the goal of re-establishing the civil rights that had been suppressed under Fascism. They disagreed, however, on how to implement this new state-of-rights; in particular, on economic policy and the distribution of powers.

On the one hand, the Constitution was influenced by the social doctrine of the Catholic Church expressed in Leo XIII's *Rerum Novarum* (1891), which fulfilled some aspirations of the liberal state while meeting socialist ideals on social justice. Secular law had to guarantee property rights for all and small private property played an essential role in limiting both 'collectivism' (meaning Communism) and 'economic imperialism' (meaning capitalism and the liberal trend towards monopolies). Paradoxically, the Catholic social doctrine met the Socialists' position as it contributed to strengthen state interventionism and the partial nationalization of industry. This last point is reflected in Article 43 of the Italian Constitution on the possibility that private property can be expropriated or transferred to the state, to other public bodies, or to workers' cooperatives.

On the other hand, the emerging power of the Communist party is vividly exemplified in the formulation of Article 1 of the Constitution, which states 'Italy is a Republic founded on work'. The idea behind this article is to promote the view of work as civic 'duty' (that is, as a contribution of the citizens to the economy of their country), rather than access to work as a right. This approach to work is found in the Communists' aforementioned opposition to the distribution of farmland and their dismissal of the peasants' resistance to collectivization as cultural proneness to clientelism. As Pardo (2017) has argued, through a selective and mechanistic application of Gramsci's views on the peasantry and on popular culture more generally, the Communists embarked on

---

[5] The names of the political parties discussed in this chapter refer to the party organization before the 1992 scandals.

a mission to 'educate' and lead the backward masses, showing ideological and cultural intolerance of values other than proletarian. However, in the late 1940s this approach was internally criticised. According to Rossi Doria (1958), the Communists overlooked the fact that the peasantry was not an 'objective class' and that a southern peasant could be at the same time a day labourer, a sharecropper, and a small holder. Rossi Doria opposed both the Right's policy of land distribution—which gave the peasants land but not the means to commercialize its products—and the Left's ideological rigidity towards the peasants' aspiration to social mobility. For him, the solution to the Southern Question was 'demographic relief'; that is, emigration abroad. Specialists on the Southern Question agree that several factors prevented the establishment of agricultural entrepreneurial activities; among them, inadequate credit institutions[6] and lack of the infrastructure and services necessary for the industrial transformation and commercialization of products.

THE FUND FOR THE SOUTH AND THE WORLD BANK

Between 1951 and 1965 Italy received a series of eight 'impact' loans from the International Bank for Reconstruction and Development (IBRD) in support of the newly established *Cassa per il Mezzogiorno*, the national government's Fund for the South.

The IBDR was established at the Bretton Woods conference in 1944; it is one of the five institutions that compose the World Bank. Its original mission was to finance European reconstruction after World War II, a mission that was later shared with the four-year European Recovery Plan (ERP, commonly known as Marshall Plan) established in 1948.

Although the IBRD loans to Europe have been widely known, several internal documents dealing with the *Cassa* were publicly disclosed only in 2010. They reveal the nature of the relationship between the Italian authorities, the *Cassa*—that is, the direct beneficiary of the loans— and the IBRD. They include evaluations and recommendations on the work carried out by the *Cassa*, how the loans were used, the public investments made by the Italian government and the state of economic

---

[6]As Pardo has shown in detail (2017), credit and access to it remain a critical problem in South Italy. See also Pardo (2000).

development in the South.[7] According to Lepore (2013), these international loans initiated a 'virtuous circle' that contributed to the industrialization of the South and the economic modernization of Italy.

The *Cassa* was established in 1950 primarily to finance public works and infrastructure projects (roads, bridges, hydroelectric and irrigation) and to provide credit subsidies and tax advantages to attract private investors. The ten-year work programme (1950–1960), later extended to 12 years, submitted to the IBRD included primarily 'land transformation and settlement'. The IBRD report of 1951 outlines 'The categories of public works which the *Cassa* is presently authorized by law to execute'—which also included the development of tourist facilities—and points out that most of these projects were not new, some had been initiated before the war and many others had made substantial progress since the end of the war. Nevertheless, the report recommends granting the loans in the belief that the *Cassa* 'should make possible substantially greater investment ... than would be possible under the old system' (p. 3). Among the geographic areas mentioned in the reports are 'the regions of southern Italy including Abruzzi and Molise and the islands of Sicily and Sardinia. Some projects have been included, however, in central Italy. These are located in the provinces of Latina and Frosinone, on the isle of Elba, in the communes of Rieti province and in the Tronto reclamation districts. Complete information as to the basis for selecting this distribution of works is not available, but it is evident to the mission that the areas included in the program either contain important works which are already planned or underway at present, or present serious political problems for the government' (p. 3).

It is argued that the IBRD loans to the *Cassa* served a dual purpose (Lepore 2013). For the recently established IBRD this was an opportunity to show that it was capable of fulfilling the mission for which it had been created. It was felt that there was a reasonable chance that the investment would be successful, in which case the Italian model would provide a template for future international development funding. For the *Cassa*, the loans in US dollars were particularly beneficial in a context marked by the 'pegged' monetary exchange established at the Bretton

---

[7]Most of these reports are now available at: http://aset.acs.beniculturali.it/aset-web/info/documentazioneIBRD. Lepore (2013) provides a 22-page long list of references that deal with the *Cassa per il Mezoogiorno*, including the role of the World Bank.

Woods Conference, especially considering that Italy's dependence on importation combined with a weak lira, and that the limited national funds were mostly directed to the northern economy.

The initial intervention for the development of the South focused on the agricultural sector. However, the Socialist and the Republican parties were enthusiastic advocates of industrialization. Prominent socialists, like Morandi, the party's theorist of industrialization, were unhappy with the outcome of the 'first aid plan' agreed to with the Allies after World War II for the reconstruction of southern industries, especially of the Naples industrial pole, at the time the second biggest in Italy. Contrary to the initial agreements, the funds had been redirected to the northern industries that needed raw material and semi-finished products to become operational again. This situation triggered the formation in 1946 of SVIMEZ (Association for the Development of Industry in the South). Morandi became its first president.

In 1955, Morandi promoted a 'dialogue' with the Christian Democrats for the industrial development of the South. Unlike the Communists, he believed that a proper 'plan' of industrialization would allow the working class to lead the transformation of society. In his view, there was no need for the working class to rise to power and expropriate the means of production and distribution; instead, he argued, it was important to free the southern industrial structure from its subordination to the northern industries. In line with this *politica di piano* (plan policy), that year the Socialists submitted to parliament a proposal for the nationalization of industry—beginning with the energy sector. They maintained that the North–South dualism would not be solved by the intervention of the private financial and industrial monopolies, as the government had proposed. They argued for a more open management of the *Cassa per il Mezzogiorno*, which was seen as an instrument of Christian Democrat power, and demanded a new programme of special intervention for the South. In 1963, the Socialists joined the national government with the explicit support of the Republicans. This was the first time that they shared power since the brief constitutional experience of 1945–1947. While participating in government, they held various economic ministries such as Public Works, Industry, the Ministry for the South and the Ministry for the State Shareholding (abolished in 1993); some of these positions were held by MPs elected in the Brindisi-Lecce-Taranto constituency. In 1965, parliament passed a new law for the South, known as the Centre-Left Law.

Throughout the 1960s economic policy in the South was increasingly characterized by two programmes: the promotion of the so-called Poles of Development and a Welfare policy. The latter took the form of assistance; derogatorily known as *assistenzialismo*; it provided subsidies without promoting development (Trigilia 1992; Pardo 1996, 2017). The Poles of Development led to the construction of large scale, technologically advanced plants that, as in the case of Brindisi, had no links with the local firms and the local economy more generally. Most of these southern Poles have become known as 'cathedrals in the desert', which is the opposite of the clustering promoted in the North. Furthermore, following Italy's entry in the European Economic Community (EEC) in 1957, it was decided that this programme of industrialization should not lead to the creation of southern industries that would 'compete' with the northern industries on the European and international markets. So, the southern 'Poles' produced raw materials that would be finished, polished, and marketed by the northern industries. This 'base' industry was mostly limited to the iron/steel and chemical/petrochemical sectors, was marked by exceedingly high capital investment per worker and employed relatively few workers who over time were made redundant, increasing local formal unemployment. Moreover, given the insufficiently developed sectors of finance, transport, and commercialization it failed to support successful economic growth.

From Peasants to Proletarians: Industrialization in Brindisi

In the 1960s, Brindisi experienced a crisis of the few local SMEs, which almost collapsed the local economy and increased unemployment. It was decided to build a petrochemical plant as part of a major industrial development in the area. The Montecatini company started construction in 1959 with the support of state funds, including the *Cassa* funds. State intervention was also crucial for Montecatini to obtain from the military a large estate on the eastern inlet of Brindisi's port. Construction was completed in the mid-1960s after several interruptions, due in part to lack of funds. On completion, the company dismissed the seven thousand local building workers, who became unemployed.

The local Communists had opposed the project because they saw it as a base of Christian Democrat power. However, they supported the government programme of the nationalization of industries, which led

in 1962 to the creation of the National Electricity Board (ENEL). The
ENEL also held shares in other sectors, including the petrochemical.[8]
In Brindisi, this development corresponded with further industrial intervention; specifically, the construction (started in 1964) of the first power
station in the area. Initially fuelled by combustible oil, the plant had a
capacity of 640 megawatt (MW). It was later expanded and in 1979 was
converted into a coal-fired plant, with the optional use of dense combustible oil. Brindisi's industrial area has continued to expand, including
pharmaceutical and chemical sectors, aeronautical production and dock-
ing stations that mainly service coal and oil tankers.

The new policy of industrialization and the attendant management of
state funds brought the question of administrative decentralization back
on the political stage. The Christian Democrats and the Communists
were against decentralization. The Socialists, instead, supported decentralization, stressing the relevant role that local authorities could play
in distributing funds and in promoting links with local enterprises.
Meanwhile, they continued to pursue industrialization 'guided' by the
state and structural reforms *within* the capitalist system. Administrative
decentralization was accomplished in 1973, giving more power to local
authorities. In Brindisi, however, the issue was far from settled and it
soon re-emerged in connection with the construction of a new power station in the rural periphery. This new plant was part of the national programme for the development of nuclear energy, in line with the European
Atomic Energy Community (EURATOM) agreement that Italy had
signed in 1975.[9] In breach of Law 393/1975 that regulates the participation of the regional government in decision-making, the Council of
the *Regione Puglia* (the Apulia Region, where Brindisi is located) was not
consulted on the construction of the new plant. While the Communists
and Christian Democrats did not oppose the decision-making process,
local minor parties and the Socialists joined an environmental protest,
arguing that more power should be given to local authorities and that
decisions had been made in total disregard of the local context.

[8]ENEL was privatized in 1999, following the liberalization of the electricity market in
Italy. It is now a multinational and, as of 2015, the Italian government owns 25.5% of
shares.

[9]Italy already had a nuclear plant in the Garigliano, built with funds from the IBRD. The
plant was operational between 1964 and 1982. It was decommissioned following a referendum on nuclear power.

Most local politicians and trade unionists who were concerned with the downturn of the industrial pole in the 1970s saw the construction of the plant as a solution to unemployment. The debate became heated in the 1980s, in the aftermath of the referendum on nuclear power (see Note 9). Elsewhere (Prato 1993, 2000, 2017), I have analysed the political events that led to the construction of the power station and the protest and legal battles that were carried out for over a decade inside and outside the institutional arena. After several interruptions in the construction process, the power station was eventually completed and became operational between 1991 and 1993 with a total capacity of 2640 MW. The plant is known as the 'Federico II-Cerano' (Cerano is the locality), or 'Brindisi South', to be distinguished from the old plant—known as Brindisi North—in the urban industrial area. Brindisi South is at the centre of a continuing saga.

Apart from the environmental pollution and the destruction of a large area of Mediterranean woodland, life-threatening health problems have emerged in connection with the soot that covers a large surrounding area, with the open-air transportation of coal from the city harbour to the plant and with its open-air storage. Brindisi South ranks 25th in the EU classification of the thirty most polluting power stations in Europe and 18th in terms of environmental costs, amounting to over 500 million euros per year. Environmental damage extends to the eradication of vast vineyards, olive groves, and artichoke fields, and the closure of dairy farms. The artificial lagoons built by ENEL to counter the natural erosion of the coast have produced a proliferation of algae, requiring expensive cleaning; they have also modified the sea currents, leading to the erosion of large stretches of beach. Moreover, the warming of seawater caused by the plant cooling system has dramatically changed the sea fauna in the area.

Since 2005, a series of legal actions have been brought against ENEL (responsible for Brindisi South) and Edipower (responsible for Brindisi North). The plaintiffs include the local authorities of nearby towns that are most affected by the plant. Following these legal battles and the intervention of the EU, in 2015 the coal-stocking area was covered, which has limited in small part the power station's disruptive impact on the environment. In February 2017, 58 farmers won compensation from ENEL for the economic losses caused by the deposit of soot on their agricultural produce *and* the consequent total loss of their livelihood. The legal battles continue.

MARKETING THE CITY: PROMOTING THE 'BRINDISI SYSTEM'

Since the mid-1990s, local politicians across the spectrum have looked at EU programmes and the creation of Euro-Regions as a way of attracting funds to the South through special intervention schemes. The end of the EU structural funding in 2006 saw the emergence of competition among the Apulian cities that had largely benefitted from these schemes.

In an attempt to 'sell' Brindisi on the national and global 'market of cities', in 2007 the local chamber of commerce (henceforth, CoC) outlined a programme, titled the Attractiveness and Competitiveness of Brindisi Economic System, adopting the 'urban market metaphor'. According to this metaphor, cities should be regarded as subfirms of a fictive national firm, which in turn would create a submarket in relation to real firms. In this scenario, the success of the Brindisi System would be assessed in terms of winning the competition against other cities that were trying to exploit the EU programmes aimed at promoting relations among regions. Accordingly, the CoC focused on the 2007–2013 Planning of European Territorial Co-operation, promoting Brindisi as a logistic platform functional to the North–South and East–West trade flows, as opposed to being merely a territory of transit. In this scenario, Brindisi would become the North of the South, thus ceasing to be the South of the more economically successful North Italian or North European cities. Inspired by the strategic role that Brindisi would play in major EU projects, the CoC proposed the development of initiatives in five major areas of freedom of movement: people, goods, capital, enterprise, and know-how. But things did not go according to the plans. Brindisi port had initially been designated as the terminal of Corridor VIII on the West Adriatic coast and as the main distribution inter-port for the gas pipeline known as the Trans Adriatic Pipeline (TAP), which will bring gas and oil from the Black Sea to Western Europe via the Balkans and Italy. Once again, vested political interests intervened to twist the local plans. While giving a new impetus to the development of Bari, they have determined a progressive decline of the importance of Brindisi and of the Salento area generally, resulting in deepening the economic downturn and environmental degradation.[10] In short, both political

---

[10] As I explain elsewhere (2017), over time, the Italian terminal of Corridor VIII has been split between Brindisi and the nearby Bari (the capital city of Apulia).

competition among parties and infighting are dictating which city wins and which loses in the city marketing system.

It has been argued that the application of neoliberalism in situations like Brindisi's is unlikely to produce healthy market competition or, as I have mentioned earlier, engender the kind of clustering promoted by the OECD. Some commentators point to the emphasis of neoliberalism on contracts rather than property (in contrast with classical liberalism, property no longer confers status); on contract maximization (splitting services, which could produce block contracts); and on a labour market characterized by the reduction of the contract period and the increase in the frequency of contracts. This would be difficult to accomplish in Brindisi, as across South Italy, because of high unemployment and the lack of a network of small-medium enterprises. The continuing difficulty to access credit is of course an additional major deterrent.

In this scenario, and given Salento's increasing development as a tourist attraction, there is now in Brindisi a push to implement environmentally oriented projects, such as the recovery of dismantled industrial areas, the re-development of the port's tourist services and the creation of protected natural parks, including the marshlands at the periphery of the industrial area and what remains of the Mediterranean woodland in Cerano. Parallel to this, various local actors show an interest in new EU strategies for regional cooperation, such as the EU Strategy for the Adriatic-Ionian Region (EUSAIR), which was launched in 2014 within the framework of the European integration of the Western Balkans. Some, however, look at these new strategies with scepticism. They note that, while the EU Action Plan promotes the involvement of the local population and different stakeholders and advocates a bottom-up approach, it also claims that it is necessary to counterbalance grassroots involvement with a carefully thought out top-down policy in order to avoid the kind of not in my backyard (NIMBY) protest that has caused the TAP route to be deviated from Brindisi to San Foca, near Lecce; an archaeological and tourist area of outstanding natural beauty.

THE MORAL OF THE (HI)STORY

This chapter raises the question, what is new about neoliberalism and the post-Bretton Woods liberalisation of the markets? Historical and ethnographic material shows that some dynamics currently singled out as the evils of neoliberalism are not new after all. Furthermore, in Italy, the shift from a centrally planned economy to a neoliberal approach has not led to extreme deregulation, thus endorsing my original argument that economic policies should be analysed in relation to relevant political approaches.

Although it has become *the* paradigm for global policies, neoliberalism is more than just an economic mechanism. It would appear to be a *total* governing system that seeks to adapt society to its needs. Politics—national or global—has not disappeared; mostly, it just tends to follow suit. Neoliberalism and market deregulation do need a supporting political apparatus. At the same time, rather than succumbing to the negative effects of market deregulation, at the local level attempts are increasingly made to adapt trendy neoliberal templates to the situation on the ground, encouraging a neo-Smithean approach to 'individual' entrepreneurial competition that would benefit society as a whole. Ethnographic analysis has the power to bring out these dynamics.

Of course, I note, for this reversal trend to succeed, a new form of political intervention would be needed. Yet, the events of the past two decades indicate that the Italian political élite appear to be inadequate to meet this challenge. Petty squabbles, political infighting, backstabbing, and servitude to purposefully not-well-defined ideologies characterizes contemporary Italian politics. Most politicians—including, often, unelected politicians—and local and regional administrators are failing to engage with the responsibilities of their office. We should perhaps ask what new alliances are ruling Italy and take a hard look at the connections between the political élite and economic powers.

References

Anderson, P.J., and S. Talani. 2000. New Wine in Old Bottles? The Problems and Future of the New Italian Republic. In *New Europe in Transition*, ed. P.J. Anderson, G. Wiessala, and C. Williams, 132–147. London and New York: Continuum.

Chavdarova, T., P. Slavova, and S. Stoeva (eds.). 2010. *Markets as Networks*. Sofia: St. Kliment Ohridski University Press.

Daniele, V., and P. Malanima. 2011. *Il divario Nord-Sud in Italia 1861–2011*. Soveria Mannelli: Rubbettino.

Federico, G. 2007. Ma l'agricoltura meridionale era davvero arretrata? *Rivista di Politica Economica* III–IV: 314–328.

Gramsci, A. 1973. *La Questione Meridionale*. Rome: Editori Riuniti.

IBRD. 1951. *South Italy Appraisal*. http://aset.acs.beniculturali.it/dm_0/00/high/IBRD/Documenti-Archivio-Cassa-per-il-Mezzogiorno-e-Banca-Mondiale/1_Rapporti-interni-IBRD/1951-South-Italy-Appraisal.pdf. Accessed 15 April 2017.

Lepore, A. 2013. *La Cassa per il Mezzogiorno e la Banca Mondiale. Un Modello per lo Sviluppo Economico Italiano*. Catanzaro: Rubbettino.

Malinowksi, B. 1922. *Argonauts of the Western Pacific*. London: Routledge & Sons.

Mauss, M. 1954 [1950]. *The Gift*. London: Cohen & West.

Nitti, F.S. 1958. *Scritti sulla questione merdionale*. Bari: Laterza.

OECD. 2000. *Local Partnership, Clusters and SME Globalisation*. http://www.oecd.org/industry/smes/2010888.pdf. Accessed July 2009.

OECD. 2004. *Promoting Entrepreneurship and Innovative SMEs in a Global Economy*. http://www.oecd.org/cfe/smes/31919244.pdf. Accessed July 2009.

Pardo, I. 1996. *Managing Existence in Naples: Morality, Action and Structure*. Cambridge: Cambridge University Press.

Pardo, I. 2000. Credit, Entrepreneurship and the Repayment of Debt: Mismatched Conceptions of Legitimacy in Italy. *Self, Agency and Society* 2 (2): 51–87.

Pardo, I. 2012. Entrepreneurialism in Naples: Formality and Informality. *Urbanities* 2 (1): 30–45.

Pardo, I. 2017. Between Stereotype and Bad Governance: An Italian Ethnography. In *Palgrave Handbook of Urban Ethnography*, ed. I. Pardo and G.B. Prato, 35–52. New York: Palgrave Macmillan.

Pardo, I., and G.B. Prato (eds.). 2011. Introduction: Disconnected Governance and the Crisis of Legitimacy. In *Citizenship and the Legitimacy of Governance. Anthropology in the Mediterranean Region*, ed. I. Pardo and G.B. Prato, 1–23. London: Routledge.

Polanyi, K. 1944. *The Great Transformation*. New York: Farrar & Rinehart.

Porter, M.E. 1998. Clusters and the New Economics of Competitions. *Harvard Business Review* 76 (6): 77–90.

Prato, G.B. 1993. Political Decision-Making: Environmentalism, Ethics and Popular Participation in Italy. In *Environmentalism: The View from Anthropology*, ed. K. Milton, 175–188. London: Routledge.

Prato, G.B. 2000. The Cherries of the Mayor: Degrees of Morality and Responsibility in Local Italian Administration. In *Morals of Legitimacy: Between Agency and System*, ed. I. Pardo, 57–82. Oxford: Berghahn.

Prato, G.B. 2017. Rethinking the City as Urban Community: Views from South Europe. In *Palgrave Handbook of Urban Ethnography*, ed. I. Pardo and G.B. Prato, 53–69. New York: Palgrave Macmillan.

Rossi Doria, M. 1958. *Dieci anni di politica agraria.* Bari: DeDonato.
Schneider, J. 2002. World Markets. In *Exotic No More*, ed. J. MacClancy, 64–85. Chicago: University of Chicago Press.
Spyridakis, M. 2012. Being an Ex-worker: The Experience of Job Loss in a Tobacco Factory in Piraeus. *Urbanities* 2 (2): 78–93.
Spyridakis, M. 2013. *The Liminal Worker. An Ethnography of Work, Unemployment and Precariousness in Contemporary Greece.* London: Routledge.
Trigilia, C. 1992. *Sviluppo senza autonomia. Effetti perversi delle politiche nel Mezzogiorno.* Bologna: Il Mulino.

CHAPTER 6

Relations with the Market: On Cosmologies of Capitalism in Greece

Andreas Streinzer

INTRODUCTION

Athina flicks through a LIDL[1] brochure that she found on the doorstep of the activist food cooperative. While looking through and commenting on the offers, she is recalling a donation the activists recently gave to poor families. They had collected money during one of their public actions, and bought as much as they could - from LIDL. I am confused and ask why they went to LIDL. Athina is surprised at me being surprised. She says: 'We can buy a lot more food for those poor families when we buy it at LIDL!'

This scene from the summer of 2015 in Volos, Greece, contains several implications of living in a market society. Athina is part of a cooperative that operates with the purpose of cutting out middlemen. The activists organise a network of suppliers to deliver food and other basic

[1] German discount retail trade company, largest discounter in Europe.

A. Streinzer (✉)
Austrian Academy of Sciences (ÖAW), Vienna, Austria

Department of Social and Cultural Anthropology,
University of Vienna, Vienna, Austria

© The Author(s) 2018
M. Spyridakis (ed.), *Market Versus Society*, Palgrave Studies in Urban Anthropology, https://doi.org/10.1007/978-3-319-74189-5_6

products from producers to consumers at a reasonable price. They see their actions as a battle against predatory pricing practices in the retail sector. In Greece, this sector has been notorious: large retail companies expanded their branch network even during recession and spiralled consumer prices down. Hence, the conditions for the supermarkets' suppliers—among them many small and medium sized enterprises and farmers—seriously worsened. The organisers of the cooperative understand their activism as a practical critique of this sector.

In early 2015, the activists advertised a boycott of German products and companies as a sign of consumer resistance. At that time, conflicts around a new debt memorandum between Greece and its lenders worsened. German politicians had been a driving force in lobbying for strict austerity measures for the Greek state. Simultaneously, German companies became the subject of widespread criticism for their involvement in the retail sector. During these weeks, the activists bought goods to be donated from LIDL—the discounter that seemed to impersonate both German retail capitalism and price-pressuring on the food sector. I was puzzled and kept asking the activists why they decided to buy from LIDL. Their answer was clear: the aim was to get as much food as possible to poor families. Therefore they had to buy cheap and the cheapest place they knew was LIDL.

This situation exemplifies a more general ethnographic puzzle that I encountered in my doctoral fieldwork between 2014 and 2017 in Volos, Greece. In this chapter, I aim to provide a critical perspective on everyday life under capitalism that asks for a nuanced analysis of ambivalence in the Greek crisis (as mentioned by Agelopoulos 2016). I do so by focusing on this specific puzzle, that during the years of economic recession and hardship through austerity, many of my interlocutors seemed to turn towards the market and neoliberal cosmologies of capitalism while at the same time rejecting them. By proposing an ethnographic approach, I do not intend to imply that analysis stops with observation. Only in contrasting the conclusions from detailed ethnographic fieldwork with other cases and by linking them to social theory can observations become comprehensible.

Where Does Society End and the Market Begin?

This book is concerned broadly with the notions of market and society, and deliberately pits them as antagonists. The conceptual distinction between market and society is the subject of epistemological controversies in the social sciences, which were already apparent in the 1880s among

German academics in the so-called *Methodenstreit* (Krul 2016: 2). One school of thought was lead by Carl Menger, who claimed that economic behaviour is the rational behaviour of individuals who maximise their interest under scarce conditions—the domain of the market. The other school, forming around the empiricist Gustav von Schmöller, understood the economic mainly from a substantivist perspective. As such, economic behaviour comprises all practices of social reproduction (Polanyi et al. 1957; Seiser 2009: 162). These lines of epistemological conflict remained basically the same in the 1960s controversy between formalists (around Herskovits) and substantivists (around Polanyi).

For understanding the current conjunctures in the Greek crisis, it is pertinent to study the interrelations between the market and other forms of social reproduction. The idea of the double movement fits in well with this conceptual perspective. Polanyi showed in 1944 how the free market requires state intervention. The concept of double movement points to processes in which different social groups slow down or alter the expansion of the free market. Such a perspective can help to analytically focus on the interrelations between different modes of economic practices, and thus shed light on rapidly transforming economic conditions, as in contemporary Greece. However, two traps need to be avoided. On the one hand, one should not content oneself with proving that there is more to economic behaviour than just the rational *homo economicus*. After all, this is what decades of substantivist economic anthropology and the new economic sociology (Granovetter 1985) have argued convincingly. On the other hand, one should not equate double movements with acts of resistance, but take them as an entry point into more detailed and nuanced analyses. In saying so, I do not intend to disregard accounts of resistance to explore the struggles of social groups for re-distribution and recognition (Fraser and Honneth 2003). However, I do intend to criticise an often all-too-fast conclusion when researching the ways in which people attempt to act ethically in troubled times.

In a setting such as Greece, where the political organisation of capitalism has led to unprecedented and rapid changes in peoples' everyday lives, this becomes especially clear. Usually, anthropological accounts of life under austerity in Greece follow a narrative such as: There are macro forces of brutal dispossession, forced restructuring as well as the success of an authoritarian Central Bank-led EU/ monetarist technocratism. At the same time, we see protest, revolt, social movements, solidarity and generalised opposition. However, to understand how everyday life, material relations, capitalist subjectivities, and the political economy of consumption are changing, another area of focus is needed.

Therefore, and this is the purpose of this chapter, the conceptual separation between market and society should be understood as being made and remade in concrete social relations that come with ideas about these relations and how they should be organised. Doing so can help avoid the variety of analytical problems that come with the reification of the categories of society and market. These categories can be made and remade through, for example, economic communitarianism (Simonic 2014: 10) or free market fundamentalism (Block and Somers 2014). I argue that economic anthropology should not leave out the latter—relating to the market and investing in its promises—but also consider how constrained and ambivalent peoples' relationship to neoliberal economic thought and practice is.

Market and Shame, Obligations and Fantasies in the Greek Crisis

In Greece, the economic shocks felt as a result of cutting social benefits, high numbers of unemployment, and sinking profits for local entrepreneurs, directly affect the circumstances of social reproduction. Income from employment or small business, or through social transfers such as pensions, provide the basis for accessing resources. After several decades of economic growth, the economic crisis abruptly reversed this process and access to necessary incomes became more difficult (for example Spyridakis 2013). Many took loans to expand consumption, cover medical expenses, or to become homeowners. When the expectations for a future of expanding earning opportunities imploded with the onset of the crisis, the consequences of these loans were still around. They tied many Voliotes to a formal calendrics (Guyer 2007) of debt repayments that required even more monetary income, and strict household budgeting (Streinzer 2016). They were exposed to the moral narratives of debt (Peebles 2010; Gregory 2012) and the punitive rhetoric of politics and media outlets across Europe.

In these circumstances, my interlocutors find themselves in a highly ambivalent setting: On the one hand, they increasingly struggle to make a living. On the other hand, the market still provides a seductive canvas for desires and the quest to live a good life as a respectable individual. They are striving to do the right thing at the right time. Following are three cases from ethnographic fieldwork that show how my interlocutors navigate market relations, social obligations, and their hope for a better life in the context of austerity of Greece.

KATERINA: EDUCATION AND THE CIRCUMSTANCES OF EARNING

Katerina told me in early 2016 about her feeling of working in an 'enemy sector'. She was in her early 30s and worked as a teacher in a school, as well as in a private tutoring institution, a so called *Frontistiro*. Such private tutoring institutes are widespread in Greece, and it is common for teachers to earn additional income by private tutoring—even more so as their salaries were slashed by state austerity measures. Teachers often meet the same children at school and in the private tutoring institutions, where they prepare them for their exams. In several of our conversations, Katerina was critical of the kinds of politics that created the *Frontistiro* system—privatised education. She was ambivalent about her income from this private industry. Yet, the reduction of her salary by almost 60% from 2009 to 2015, as well as caring for her chronically ill mother, left her little choice, she said. She asked herself if she is morally right or wrong in having this kind of ambivalence to her sources of income. She told me she would like to ignore where her income was coming from and rather focus on its use—her mother's treatments. Yet, she was always ambivalent about her own role in seemingly perpetuating her students' dependence on her private tutoring.

She is not alone in this ambivalence. Greeks are faced with high unemployment rates, a difficult environment for starting up businesses, and the fact that many people who still have jobs don't get paid anymore. Katerina still considers herself lucky, even if her salary as a public school teacher was cut and the *Frontistiro* did not always pay on time or at all. Her example shows the constraints that she, and many others, operate within.

Her reflection on these constraints points to large questions—of the implications of her decisions as well as her being implicated in structures that she reproduces. In short, it is exactly her ambivalence about needing the private market to support her ill mother and what she sees as the consequences of this earning possibility that can show how constraint, obligation, and opportunity are intertwined.

Ioanna: Fantasies of Pure Meritocratic Market Relations

For some, the imaginary of idealized market settings provide a way to escape certain kinds of social obligations. Ioanna, working in a private health facility, complained about Greek entrepreneurship when I met her in summer 2015. She was in charge of supplying the facility with goods, from vegetables to technical equipment. She said she was sick of having to deal with her boss's friends, cousins, and acquaintances, who, as she told me, offered poor quality at high prices. Impersonal supplier relations, she imagined, would put an end to this. She told me about a potential solution: to change suppliers every three months by default. Not even one should get two contracts in several years. Every three months, a new call should be issued to supply the facility with goods. Only the best offers should be taken, eventually leading to low prices and high quality. She praised the meritocracy that would then supposedly dominate their relations and that such a system would push the suppliers into entrepreneurship as a necessity. Faced with unfavorable market conditions, they would thus not rely on their personal ties to the boss as the basis for their economic relationship but on the very commodities that, in Ioanna's account, should be the means and ends of their relation to each other. This situation would make them concentrate less on drinking coffee with the boss and more on efficiently producing high quality goods, she said.

Her solution is clearly informed by mainstream economic thought, which is a major source for her cosmology of capitalism. For her, this solution would provide a way out of her social position between the suppliers, her boss, and the clients of the health facility. Ioanna presented the market as a moral obligation in that it can provide an efficient mechanism for reducing health risks in the commodified care relation.

Kalypso: Avoiding Shame and Causing Ripple Effects

Kalypso was in her 40s and had been unemployed for several years when I met her in late 2014. She was providing the household with necessary goods and told me about her strategies for finding great products cheaply—through browsing the internet and comparing prices until she found the best offer. One day in 2015, she was looking for a spare part for her mother's water boiler. We clicked through websites, when I asked whether there were local shops she could go to, or people she could approach to help with the search. She replied negatively because she knew them too well. Kalypso explained to me that asking for prices in the local shops would result in a difficult situation, as she felt she couldn't decline their offers.

In the boom years, Kalypso used to be a successful entrepreneur, and never looked at price tags. If people would see her today, negotiating price reductions, her thriftiness and personal austerity would become apparent and this would bring shame on her and her family. Ordering from the internet, in impersonal trade relations, offered an easy way out, she said. She could endlessly browse for cheaper prices, make profitable deals, and feel again as an entrepreneurial person she sees herself as.

Her shame points to the interdependence of personal recognition and economic success that was severed, in her view of the world. Kalypso believes the failure of her own business was due to the thriftiness of others, and that she was aware that she was doing the same thing to local shops. 'It is a cycle (kyklos)', she said, 'If someone has money again, we will restart and one will give, one will take, one will order, one will pay!'. Her lack of personal income, fear of social stigma, and the possibilities of a global retail market facilitate her economic practices. Kalypso, too, was ambivalent about the role she played in this process. By avoiding personal trade relations, she was passing on economic problems to others in the local economy. Here, personal achievement and the possibility of having close social relations are tied to a functioning local market sphere. In her account, resorting to supra-regional forms of retail capitalism is only a temporal bridge until money re-appears again to restart the local market economy.

The Market as Material Relation and Its Cosmologies

These three ethnographic cases point to some of the investments that people make in the promises of the market relation as a resource for recognition. Other scholars have as well taken such a route and asked about the relations between market involvement and assessments of worthiness. In her account of the absurdities that living in contemporary capitalism brings with it, Neni Panourgiá supports understanding the ambivalence of people acting under the current conditions in Greece (Panourgiá 2016). Manos Spyridakis has shown how labourers criticize market arrangements that increased their precarity with the outsourcing of industrial work in Piraeus (Spyridakis 2012, 2013). The productive subjectivities—and their material arrangements—of the past are crucial resources for thinking about cosmologies of capitalism. Bakalaki (2003) has shown how Greeks deal with new kinds of troubles that come with economic growth: burglaries. Bakalaki describes how this growth has been accompanied by a surge in privatised security and the view of the state as a structure that can no longer take care of people's safety. Phaedra Douzina-Bakalaki discusses the orthodox organisation Bank of Love and gives detailed accounts of ethical religious volunteering practices, while carefully navigating a critique of them (Douzina-Bakalaki 2016).

These and other accounts provide a nuanced perspective on living and acting in contemporary Greece. In this chapter, I have aimed at bringing notions of progress, care, and the ambivalent and often paradox relations that make capitalism function, and indeed sometimes longed for, into focus when analysing everyday economic lives.

But how can the cosmologies of capitalism seem severed, yet not deeply devastated, in Greece? James Carrier's work, 'Meanings of the Market: the Free Market in Western Culture' provides an analytical conception that helps to answer this question. Carrier understands the Market (with a capital M) as 'conception(s) people have about an idealised form of buying and selling, and that this conception comes with a claim and a belief that a certain sort of buying and selling benefits all those involved economically, politically, socially and even morally' (Carrier 1997a: vii).

This point has been raised by several others, I want to quote two here. Somers and Block have shown how the ideas of the market promise a reduction of the political in social life and in which ways this is a seductive idea in the United States. The promise of replacing coercion with choice, and compromise with freedom, is key to the success of what they call market fundamentalism (Block and Somers 2014). Mirowski describes how neoliberalism, as thought collective and political program, consists of a very scattered and fragmented bunch of ideas and people. In analysing what he calls 'everyday neoliberalism', he shows that the very idea of the neoliberal market as coherent and nonparadoxical is one of the strengths of neoliberal thought and praxis (Mirowski 2014).

From these scholars, I take inspiration to emphasize three crucial dimensions for an analysis of market relations in contemporary Greece: first, the political economy of the Greek crisis and attempts of the Greek and other governments to secure economic value for capitalist circulation; second, idealised conceptions of what the market is and can offer, which provide seductive potentialities of less social conflict, less messiness, and less difficulties in everyday life; and third, the scattered nature of the market as thought and everyday practice. The political economy of austerity employed powerful narratives of the market to gain political support for the restructuring of the state. One such narrative held that the Greeks are inadequate market subjects and that cultural change was necessary to achieve economic prosperity. Carrier observes that often, the market is a form of Occidentalism idealising Western society (Carrier 1997b: 31), which hints at the direction that this change is supposed to take. The threat of being excluded from the market comes with a threat of not being 'European'. Market thinking rests on social philosophical models that equate human reason with the rationality of the *homo oeconomicus*. Economic relations and political systems, according to this logic, need to be fashioned after these models (see Carrier and Miller 1998). These idealised conceptions of the market do not stop at the macro level of austerity negotiations, but also influence everyday economic practices and how people make sense of them. The economic anthropology of life under capitalism must consider these models as not only top-down imposed expressions of material value extraction, but as ones that inform everyday market thinking. This means taking the notions of 'society' and 'market' seriously as notions that structure how people make sense of economic relations.

Conclusion

The chapter started with an ethnographic vignette about activists from a Volos food cooperative purchasing goods at a large German retail company. From there, I reflected on my own puzzlement at this purchase, which was contradicting their hard stance in the boycott of such companies. I took this vignette as an entry point into asking about the notions of society and market in the anthropology of the Greek crisis and in economic anthropology at large. Then, I gave an overview about the conceptual split of these categories in economic anthropology. From there, I argued for taking the economic relation in market exchange as important, and understanding the normativity of economic practices as part of the cosmologies of capitalism. The key question of my chapter was: How can the capitalist market still offer such a seductive potential for the people of Greece, after several years of enforced economic restructuration, value extraction, and state austerity?

To give ethnographic entry points into an exploration of this question for Greece, I presented three cases from my ethnographic fieldwork in Volos. Each portray a specific kind of relation that my interlocutors had to the market. In the first one, Katerina works both as a public school teacher and in a private tutoring center. Because her salary as a teacher was cut, the tutoring became more important for her in terms of income. She considers this income arrangement as highly problematic for her and Greek society. Yet, she justifies her action as she is also the primary caregiver for her mother, who suffers from a medical condition and requires treatment that is not paid for by the social insurance. This case illustrates the constraints as a result of state austerity. The capitalist market is an important source of employment, even more so in times of state withdrawal from major sectors like education.

The second case revolves around Ioanna's position in charge of supplying a private health facility with goods. She is indignant with her boss and his way of organising supplier relations around his acquaintances, friends, and kin. Ioanna attributes technical failures and poor quality to this arrangement. She would like to change all suppliers every three months, which she believes would lead to more pressure on the suppliers to provide higher quality and lower prices. Here, market exchange between actors meeting for the transaction and spending less time in social obligations were thought of as part of a moral obligation to put patients and the quality and reliability of care first.

In the third case, Kalypso oversees household provisioning while facing reductions in available income. She has turned to the impersonality of the internet as a way to find the best prices. Doing so means she spends less time in local shops, trying to avoid the shame of others noticing that she is not longer the prosperous entrepreneur that she used to be. She admits to feeling ashamed of having to search online for goods. Trapped in the attempt to conserve her image of herself as an entrepreneur who does not have to turn a coin, she turns to the internet to window-shop. As she had to close her business due to such thriftiness by others, the online browsing feels wrong for her, but nevertheless she uses it as a strategy to get by.

After presenting these cases, I turned to scholarly work to support my analysis of the cosmologies of capitalism. I discussed James Carrier's definition of the Market as an idealized conception about the world and a claim that ultimately everybody will benefit from meeting one another as buyers and sellers. Then I introduced Fred Block and Margaret

Somers because they have—in taking Polanyi's thinking further—analysed how the Market offers several promises, one being the replacement of coercion and obligation with freedom and choice. Finally, I presented Philip Mirowski's analysis on why neoliberalism got even stronger with the financial crisis. In his work on everyday neoliberalism, he shows how scattered and paradoxical neoliberalism as thought and practice is.

The aim of this chapter was thus less to do away with a certain reading of Polanyi, which looks for resistance and antagonism in capitalist societies, but to add to it. I propose a serious consideration of the cosmologies of capitalism that can not only tell us about the material and symbolic rationales of getting by in crisis, but also about the promises that the Market offers. This is ultimately a political project, because if there are no other promises to be made, and ways out to show, then it seems unlikely that people will turn away from the scattered array of conceptions and practices associated with the Market.

REFERENCES

Agelopoulos, G. 2016. Ex Nihilo Nihil Fit: On the Greek Crisis. *Cultural Anthropology Website*. https://culanth.org/fieldsights/863-ex-nihilo-nihil-fit-on-the-greek-crisis.

Bakalaki, A. 2003. Locked into Security, Keyed into Modernity: The Selection of Burglaries as Source of Risk in Greece. *Ethnos* 68 (2): 209–229.

Block, F., and M.R. Somers. 2014. *The Power of Market Fundamentalism. Karl Polanyi's Critique*. Harvard: Harvard University Press.

Carrier, J.G. 1997a. Preface. In *Meanings of the Market. The Free Market in Western Culture*, ed. J.G. Carrier, vii–xv. Oxford and New York: Berg.

Carrier, J.G. 1997b. Introduction. In *Meanings of the Market. The Free Market in Western Culture*, ed. J.G. Carrier, 1–67. Oxford and New York: Berg.

Carrier, J., and D. Miller (eds.). 1998. *Virtualism: A New Political Economy*. Oxford and New York: Berg.

Douzina-Bakalaki, P. 2016. Volunteering Mothers: Engaging the Crisis at a Soup Kitchen in Northern Greece. *Anthropology Matters* 17 (1): 1–24.

Fraser, N., and A. Honneth. 2003. *Redistribution or Recognition?: A Political-Philosophical Exchange*. London and New York: Verso.

Granovetter, M. 1985. Economic Action and Social Structure: The Problem of Embeddedness. *American Journal of Sociology* 91 (3): 481–510.

Gregory, C.A. 2012. On Money Debt and Morality: Some Reflections on the Contribution of Economic Anthropology. *Social Anthropology* 20 (4): 380–396.

Guyer, J. 2007. Prophecy and the Near Future: Thoughts on Macroeconomic, Evangelical, and Punctuated Time. *American Ethnologist* 34 (3): 409–421.

Krul, M. 2016. Institutions and the Challenge of Karl Polanyi: Economic Anthropology After the Neoinstitutionalist Turn. Max Planck Institute for Social Anthropology. Working Papers, No. 168.

Mirowski, P. 2014. *Never Let a Crisis Go to Waste: How Neoliberalism Survived the Financial Meltdown.* London: Verso.

Panourgiá, N. 2016. Surreal Capitalism and the Dialectical Economies of Precarity. In *Impulse to Act. A New Anthropology of Resistance and Social Justice,* ed. O. Alexandrakis, 112–131. Bloomington and Indianapolis: Indiana University Press.

Peebles, G. 2010. The Anthropology of Credit and Debt. *Annual Review of Anthropology* 39 (1): 225–240.

Polanyi, P. 1944. *The Great Transformation.* Boston: Beacon Press.

Polanyi, K., C.M. Arensberg, and H. Pearson (eds.). 1957. *Trade and Market in the Early Empires.* Glencoe: The Free Press.

Seiser, G. 2009. Neuer Wein in Alten Schläuchen? Aktuelle Trends in der ökonomischen Anthropologie. *Historische Anthropologie* 17 (2): 157–177.

Simonic, P. 2014. Solidarity and Reciprocity in Times of Recession. Understanding the Old and New Values in Late Capitalism. *Ars & Humanities. Revija za umetnost in humanistiko/Journal of Arts and Humanities* VIII (1): 9–14.

Spyridakis, M. 2012. Being an Ex-worker: The Experience of Job Loss in a Tobacco Factory in Piraeus. *Urbanities* 2 (2): 78–94.

Spyridakis, M. 2013. *The Liminal Worker: An Ethnography of Work, Unemployment and Precariousness in Contemporary Greece.* Burlington: Ashgate.

Streinzer, A. 2016. Stretching Money to Pay the Bills: Temporal Modalities and Relational Practices of 'Getting by' in the Greek Economic Crisis. *The Cambridge Journal of Anthropology* 34 (1): 45–57.

CHAPTER 7

'We Are All Socialists':
Greek Crisis and Precarization

Manos Spyridakis

Precarization is a term very much heard in the current period. In general it refers to the creation of insecure and uncertain conditions of existence as the result of remote decisions made at the expense of ordinary people's life trajectories (Spyridakis 2017). Hence, the term encompasses not only nonstandard employment and worse labour conditions but life itself. 'Precarization means more than insecure jobs, more than the lack of security given by waged employment. By way of insecurity and danger it embraces the whole of existence, the body, modes of subjectivation' (Lorey 2015: 1). Precarization is strongly connected to a status of vulnerability where people cannot schedule their future lives, they tend to be isolated and socially excluded, doing short and dead end jobs and mostly they are forced to find recourse on public programme schemes in order to get by. Far from being a homogeneous category, precarious people can be thought of as second class citizens since they are denied a range of rights, the main being the equal access to forms of protection

M. Spyridakis (✉)
Department of Social and Educational Policy,
University of the Peloponnese, Corinth, Greece

M. Spyridakis (ed.), *Market Versus Society*, Palgrave Studies in Urban Anthropology, https://doi.org/10.1007/978-3-319-74189-5_7

and the equal possibility to live with dignity. They are the product of a process owing much to the way the global market works: backed by political decisions made by neoliberal governments, every aspect of human life is commodified fully and intensively, thus eroding regulated safety nets. In such a system, the reproduction of labour power as a pure commodity dissembedded from society becomes the norm. In this connection, Zygmount Bauman argues that precarious people are those who are rejected from the process of consumption; they are imperfect consumers and for this reason they are deemed unable to achieve any sort of contemporary freedom, that is choice. To the extent that precarious people have no role in contemporary society, they 'serve' as the negative example of personal failure and of a useless, redundant workforce in a very delicate, cloaked form (Bauman 1998).

As far as Greece is concerned, neoliberalism, especially by 2010, took the form of imposed economic austerity, internal devaluation, and reductions in public deficits and spending in exchange for financial support from the International Monetary Fund (IMF), the European Community (EC), and the European Central Bank (ECB), and lately the ESM, worsening an already problematic economy. This oppressive condition led to a series of deregulations in the Greek labour market, which in turn ended up in significant wage cuts, the introduction of lower minimum income scales, the easing of employers' dismissals by reducing compensation payments, and in the relaxing of justifications required of employers when making redundancies (Kretsos 2014). However, the most serious and permanent effect was the decline of people's living standards in material and social terms and the increase of inequality. According to the Greek Statistics Authority and the European Union Survey on Income and Living Conditions (EU SILC) sample survey (reference period 2015), people at the edge of social exclusion, despite some light fluctuations, have been increasing since 2010, reaching the 35.6% of the population, that is 3,789,300 individuals. Households on the edge of poverty are estimated at 832,065 out of a total of 4,168,784. At the same time, the data show that the deprivation of basic goods and services affect not only the poor but a significant part of the well-to-do population as well. Since 2009, material deprivation related to crucial dimensions such as food provision, heating, basic goods, purchasing with installments, coupled with an inability to secure loans and bill payment schedules has been increasing steadily. The gap between rich and poor has consequently been widening. In 2015, the income of the richest 20% of the population grew by 6.6%, in Gini's indicator terms, than that of the poorest 20%. On top of that, according to Eurostat, Greece currently has the highest unemployment percentage (22.5% in March 2015) among the EU-27.

A Sketch of the Greek Economic Crisis

Greece wasn't the exception or the trouble maker of a well functioning global economy, it was the tip of the iceberg. The financial crisis, which emerged with subprime loans in August 2007 and heightened in September 2008 with the collapse of Lehman Brothers, required an unprecedented mobilization of public sources in order to prevent a bank run. National states, hypocritically enough, set aside their neoliberal principles about the diminished role of government on economy and began to compete with each other in supplying banks with cornucopian sums of money. From 2008 to 2012 a financial aid package for the banks of the 27 countries in the European Union came from public coffers, amounting to the unthinkable sum of 5085.95 billion euros (or 40.3% of 2011 GDP). This money included recapitalization measures, guarantees, asset relief interventions and liquidity measures other than guarantees. It was the first time since 1980s that neoliberal doctrines gained the hearts and minds of governing parties almost all over the world, as states unanimously agreed to rescue a system which was on the edge of collapsing. The contradiction with what happened a couple of decades before with the textile or shipyards industries, when one after the other was closed down, hurting the industrial base of the whole European South and making its economy much more vulnerable to the gradations of the economic circle, is more than striking. In this context, sovereign debt crisis can be seen as a metastasis of the banking crisis and it is not surprising to notice the stable increase of sovereign debt throughout these years in advanced economies. Namely, in the United States, the debt increased from 72.8% in 2008 to 104.5% in 2013; in the Euro Area from 70.3 to 95.2%; and in the United Kingdom from 51.9 to 90.1% etc. (IMF 2016). One can logically claim that neoliberals directed their hatred to the state in high levels, turning it into a hostage of the private sector. Hence, the persistence of debtocracy (Vatikiotis 2015), so many years after the onset of the crisis, is worth noting if we bear in mind the draconian austerity measures that have been implemented after 2010, especially on these countries that were found on the frontline of the crisis, like Greece.

Obviously, the issue of 214.9 billion euros (the amount the 'rescue' of Greece has cost, through December 2013) is related to the peculiarities of Greece. However, what happened in this part of Europe, feeding, once more, the most unfoundedly stereotypical comments about Southern laziness, threatening the supposed coherence of the inherently fragile Eurozone construction? Data about debt and budgetary deficit of Greece are eloquent, even if one omits the condemnation of Greek justice about the alchemies which led to the abrupt increase of debt and deficit. No other country in the European Union or the Euro Area had a budgetary deficit of 10.9% and a sovereign debt of 148.3%, simultaneously in 2010 when rescue officially began. There are seven main reasons for the Greek fiscal derailment, which by no means justifies the solutions that were imposed: (1) The very low real (no nominal based on official rates) taxation of capital achieved mainly by tax exemptions. In 2009, business taxes were equal to 16.5% of GDP when the EU average was 28.8%. No doubt Greek governments disagreed fully with Thomas Pickety's conclusion that, 'from the standpoint of general interest, it is normally preferable to tax the wealthy rather than borrow from them' (Pickety 2014: 540). Greek political elites chose to borrow from the rich instead of taxing them; (2) The addiction of Greek business to state subsidies, which culminated in the 2004 Olympic Games, which cost more than 20 billion euro (2.5 times more than their initial forecast of 8 billion euro). Their final cost is very close to the deficit of 2010, 24.11 billion euro. The second tranche of state generosity occurred in 2008, when the government gave the banks 28 billion euro (in the form of cash and guarantees), paving the way to their continuous funding that has cost more than 146.35 billion euro, according to the Preliminary Report of the Truth Committee on Public Debt (2015); (3) The provocative record, in European terms, of military spending (as percentage of GDP), which is due only partially to the Turkish aggressiveness, the main reason being NATO's imposed policy. In 2009, Greek military spending was equal to 3.2% of GDP, when according to the Stockholm International Peace Research Institute (2015), Germany's was 1.4%, and both the UK's and France's spending were 2.5%! Ironically enough Greece should by now be the superpower of Europe, confirming, *mutatis mutandis*, the view that 'national debt is first, born of war' (Graeber 2011: 358); (4) The vicious circle of servicing the public debt reveals the trap where any indebted country is caught. From 1992 to 2016 the servicing of sovereign debt or, in other words, the fee of keeping it viable, referring to the debt of general government and not of central admin-istration, cost Greek taxpayers 640.157 billion euro on December 31, 2016! (Ministry of Finance 2017); (5) The participation of Greece in 1981 in the (then) European Economic Community and in 2002 in the Eurozone. The economic integration of Europe helped German manu-facturers and others from northern countries with productivity benefits. These benefits helped to transform the whole continent to an internal market through the intensification of the competition and the assistance of visible hand of the European Commission, which led to the bank-ruptcy of industries who historically lagged in productivity. The result wasn't so apparent in the 1980s and 1990s because of the influx of sub-sidies from EU funds, basically in primary sector. However, it became thoroughly apparent recently due to diminishing tax revenues and a huge deficit on the foreign account balance; (6) The integration of Greek finance and the international financial system which facilitated the con-tagion of the 2008 crisis; (7) And, finally, and more important, is the underlying crisis of Greek capitalism. This crisis was evident in the falling rates of increase of the GDP, which in 2008 turned to a reduction in the third quarter of 2008 (for first time since 1993), ending a long period of increases; increases that were higher than European ones. The capital-ist crisis goes back to the international crisis of the 1970s and the falling rate of profit; and it can be noted that Karl Marx wrote about such crises in the third volume of *Capital*.

This picture obviously contrasts not only with the official narra-tive repeated by the international press (including the intensive cover-age in the German press), but even by the Greek press and politicians. The convenient explanation is based, briefly, on two interpretations, the first being that Greeks don't work; the second referring to the 'waste-ful' Greek welfare state and its hydrocephalous public sector. Yet, offi-cial data tell a different story. In 2011, according to the Organisation for Economic Co-operation and Development (OECD), Greece got the third position on the average ranking of actual annual hours worked per worker, with 2032 hours. In the first two positions were Mexico (with 2249 hours) and Chile (2047 hours), while the average of OECD coun-tries was 1.776 and Germany had one of the lowest records with 1413 hours. Social spending in 2009 in Greece was 28% of GDP when in the EU-27 it was 29.5%. In 2011, public servants in Greece represented 7.9% of the labour force when in Germany, for example, they represented 10.6% (OECD 2011).

The economic collapse that followed the implementation of the classic receipt of IMF by Troika through Memoranda was anything but unexpected. Spending cuts, reductions in wages, sell-off of public enterprises, and massive redundancies of public servants failed to confront the fiscal wreckage because Greece's problem wasn't excessive expenses but the deficient revenues. As a result, the initial Memorandum (of May 2010) that accompanied the first loan agreement of 110 billion euros is a monument of epic failure. It predicted that unemployment would reach its highest level of 14.8% in 2012 and then would begin to fall. However, the unemployment rate during the last two years is still higher than predicted. The Memorandum had also predicted that 2011 would be the last year of GDP reduction. Yet, in 2013 it kept on falling. It predicted that in 2012 public debt would reach its peak at 149% of GDP. On June 2014 it reached 176.9% of GDP, despite the haircut of 105 billion euro in 2012, which was countervailed by a new loan of an initial high of 109 billion euros, recording on these rescue years the biggest increase during the last decades.

The sharp increase of sovereign debt both as a percentage and an amount since 2009, when the government began implementing the first austerity measures—from 129 to 177% and from 299 to 323 billion euro (Ministry of Finance 2017)—is telling. It shows that Troika's short-term aim wasn't budgetary discipline or fiscal recovery, but, the rescue of foreign banks, namely French and German ones, which had been exposed to the Greek bonds. The long-term aim is a much larger effort: to demolish the European welfare state and reform it by reducing public spending and privatizing social security, health, and education services—starting with Greece. The finance ministers of Germany and the UK, Wolfgang Schäuble and George Osborne, respectively, illustrated well this goal by writing in the *Financial Times*, on March 27, 2014, 'Our continent has just over 7% of the world's population but 50% of global social welfare spending'!

It was apparent from the beginning that Greek sovereign debt couldn't be paid. And even though a serious 'haircut' on the nominal value of bonds was characterized as inevitable since 2010, this was a forbidden discussion. Up front, in Greece and abroad, governments made assurances that the full repayment of the debt was a 'matter of honor'. However, in practice, different plans were in the works. At stake was the very big exposure of foreign banks to Greek debt. As revealed by the annual surveys of the Basel-based Bank for International Settlements, the 'mother' of central banks, as well as from data the Bank of Greece provided to Greek parliament in September 2012, foreign banks' exposure to Greek bonds on March 31, 2009 was 123 billion euros (Vatikiotis 2015). Two years later it had been decreased to 65 billion euros with the help of Troika's funding and the ECB, which helped ease French and German banks in getting rid of their Greek bonds before a 'haircut' measure was decided. Yet, just the opposite happened; Troika with the help of the Institute of International Finance decided to proceed with the 'haircut' of Greek bonds. In a confidential IMF document (*'Board meeting on Greece's request for a Stand By Agreement – May, 9 2010'*), the hypocrisy of the Northern capitalist interests and its well planned decision to use rescue funds and time to sell off Greek bonds before the inescapable haircut, was revealed on May 10, 2010. The document stated: '*The Dutch, French and German chairs conveyed to the Board the commitments of their commercial banks to support Greece and broadly maintain their exposure'*.

The lasting effort to demolish the European welfare state peaked under the terms that accompanied the haircut, which took the form of private sector involvement (PSI), implying that private investors (banks, insurance schemes, etc.) would bear the cost of it. The new Memorandum (part and parcel of the new loan agreement) foresaw reductions in wages, the abolition of collective bargaining and, among other things, the biggest wave of privatizations of public property for paying off the public debt, the effectiveness of which is highly debatable. The PSI led the indebtedness of Greece in unprecedented levels, succeeding at the same time in fundamentally transforming the profile of Greek debt, from mostly private (in the form of bonds) before the crisis, to official (that is, owed to IMF, Eurozone, EFSF and ESM) after the 'rescue'. On June 30, 2014, 68.4% of Greece's debt was owed to Troika. In this way debtors of Greece passed to the European people the banks' debt; truly, a very extraordinary expression of European solidarity.

During this period, sovereign debt increased not only in Greece, but in Ireland, Portugal and Cyprus too—the three other countries that adopted the strict austerity measures under Troika's monitoring. Undoubtedly the rescue's aim wasn't the decrease of debt or the rescue of the country as was said in dramatic tones as soon as the measures were implemented. European elites knew very well that the price of the fiscal consolidation would be the recession, as was observed in the whole Euro Area, where GDP six years after the collapse of Lehman Brothers hasn't came back to its pre-crisis levels—contrary to what was happening in US and the UK, where the mixture of economic policy was more flexible despite the implementation of austerity measures.

History is teaching us that debts in general are a mechanism of dependence and a way of limiting a country's sovereignty (Chossudovsky 2003: 5). Further, as Carmen Reinhart and Kenneth Rogoff (2009) have shown, the debt trap stopped by declaring unilateral cessation of payments. Troika's loans rescued European and Greek banks while failing even to maintain the sovereign debt at its initial levels. Also, as seen in Russia (1998), Ecuador (2008), Iceland (2010), and even Argentina (Research on Money and Finance 2010) the social struggles these events caused threaten not only the stability of debtocracy's regimes (while servicing of the debt means increasing poverty, unemployment and migration), but its feasibility too. Debtocracy is Troika's creation.

The Greek debt crisis and other similar crisis in other European countries was a gift for the ruling class because it paved the way for European elites to undermine and abandon social spending while at the same time incriminating the whole population in order to accept these odious changes. As Lazzarato said, 'Debt constitutes the most deterritorialized and the most general power relation through which the neoliberal power bloc institutes its class struggle. Debt represents a transversal power relation unimpeded by state boundaries, the dualisms of production (active/ nonactive, employed/unemployed, productive/nonproductive), and the distinctions between the economy, the political and the social. It immediately acts at the global level, affecting entire populations, calling for and contributing to ethical construction of the indebted man' (Lazzarato 2012: 89). In this long course, more of a marathon than a sprint, its ending not yet predictable, social security, health, and education have been caught in the frontline of the neoliberal attack.

GOVERNING THE VULNERABLE

It is against this adverse economic canvas that the production of vulnerable people should be seen, at least in the Greek case, for the simple reason that precarization does not emerge out of parthenogenesis. Ironically enough, the rescue policies imposed produce, as Lorey states, the conditions that maintain people's life as precarious (Lorey 2015: 20). Yet, the question remains, who exactly is the savior? There are many candidates, the main being the four so-called institutions previously mentioned. Keeping in mind the socially deleterious mixture of the policy they implemented, which their internal machine politics apparatus called *necessary sacrifices*, they bring to mind what Hanna Arendt (1969) describes as the ruling of *Nobody*. The trick is an old one, as Ulysses taught us, but always works: *Nobody* means that literally no one has a specific responsibility for the decisions made since this entity helps, in theory, those who badly need to correct their own mistakes. In this light, as Cris Shore claims, with reference to the similarly remote, untouchable and in essence undemocratic structure of decision-making in the EU, 'With nobody left with who one can argue or to whom one could present one's grievances. This is perhaps the greatest danger of governance without government' (Shore 2006: 721). The degrading acronym, P.I.G.S. is but the relevant exemplary metonymy of a *Triste Tropique* representing a specific way of governing and signifying a realm of economic and political experiment where governments, whose members in some cases are not even elected, succumb to the wills of supranational economic powers, thus organizing capital accumulation on a world scale (Narotzky 2016: 84). Hence, the notion of governing entails a polycentric vague state and a centreless society which, according to Shore—resting on Foucault's ideas—is regulated and manipulated by market forces and through inexplicit processes of intra-institutional bargaining (Shore 2006: 12), which, however, have the power to impose and implement specific policies.

From an anthropological point of view, this condition is of primary importance, since modern society is regulated, organized, and defined by policy discourses and measures that shape and formulate the conditions of our existence. To the extent that our contemporary life is subject to policies, decision-making and to their respective implementation, it is analytically important to think not only of the ideological orientation they convey but also of the constraining way they fashion the modern citizen and his identity, as well as his perceptive categories about his social milieu. In that sense, policy discourses tell their own stories concerning the classification of people and of problems as particularly reified categories of social, economic, and political life. Hence, similar to the clinical Foucauldian gaze, mainstream policies attempt to construct regimes of etiologies for social issues rendering them into common sense phenomena and ascribing to them a programmatic character (Goode and Maskovsky 2001: 7). As the British governmentality school argues in referring to the relation between the evaluation process of policy and governmentality, the latter: 'Is programmatic, not simply in that one can see the proliferation of more or less explicit programmes for reforming reality government reports, white papers, green papers, papers from business, trade unions, financiers, political parties, charities and academics proposing this or that scheme for dealing with this or that problem. It is also programmatic in that it is characterised by an eternal optimism that a domain or a society could be administered better or more effectively, that reality is in some way or another, programmable' (Miller and Rose 1990: 4). This optimism, coupled with the knowledge produced by experts that were called upon to monitor the design and the institutional process of active transformation, is effused as a normative behaviour to other experts as well as to individuals who should reform their conduct in line with the new imposed and internalised archetype of work and getting things done (Shore and Wright 1997: 9). Therefore, it is more than obvious that the co-dependent relationship between the notions of knowledge and bio-power as dominant political technologies in the modern mode of government shapes and subjectifies the 'active citizen'. At the same time, the power of knowledge creates a normalising imperative influencing the personal judgment and self disposition of individuals as well as the disposition of social groups and populations based on intellectual technologies like social statistics, census taking, tables, and graphs. The power of knowledge produces subjects and manipulated beings—docile instruments—while it imposes itself as something natural, through applied policies and leverage. It is through this theoretical background that programmes issued to absorb the pain sprung by the economic crisis that *Nobody* caused can be analysed, and in particular their implicit aim: the regulation of social asymmetries via the governance of the new 'dangerous classes'.

In 2015 I was responsible for the implementation of such a program coming from EU headquarters. Its logic was based on the 'Europe 2020' paper for smart, sustainable, and inclusive growth. According to this report, the Union and the member states have set themselves the objective of having at least 20 million fewer people at risk of poverty and social exclusion. Nonetheless, in 2011, nearly one quarter of people living in the Union (119.82 million) were at risk of poverty or social exclusion, approximately 4 million people more than in the previous year.

From the end of 2014 onwards, the European Commission has promoted an operational program of basic material assistance, called the Fund for European Aid to the Most Deprived (FEAD) (2014). The Fund offers assistance to individuals, families, households, or groups of people in the EU member states. The assistance may take the form of food, clothing, and other essentials, accompanied by advice, counselling, or other help to re-integrate into society. The FEAD may also finance standalone social inclusion activities, which are designed to strengthen people's skills and capacities so that they can overcome the difficulties or discrimination they face in everyday life, for the most deprived persons.

Each EU country has adapted the assistance it provides to the specific needs in their region. The country may, for instance, focus on food aid or on basic consumer goods for the most deprived people. Or the country may provide social inclusion activities in order to best meet local needs. The assistance available is comprehensive and has included: food support, e.g., food packages, meals, collection and distribution of donated food; material assistance, e.g., basic hygiene items, clothing/sleeping bags, school supplies; assistance in the form of accompanying measures, e.g., information about available social services, temporary shelter, financial literacy and debt mediation, information about maintaining a balanced diet, access to health and education services, psychological support and empowerment; other social inclusion activities, e.g., outreach activities, socialisation and networking activities, training for improved self reliance, a healthier and more active lifestyle, and improved skills, orientation activities, and information about rights and obligations; as well as language training.

Each member state must adopt focused solutions that fit their national circumstances. The FEAD allows them the flexibility to do so by identifying the specific groups of people that the Fund will support. While national approaches differ and may address specific needs or challenges facing a particular region, some of the groups targeted for food and/or basic material assistance or social inclusion measures are people experiencing poverty, the homeless, children, seniors, the disabled, people living in remote areas, and immigrant families.

The FEAD assistance is supposed to reach deprived people through partner organisations approved by EU. These organisations are mandatory for all FEAD programmes and may be national, regional, or local public bodies or nongovernmental organizations (NGOs). They are charged with the actual distribution of assistance and/or the provision of social inclusion measures to the most deprived. They are expected to have relevant expertise that would make them best placed to reach FEAD target groups, which can sometimes be hard to find. The exchange of information and best practices between partner organisations is a key part of the FEAD platform and a way to develop synergies within Europe.

FEAD's total budget is approximately 4.5 billion euros for 2014–2020. The bulk of it—3.8 billion euros—comes from the EU budget, while member states will top this up by 674 million euros as national co-financing. As far as Greece is concerned, the budget allocation is 280.9 million euros; the national contribution is 49.6 million euros.

The funds are being spent by tackling food and material deprivation of those most in need, with a focus on families, in particular single-parent or multichild families, as well as the homeless. Material aid includes food packages or ready made meals (mostly for the homeless), as well as shoes and clothes, school items, and baby equipment. The target group in the Greek version of the program are those: (1) with an annual income not exceeding, for each individual person, 3000 euros, for two-member families 4500 euros, for a three-member family 5400 euros, for four-member families 6300 euros, and for five-member families 7200 euros; (2) the total taxable value of their property must not exceed 115,000 euros per person and 250,000 for the whole family, plus 20,000 euros for each additional adult and 15,000 for each dependent minor, with a maximum total value for each individual or family of 250,000 euros.

What is the point of all these? In the above description the important role is played by the content of the social protection. Based on the principle of personalization each time a beneficiary target group is sought to get assistance with expiration date which is close to a kind of philanthropic action and administrative job.

In anthropological terms, a conceptual intervention territory is constructed, that is, a specific discourse that calls for interference and regulation. As a case study the FEAD program shows how the microphysics of power, to use Foucault's term, constructs those whom it aims to control and regulate and who at the same time are the outcome of the policy it implements. An apparatus comprised of professionals and experts (economists, lawyers, agencies, management authorities, civil society organizations, as well as censuses, electronic databases, monitoring and control bases, applications and reports) rearranges social categories by creating new classifications and subjectivities. This kind of governmental functioning has the potential to transform social issues and needs into mere data, which in turn are reified, becoming cases requiring study, diagnosis, and treatment. Within this constructed objectivity the experts are invited to submit their know-how so as to achieve a common sense solution. This solution turns out to be nothing more than the conventional implementation of the principles of a formal instrumental bureaucracy consisting of unending evaluations, reports, and recommendations for the future. This political technology, however, does not simply identify issues to be resolved but also those people whose identity should be reformed and re-categorized as poor, deprived, deserving, undeserving unemployed, socially excluded, etc. In other words, their citizenship is reframed in terms of its vulnerability. Thus, through a pedagogical discourse about who and what qualifies as a beneficiary—or as partner, contractor, end recipient, insiders and outsiders, accompanying measures, irregularity, systemic irregularity, operation, as, etc.—a rhetoric is being developed in order to persuade and discipline. The more focused this rhetoric claims to be, the more legitimate it is considered, thus becoming a panoptically powerful tool of control.

Back to FEAD as a program, the external observer, the beneficiary or even the benefiter, may possibly consider that it is a significant assistance in a recessionary environment. I now take a brief look at the ethnography of an ongoing research project taking place in social assistance structures in Athens. Petros is a forty five years old and is unemployed. He had an auto repair garage near his place of residence in Athens and employed his oldest son occasionally. The garage used to be a family business from father to son and Petros managed to expand it and succeeded in having a steady cycle of clients every week. The economic recession operated as a chain reaction for his shop, as his clients were mostly big companies they could not, especially after 2011, afford to make any payments. Petros said:

> None could anticipate this would happen. This crisis is like a cancer. If you don't anticipate it then it spreads rapidly and infects all healthy parts of the economy. I had a very well-to-do business and now I have got nothing. I still simply cannot take it, cannot really explain it, I just laugh.

Petros' account highlights what remains unsaid in the rhetoric of the political elites of neo liberalism. He used to work very hard trying to make his way among a sea of opportunities. However, he lost his job mainly due to the austerity measures whose main effect was to constrict money circulation. Indeed, as very ironically many informants said during the interviews, they had a sense that they did not live and act in a free market system, but in a centrally planned economy! Anna, fifty five years old, used to have a franchise outlet store in the north of Athens, commented:

> I feel like I am a forced socialist now. I have nothing in my disposal, I sold all of my property to make ends meet but this cannot last forever. I am relying on programs like FEAD and on the public assistance coming from social services. Well, we are all socialists now, aren't we?

The majority of the informants of this ongoing research have been pushed out of the labour market contrary to their own will. Many experienced multiple deprivations as the outcome of their inability to meet daily expenses and cope with health problems. They started losing their optimism for life and most importantly their social connections, bonds, and networks. At the same time, they gradually came to rely on public assistance, either in the form of common meals or of a minimum guaranteed income, which only very recently has been introduced into the Greek social policy toolkit. What is very revealing is that none of my informants have any feelings of shame or of stigmatisation. They develop a critical stance in relation to what currently is happening in Greek society in general and economy in particular, stressing that they feel like they are living in a context where anyone runs the danger of becoming a vulnerable person. Petros, for example, explains:

> Look, I don't really care going to get some food or my MIG (minimum guaranteed income) now. I am entitled to them, it is the only benefit I can get after all these years of employment. Can you imagine it? But I am not the only one, I don't mean to say that I like this thing, but I don't mind what people might say. There are many to come along with this thing, Greeks are only in the beginning.

However, one of the most important accounts concerns the way informants see their employment future. What is very telling is that they feel angry because although they try to find employment, they simply cannot because of the existing prejudices in the labour market. This goes against the implied rhetoric of neoliberalism's ethic, which blames the victim for his own inability either to make a living or to snatch the opportunities the invisible hand creates (Bauman 1998). As Anna, said:

> I feel hatred and anger because I feel that the system I supported for so long time ago do not allow me to escape from this condition. I tried to find a job, to become employee, so to speak, from employer that I used to

be. I got nothing. Most of companies reject me as soon as they see my age and that I know the market very well. They want stupid people; they want people who don't think. But this is not me. I want to work and this system throws me out, it is like vomiting.

Anna's experience describes not a neutral instrumental labour market but an imperfect system, which very selectively decides who will be categorized as socially outcast, excluded as vulnerable. The policies in place have not improved the medieval conditions of the Greek labour market; it is the centrally planned social policy programs, like FEAD, which are in place to make a help the increasing vulnerability so many people now face. For this reason, it is of utmost importance not only what social policy is instituted, but what happens in the name of such a social policy (Wedel et al. 2005).

In the FEAD case there is an attempt to absorb the social shock coming from the economic crisis through philanthropy and a specific understanding of how a normal citizen should be. This citizen must necessarily take advantage of the program's social partnerships. He should act with celebrated individual responsibility (Wacquant 2009: 5), accountability, self interest and proactively, as is expected (theoretically) of all the relevant assistance mechanisms that start from EU offices and reach local authorities. In this way, eventually, he becomes a biopolitical subject, a visible personality ready to be adjusted and re-arranged through the art of governing.

CONCLUSIONS

Anthropology has not so far been engaged systematically with several kinds of vulnerabilities and their relation to policy regimes. Understanding these differences is important in order to make sense of contemporary society and its culture (Prato 2011; Kingfisher 2013: 2). Be that as it may, anthropology is in the unique position to analyze the rhetoric and the aims lurking behind policy programs emanating from professional policy makers or, to put it in differently, from those who have the power to define other people's lives (Durrenberger 2017). In line with Shore and Wright, in fact, policies and their products like FEAD are inherently and unequivocally anthropological phenomena. Not only do policies codify social norms and values, and articulate fundamental organizing principles of society, they also contain implicit (and sometimes explicit) models of society (Shore and Wright 1997).

By reading FEAD texts, one gets the impression of a simple equation: deprived and vulnerable people (e.g., beneficiaries) plus assistance mechanism, gives us in normative and irrevocable terms a positive thing for society's homeostasis. Although not a poststructuralist, E. Durkheim drew our attention to social facts which, while 'they place constraints upon us, and yet we find satisfaction in the way they function, in that very constraint' (Durkheim 1982: 47). A social program of this economic magnitude seeks to render vulnerability a natural condition by depoliticizing the changed structural conditions that led to its increase and by mystifying the mechanism through which it came into being. For although it is true that globalisation is used as the aetiology toolkit for every evil in this fatal world, at the same time this usage obscures the specific responsibilities of a chain of politicians and economic experts who orchestrated the effects of radical alteration of income distribution (Lyon-Callo and Brin Hyatt 2003: 190).

This takes place in the Greek version of post-Keynesian social policy framework where social protection is under constant fire, state spending as a toolkit for job creation is severely limited, full-time employment is substituted by low-paid and dead-end jobs, informal labour relations tend to thrive and activation rhetoric prevails, obscuring the absolute freedom of employers to hire and fire at will, against the background of a permanent and still ongoing economic recession. This situation should be read within the uneasy relationship between top political decision-making and the management of those affected by it conditioned by the gradual revision and rearrangement of both social rights and citizenship. As I have argued elsewhere (Spyridakis 2011), it is important to take into account that citizenship currently takes place in a context in which people are constantly witnessing structural transformations in the power and the nature of the welfare state in the western world. This is a process affecting national public policies that aim at implementing and reproducing particular ideological visions of the world through their decisions.

As the economic account of the present crisis has shown, the production of precarization is not a natural process but in essence a production of a neoliberal political technology that praises the realm of market rationality where the fittest is surviving. The next step is to present the vulnerable and the weak in a series of censuses thus creating tangible homogenised entities (Green 2006) which require philanthropic assistance due to their own inability to enter the culture of competition the market system requires. By that means the precarious, no matter how much they try to face the structural conditions of their existence, as these short ethnographic accounts have shown, are made invisible (Susser 1996) to society, a legitimate 'Other' (Pardo 2001) and at the same time visible to state's clinical apparatus through a chain of policy makers who structure themselves by structuring others. On this view, understanding the precarious Other presupposes understanding the way it is constructed and managed.

REFERENCES

Arendt, H. 1969. Reflections on Violence. *New York Review of Books*, February 27, 24–26.

Bauman, Z. 1998. *Work, Consumerism and the New Poor*. Buckingham: Open University Press.

Chossudovsky, M. 2003. *The Globalisation of Poverty and the New World Order*. Quebec: Global Research.

Durkheim, E. 1982. *The Rules of Sociological Method*. London: Macmillan.

Durrenberger, P. 2017. Introduction: Hope for Labor in a Neoliberal World. In *Uncertain Times. Anthropological Approaches to Labor in a Neoliberal World*, ed. P. Durrenberger, 3–31. Boulder: University Press of Colorado.

Fund for European Aid to the Most Deprived. FEAD. Regulation (EU) No. 223/2014 of the European Parliament and of the Council of 11 March 2014 (OJ L 72, 12.3.2014).

Goode, J., and J. Maskovsky. 2001. Introduction. In *The New Poverty Studies. The Ethnography of Power, Politics and Impoverished People in the United States*, ed. J. Goode and J. Maskovsky, 1–34. New York: New York University Press.

Graeber, D. 2011. *Debt, the First 5000 Years*. New York: Melville House Publishing.

Green, M. 2006. Representing Poverty and Attacking Representations: Perspectives on Poverty from Social Anthropology. Q-Squared Working Paper, No. 27, June, University of Manchester.

Hellenic Parliament. 2015. *Truth Committee on Public Debt*. Athens: Hellenic Parliament.

IMF. 2010. *Board Meeting on Greece's Request for a Stand by Agreement—May 9*.

IMF. 2016. *Fiscal Monitor*, October. Washington, DC: Publication Services.

Kingfisher, C. 2013. *A Policy Travelogue. Tracing Welfare Reform in Aotearoa/New Zealand and Canada*. Oxford: Berghahn.

Kretsos, K. 2014. Youth Policy in Austerity Europe: The Case of Greece. *International Journal of Adolescence and Youth* 19: 35–47.

Lazzarato, M. 2012. *The Making of the Indebted Man: An Essay on the Neoliberal Condition*. Los Angeles: Semiotext(e).

Lorey, I. 2015. *State of Insecurity: Government of the Precarious*. London: Verso Books.

Lyon-Callo, V., and S. Brin Hyatt. 2003. The Neoliberal State and the Depoliticisation of Poverty: Activist Anthropology and 'Ethnography from Below'. *Urban Anthropology and Studies of Cultural Systems and World Economic Development* 32 (2): 175–204.

Miller, P., and N. Rose. 1990. Governing Economic Life. *Economy and Society* 19 (1): 1–31.

Ministry of Finance. 2017. *Introductory Budget Report*. Athens: Ministry of Finance.

Narotzky, S. 2016. Between Inequality and Injustice: Dignity as a Motive for Mobilization During the Crisis. *History and Anthropology* 27 (1): 74–92.

OECD. 2011. *Government at a Glance*. Paris: OECD Publishing.

Osborne, G., and W. Schäuble. 2014. Protect Britain's Interests in a Two-Speed Europe. *Financial Times*, March 27.

Pardo, I. (ed.). 2001. *Morals of Legitimacy. Between Agency and the System*. New York: Berghahn.

Prato, G.B. 2011. The 'Costs' of European Citizenship: Governance and Relations of Trust in Albania. In *Citizenship and the Legitimacy of Governance. Anthropology in the Mediterranean Region*, ed. I. Pardo and G.B. Prato. Farnham: Ashgate.

Pickety, T. 2014. *Capital in the Twenty First Century*. Cambridge: Harvard University Press.

Research on Money and Finance. 2010. *The Eurozone Between Austerity and Default*, September. www.researchonmoneyandfinance.org.

Reinhart, C., and K. Rogoff. 2009. *This Time Is Different, Eight Centuries of Financial Folly*. Princeton: Princeton University Press.

Shore, C. 2006. 'Government Without Statehood'? Anthropological Perspectives on Governance and Sovereignty in the European Union. *European Law Journal* 12 (6) (November): 709–724.

Shore, C., and S. Wright. 1997. Policy: A New Field of Anthropology. In *Anthropology of Policy: Critical Perspectives on Governance and Power*, ed. C. Shore and S. Wright, 3–30. London: Routledge.

Spyridakis, M. 2011. Between Structure and Action: Contested Legitimacies and Labour Processes in the Piraeus. In *Citizenship and the Legitimacy of Governance. Anthropology in the Mediterranean Region*, ed. I. Pardo and G.B. Prato, 153–170. Farnham: Ashgate.

Spyridakis, M. 2017. Coping with Uncertainty: Precarious Workers of the Greek Media Sector. In *Mapping Precariousness, Labour Insecurity and Uncertain Livelihoods. Subjectivities and Resistance*, ed. E. Armano, A. Bove, and A. Murgia, 98–109. London: Routledge.

Stockholm International Peace Research Institute. 2015. https://www.sipri.org/databases/milex.

Susser, I. 1996. The Construction of Poverty and Homelessness in US Cities. *Annual Review of Anthropology* 25: 411–435.

Vatikiotis, L. 2015. Towards Debt Sustainability in Europe? The IMF's Role in the Eurozone Debt Crisis. Paper delivered on IMF Conference, October, Lima.

Wacquant, L. 2009. *Punishing the Poor. The Neoliberal Government of Social Insecurity.* Durham: Duke University Press.

Wedel, J.R., C. Shore, G. Feldman, and S. Lathrop. 2005. Toward an Anthropology of Public Policy. *The Annals of the American Academy of Political and Social Science* 600 (30): 30–51.

CHAPTER 8

'*De proletarios a propietarios...*' Neoliberal Hegemony, Labour Commodification, and Family Relationships in a 'Petty' Steel Workers' Firm

Julia Soul

INTRODUCTION

In Argentina, neoliberal policies were consolidated by the end of the 1980s. Their implementation was the response to a profound social crisis that included several pillaging episodes at large supermarkets. This crisis paved the way for a restructuring process that has been confronted by labour movements since the 1980s. The consolidation of neoliberalism was based on privatization processes and a set of government measures that resulted in a depreciation of wages, labour rights, working conditions, and employment levels. Thus, through the 1990s, medical care, education, the state managed pension system, water, and the provision of urban services (and a long etc.) were sold and passed into private hands, becoming directly subordinated to market rules (Bonnet 2008). The consequences

J. Soul (✉)
CONICET (Consejo nacional de Investigaciones científicas y tecnológicas - National Council of Scientific and Technological Research), CEIL (Centro de Estudios e Investigaciones Laborales), Buenos Aires, Argentina

© The Author(s) 2018
M. Spyridakis (ed.), *Market Versus Society*, Palgrave Studies in Urban Anthropology, https://doi.org/10.1007/978-3-319-74189-5_8

of neoliberal hegemony over social reproduction have been considered in a twofold perspective: On the one side, from the viewpoint of subordinate classes, the privatization process resulted in a deprivation of rights and common goods. This situation changed the social form of many means of livelihood, which were directly subsumed by market rules, becoming commodities, compelling communities to defend their common possession (Nash 2006). On the other side, a deep restructuring process changed the configuration of productive relations, which paved the way for a variety of forms of subsumption of labour by capital and for the rising of labour collectives embedded in different sets of relations with the market.

Insights from anthropological research highlight the interconnections between the process of commodification, different forms of social labour mobilization, and market relations as the core of social reproduction through a broad array of concrete social formations (Wolf 1982; Narotzky 1997). Workforce availability is the result of a continuous process of separation between workers and their working conditions, which in turn triggers a continuous process of making and unmaking of the working classes (Carbonella and Kasmir 2014). Workforce commodification and its reproduction and availability as a commodity are the cornerstone of capitalist development. According to Marx (1993), the 'commodity' as a social form is in the surface of a production process that occurs 'behind subjects' backs'. Such a process involves an increase in surplus value and its circulation through labour exploitation. As much as labour, in its different expressions, has been considered the main actor in struggles for de-commodification (Silver 2003), the relationship between commodification and labour subsumption rises as the theoretical link in the dynamic between market and productive relations in the making of the working class.

In this chapter, I aim to discuss the relationship between the commodification of labour spurred within the neoliberal hegemony and the working-class disorganization/reorganization dynamic in Argentina, pointing to changing forms of labour subsumption. I do this through a medium-term ethnographic study of a group of steel workers from San Nicolás de los Arroyos, the city where SOMISA—the state-owned steel mill privatized in 1992—was located. The privatization process is an historical landmark in workers' experience, for since then labour and community relationships have been profoundly transformed (Soul 2014). New owners introduced a restructuring process, which set lasting differences among workers, establishing the basis for a broad array of contractual relationships. One of the most interesting configurations that emerged from the proliferation of contractual work are the microfirms, a multiplicity of small firms formed on the basis of former productive sections and workers within the company.

The analysis will be focused on one of these microfirms, which is actually the first one with a union delegate elected by its employees. The proliferation of a small firms in the contemporary capitalist configuration has been researched, pointing to their role in subcontracting and commodity chains (Starosta 2010). Spyridakis (2006) and Mollona (2009), among others, have registered how labour precariousness, subcontracting, and the spread of capital are intertwined in deindustrialization processes. Additionally, an anthropological approach to 'petty capitalists' highlights their 'inherently unstable' status in the capitalist social reproduction process (Smart and Smart 2005: 4). I am interested in the interplay between commodification and labour subsumption that the microfirms hold and the role played by their workers in broader working class disorganization/reorganization processes. In the course of my fieldwork, the question emerged as to why the sons of shareholders, future owners of the firm, supposedly called to manage it, ended up becoming union activists. This question was followed by another one: what does this activism tell us about the contemporary configuration of the working class? As former employees are their owners, these microfirms entail both the neoliberal promise of property democratization and the neoliberal disappointment of labour precariousness.

The historically informed ethnographic approach allows for the identification of changing relationships, expectations, and values, within which a new working-class generation experience is forged. I have identified two landmarks in the steel workers' experience: the first one, during the 1950s and 1960s, was structured by the building and the inauguration of the steel mill. The second one was marked by the crisis and transformations suffered by the working class as a consequence of neoliberal policies. I argue that, in the interplay between, on the one hand, the daily experience of labour subsumption and domination that subcontracted workers experienced, and, on the other hand, the improvement in wages and working conditions that direct workers—those employed by the main firm—obtained through the union, young workers abandoned entrepreneur expectations and assumed the proletarian ones. The daily experience of labour subsumption and failed expectations about labour process control are at the core of the unrest. Thus, through the reassessing of organizing traditions and their integration in the union, the new working-class generation is part of an uneven and slow process of class reorganization, involving the struggle for the improvement of daily labour relationships.

THE SOMISEROS AS WAGE LABOURERS: SACRIFICE AND SOCIAL MOBILITY

The privatization of SOMISA in 1992 was preceded by an accelerated rationalization process whose outcome was more than 6000 steel workers became unemployed. For some years, the Steel City, with 140,000 inhabitants in the north of the Buenos Aires province, was mired in a profound social crisis and faced deep changes in community relationships. According to Daniel, office coordinator of the Urban Development Department, 50% of the local workers were employed in the steel mill, in one of the big subcontractors or in a supplier workshop. 80% of the steel workers lived in San Nicolás, and the other 20% come from neighbouring cities. Massive redundancies were a novel—and traumatic—experience for a local working class that had structured its social experience through steel jobs.

In Argentina, post-World War II capitalist development was led by the expansion of the manufacturing sector, supported by the intervention of the central state, which shaped the productive structure of strategic industries. Thus, the building of the steel mill and the roads and docks linked to it attracted a generation of migrant workers from rural zones, who were being expelled by the expansion of the mechanization in agriculture or by the exhaustion of natural resources exploited by large firms. The three Population Censuses run between 1947 and 1980 show a population growth rate in San Nicolas from three percent to five percent, far from the rate of less than one percent registered in the previous period.

Manufacturing jobs were at the core of rural workers' expectations since the 1940s, when the affluence of migrant workers to urban centres contributed to reshaping the working class' social being. This massive shift from daily labourers or semi-peasants/semi-proletarian workers to full wage-labour relationships was framed by an early labour movement that had achieved key protective regulations—such as a set of union supportive laws and progressive direct and indirect wage regulations—through nationally organized unions. Through this institutional structure, health care, pension funds, education, and even recreational issues, among other factors of working-class reproduction, were split off from direct market rules. Managed by the state or by the unions, those issues entered the reproduction process in the form of collective rights or public services, rather than in the form of commodities.

Since the mid-1950s the expectations of working-class families in San Nicolás were structured by the access of men to a direct job in the steel plant. Broad neighbourhood, family, and labour networks may support the path to be a *Somisero*. It was the self-identity category for SOMISA workers, extensive to families and neighborhoods. A *Somisero* should be able to talk to his supervisors, foremen, bosses, even to union delegates and representatives, to get a job for his son, his nephew, or a friend's or relative's son. It could take more or less time, but it was almost sure that, after some time working for a subcontractor, the boy would finally become a *Somisero*. If the father, coming from a rural area, was mainly an unskilled worker and suffered from heavy working conditions, the son would achieve technical skills in one of the six technical schools established in the city, which could allow him access to maintenance or supervisor's jobs (Soul 2014).

During my fieldwork,[1] I understood that being a *Somisero* involved contradictory meanings, expressing workers' dual conditions under wage relationships: being at the same time workforce sellers and direct producers (Gramsci 1977). On one side, as a workforce seller, to be a *Somisero* meant to be part of a workers' collective with access to relatively better reproduction conditions than other groups, because of higher wages and a set of corporate policies linked to household reproduction. However, these conditions were considered the reward for years of sacrifice, suffering heavy conditions, long workdays and oppressive relations in order to get better wages. These meanings illuminate Virginia Manzano's (2002) argument about the expectation of ascendant social mobility as the key issue structuring Argentine working-class families' practices, feelings,

---

[1] I have conducted a long term fieldwork in San Nicolás, focused on different research problems and inquiries. The first stage, between 2000 and 2002, was focused on workers' restructuring experience. The second phase, run between 2005 and 2008, studied a set of molecular conflicts that emerged in different plants of the company. The third phase, between 2011 and 2013, was focused on young workers' experiences and union policy shifts. Since 2014, participant observation in annual international union meetings has been conducted.

values and expectations since the post-World War II era. Thus, the sacrifices and pain suffered as a direct producer are underestimated as negative meanings, considered necessary in order to achieve better conditions and ascendant social mobility. Social mobility has three clear landmarks: to own a (nuclear) family house, superior education for children, and to be able to keep the breadwinner role as a masculine one.

On the other side, as a direct producer, to be a *Somisero* meant to be part of a collective labourer and thus a bearer of strategic knowledge about the labour process. Workers' memories describe daily work as a set of relationships entailing discipline and hierarchy but also cooperation, discussion about problems and solutions, and the unfolding of collective knowledge. The labour process was organized through direct operations over mechanical devices and hydraulic systems requiring sensorial skills, so discussions and different opinions were a matter of daily labour relationships. When workers talked about their daily activities, impersonal and bureaucratic relationships, expressed by hierarchy and discipline, by punishment, work orders and strict control measures were interwoven with partnership and cooperation that stemmed from concrete tasks. In this period and within steel production, subsumption of labour by capital developed through a labour process based on the specialized and semi-skilled workforce, bearer of a body of knowledge that was daily built in and incorporated into the labour process. Although there were a multiplicity of segmentations (according to skills and hierarchical structures, work sections, political attitudes), most workers were employed by the same company and an important share of their reproduction conditions were partially split off from market regulations. This set of regulations were considered by workers as a product of the steel mill's social goals, opposed to profit goals, which would orient the company after privatization.

In sum, since the building and operation of the steel mill, former rural workers and their sons were able to build their own homes, lengthen their children's educational trajectories, and keep households financially supported by male breadwinners. Through sacrifice and suffering they were able to improve their families' living standards. Proud of those achievements, older workers may understand them as individual and family success, as they are the result of their own sacrifice and suffering: 'Nobody gave me anything' is the common expression for referring to what they own. This individualism is part of the common sense and coexists with solidarity and collective contents that are also part of the working-class experience (Nash 1989).

In short, living standards and expectations, associated with ascendant social mobility, stemmed from a set of conditions shaping workers' reproduction, which involved, as was mentioned above, state and union policies that were the result of a long term working-class dispute for its 'expanded reproduction' (Lebowitz 2003). While the 'expanded reproduction' has historically entailed de-commodified conditions for the working-class reproduction, it maintains labour commodification under wage relations as its condition. This process unfolded in Argentina between the 1930s and the 1950s when along with the subsumption of an increasing mass of population by the factory system through its incorporation to manufacturing industries, the labour movement achieved the de-commodification of key reproduction conditions. The key social commodification was of course labour commodification, which remained the condition for access to those de-commodified reproduction conditions, through union membership associated with wage labour (Lazar 2013) or through state social policies associated with Argentina's particular welfare regime.

The Shareholders: Privatization and Commodification as Landmarks of Working Class Disorganization

The reproduction conditions for working-class families have been profoundly changed during the last four decades. Through repression and forced disappearance of union activists, delegates, and leaders and of political and social militants, Argentina's dictatorial government, which took power in 1976, dismantled the nuclei of working-class social strength—such as unions and neighbourhood and community associations. Since then, neoliberal hegemony unfolded through an unstable interplay between repression and consent. Although during the 1980s there were some molecular advances in restructuring processes, the main corporate and government policies involving the commodification of former wage social components as much as the shifts in labour subsumption were applied during Carlos Menem's first term, between 1989 and 1995. During that period, government and employers promoted a set of practices and institutions aimed at reinforcing capital accumulation. Rather than through direct repression, during the 1990s advances against working-class living and working conditions unfolded through a hegemonic process (Williams 1977) involving the disorganization of working class.

SOMISA's privatization process is a landmark in workers' experience—as it is in the broader community—for it involves deep regressive changes in their everyday lives. During the privatization crisis, as the period between 1989 and 1992 is called, working conditions, as did much as the productive dynamics, seriously deteriorated. When the privatization law was passed in 1991 an auditor was designated and a rigid rationalisation plan was applied. The core rationalization strategy was a voluntary retirement plan. The auditor asked each section manager to list the names of those workers to be retired and to offer them the retirement compensation. Steel workers' first reaction was to ask for delegates' and union representatives' advice, who told them to decide it at home. As Peter Richardson (2010) recorded in the case of the car industry, the voluntary retirement programs turned unionised protected jobs into workers' individual, private possessions.

Thus, the interplay between management and union delegates' practices resulted in an individualizing dynamic through which retirement was a personal family decision (Soul 2009). In contrast with the strong opposition held by the union to the privatization plan in 1986, when delegates confronted communications between managers and single workers, this time management and the union agreed upon the private character of the retirement decision. In fact, although uncertainty and anguish about the future were shared feelings, steel workers' memories of the privatization crisis highlight the private character of the retirement decision (Soul 2014).

These novel individualistic practices related to jobs and layoffs engaged with dominant discourses about property and private initiative. On one side, President Menem repeatedly announced their goal of 'diffusion of personal property, in order to achieve the decrease of proletarians and the increase of private owners' (my translation) through the spread of financial assets property (Opening Conference Stock Exchange Annual Meeting, July, 1989). In 1998 he highlighted this transformation with the case of the employee stock ownership plans, by which the workers of a privatized firm could purchase ten percent or twenty percent of the company's stock (Pagina/12: 16 May 1998). The steel workers employed by SOMISA did the same, purchasing twenty percent of the stock assets of the new company, through an investment firm created by the union, which designated the worker member of the Directive Board. Although by the time of my fieldwork most steel workers did not feel like owners, an increasing share of their family incomes (usually meant to buy cars, domestic appliances, or holiday trips) depended on their shares.

Private individual initiatives were promoted by the new owners through social and labour policies such as 'benefits with gains' or 'internal client-supplier'. Unfolding these initiatives, managers aimed to translate labour rights into commodities subordinated to profits and cooperative relationships into market relations. This involved the commodification of a set of corporate social services and the setting of horizontal control relations among workers' collectives. Workers' transportation, daily lunch, or workplace medical services were reduced and rationalized according not to workers' needs or comfort, but to management's desire to trim costs. Extended subcontracting policies became part of this commodification movement, for they stem from the transformation of former labour process components into commodities that are sold to the main firm.

As a commodification process, subcontracting policies subordinate smaller and specialized groups of workers to direct market rules, triggering a process of differentiation of wages, job rankings, and working conditions, as it has been broadly registered for the steel industry (see also Fevre 1987; Esponda 2012; Vargas and Perelman 2013; Soul 2013, 2015a). This broad commodification movement also involves the blur of labour relations and the rise of forms of non-formally waged subsumption. Mollona (2009) identifies the chain of links between subcontracting and the provision of cheap labour in the case of the United Kingdom's steel industry. I identify a specific social form for this cheap labour provision in Argentina Steel Industry: the microfirms.

Microfirms are a special kind of service subcontractors, deeply specialized in areas such as classification of raw materials and logistics, internal transportation, maintenance of heat-resistant materials and cooling services, for example. The microfirms were created by the mid-1990s, when the situation of the former *Somiseros* was worrying: 3000 of them hadn't been able to access the formal labour market again, and 34% of the economically active population was unemployed and underemployed (Peñalva 2003; PLESAN—San Nicolás 1999). According to union officials and former workers, about twenty microfirms were established on the basis of productive areas and workers' collectives. Although many of them employed less than 50 workers, there were a few with more than a hundred employees. Their creation was promoted by the company, which proposed to particular groups of workers to take retirement compensations, invest in them as capital and become shareholders of independent firms. If it was necessary, the company might support the initial investment, funding expensive machinery and equipment. Thus, the main company replaced employment relationships with commercial ones and former wage workers became "shareholders".

This is the origin of Tectel, a limited liability company formed by more or less 20 shareholders, former workmates from the communications area, who were asked by the managers to accept layoffs and to form their own firm. Once it was established, Tectel hired about fifteen employees who were, actually, "son of shareholders". The tasks performed by Tectel's employees are the same the shareholders performed as wage workers: the installation and maintenance of communication networks and computing equipment (for users and for equipment command). In 2011, there were 48 Tectel workers, both on project contracts and frame contracts.[2]

Frame contracts are keys for the continuity of Tectel because of their length. They set up the amount of labour, the conditions and the values for labour-hour. The discussion about the values, involving the labour-hour price, is led by Lewis, the only engineer in the microfirm, who was the former director of the section. Eventually, shareholders try to avoid decreasing their own labour prices, increasing either the work hours or the price-per-hour charged in the contract. However, this is not always possible if they want to get the contracts. According to shareholders and union officials, the managers of the steel mills are used to haggling around the contracts' final costs before signing them.

Labour organization and organizational hierarchy are an extension of those prevailing in the former company. In this way, Lewis became the actual manager of the microfirm. As one of the shareholders told me in a chat,

> [the engineer] had the capacity and the skills needed to manage the company. He was used to talking to managers and directors. Can you imagine? We never talked to SOMISA's bosses. They were the heads and we were the toenails!

[2]There are two kinds of contracts. "Frame Contracts" are signed for a period of 2 or 5 years and stipulate terms and conditions of work and inputs. They are expressed in man-hour, fixing the hour value. "Project contracts" provided by tenders, usually involve larger sums of money and skilled tasks (see also Esponda 2012: 126 ss).

As before, section directors were those in direct contact with the company's faces: in this case, the ones responsible for preparing the contract offers to the main company and for microfirm management.

Furthermore, because of the small scale of the microfirm, the shareholders' status does not release them from direct tasks, although they play mainly supervisory and control roles—especially in coordination with the steel mill managers as the microfirm runs different contracts. This usually causes misunderstandings, contradictory directives, and arguments between the workers—sons of shareholders—their fathers and the main company managers.

While leading with their new 'owner' status, former *Somiseros* maintain the goal of getting a job for their sons, many of whom may have attended a technical school. In contrast with their former mates, shareholders could offer the positions to their sons, but in worse working conditions. The creation of the microfirm embedded the former *Somiseros'* expectations of getting a job for their sons in a set of commodified relationships. As employers and employees, they were placed in potentially contradictory market roles, which were initially reconciled by the expectations of firm growth and future management positions for the sons.

The microfirm was initially assumed by shareholders and sons of shareholders as a sort of family heritage, just as direct jobs used to be. Direct cooperation and teacher–apprenticeship relations reinforced this assumption. When Cirilo (a son of a shareholder) told me that some microfirms were called back after the firms that had won the contract failed in performing the work, he assumed it was

[b]ecause this plant is a world. You can't just arrive and start to work... you need somebody to guide you, to teach you. Instead we have been walking this factory for twenty years with my dad with the old mates... they taught me everything I know.

In contrast, the idea of family heritage was mediated for the sons of shareholders as the main labour suppliers of their fathers' firm. In fact, until the sons of shareholders were able to be in charge of the microfirm, they felt they should resign their demands as workforce sellers on behalf of the contracts' continuity. The role that microfirms played in providing cheap, specialized, unskilled labour for the steel mill was the main constraint for the continuity of the microfirm and, thus, a serious obstacle for growing the family heritage.

By the end of the 1990s, neoliberal policies had seriously deteriorated the working-class conditions of reproduction. Frozen wages, high unemployment rates, precarious jobs, and the commodification of most social rights were the outcome of the capitalist advance. In this context, government promotion of private initiatives and assets ownership as natural rights, the entanglement of workers' goals with companies' goals through the employee stock ownership programs, the promotion of market rationality through corporate policies, and the union support for individualistic practices combined to increase working-class disorganization. Thus, the commodification of kinship relations involved in familiar firms owned by former *Somiseros* was part of this disorganization.

The XXIst Century: Reassessing Commodification Through Working Class Reorganization

I met Tectel workers via two common friends—who are, in turn, sons of a steelworker—and former neighbors in a *Somisero* neighbourhood located in the south of the city. While my friends' father had maintained his job at the steel mill and his sons were attending university, Cirilo and Jenaro were working in their fathers' microfirm. In the course of that chat, I heard about the notion of sons of shareholders for the first time. It was a self-referential notion that expressed the instability and the ambiguity of their position in the microfirm.

As sons of shareholders, they were expected to assume their work with high responsibility and initiative. The better they performed the tasks assigned in the contracts, the higher the microfirm's possibilities for renewal and growth. Tectel's expansion was a shared goal of shareholders and sons of shareholders, as the latter were expected to be the future managers. At the same time that they were sons of shareholders, they were also employees. Just like their fathers, they were not released from direct tasks for being members of shareholder families; on the contrary, this status transferred to their own workforce the needs of lowering costs imposed by the contracts, since the wages were set up in the form of man-hours. Furthermore, the metalworkers' national collective agreement set up special bonuses for extraordinary time, overnight work, or dangerous tasks that were not incorporated in the contracts' labour cost estimations.

Besides, they told me about workdays that started at 6 a.m. but finished 'when the work was finished', which meant staying more than twelve hours in the plant, working on holidays or at night. They also were exposed to high temperatures or to hazardous powders, sometimes without the needed protective procedures. Sons of shareholders also faced the fragmentation of the labour process organization, thus they were in daily contact with the Tectel foremen but also with supervisors and managers of the main company. Cirilo and Jenaro bitterly complained about the treatment they received, about the disorganization of tasks and because they 'had to run from one production line to another to fix others' troubles'.

For most of the sons of shareholders, it was their first job. They were young when they started, no more than 20 years old, and they were spurred by what Jenaro calls the illusion:

> We had the idea... it was supposed that the firm would continue, and would continue under our orders, for us... I don't know. We had the illusion... mainly because we were sons of shareholders... but it was just an illusion.

The sons of shareholders' illusion stemmed from family ownership. That illusion was blurring as they started to question their fathers, who acted as supervisors. In the questioning they focused on the engineer as the one responsible for the conditions in the contracts. He was the one who centralized planning and cost estimations. The role played by the engineer was another reason for frequent rows between the sons of shareholders and their fathers. The young ones considered him responsible for their low wages and poor working conditions. Nevertheless, their fathers asked them to stay calm and patient. They were afraid of the impact of their sons' wage demands on the offers performed by the microfirm.

In the meantime, direct workers' wages and working conditions had been improving since 2003, when the beginning of an economic expansive cycle triggered the labour movement mobilization. A broader rank-and-file movement expressed waged workers' unrest and a set of open conflicts questioned the worst consequences of restructuring processes, such as wage flexibility, temporary contracts, outsourcing, corporate medical services, and so on. Among the steelworkers, some delegates promoted the organization of a national steel workers' delegates conference with three goals: to discuss a national wage agreement for the whole branch (including subcontracted workers), to put an end to precarious contracts and employment agencies, and to stay within the metalworkers' national contract.

These auspicious union policies deepened the gap between those workers included in the annual rounds of wage bargaining and those employed by the microfirms, whose earnings were set up through the contracts. This situation has changed since 2004 and daily relations between sons of shareholders and direct workers in the company and in the neighbourhood have spurred the vanishing of the illusion of ownership as the path to ascendant social mobility. In fact, in the struggle for their expanded reproduction, the sons of shareholders shaped their expectations referring to the bundle of direct workers' needs.

In 2004, Jenaro, Cirilo, and most of their workmates had got married and had had children, so they felt they should be able to maintain their wives and children in their own family house. By the time I met them, Cirilo had gotten divorced. He would have liked to rent an apartment alone, to spend time there with his daughters. In contrast, he came back to his parents' house and his mother took care of the girls when he was working, because he couldn't afford a double-shift school. Both issues (children's double-shift school and an exclusive apartment if they got divorced) were easily afforded by the steelmill direct workers. Jenaro hadn't been able to buy his family house and couldn't even think of building one. Again, the comparison was with direct workers, who could buy houses and had access to credit. As for most working-class young men, these were vital landmarks in Cirilo's and Jenaro's experience as their expectations were shaped by being sons of steelworkers. They had hoped to provide their children and wives with the goods and services involved in steelworkers' contemporary consumption bundle, which entailed private schools and health services.

The conditions of the sons of shareholders were worsening in comparison with those of direct and subcontracted workers covered by the national agreement. Slowly they shifted their role as sons of shareholders to troublemakers, stopping the work if they considered it hazardous or refusing to start working if the tools or equipment were missing. These self-organized protests caught the attention of union delegates, who offered to channel their claims. It was not an easy process, as many delegates were shareholders' friends or former mates. But in the meanwhile, Cirilo, Jenaro and Nick looked for collaboration to understand their pay check stubs, asked former steelworkers about bonuses, organized meetings with the other sons of shareholders and even secretly collaborated with other precarious workers' claims.

Finally, in 2009 the union's local committee approved the delegates' election in the microfirm, Jenaro was elected delegate by his workmates. Since then, he speaks in their name to the microfirm management and bears their specific claims, mainly around wage and working conditions. Elder delegates collaborate with him, especially in the presentation of complaints and demands. Other sons of shareholders support him in meetings and interviews with management. At the same time, Jenaro takes part in delegates' meetings and training courses organized by the union, where he meets delegates from other plants. Since they have their own delegate, Tectel's sons of shareholders were able to improve their wages, especially payment of bonuses for extraordinary hours and night work. In turn, they improved the conditions of their rest areas and the quality of work clothes (provided by the firm).

They did so bargaining with their direct employer (i.e., Tectel), not with the main company. Jenaro and Cirilo consider the engineer as the one responsible for their working conditions, and so do the union representatives. The mechanism established by the main company for setting conditions through the contracts hasn't been explicitly questioned. Nevertheless, since 2007 and after a claim by the local directive board, the steel mill managers agreed to pay Tectel workers the annual wage increase, beyond the contract clauses.

Thus, during the 2000s, this small group of young workers, initially called to act as petty capitalists, fully assumed traditional working-class organizing practices. In fact, the sons of shareholders have retrieved the practices that the generation of their fathers had implemented twenty years ago, when they rebuilt the workplace union organization after the dictatorship. They have done so in the context of a broader working-class reorganization process in Argentina that started with the organization of unemployed workers at the end of the 1990s and continued with the union revitalization process (Senen Gonzales and Haidar 2009; Atzeni and Ghigliani 2008, 2007; Etchemendy and Collier 2007).

The interplay between the working-class background of the sons of shareholders, underlying their daily practices, and the failed expectations stemming from family ownership were key issues in the displacement of their practices from the individualistic logic of profits to the collective logic of working conditions improvement. The instability inherent at the microfirm scale and its role as a supplier of cheap labour became evident in a context of growing union militancy and working-class acti-vation. Daily relations with delegates and union members, as much as their family backgrounds, allowed Tectel workers to assess their objec-tive market role as workforce sellers and to retrieve workers' classic protest practices.

Conclusion: Commodification and Subsumption in Working Class Reorganization

A historically informed ethnographic approach to particular work-ing-class groups provides further insights on the variety of social forms assumed by capital and labour practices in the process of working-class making and remaking. Exploring the broader field of a steel mill commu-nity, I focused on the creation of microfirms as a novel corporate strategy entailing, in succession, the advance over working-class strength posi-tions (expressed by the rise of individualistic and profit-oriented behav-iour and the illusions of self-control and social mobility originated in property relationships) and traces of uneven and molecular working-class reorganization processes. Disorganization and reorganization practices are better expressed by the practices and expectations of two working-class generations. In the microfirm, generational cleavages match property ones: shareholders and sons of shareholders.

As microfirms come from a broader advance over working-class posi-tions, instability becomes a part of the workers' experience at Tectel. In the interplay between labour commodification and labour subsumption, the working-class experience is reshaped in a novel reorganization pro-cess. I identify two issues through which microfirm shareholders and workers' relationships go into conflict with their working-class experi-ence: the continuity of labour subsumption through re-commodification and the changing role of union mediation. Based on these two dynam-ics, I present a balance between continuity and change in the histor-ical working-class experience to highlight the shaping of contemporary workers' practices.

Labour subsumption: I described how the formerly state-owned steel mill project developed through the incorporation of a growing amount of non-waged workers to the factory system. The restructuring process produced a set of non-waged and precarious workers. The non-waged status of Tectel shareholders placed them in an ambiguous relationship with their own labour practices. The main company transformed those practices, formerly integrated in the general steel production process, into a service to be provided; and Tectel's main competitive input is labour price, as the rest of the productive conditions are stipulated by the main firm through the contracts.

As direct producers, conditions set by the contracts affect the daily working conditions of shareholders and their sons. They are aware of the amount of specialized knowledge that they command, as they have a detailed knowledge of the facilities. This is their bargaining chip with the steel mill managers. In contrast with the cooperation developed in the daily labour process, the shareholders' role is to convince their sons to sell cheaper their workforce, thus worsening their conditions of reproduction. Hence, common interests involved in the notion of family heritage were undermined by the contradictory role played by shareholders and their sons in the labour market.

In this scenario, the union became a mediator of microfirm contracts, asking for the restarting of bargaining if the company refused to renew the contract. The shareholders need union support to maintain their labour price. Inversely, the union channels the new profit-oriented premises, compelling the microfirm managers to adjust costs. In this respect, union leaders severely disapproved those practices that raised the labour price because of what they call the 'maintaining of old habits', like the rigid eight-hour workday or long break times.

The recognition of the wage worker status for the sons of shareholders with the delegate election involved a shift in union mediation policy that split off in two directions. On one side, channelling daily claims about bonus payment, tool provisions, and working regimes to the microfirm management; and on the other side, setting up a mechanism for wage increases beyond the contracts, in an implicit recognition that they characteristically lowered labour prices. In sum, as evidence of the mechanism for cheap labour subsumption involved in microfirms' policy, the union plays a role at each stage of the labour price discussion. This role shows that union practices are active forces in the shaping of workers' reorganization processes.

With the advance of neoliberal hegemony, an individualistic aspect of workers' practices concerning the notions of personal sacrifice and pain involved in the social progress of the family became entangled with corporations and government promotion of profit-oriented practices through a set of interventions aimed at displacing workers' collectives.

This entanglement, along with the spread of heterogeneous labour relations in the context of productive restructuring, were key factors in the disorganization of Argentina's working class.

The assumption of the microfirm as a sort of family heritage—not only because of the common tasks and skills shared between fathers and sons, but also because of the common expectation that through daily sacrifice they would achieve social mobility—expresses the moment of disorganization, which involved the commodification of parental relationships.

The undermining of the family heritage expectation is closely linked to the reactivation of union activism in the workplaces, spurred by a set of claims that stemmed from the consequences felt by the working class of the restructuring process. In a general outlook, the working-class struggle was oriented towards the improvement of labour prices and working conditions, as the employment levels were improving. Thus, solidarity emerging from the daily labour process of cooperation (Atzeni 2010) was the first step in the reconstitution of traditional working-class links by the former sons of shareholders turned into union activists, retrieving practices that are part of a 'class heritage' (Soul 2015b).

References

Atzeni, M., and P. Ghigliani. 2007. The Resilience of Traditional Trade Union Practices in the Revitalisation of the Argentine Labour Initiative. In *Trade Union Revitalisation: Trends and Prospects in 34 Nations*, ed. C. Phelan, 1–13. Düsseldorf: Peter Lang.

Atzeni, M., and P. Ghigliani. 2008. Nature and Limits of Trade Unions' Mobilisations in Contemporary Argentine. *Labor Again Publications*. Available at www.iisg.nl/labouragain/.../atzeni-ghigliani.pdf.

Atzeni, M. 2010. *Workplace Conflict Mobilization and Solidarity in Argentina*. Basingstoke: Palgrave Macmillan.

Bonnet, A. 2008. *La hegemonía menemista. El neoconservadurismo en la Argentina 1989–2001*. Buenos Aires: Editorial Prometeo.

Carbonella, A., and S. Kasmir (eds.). 2014. Toward a Global Anthropology of Labor. In *Blood and Fire: Toward a Global Anthropology of Labor*, 1–29. New York: Berghahn.

Esponda, A. 2012. *Tercerización en la Industria. El caso de la formación de empresas de extrabajadores en la ex–Propulsora Siderúrgica (Siderar-Ensenada)*. Mg thesis, PPGAS—UNAM. Misiones.

Etchemendy, S., and R. Collier. 2007. Down but Not Out: Union Resurgence and Segmentated Neocorporatism in Argentina (2003–2007). *Politics and Society* 35 (3): 363–401.

Fevre, R. 1987. Subcontracting in Steel. *Work, Employment and Society* 4: 509–527.

Government Document. 1999. Plan Estratégico San NIcolás (PLESAN), viewed August 2008, from www.sannicolas.gob.ar.

Gramsci, A. 1977. Sindicatos y Consejos (I and II). In *Escritos Políticos*. México: Siglo XXI Editores.

Lazar, S. 2013. Citizenship, Political Agency and Technologies of the Self in Argentinian Trade Unions'. *Critique of Anthropology* 33: 110–128.

Lebowitz, M. 2003. *Beyond Capital. Marx's Political Economy of the Working Class*, 2nd ed. New York: Palgrave Macmillan.

Manzano, V. 2002. Del ascenso social a la precarización. Un análisis sobre la producción de significados en torno al trabajo en el sector metalúrgico a fines de la década de 1990. *Cuadernos de Antropología Social* 15: 71–90.

Marx, Karl. 1993. *El Capital t I v II*. México: Siglo XXI Editores.

"Menem bajo a Las Parejas para resaltar su gestión de Gobierno. La Argentina según el Presidente", Pagina/12 (16 May 1998) from https://www.pagina12.com.ar/1998/98-05/98-05-16/rota3a.htm.

Mollona, M. 2009. *Made in Sheffield: An Ethnography of Industrial Work and Politics*. New York: Berghahn Books.

Narotzky, S. 1997. *New Directions in Economic Anthropology*. London: Pluto Press.

Nash, J. 1989. *From Tank Town to High Tech. The Clash of Community and Industrial Cycles*. New York: State University of New York Press.

Nash, J. 2006. *Visiones Mayas. El problema de la autonomía en la era de la globalización*. Buenos Aires: Editorial Antropofagia.

Peñalva, S. 2003. *Desafiliacion, precarizacion y desintegracion social en la argentina de los noventa. Un análisis regulacionista e institucional a propósito de las reestructuraciones de la intervención del Estado y de la relación salarial.* CONICET—Research Report.

Richardson, P. 2010. Buying out the Union: Job as Property and the UAW. In *The Anthropology of Labour Unions*, ed. P. Durrenberger and K. Reichart, 79–103. Colorado: University Press of Colorado.

Senen Gonzales, C., and J. Haidar. 2009. Los debates acerca de la revitalización sindical y su aplicación en el análisis sectorial en la Argentina. *Revista Latinoamericana de Estudios del Trabajo* 22: 5–31.

Silver, B. 2003. *Forces of Labor. Workers' Movements and Globalization Since 1870*. New York: Cambridge University Press.

Smart, A., and J. Smart (eds.). 2005. *Petty Capitalists and Globalization. Flexibility, Entrepreneurship and Economic Development.* New York: State University of New York Press.

Soul, J. 2009. Procesos hegemónicos y cotidianeidad. Prácticas obreras en la privatización de la Sociedad Mixta Siderúrgica Argentina. *Cuadernos de Antropología Social* 29: 85–102.

Soul, J. 2013. Las relaciones capital-trabajo en el sector siderúrgico. Expresión de una nueva legalidad industrial? en *Revista Estudios del Trabajo* N° 43: 81–112.

Soul, J. 2014. *SOMISEROS: configuración y devenir de un grupo obrero desde una perspectiva antropológica.* Rosario: Editorial Prohistoria.

Soul, J. 2015a. A 40 años de Braverman. Reflexiones sobre el devenir de los procesos de trabajo y control en la Industria siderúrgica argentina. In *Control del Trabajo Hoy: a 40 años de Trabajo y Capital Monopolista,* comp. M. Zangaro, 132–157. Quilmes: Quilmes University.

Soul, J. 2015b. New Times Are Still Coming, Old Times Are Still Leaving: Notes About Young People's Participation and Union Traditions in Contemporary Argentina. In *Young Workers and Trade Unions. A Global View,* ed. A. Hodder and L. Kretsos, 37–53. London: Palgrave Macmillan.

Spyridakis, E. 2006. The Political Economy of Labor Relations in the Context of Greek Shipbuilding: An Ethnographic Account. *History and Anthropology* 2: 153–170.

Starosta, G. 2010. The Outsourcing of Manufacturing and the Rise of Giant Global Contractors: A Marxian Approach to Some Recent Transformations of Global Value Chains. *New Political Economy* 15 (4): 543–563.

Vargas, P., and L. Perelman. 2013. Los propios y los de las compañías: efectos de la tercerización entre los trabajadores siderúrgicos. *Papeles de Trabajo* 12: 84–101.

Williams, R. 1977. *Marxism and Literature.* London: Oxford University Press.

Wolf, E. 1982. *Europe and the People Without History.* California: University of California Press.

CHAPTER 9

At the Periphery of Development: Scenarios and Actors of an Industrial Settlement Experiment and Its Crisis in the Case of FIAT-SATA in Melfi

Fulvia D'Aloisio

THE ANTHROPOLOGICAL APPROACH TO A CASE-STUDY OF INDUSTRIAL DEVELOPMENT IN A DIACHRONIC PERSPECTIVE

This chapter analyses in a diachronic perspective, an industrial event and its evolution in a small town in the Basilicata region (Southern Italy). The economic downturn, the fragmented industrial policies, and the political clientelism as a diffused system of relationships are some characteristics of this less industrialised part of Italy, where historically development has had problematic and contradictory results. The anthropology lens on this case of industrialisation, belated with respect to the national development and the role that big industry has had on it, allows us to analyse on a local scale the aspects of a global process connected to the transformation of the car market and the role of the Italian Fabbrica Italiana Automobili Torino (FIAT) inside it; at the same time, we can

F. D'Aloisio (✉)
Department of Psychology, University of Campania Luigi Vanvitelli, Caserta, Italy

M. Spyridakis (ed.), *Market Versus Society*, Palgrave Studies in Urban Anthropology, https://doi.org/10.1007/978-3-319-74189-5_9

153

analyse the relapses of this process on the life trajectories of the workers employed in the last Italian FIAT factory. The sense (mean and value) of work and the perspective on the present and the future have been deeply changed by this process; the ethnographic approach also allows us to observe the strategies put in place during the crisis, which has diffused since 2008, and, by and large, the modalities in which role and configuration of a peripheral area in the national development have been redefined, up to the parallel transformation of FIAT into Fiat Chrysler Corporation (FCA) in 2014.

The theoretical perspective I take here moves from a typical articulation of anthropology, that is the connection between local and global, in its more recent formulation, not as a reality in itself, but as a way in which the anthropologist puts into relation different levels of the phenomena facing them during the construction of his/her anthropological object. As noted by several scholars, the constitution of the fieldwork requires, in the globalised era, instead of studying "in the field" the study of the conditions producing the field (Appadurai 1996; Comaroff and Comaroff 2003; Hannerz 2010; Kilani 2009). Regarding this, from the Comaroffs' point of view, one of the most crucial difficulties is that 'almost everything which falls within the discursive purview of contemporary anthropology exists, in the phenomenal world, on a scale that does not yield easily to received anthropological theories and methods' (Comaroff and Comaroff 2003: 152). In the face of these difficulties, both the anthropological theory and ethnographic practice need important re-formulations that find in the interconnection global/local an important access channel. In front of globalisation, Anthropologists who have picked up the heuristic challenge, 'have tended not to decry 'localised' ethnography, but to insist on its unique value in plumbing the nature and effects of large-scale social, economic and political processes' (Comaroff and Comaroff 2003: 156).

The Anthropological perspective of the enterprise by Monique Sélim has helped us, during the last twenty years, to consider the enterprise as a field of forces (similar to Bourdieu) in which we can read economic and political processes that, on a global scale, affect the shape of organisations and work on the local scale (Selim 1996; Althabe and Selim 2000; Hours and Selim 2012). Considered as porous organisations, enterprises thus became agents of change, both inside and outside of the company walls, with an interchange able to explain the graft of the global economic and productive logics in the areas where the enterprise concretely acts.

The ethnographic research in Melfi, where the settlement is collo-cated, was held in two different phases, the first one from 1999 to 2003, and began six years after the opening of the factory. The second phase was held from 2011 to 2014, in the midst of the production crisis, and into the transformation into the FCA corporation (D'Aloisio 2003, 2014). The two phases will be described briefly in this paper, with a focus on the strategies implemented to tackle the economic constraints and the huge uncertainties of the even larger crisis, from 2011 to 2014; more recently, in 2016, a new phase has begun with the assumption of approximately 1000 new workers, younger than the first generation and with new and different employment contracts. It should also be said that, in the current phase we have found new uncertainties, which are a matter of ongoing research activity (D'Aloisio 2016, 2017).

The ethnography here is a long-term dialogic work, grounded on a hermeneutic and interpretative perspective, which has been opened since the famous Santa Fé seminar and has continued in the interna-tional debate up to the more recent formulations (Agar 2010; Clifford and Marcus 1986; Faubion and Marcus 2009; Gallini and Satta 2007; Marcus and Fischer 1986). As a result, we are now more conscious of the scale in which ethnography has to be practiced, re-constructed, and returned in the analysis and in the writing. We also have to bear in mind that in the Italian tradition, the anthropologist Ernesto De Martino, reflected on the issue of the 'ethnographic encounter' and on the spe-cific knowledge produced by the constant 'query and query themselves' (De Martino 1966, 2005). In this perspective, before the American debate, we can find the first traces of an ethnography as a multi-entry dialogue, a constructive process that today represents the focus of the anthropological approach.

The Industrial Settlement at Melfi. Scenarios of a Belated Development

When its production begun, finalising the production of cars from seg-ment B, the Melfi settlement had been anticipated as a big event, both at the popular level and from the local political class: the Fabbrica Italiana Autobili Torino had been the historical goal of many emigrants from Southern Italy who, after the Second World War, moved to Turin aban-doning the countryside and the rural life to construct a better future for themselves and their children. The migration from the South to Northern

Italy, especially in the period 1955–1970, was complemented by the larger flow to European destinations (France, Belgium, and Switzerland): in these flows the aspiration to became a metalworker, in FIAT and especially in Turin, represented the top, because it marked the detachment from hard, fluctuating, precarious work, associated with the frequent and typical turnover of the urban building labourers (Alberoni and Baglioni 1965; Berta 1998; Signorelli 1995). The memory of this, still alive in the local migrants, played an important role when one of the most important Italian factories landed in Melfi, at the beginning of the 1990s. The lack of industrial and economic development, up to that moment, created the expectation of trust and hope in the form of the new settlement, realistically disproportionate to the real ability of economic development for the local area. The settlement then configured, on the one hand as a millenaristic occurrence, on the other generating an attitude of paralysis and suspension of the trial by the local political institutions. These are the words of one of the local politicians, the vice-president of the provincial council, remembering the discussion in 1999 regarding the arrival of the factory:

> We were conscious that an entrepreneur had arrived, and he had decided to locate a factory with 7000 workers in the northern part of Basilicata, and then he told the political class 'I need all these things'. (…) So the political class had in front of them a strong interlocutor, able to dictate the rules, an interlocutor that had to be respected, pandered to, and also he proposed the need to review their projects and their regional programmes. During that period I realised that not only FIAT had opened a factory, but, because of its role as the most important economic protagonist in this area, he could state his opinion on everything, and then the institutional choices made sense if it was the conciliation with FIAT, otherwise, if FIAT didn't show their interest, probably these choices were not destined to continue, to become final choices. (Interview to G. A., Melfi, 1st of July 1999; D'Aloisio 2003: 56)

The fieldwork, at that time, underlined a relationship between the company and the local government that was completely asymmetrical. The politicians of various currents had enthusiastically shared the choice of location operated by FIAT; some voices out of the chorus, however, had pointed out, for example, the need for an environmental impact assessment and the major problem of the plant's waste, but those concerns had been isolated as senseless opposition. A few years later, in October 2011, Vincenzo Sigillito, former director of Agenzia Regionale Protezione Ambientale Basilicata (ARPAB), and Bruno Bove, coordinator of the provincial department, were arrested, charged with negligence and withholding (literally leaving in a drawer) the data on environmental pollution by the FIAT incinerator named 'Fenice'.[1] The episode denotes that institutional subalternship has been accompanied by episodes of corruption and collusion that allowed actions outside the law, with the aim of private speculation grafted on the edge of the industrial project.

During the years of construction of the settlement (1993–1994), the local people had the widespread expectation of a great economic event: 7000 jobs for a complete production plant (molding, body shop, painting and assembly), with a further 3000 places planned. In addition to this, the expectation widened even further to imagine a sort of economic revolution, an industrial transformation that would drive the local economy towards a development that was finally comparable, after decades of delay, with the North and Central Italy.

The major national newspapers spouted headlines such as 'Enthusiastic about the stars in Basilicata,' 'A challenge, a bet', 'Courageous Choice', seeing the location selection as a prize for an area that saw transforming its economic delay into a sort of merit note, able to guide the choice of location.[2]

In reality, the SATA factory represented an important organisational turn for the FIAT Company, that is to say the Italian interpretation of the so-called Japanese model, inspired by Thaicj Ohno's philosophy (Nakane 1992; Ohno 1988). Inspired by just-in-time production and the total quality model focused on the progressive and stable

---

[1] The 7th of October 2011 the newspaper *Repubblica* broke the news: Raffaella Cosentino, Falde avvelenate e dati fantasma. I misteri dell'inceneritore francese, *La Repubblica*, 7 October 2011.

[2] *La Gazzetta del Mezzogiorno*, one of the most important newspapers in Southern Italy, the day after the news (30th of November 1990) headlined "The big gift by the Avvocato (Lawyer) as a tribute for a healthy Region", referring to the President of FIAT, Gianni Agnelli (known in Italy as 'The Avvocato'), who had gifted the plant to the region, thus transforming its backwardness into a favourable state for new development. The idea of a gift, is a particularly interesting form, from an anthropological point of view inasmuch as recalling the reciprocal logic, inserts a free content where there is a cheap economic choice, as in the case of location choices; in this case, it was linked to the great availability of manpower and the existence of a 'green field', lacking industrial memory and union organisation.

improvement of product quality, the model overwhelmed the pillars of the old Fordist model and, above all, redefined the terms of market competition as it was happening in those years with the predominance of Toyota's Japanese manufacturer on international automotive markets (Bonazzi 1993; Rieser 1993; Volpato 1993).

From the enterprise's point of view, the Melfi plant constituted an important productive turn, which would reposition an industry characterised for decades by crisis (Volpato 2004, 2008). The choice of location was guided from the necessity to have manpower equipped with the necessary features for the construction of the new organisational model, such as higher education, shortage of other job opportunities and therefore also willingness to accept strict working conditions. In this regard, the second-level employment contract, concluded in 1993 before the factory began production, included lower wage levels than in the Northern factories, a sharper turnaround shift scheme, and tax reductions for recruitment according to the law in force at the time.[3]

In short, the company was set up in while the local workforce (including metalworkers) was weak. Politicians saw the importance of the operation, with attitudes between the lack of awareness and vice versa a certain complicity: 10,000 new jobs, albeit subordinated to contractual terms, would be a useful resource for the local population, suffering from a historic unemployment.

The third and most important social actor is the young adult manpower of the new 'amaranth suits', the new colour of the metalworker overalls adopted at Melfi; the new metalworkers came to the factory full of enthusiasm and relief at finding a stable job, with all the guarantees and safeguards of a formal contract, leaving behind the precariousness typical of temporary and moonlighting job which had been widespread in that area. However, the new state of well-being has been paid at the price of harsh working conditions; and above all, the unsettled precariousness has not disappeared altogether, but rather has returned, with even more worrying features less than twenty years since the plant opened.

---

[3]The so-called salary cages expected lower wages of about 20%, compulsory working Saturday, Sunday night shift, night shifts for women, in derogation of the national law prohibiting it. In the local contract of 1993, however, the percentage of women employees was expected to be 18%, exceeding the FIAT average of 12%, on the basis of agreements previously taken with the Basilicata Region and consistent with the high local female unemployment rates (Agreement Sata SRL—FMA 11th June 1993, Editing Center FIAT Auto, Turin).

The Crisis 2011–2014. The Protagonists of Daily Constraints and Livelihood Strategies

Now we go ahead with uncertainties. A few years ago we never thought that we would have come to the time where we would work three days a week ... Now we go ahead, you know, with fear, not knowing how many days we'll be working next month. Look at it this way, we are now in November, I still don't know how many days we'll work this month. There is a lot of worry. Worry for the future, because here the area where we are, is an area too poor - if we lose the little we have. ... The FIAT at Melfi has brought a lot of well-being into the area, if this factory fails it would be a tragedy! (Massimo, age 36, assembly-line metalworker, average education, single, November 2011).

This story, in the Autumn of 2011, in the second phase of field-work, refers to the contraction of production and the use of the Cassa Integrazione Guadagni (CIG), the supplementary wage authorised by the Italian State to integrate the salary during the reduction or stoppage of production. These comments reflect the widespread change in perspective that occurred in the area, leading to a new phase of uncertainty about jobs and the fate of the factory.

The difference between the interviews conducted in the first phase of research, six years after the factory's opening, and the interviews conducted ten years later, shows a clear change in the meaning of and value attributed to holding a job at FIAT. During the early years after the opening, a clear line was drawn between those who were able to enter FIAT, 'the lucky ones', those who had been given a big new opportunity, and those who looked 'from the outside of the factory' at new and privileged job positions. Those on the outside looking in could appreciate that the town itself had remained largely unchanged, with its shortcomings and dysfunctions. Working at FIAT gave those workers security and worker rights' protection, very different from the widespread forms of temporary and moonlighting characteristic of southern Italy (Ginsborg 1998). Therefore, the amaranth suits were considered truly privileged in the town and in the surrounding areas. They had a good wage and job security guaranteed by FIAT, whose international position, although already critical in those years but by no means was tarnished, thanks to the persistent myth of the celebrated brand (D'Aloisio 2003).

In the autumn of 2011, nearly twenty years after the plant first opened, effects of the 2008 financial crisis began to be felt at FIAT. The factory decreased its production and began part-time work and reduced salaries. As a result, in the following months daily life began to change dramatically in the area. Shops began to close down in and around the town, as well as a shopping mall in the area. There was talk of the local banks suspending debts, as they had given loans to workers for houses. Now on reduced hours and salaries, many were therefore were unable to pay. The restriction on everyday lifestyles hit precisely those improvements to consumerism that had characterised the local workforce: holidays, fashion clothing, showy consumption (from mobile phones to furniture), leisure activities, to name some. Thus explains a worker:

> I went to the bank for my own personal business … luckily I was able to weigh up my possibilities because I couldn't do anything else. I can't take out a mortgage, it's not convenient. I'll rent a home, I'll have to pay a lot of backhanded money, it's a small house, I'm happy: there are people who have taken out mortgages and now they're going to say to their banks that they don't have enough money to pay. With the integrative salary we've been able to make do up until now, we've lost three, four hundred euros a month. (…) Now we have to cut back. I'll show you my example. Last year I sent my little girl to a dance school because there was a problem with her left foot. This year I couldn't send: with this present situation, if I send her to dance school, what should I cut? (Antonio, assembly worker, age 43, school leaving diploma, married, one child).

> I'm seeing a big difference in salary now, and I lose almost 300 euros a month. I went from 1250 to 1000 euros. And for me it's difficult, but I live at home with my mum and dad, they don't let me pay anything. But I have to tell you, I'm suffering for this, because of university, the car, I go back and forth… But I see who has family they really are in great difficulty. Many here have mortgages, or children who go to college, or go to high school and they have big expenses. Unfortunately, we're all at this stage both young and old. The difference doesn't affect me, but with a family, it weighs very heavily on them. And fortunately here all we're still close to the family, with parents, kin, with the land, which maybe is not so in cities like Turin or Milan. So, anyway, we're on reduced working hours and reduced salary since November, but almost all of us have our 40 or 50 olive trees…

> (Iolanda, age 35, metalworker and university student, school leaving diploma, single, February 2012)

Looking back to the 1960s, we can see that the Italian economic boom favoured the wage increase of the working class, especially with a reduction in differentials separating blue collar workers from skilled and specialised categories (Musso 2006). It was a long-term process, which also led to wage bargaining between men and women, as well as increasing individual and collective incentives. Authoritative members of the Italian Marxist Left viewed this process as the end of the labour struggle and as an increase in the progressive imitation of the American way of life by the workers, played under the hegemony of well-being and the progress embodied in some symbols such as cars, refrigerators and televisions (Berta 1998). What can we learn from the economics of the 1960s?

The Melfi plant, the late action by the Italian industrial policy and the example of the FIAT strategy within the national borders, seem to retrace a curious parable with opposite sides of the coin, depending on whether it is viewed on a national or local scale. On a national scale, it represented a revival of the company in crisis, which used state funds and the opportunity to begin a business plan to relaunch. On a local scale, as we have illustrated here, it helped an all-round economic opportunity far beyond the employment figures offered. When the crisis phase began in it became clear that there had been no development outside the boundaries of the establishment, and that the company was not so solid. At the same time, the new local workers had increased their consumption and approached and embraced middle-class lifestyles.

Faced with the decrease in production and the resultant abrupt decline in wages, which lasted about three years, the livelihood strategies workers used took many forms. Susana Narotzky underlines "the means of livelihood thesis point out how people manage to get the necessities of life. Formal, market-mediated, economic relations such as employment and informal, non-market systems for getting hold of resources are considered on an equal methodological standing" (Narotzky 1997: 39). The role of kinship, friendship, and neighbourhoods is all importance, especially in the Italian case: both anthropological studies from earlier times in Basilicata (Banfield 1958; Davis 1973) and recent sociological studies (Fine-Davis et al. 2004; Naldini and Saraceno 2011), testify to the relevance of supportive networks in Italy, which can act in front of the absence or as a substitution for the public welfare, especially in times of crisis. Many strategies have been activated in Melfi: the support of the origin families (parents of the families in crisis), who support workers, especially by guaranteeing daily meals; and the networks of friendship and neighbourhood, including small services of a technical and/or domestic nature to reduce costs, such as collective car-sharing.

These strategies were also accompanied by the resumption of part-time and moonlighting jobs, which many FIAT workers had abandoned once they reached the position of metalworkers. In my ethnographic snowball sample, a working woman has resumed paid domestic work during her off-shift hours, another one supplements her salary as a home-to-home beautician, another one rents a room in his apartment; others work as waiters in restaurants, at parties and ceremonies during the weekends; some also have resumed working on their own or friends' land, in conjunction with the seasonal farming needs (harvesting fruit, olives, wheat, sowing, etc.).

The increase of occasional jobs, mostly moonlighting, obviously marks a brisk return back to the past: the local metalworkers, in the past unemployed and involved in various forms of job precariousness, had been transformed into new workers with a stable contract and a guaranteed status. Now, however, the new precariousness, twenty years after the opening of the plant, affecting these same workers, who are no longer young, has opened up concerns in new areas outside of the factory as the lack of work is felt throughout the region.

THE MULTINATIONAL SETTLEMENT AND THE NEW UNCERTAINTY BETWEEN GLOBAL AND LOCAL DIMENSION

In 2014, FIAT's chief executive office (CEO) Sergio Marchionne concluded the merger with US Chrysler, creating the Fiat Chrysler Automobiles corporation (FCA). As noted by Berta, Marchionne, the first international manager to run FIAT since 2004, marks a clear discontinuity with respect to the previous business history; his nomination was a result of the company's most acute phase of crisis, from 2002 to 2004 (Berta 2011). When the merger was announced in 2009 it generated an outpouring of nationalism by many observers. It was almost as if 'that acronym capable of evoking, in only one stroke, automotive production, Italy and their home town was not already depopulated' (Berta 2011: 26). With this important step, FIAT became an international corporation, a step necessary for its survival (for both Chrysler and FIAT). However, in recent years industrial relations and the business climate have become more strained, both nationally and locally, with Marchionne intolerant of the weak governance of the plants. Marchionne's actions are reminiscent of the history of FIAT and the Melfi plant; for example, the exemplary redeployments carried out at Melfi in 2010, the result of the exasperation of the factory climate, but still aimed at intimidating workers and making them more docile (Barozzino 2011).

The workers' perception of these steps illustrate the complexity of the situation. With their daily life radically changed due to economic constraints, their frustration towards jobs that no longer guarantee material security or satisfaction, the growing awareness of an uncertain future shows in their comments:

> We are here, Basilicata, all the invaders have moved up to become bosses, it has happened for centuries, millennia those who have come here. The last one, it turns out, to bring us anything was Frederick II, then all the others came only to spoil. Then Marchionne came too. He brought wealth, but he didn't appreciate us. I find this role within the FIAT world rather humiliating for us. That is, slaves, with a very negative meaning, in the sense of manpower, here it is. Consensual manpower, nothing else. (...). In my opinion, he's setting sights right now, just with his eyes not with a compass. And we all know... but we don't say anything, we keep quiet. If Marchionne finds different opportunities ... And since we know that he is navigating only by sight, our perception is this, so let it be. Because we don't want to give support to this ... But, what can we give to FIAT that can't be done in Serbia or China? What do we give him? Do we have peculiarities for which he sees Melfi as an irreplaceable pole of excellence? All right, in today's world - nothing is irreplaceable. But if I think about Ferrari, in Maranello, there's something ... but why? Because they do have a special product: why can't we do a special product here too? (Luigi, age 42, assembly worker, up to Junior school educated, married, two children, November 2011)

> I must say that the future is pessimistic. I'm pessimistic because I'm seeing not only in Marchionne, but in many entrepreneurs the idea of leaving Italy. So I don't know, this idea of going to America to buy this slice of business, going to Serbia to buy an abandoned company, going to Mexico to produce the FIAT 500, I see it as a departure not only from Italy but from a whole country that has good rules, certain benefits for the workers, especially if you compared it to developing countries, where there are certainly many more benefits for entrepreneurs than here. So I think that when they get stability and earnings elsewhere, out of Italy... Why?

Because I can't see him leaving it to his children, then to his children's children. I see the entrepreneur as a speculator: today it's possible to earn in Basilicata, so I'll go there, tomorrow Serbia opens the door to me, so I'll leave Basilicata and go to Serbia.

(Iolanda, age 35, metalworker and university student, school leaving diploma, single, February 2012)

As these interviews show, the workers saw early on what the future scenario was shaping up to be during the merger between FIAT and Chrysler. Likewise, in the testimonials shown, insights emerge on the broader reasons explaining the origin of the industrial operation in Melfi. Much research has dealt with the temporal modification of capitalism introduced by globalisation, highlighting how global-local interrelationship is being configured in new forms. In Herod's thesis, supported by his case studies, the relationship between the global dimension and the local has to be rethought in a more dynamic and changing direction, since, occasionally, local workers' actions can use global solidarity and so be able to have a positive impact on the course of globalisation or, vice versa, they can claim local specificities to counter global actions According to the author, as the case may be, acting globally can reinforce local claims, or even, on the contrary, local struggles can claim larger global instances (Herod and Aguiar 2006; Herod 2011). In this sense, world labour geographies seem to be different depending on the scale at which workers, or even businesses, are able to place themselves on the basis of variable factors that are not so clearly predictable (Crouch 2011; Moretti 2013); it is therefore with a variable scale that the contrastive actions or corrective interventions regarding globalisation processes must be analysed and understood.

Starting from this analytical premise, it is possible to understand better the evolution of the industrial site of Melfi, and also the characteristics of the new form of insecurity the workers experience as a consequence of the new multinational structure. The plant's deed of establishment, in 1993, represented for FIAT a useful internal relocation act that could enable it to modernise and relaunch the company out of the crisis. A local contract, which concerned both salary and labour rights, placed the Melfi workers in a subordinate position compared to the FIAT workers in Northern Italy. The local absence of an historically organised and solid trade union made such a local contract possible, and the slow organisation of the new trade unions didn't facilitate the improvement of the work conditions in the factory.

The old Italian FIAT changed, in a period of approximately twenty years, the scale with which we can observe the metalworkers' job and life conditions. The merger, started in 2009 and finalised in October 2014, determined the new international context of FCA, a company which has moved its legal headquarters from Italy to Holland and collocated its core business at the Chrysler plant in Detroit.

As described by many analysts of globalisation, insecurity is a condition deeply tied to the global dimension of production and businesses: as Standing describes in his analysis, the new class of precarious crosses the 'traditional' boundaries between groups and classes of workers, and it forces us to get out of the old bipartisanship between stable and precarious workers. In fact current precariousness is a condition concerning both young people entering into the labour market and also the old so-called stable workers; finally, it includes managers and management groups, traditionally considered more protected from layoffs (Standing 2011).

More generally the set of global companies mixes conditions and opportunities for precariousness, through the de-localisation of production, the distribution of value chains of the products, spread in different countries with different legislative frameworks, and finally through changes in company set-up and corporate changes of ownership, which also make managers, who are involved in these steps, precarious (Bauman 1998; Standing 2011). In addition, the unpredictability of these moves and often the rapidity of their implementation only increases the precarious size of the work position, which, however stable, can become susceptible to change, even to the loss of work.

The uncertainty expressed by workers at Melfi after the constitution of FCA can be traced back to the awareness that the expansion of the enterprise and production on a planetary scale makes it difficult to understand what will happen tomorrow; i.e., what choices will be made on the distribution of production and work at a global level. In the frame of the new geography of work that FCA is designing, therefore, hard work engagement, high productivity rates and willingness to change may not be sufficient to help successfully execute global business decisions, and some workers describe with great effectiveness the uselessness of all this. These descriptions echo Standing's observations when he speaks of the functional flexibility of the enterprises: it is the opportunity to intervene quickly and without cost on the division of labour, either by modifying positions and places of work, or modifying assignments in the same company. Accompanied by governments in response to global competition, this form of flexibility increases the insecurity of the professional role and adds to job insecurity more closely linked to employment numbers and cuts.

The history and constitution of the industrial settlement of Melfi do not encourage a positive outlook on the future: the economic downturn in local development has made it possible to establish a plant that has strongly downgraded the wage and working conditions of new workers. The protagonists of the operation, the metalworkers of Melfi, have discounted the price of the weakness of local institutions: they accepted the establishment without being able to govern the course of its evolution. In addition, the newly formed trade unions were not able to measure themselves with the company. Hence, the workers have gone from the precarious state and absence of a certain working future when, in the 1990s, the local employment landscape was devoid of opportunities, to a condition of new uncertainty, deriving from the multinational structure of the factory and the new situation in which production decisions are now anchored to global scenarios, constantly changing and connected to the economic conjunctures, impossible to predict at the local scale only.

CONCLUSION

Over a period of just a decade, the production cycle of the Melfi plant has undergone several phases, in which we can recognise the transition of the largest Italian car manufacturer into a multinational and global corporation (Stocchetti et al. 2013; Volpato 2004). During the mid-1990s, the Melfi plant, the last Italian investment, had undergone a long, full-scale production phase with intense work rates due to the good holding of the Punto model on the car market. Beginning in 2009, the acquisition by Chrysler began trying to lift the company out of a long crisis, repositioning it on the global scale. Experts agree that the acquisition, completed in 2014, had re-established the company's fate, but the extended crisis of 2011–2014 and then the transition to FCA profoundly marked the course of the workers in Melfi The workers faced producing daily economic difficulties, uncertain future scenarios, and renewed fear of losing their jobs. The strategies employed by workers to cope with the difficulties caused by the long-term production reduction have included forms of circularity and support of kinship, and in some cases also the neighborhood, a form of solidarity typical of rural Italy, especially Southern Italy, while also consistent with the lack of a national welfare system.

Kinship support and networking between colleagues have provided efficient livelihood strategies to cope with the crisis, upholding expenses and debts contracted in a period of full-year earnings. However, the prospect of the long-term future marks a halt compared to what the plant had expected. Considered a definitive existential turning point, which had in the past delivered a precarious condition and no prospects, FIAT's workplace revealed a new uncertainty, even more difficult to face for the fifty-year-old workers, tired and fatigued, unable to find job alternatives.

Obviously, the two different phases, the starting and rising of the plant and the current one, before the crisis and now with its new multinational status, are not independent, but closely related: the economic delay transformed into further subordination, which allowed the industrial location, followed by the weakness of a political class incapable of coping with the local industrial process, coupled with an objective weakness of the young local trade unions. However, this economic and institutional weakness is the problem that the workforce has to face, taking into account the scale of global business decisions and the geographies of labour that they draw from. As a result, workers have little chance of determining their own workplace destinies. The efforts and the profound commitment seem to be a parable of the unpredictable and ungovernable outcomes. Melfi and its industrial settlement thus seem to be one of the new, multiple suburbs that in the perspective of Mollona characterise the present phase of globalisation, where we can no longer find a single centre converging into a model conceived as Western: on the contrary, as he points out, not only the distinction between the industrial North and the underdeveloped South is less clear and more problematic, but also the same production and service chains are shaken in new directions (Mollona 2009). The new dystopian landscapes that this globalisation produces seem to justify the foggy future perceived by Melfi's workers.

From an anthropological point of view, the workers have not escaped the sense of emptiness and ineffectiveness of working practices, engagement and daily labour efforts within a project that remains foreign. Represented as the protagonists of an organisational change and epoch-making, they almost seem to pick up pieces of failure. As actors involved in keeping together old and new strategies to cope with the crisis, they are now engaged in the new stage of the plant, with the promise of a new model in production (Jeep Renegade, exported to the American market), under the uncertainties of market trends and future production locations. Overall, they stand strong trying to ensure the best work and production, for goals that do not see them as protagonists on the new scenario of globalisation.

REFERENCES

Accordo Sata SRL—FMA. 1993. Editing Center FIAT Auto, Turin.

Agar, M. 2010. On the Ethnographic Part of the Mix. A Multi-genre Tale of the Field. *Organizational Research Methods* 13: 286–303.

Alberoni, F., and G. Baglioni. 1965. *L'integrazione dell'immigrato nella società industriale*. Bologna: Il Mulino.

Althabe, G., and M. Selim. 2000. *Approcci etnologici della modernità*. Turin: Harmattan Italia.

Appadurai, A. 1996. *Modernity at Large: Cultural Dimnesions of Globalization*. Minneapolis and London: University of Minnesota Press.

Banfield, E.C. 1958. *The Moral Basis of a Backward Society*. Glencoe: The Free Press.

Barozzino, G. 2011. *Ci volevano con la terza media. Storia dell'operaio che ha sconfitto Marchionne*. Rome: Editori Internazionali Riuniti.

Bauman, S. 1998. *Globalization the Human Consequences*. Cambridge and Oxford: Polity Press and Blackwell.

Berta, G. 1998. *Mirafiori*. Bologna: Il Mulino.

Betra, G. 2011. *Fiat Chrysler e la deriva dell'Italia industriale*. Bologna: Il Mulino.

Bonazzi, G. 1993. *Il tubo di cristallo. Modello giapponese e fabbrica integrata alla Fiat Auto*. Bologna: Il Mulino.

Clifford, J., and G.E. Marcus (eds.). 1986. *Writing Culture Poetics and Politics of Ethnography*. Berkeley: University of California Press.

Comaroff, J., and J. Comaroff. 2003. Ethnography on an Awkward Scale. Postcolonial Anthropology and the Violence of Abstraction. *Ethnography* 4 (2): 147–179.

Cosentino, R. 2011. Falde avvelenate e dati fantasma. I misteri dell'inceneritore francese. *La Repubblica*, October 7.

Crouch, C. 2011. *The Strange Non-death of Neoliberalism*. Cambridge: Polity Press.

D'Aloisio, F. 2003. *Donne in tuta amaranto. Trasformazione del lavoro e mutamento culturale alla Fiat Sata di Melfi*. Milan: Guerini & Associati.

D'Aloisio, F. 2014. *Vita di fabbrica. Cristina racconta il decollo e la crisi della Fiat Sata di Melfi*. Milan: Franco Angeli.

D'Aloisio, F. 2016. Work Inequalities Between Global Trasformation and Local Embedment: The Case of Fiat-Chrysler and the New Course at Melfi's Factory. *Antropologia* 3 (1): 53–68.

D'Aloisio, F. 2017. Postfordist Work Organization and Daily Life in a Gender Perspective: The Case of FIAT-SATA in Melfi. In *Work and Livelihoods—Ethnography and Models in Times of Crisis*, ed. S. Narotzky and V. Goddard, 77–92. London: Routledge.

Davis, J. 1973. *Land and Family in Pisticci*. London: Athlone Press.

De Martino, E. 1966. *La fine del mondo. Contributo all'analisi delle apocalissi culturali*. Torino: Einaudi.

De Martino, E. 2005. *The Land of Remorse*, trans. D. Zinn. London: Free Association Books.

Faubion, J.D., and G.E. Marcus (eds.). 2009. *Fieldwork Is Not What It Used to Be. Learning Anthropology Method in a Time of Transition*. Ithaca and London: Cornell University Press.

Fine-Davis, M., J. Fagnani, D. Giovannini, L. Højgaard, and H. Clarke (eds.). 2004. *Fathers and Mothers. Dilemmas of the Work-Life Balance. A Comparative Study in Four European Countries*. Dordrecht: Kluwer Academic Publishers.

Gallini, C., and G. Satta (eds.). 2007. *Incontri etnografici. Porcessi cognitivi e relazionali nella ricerca sul campo*. Rome: Meltemi.

Ginsborg, P. 1998. *L'Italia del tempo presente. Famiglia, società civile, stato*. Turin: Einaudi.

Hannerz, U. 2010. *Anthropology's World: Life in a Twenty-First-Century Discipline*. London: Pluto Press.

Herod, A. 2011. *Labor Geographies. Workers and the Landscapes of Capitalism*. New York and London: The Guilford Press.

Herod, A., and L.L.M. Aguiar. 2006. Introduction: Geographies of Neoliberalism. *Antipode* 38 (3): 435–439.

Hours, B., and M. Selim (eds.). 2012. *Fare Antropologia nella realtà globale*. Turin: Harmattan Italia.

Kilani, M. 2009. *Anthropologie Du local au global*. Paris: Armand Colin.

Marcus, G.E., and M.J. Fisher (eds.). 1986. *Anthropology as Cultural Critique an Experimental Moment in the Human Sciences*. Chicago: University of Chicago Press.

Mollona, M. 2009. General Introducion. In *Industrial Work and Life. An Anthropological Reader*, ed. M. Mollona, G. De Neeve, and J. Parry, XI–XXVIII. Oxford and New York: Berg.

Moretti, E. 2013. *The New Geography of Jobs*. New York: Mariner Books.

Musso, S. 2006. *Operai*. Turin: Rosemberg & Sellier.

Nakane, C. 1992. *La società giapponese*. Milan: Cortina.

Naldini, M., and C. Saraceno (eds.). 2011. *Conciliare famiglia e lavoro. Vecchi e nuovi patti tra i sessi e le generazioni*. Bologna: Il Mulino.

Narotzky, S. 1997. *New Direction in Economic Anthropology*. London and Chicago: Pluto Press.

Ohno, T. 1988. *The Toyota Production System: Beyond Large Scale Production*. Portland: Productivity Press.

Rieser, V. 1993. Crisi dell'automazione e riaggiustamento organizzativo alla Fiat di Cassino. In *Fiat punto e a capo. Problemi e prospettive della fabbrica integrata da Termoli a Melfi*, ed. M. Carrieri, 399–455. Rome: Ediesse.

Selim, M. 1996. L'entreprise: emprise idéologique, mondalisation et évolution des problématiques. *Journal des Anthropologues*, 19–28, 66/67.

Selim, M. 2000. L'impresa. In *Approcci etnologici della modernità*, ed. G. Althabe and M. Selim, 63–106. Turin: Harmattan Italia

Selim, M. 2012. Verso un sistema di lavoro globale. In *Fare Antropologia nella realtà globale*, ed. B. Hours and M. Selim, 59–76. Turin: Harmattan Italia.

Signorelli, A. 1995. Movimenti di popolazione e trasformazioni culturali. In *Storia dell'Italia Repubblicana*, II, 1, ed. F. Barbagallo, 589–658. Turin: Einaudi.

Standing, G. 2011. *The Precariat: The New Dangerous Class*. London and New York: Bloomsbury Academic.

Stocchetti, A., G. Trombini, and F. Zirpoli (eds.). 2013. *Automotive in Transition. Challenges for Strategy and Policy*. Venice: Edizioni Ca'Foscari.

Volpato, G. 1993. Lo scenario della competizione automobilistica internazionale e la strategia di rilancio del Gruppo Fiat Auto. In *Fiat punto e a capo. Problemi e prospettive della fabbrica integrata da Termoli a Melfi*, ed. M. Carrieri, 11–14. Rome: Ediesse.

Volpato, G. 2004. *Fiat Auto Crisi e riorganizzazioni strategiche di un'impresa simbolo*. Turin: ISEDI.

Volpato, G. 2008. *Fiat Group Automobiles Le nuove sfide*. Bologna: Il Mulino.

CHAPTER 10

Workers' Committees in Israel in the Heyday of Neoliberalism: From Consent to Professionalisation to Alternative Solutions

Gadi Nissim

Mindset becomes hegemonic when alternative ideologies or social orders cannot be imagined. This occurs when those who are most marginalized by the social order internalize it. Hegemonic order does not mean the elimination of all struggle, but the transformation of political and strategic conflicts into mere tactical disputes that deny their political character and succumb to objective standards. This chapter demonstrates how stewards of Israeli workers' committees (the union's unit at the workplace level) grasped the market as a natural entity with objective rules. As a result, they channeled their efforts from confronting the employers to the more complicated position of coping both with employers and with the abstract concept of market rules. Confronting natural forces also led workers' committees to abandon political orientation and embrace professionalism, which was perceived as the only way to understand the

G. Nissim (✉)
Department of Behavioral Sciences, Ruppin Academic Center,
Netanya, Israel

© The Author(s) 2018
M. Spyridakis (ed.), *Market Versus Society*, Palgrave Studies in Urban Anthropology, https://doi.org/10.1007/978-3-319-74189-5_10

171

market and adjust to its dictates. However, the harsh labour conditions in which the committees operated also led to the development of the seeds of radical alternative thought.

INTRODUCTION

Hegemony is an oppressive social order in which the rulers gain control of the economic, political, and cultural institutions. In a hegemonic order, the mindset serving the rulers' narrow interests becomes the common, objective mode of thinking about reality. Hegemonic order is not free of tensions; but since no alternative is even imagined, these tensions are manifested as isolated skirmishes and not as part of a counter-hegemonic movement (Filc 2006: 29; Khenin 2000: 69, 72).

Over the past four decades, capitalism has changed its course. It has become global (Sklair 2009), shifting away from being productive and industrial (the 'gospel of work') to being more financially inclined (the 'gospel of wealth') (Durrenberger and Doukas 2008). The new capitalism is hectic, in greater flux than previously. It is often praised for being more open to new forces (for example, to high tech entrepreneurs). But in this new cannibalized world, we still see clear advantages of employers over employees, of capital over work, and of corporations over unions. The outcomes are growing inequality and insecurity and the emergence of the precariat (Standing 2011; Spyridakis 2017).

The new polarized order needs legitimacy. A key role in this process is played by the neoliberal project. David Harvey defines neoliberalism as 'a theory of political economic practices that proposes that human well-being can best be advanced by liberating individual entrepreneurial freedoms and skills within an institutional framework characterized by strong private property rights, free markets and free trades' (Harvey 2005: 2). The ultimate achievement of neoliberalism is to create the perception that the capitalist order is natural and neutral, and therefore to conceal its social and political character: 'Such a view of the economy is, for better or worse, a disembedding vision since it sees the economy as lifted out of social relations, following its own logic and its own dynamic, driven by anonymous market forces' (Eriksen 2014: 34).

According to the neoliberal mindset, the only alternative for an economic system is a market system (Fourcade-Gourinchas and Babb 2002). Although the market appears as a natural entity, however, it is actually part of a class struggle; that is, it is part of the strategic move of the old economic elites to regain their power, which had been restricted since World War II, and to free themselves from any control or interference by the state and working class (Harvey 2005: 19, 152–153, 187–188).

In this context, one might expect that workers, and their representatives, would object to neoliberalism and offer an alternative mindset. But is this always the case? In studying this issue, I examined twenty workers' committees affiliated with the Histadrut, Israel's largest and most prominent union. Workers' committees comprise the union's representatives at the workplace level. I studied these committees in 2007–2008, at the height of neoliberalism, when private employers were at the peak of their strength, just as the global economic crisis was about to erupt. The methodology used was ethnographic; I was mainly interviewing and observing the workers' committees' stewards in their natural settings, at the workplaces. All the names mentioned in this chapter are pseudonyms.

The Israeli case is useful for an inquiry into contemporary labour relations and trade unions. Like many other countries, Israel has been transformed from a state-led capitalist economy, dominated by a social-democrat party and collective ideology, into global capitalism, dominated by liberal-conservatives and the rise of individualistic ideology. In Israel, however, these transformations were more intensive and radical (Bareli et al. 2005: 1–4) than elsewhere. Consequently, the Israeli case exemplifies, more vividly and explicitly, trends that have taken place globally. In addition, the cultural, political, and economic vision of Israel was to a large extent shaped by the dominance of the Israeli labour movement. Thus, it is interesting to consider whether the imprint of this legacy still exists, and to ask whether there is any cultural or political agent with the potential to block, or at least thwart, neoliberal capitalism.

Workers' Committees: Observation and Policy

Workers' committee stewards negotiate and struggle with employers, but they also look beyond them. They refer to the whole industry and to what they observe as the objective market's reality.

In April 2008, I visited the workers' committee of one of Israel's famous textile companies. The giant factory, located near a southern rural town, had closed its gate the day prior to my visit, after decades of activity. All the workers were dismissed. The deterioration had started years earlier when the company was sold to foreign investors; immediately a series of unsuccessful 'recovery' steps were begun, until the closure in 2008. The brand, one of the Israeli industrial symbols, still exists, but manufacturing takes place in East Asia.

I was sure I would find Dani, the workers' committee chairperson, in a combative mood; but instead he calmly told a story of uncontrollable forces—globalization, investors, the garment industry, the Chinese—that had left no alternative but to shut down production in Israel. There was no anger in Dani's voice, just sorrow: 'They said we were too small for the big world'. The struggle was not for the survival of the factory or to save jobs. They had given up on these. The struggle was rather to secure workers' rights after the company's liquidation—their pensions and compensation—and to pressure the liquidator to give priority to workers' rights over other company stakeholders.

In the case of a weak industry like textiles, it might be understandable that workers would give up the idea of winning and strive to minimize their losses. However, this approach also appeared in much stronger industries. Following my meeting with Dani, I had an interview with Ronen, chairperson of the workers' committee of an oil refinery at a city in a northern district. The refinery was privatized in 2007—an act that, according to Ronen, was unreasonable since the company had been strong and the industry was solid. Moreover, the workers' committee had been successful for years in its efforts to block privatization, using its power among the workers and effective networking in the political playground. Nevertheless, the workers' committee finally decided to accept privatization, after negotiating what had been seen as a good deal for the workers. Ronen explained the logic of the move: 'An opportunity came in 2006. The company—which had been previously owned by the government—had substantial profits, so we could privatize it and at the same time finance and secure workers' rights. After all, this trend of privatization is natural and bound to occur, so why not do it in a timing that serves us?' Privatization, perceived by Dani as a natural outcome in 2006, would have been unknown to him only a few decades before, as it appeared in the dictionary only in 1983 (Peleg 2005: 1).

Although the two cases represent different industries—weak and competitive versus monopolistic—both committee chairpersons surprisingly shared the assumption that political-economic trends are deterministic. Therefore, they referred not only to their employers, but added another layer—the assessment of 'objective' conditions—and anchored their expectations in the context of that reality. Viewing the economy as a supra-social entity is a pillar of neoliberal thought. By internalizing it,

Dani and Ronen felt they could negotiate only about compensations, but not about the 'big decisions' (that is, whether the workplace will survive, who will own the company, and so on).

Treating the market as an ontological entity has additional consequences. In the context of the market's harsh rules, the workers' relationship with the employer could be perceived either as a collision of interests or as mutual destiny. Take, for example, the case of a chemical product factory in the north of Israel. In the 1990s, the company was profitable; however, instead of sharing the profits with the workers, the owner tried to increase profits by worsening employment terms and even abolishing the collective agreement. The owner—a tycoon with many other holdings, including a new branch of the company in a southern district of the country—could afford to shut down the factory and sacrifice short-terms profits in order to break organized labour. Although he did not in the end shut down the factory, his position gave him increased manoeuvring ability and restricted the company's workers' committee. The chairperson of the workers' committee, Michael, concluded that combative acts like striking were useless. More than ten years prior, the committee led a strike that lasted four months without any positive results. The lesson they learned was that the owner was too greedy and they were too weak. In examining the southern branch of the company a few years later, I found that by the turn of the millennium the company had begun to lose money in the more competitive global market. The workers' committee in this case was also restrained; however, this restraint was not out of fear of the owner, but because the entire company was vulnerable.

Company vulnerability can also lead to cooperation between employers and workers' committees. This was the case in a metal product company at the beginning of the global crisis in 2008. The stewards of the workers' committee became convinced that the company would collapse unless 20% of the workforce liabilities were cut. However, they insisted on controlling how the cuts would be made, demanding that all workers would give up one workday a week in exchange for the promise that none of workers would be laid off. The workers' committees thus would accept the laying-off of employees if they thought it was inevitable; but at the same time, they expected management to be fair and honest with them. In addition, they expected to be partners in decision-making. When harsh measures seemed inescapable, they wanted to influence the process and have the power to suggest alternatives. In a number of companies, the workers' committees insisted that management could not arbitrarily decide who would be laid off, but that the committee would have the option of suggesting workers who had already expressed a desire to retire, and that these workers would be generously compensated. Workers' committees also insisted on ensuring that recovery measures would not endanger the existence of organized labour and collective bargaining in the company.

Perceiving the market as deterministic has also led to a personalisation of the capital-labour conflict. Contrary to the Marxist notion that this conflict is structured within the capitalist system, the perception of capital as an external force has led, ironically, to its personalisation. A number of the committee stewards I interviewed referred to good or bad owners, assuming that when the system is unchangeable, the only thing that matters is the person behind the class position, and that social action is aimed to influence the extent of a given relationship, not its content. For example, Ronen, the chairman of the northern oil refinery in mentioned above, justified his cooperation with privatisation by emphasizing the identity of the buyer. He said that he was glad that the new owner, a well-known Israeli tycoon, was 'solid' and not a 'speculator'.

Given the structural relationship dictated by the market and the power gaps between employers and employees, the main task of workers' committees became assessing what was reasonable to achieve in such a context. Hence, Tuli, the committee chairperson of a famous hotel in Tel Aviv, reported that he was proud of his success in limiting the share of temporary workers to no more than 15% of the workforce. The goal of the committee had become to act as a kind of shock absorber, or as one chairperson defined it, 'a layer that protects the workers from the arbitrary and harmful behavior of the management'. So, for example, when one of the chairpersons I interviewed assessed that their employer had the power to outsource the entire workforce and abolish organized labour, his priority was to allow the management to reduce the number of regular employees in the company while at the same time enforcing an agreement that the number did not go below the minimum required to secure the existence of organized labour in the company.

As workers' committees internalised neoliberal concepts, their chief agenda had become to achieve what is feasible in the context of objective market conditions. In this respect, in my interviews I found that chairpersons even justified the existence of organized labour in terms of business utility. One assertive character in the field was Chemi, the committee chairperson in a telecommunication company. He argued that company managers oppose workers' committees because they mistakenly interpret organized labour as a threat to the company. Instead, Chemi passionately asserted, workers' committees should be seen as providing feedback to the management, creating a permanent 'quality circle'. According to Chemi, instead of undermining managements' prerogative in salary policy or other issues (except for when it came to laying off workers), these committees help in running the business and contributing to its efficiency. Chemi was proud of the efficiency process he had led in the committee, which saved working hours for the company through improvements. Indeed, many of my informants stressed that the committees are as committed to the companies' interests as they are loyal to the workers', and are certainly no less committed than management. One of them even argued that committee stewards are *more* loyal to the company than the owners, as the latter seek to maximize private gains in the fastest way, while stewards are the true guardians of the enterprise. He concluded: 'I won't fight or sacrifice myself for an undeserving worker ... We have a responsibility to the system. There is a mutual interest for the workers and the management. Bad workers don't provide work for the others. We don't want these kinds of workers here'.

The ultimate example of committees' loyalty to the company can be seen in the case of a chemical materials factory in the south of Israel. In the past, the company bought raw materials from another company, which, functioning as a monopoly, used its position to raise the prices. As a result, the chemical factory management (which had previously tried to prevent workers from organizing) recruited the workers' committee to entice protest against the monopoly. They wanted to pressure the other company to cut prices and force the government to regulate the monopoly. Workers' committees thus justify their existence not only in terms of worker solidarity or interests, but also in terms of loyalty and professional contribution to the business. These terms correspond with the neoliberal mindset that business is the only relevant thing.

To sum up, the perception of market rules as objective and deterministic led workers' committees to develop a conditional logic. They assessed reality through the available neoliberal cultural tools in determining whether they should cooperate with or contest the employers.

PROFESSIONALISATION OF WORKERS' COMMITTEES

The view of the market as a decipherable given, together with the perception of workers' position as inferior vis-à-vis the owners, has led committee stewards to conclude that they should handle their struggles cautiously and wisely. Their mutual guidelines were not based on creating new and better labour relations, but rather on showing 'responsibility for the business' and on responding to violations that had already occurred. The workers' committees, then, had to be prudent. Consequently, they developed an ethos of professionalism.

Many of my informants found ideology to be mere 'talk'. They identified ideology as the software of the political sphere, which they saw as an arena not of social change or justice but where narrow interests are fulfilled. Therefore, they saw ideology as fantasy. Meir, the young committee chairperson of a southern branch of the chemical factory mentioned above, clearly expressed this attitude. He declared that he did not watch the news or read newspapers because he did not want to be exposed to politics. Despite this position, Meir and his committee successfully attained the first collective agreement for employees in their factory. In fact, most other chairpersons in the field made use of the political sphere only as a means of establishing instrumental relationships with members of the Knesset (the Israeli parliament) to gain their support. Here, as in the case of the employers, committee chairpersons tended to personalise politics. They believe that since parties do not really represent distinct alternatives, they do not matter. The only thing that can help is a sympathetic politician of good character or one who will personally benefit by assisting. The chairpersons interviewed did reveal ideologies when they spoke about justice, but they articulated their claims using the raw language and basic terms of what E. P. Thompson (1971) referred to as the 'moral economy'. Thus, they treated justice using simple terms, while referring to the realm of the economy with sophistication.

In this way, the chairpersons I interviewed abandoned ideology on the one hand while seeking professional training or assistance, finding it in the business world. Some of them went to college for academic degrees in business administration, others tried to educate themselves through economic newspapers saturated with neoliberal rhetoric and content. They also began to use the services of 'cutting edge' professionals. For example, a few committees hired accountants to monitor company finances in order to decide whether management was sincere in its reports and demands. Committees also use the services of public relations consultants to advocate for workers or to damage the employers' public image when needed. Another popular procedure is to use legal practitioners. Many committee chairpersons view labour lawyers as experts when it comes to difficulties in dealing with employers. While the Histadrut symbolizes an anachronistic world, lawyers are seen as the most informed actors for the job; and chairpersons often prefer lawyers who, ironically, advise employers against organized labour. Indeed, hiring lawyers has become so common that committee chairpersons describe their own role to be the lawyers of the workers.

Lawyers also symbolize the option of being assertive winners without inhibitions. A joint consultation forum of workers' committee chairpersons, all affiliated with subsidiaries of the same company, used to gather every few weeks in a town near Tel Aviv, to discuss matters of mutual concern and coordinate their activity. I was introduced to the forum by Chemi, the committee chairperson of the telecommunication company mentioned above. Chemi invited me to observe one of the forum's meetings. On this occasion, the issue was whether to hire a well-known but expensive lawyer against the management of one of the companies. This company had had a crisis few years before and the workers had been asked to reduce their salary until the company recovered. After the company became profitable again, the chairpersons were convinced management was withholding money belonging to the workers and taking legal maneuvers to conceal it. Chemi, who was the unofficial leader of the group, offered to give up the money allocated for welfare services of the workers (gifts for holidays, trips, and so on) and pay the expensive lawyer fees. He urged his friends to see it as an investment: 'All you have to do is to put in a few dimes and you will get ten to fifteen thousand back'. His friends, however, were more reserved, one of them suggesting that they use the legal services provided by the Histadrut. Chemi, in response, criticized their wavering: 'Hearing the word 'money' makes you run away'.

This story encapsulates the neoliberal logic of the new labour struggle. The classic socialist tool-kit is seen as too altruistic, too 'union,' and too ideological. The neoliberalising labour struggle means embracing market logic and business tools: that is, to be assertive, professional, selfish, and materialistic. Thus, some chairpersons saw the business world as a benchmark. In an interview, Paz, the committee chairperson of a company that manufactured items for the military, declared, 'The age of burning tires is over'; meaning that the known and popular spontaneous acts of violence during workers' rallies are archaic and should be abandoned. Professionalism, instead, has been grasped as a realm of concrete and up-to-date practice, ascribed to winners. Chemi added, 'Only wisdom will empower you ... You mustn't arrive inferior to the negotiations with the management. This is the new era and we need to adjust ... So far it was our Achilles' heel as workers' committees. We should overcome it and look management straight in the eye'. Chemi was one of the optimistic chairpersons in the field. He even stated the belief that a professional and 'cold-blooded' approach would not only enable workers to mitigate the damaging effect of globalisation, but also to 'win'—in this case, 'winning' refers to increasing workers' benefits. For example, some of the committee chairpersons demanded bonuses and dividends from the company's profits.

In brief, assuming that the days of political ideology were gone, the stewards of workers' committees professionalised: referring to the business world as a benchmark and using the services of cutting-edge business experts.

ALTERNATIVE THINKING OF THE WORKERS' COMMITTEES

Workers' committees also turned from defensive to a more ambitious orientation. Further, their adaptive logic was followed by a more subversive logic, characterised as socialist (or social-democrat) and articulated in neoliberal terms. In my research, examples of this trend were easy to find. Weekly meetings of the workers' committee of the metal company in Israel's south were full of these expressions. On one of these occasions, for example, a steward declared, 'it is well known that people [workers] bring profits, not machines'. This quote, accepting the assumption that the company's raison d'être is to profit, at the same time declares that workers, and not the owners or management, are the source of profits. Stewards often criticized the government for preferring the interests of investors and corporations over those of the workers. They were also preoccupied with the unfairness of the company's bonus system. On the one hand, they accepted the principle of individual bonuses for high production rates; but on the other hand, they did not believe that the goals defined by the management were feasible, and complained that workers had little influence on the production rates entitling them to bonuses. One of the stewards, for example, was furious that to achieve their bonus, they were forced to push the machines beyond their limit. The committee's stewards often discussed the need to open the collective agreement and renegotiate the bonus system. However, they did not really believe they had the power to bring change, or that the Histadrut would actively support them if they declared a labour dispute. In these moments, when anger met frustration, radical thoughts rose. One steward declared that the whole system was exploitive: minor raises would not improve workers' conditions, and to bring justice they needed to define a 'maximum wage' and not just minimum wage. He meant that limiting the seniors' salary would free money for the middle and the lower wage earners. He was thus speaking quite radically, then, on redistribution and allocative justice. Here it is worth mentioning that the production process has been known for decades as a complicated arena of consent and struggle between the management and the workers. The consent or the struggles evolve over the creation of surplus value by methods like price/rate per piece; as it is shown in the seminal work by Michael Burawoy about a factory in a town near Chicago, from 1944 to 1975 (Burawoy 1979).

Radical views about the economic structure and allocative justice were also heard among chairpersons of other committees, mainly regarding the issue of company ownership. Chemi, the telecommunication company's committee's chairperson, had an innovative idea. He declared that he had had enough of useless exertion of force and that he sought real power. His vision in the long term was for workers to become major shareholders. In order to achieve this, the workers needed a business partner, a serious investor, to join them. Afterward, they could become partners in the corporation: 'I want the workers' to be the real owners. Why are the rich holding it all? After all, they are turning the workers into nothing, treating them like trash. We need to have a smart change—silent but substantial'.

The idea of workers owning corporations was also promoted by Joel, the committee chairperson of a newly privatized oil refinery in a southern city in Israel (this is not the oil refinery mentioned earlier in this chapter, which was located in a northern city). Joel had been fighting against privatisation for twenty years. He claimed that the refinery had been privatised for no good reason, as it had been prosperous under public ownership. Furthermore, it was sold for much less than it was worth to the private holdings company of a local tycoon. The workers' committee eventually consented to privatisation after successfully negotiating an agreement that secured workers' rights. The most striking element in Joel's story of privatisation, however, was the connection established during the process between the workers' committee and a well-known Russian tycoon with controversial business dealings who had recently immigrated to Israel. The tycoon had tried to gain legitimacy and political and economic power in Israel through, among other things, philanthropic acts and the purchasing of Israeli corporations (for example, buying a famous soccer team). He offered to enter into a partnership with the refinery's workers, suggesting that they establish a joint company and offer the state's treasury a high price for the refinery, with the tycoon taking 60% of the joint company's shares and the workers 40%. Moreover, the tycoon offered to lend the workers the money to buy their shares, and agreed that they would pay him in the first ten years of joint ownership. He also agreed that the payments would be made from the profits made up to that point. The tycoon did not suggest this deal out of pure altruism, but in the hope of controlling the second biggest refinery in the country; but this fact was agreeable to the workers' committee: as Joel told me, 'He had his interests, and so did we'.

Despite their efforts, however, the government declined their offer, selling the refinery to another investor. Joel reiterated that the process was biased and unfair. Their offer, he claimed, was generous and met all the criteria. He assumed that government officials wanted to sell the company to an investor they favored, and to avoid selling to one they could not control. Moreover, according to Joel, government officials and local investors definitely did not want the workers to be owners, even partially, of the company, regardless of how much money they were willing to pay. Joel concluded, 'If I had succeeded in my move, all the workers here, including myself, would have been millionaires'.

To sum up, despite the depth of the stewards' internalisation of the neoliberal cultural world, they were still able to think alternatively about reality. On the one hand, they shared with owners and managers the assumption that profits are the ultimate goal of the enterprise. On the other hand, some of the stewards' and chairpersons' views undermined the logic and values of the current system. They did not accept a distorted allocative system in which owners and managers received most of the benefits, and they even considered an alternative structure of ownership. However, the political dimension of their views and deeds was conveyed through a rhetoric congruent with neoliberal order.

DISCUSSION: THE IMPORTANCE OF ORGANIC INTELLECTUALS

This chapter proposes an inquiry into the world of Israeli workers' committees in 2007–2008, when neoliberal hegemony was at its peak. The aim was to find out whether and how workers' committees' stewards internalised neoliberal discourse. Findings show that the culture of workers' committees was incorporated into the neoliberal hegemony. The stewards perceived the market as an ontological entity and not as a social phenomenon. They saw market rules as universal, deterministic, and beyond the influence of social forces. People can only succumb—or better, adjust—to these rules. Hence, workers' committees developed the notion they could not change reality, but could only maneuver in the narrow margins left in order to mitigate the severe outcomes for lay workers. Stewards also developed a sense of personalised justice, judging employers on their fairness in the context of the market. Furthermore, the need to make accurate choices led stewards to seek calculated action. Turning to professionalism, they gave up political ideologies and actions. The business world became the benchmark. Finally, not all workers' committees merged smoothly into the neoliberal order. Some stewards defied this order in various ways, such as trying to alter company ownership to change the power balance with the employers. However, even these alternative stances were often articulated in the language of business world.

How can these findings be explained? To do so, we need to address two issues: the first pertains to how hegemony functions, and the second pertains to the history and character of labour unions. I will consider both of these.

The question of how hegemony functions can be answered in two ways. In the first, hegemony is viewed as absolute control of the dominant class over the subordinate, a situation in which thought becomes unified and no resistance arises (Khenin 2000: 69, 72; Scott 1990: 70–84, 198–201). The second views hegemony as a wide, deep control that leaves place for tensions and struggles. But these skirmishes remain in the boundaries of the hegemonic order; they are articulated by principles of the dominant mindset, or manifest original ideas through the hegemonic language (Khenin 2000: 69, 75–77; Scott 1985: 326). This latter view of hegemony can explain how workers' committees tend to take market reality for granted (and therefore focus on the mitigation of its damages), and also how the stewards can develop subversive ideas but wrap them in the terms of the business world. Neoliberalism has the clear features of a political movement since its vision is not confined to running the economy but also includes the ambition to transform government, individual morality, education, welfare, labour relations, and so forth. However, the power and legitimacy of neoliberal hegemony is dependent upon denial of its political character. Neoliberal assumptions and rhetoric appear as objective, technical, or scientifically true. Here the prominence of professional knowledge, jargon, and experts becomes crucial—we are expected to accept instructions without questioning— and at the same time there is de-legitimation of the public arena, political sphere, and representative institutions (Jessop 2002: 467–469; Peck and Tickell 2002: 398). The outcome is that resistance to neoliberal order, no matter how oppressive and full of contradictions it is, remains non-radical and local. It does not change the system (Peck and Tickell 2002: 399–401). We can understand the range of the reactions of workers' committees to neoliberal reality in this context: from negotiating (or fighting) for the minimum that workers can receive in inferior conditions to fighting for 'more' and suggesting radical solutions, but staying within the boundaries of the neoliberal economic-cultural system.

The second issue to consider in explaining the research findings pertains to the history and character of labour unions. From their outset, trade unions have not always been considered as revolutionary, creating controversy not only among capitalists but also among socialists. Radical socialists saw trade unions as accepting—or cooperating with—the capitalist order. Lenin contended that when left alone, the working class is bound to stay within 'trade union consciousness', which means it fights to improve its working conditions without changing the system (Filc 2006: 202). Therefore, radical Marxists saw unions as too compromising. According to this explanation, workers' committees have missed their calling as agents of social change.

I argue that this view ignores the vitality and independent logic of workers' committees. Committee stewards should not be seen as submissive in their essence, nor treated as if their consciousness is necessarily false. In a way, we cannot judge them for their consent to 'recovery' measures or for the limited scope of their goals. Their problem is not a matter of essence, but is structural:

> If their consciousness can be said to be false, it is at least realistic—it reflects the realities of power at their workplace. If their consciousness is

false, it may not be so much because of the hegemony of another class over the cultural apparatus or their ability to shape ideas that form culture. It is because the capitalist class has the power to shape the daily lives of workers in their workplaces. Workers encode these realities as patterns of thought, culture. (Durrenberger 2002: 101–102)

The conclusion, therefore, is that class-consciousness is not separate from concrete reality, but at the same time it is not automatically determined by this reality. It is generated when real conditions meet the cultural tool-kit (Swidler 1986). Cultural work is needed to constitute the working class (or any other class) as a subject. In this respect, the ultimate success of the neoliberal project is the ability to transform its particular truths into universals. One of the ways to do this is to nurture organic intellectuals.

There are a number of prevalent types of intellectuals. Critical intellectuals judge social order from an external point of view without being involved in the community. Traditional intellectuals introduce to the public the character and virtues of social order that no longer exist. And finally, organic intellectuals are integrated into the fabric of community life, therefore articulating the reality experienced by the collective, putting it into context and providing a wide explanation for it. Organic intellectuals have a critical role in transforming the potential collective subjectivity into a real one. They do so by facilitating the constitution of intersubjective cultural truth (Filc 2006: 199–220).

The ultimate success of the hegemonic project is dependent upon nurturing the strata of organic intellectuals who are active in various cultural fields. The neoliberal project has been more than successful in this aspiration. Jamie Peck and Adam Tickell (2002: 380) defined neoliberalism as the 'ideological software' for the establishment of the global capitalist order. It does this by instilling the values, assumptions, and interpretation of the neoliberal ideology in business schools, churches, mass media, and so on. This way, the particular culture that serves the giant corporations and financial world has become accepted as universal and neutral.

In this context, we can also understand the adaptive, as well as subversive, worldview and practices of workers' committees in Israel. Their exposure to the activity of neoliberal organic intellectuals can explain why they treat the market as natural and deterministic, perceive ideological issues as technical, and prefer business professional experts over political action (Filc 2006: 221). Even as they developed alternative thoughts, these remained confined to the boundaries of the neoliberal tool-kit. It appears, then, that grassroots resistance to neoliberalism exists, but there is still a vacuum in socialist organic intellectuals. Anthropology, sociology, history, and other fields do provide critical and traditional intellectuals that analyze social order from an external point of view. Yet, these do not infiltrate workers' daily lives. The lack of socialist organic intellectuals is therefore conspicuous in Israel, especially when considering its recent history.

Israel's modern nation, economy, and state were shaped under the strong influence of the Zionist labour movement. Though the Zionist Labour movement was criticized for being more nationalist than socialist, it was still successful, particularly in its early days, in nurturing a strata of organic intellectuals: that is, popular philosophers, writers, educational figures, newspapers, and many others (Filc 2006: 220). Therefore, one of the major causes for the decline of that movement was the diminishing of its intellectual enterprise. Even at the peak of its hegemony, the Israeli labour movement had major deficiencies: for example, it failed to nurture a strong trade union wing (Shalev 1996). Nevertheless, the labour movement did provide a cultural tool-kit that influenced the mindset and vocabulary not only of its constituency but also of the public (Khenin 2004: 131). Not much was left of this enterprise in the first decade of the twenty-first century, so workers committees used the only tool-kit available (Nissim and De Vries 2017), thus expressing the most subversive thoughts against capitalist logic in capitalist terms.

After this time, although a grassroots working-class resistance continued to exist, class struggles tended to be tactical (and not strategic): in a sense, this fight was incorporated by the body it resisted, was nurtured by its materials, and searched for the opportunities it enabled (De Certeau 1984). It is a resistance that recognizes its limits and does not challenge the existing order (Scott 1976, 1985: 326).

EPILOGUE

This chapter introduces a working class that is controlled, in the deepest way, by the system of capital accumulation. Workers' committees are enmeshed in the cultural world that oppresses them. Struggles are local and limited in scope, and though some have produced radical seeds, these have not led to radical action. In the current Israeli context we see that, as in many other countries, social unrest has also come to Israel. A new nationwide radical union, *Koach La Ovdim*, has emerged, challenging the Histadrut and stimulating it to be more active and innovative. After decades of stagnation, new spontaneous workers organizations are arising in work places, affiliating themselves with the national unions. Socialist content and rhetoric is back again. However, these new trends are incoherent and incomplete. The neoliberal order, accompanied by the strengthening of nationalist-religious political ideologies, is far from collapse. But more research is needed to investigate these new developments.

References

Bareli, A., D. Gutwein, and T. Friling. 2005. Society and Economy in Israel: A Historical and Political Overview. In *Society and Economy in Israel: Historical and Contemporary Perspectives*, ed. A. Bareli, D. Gutwein, and T. Friling, 1–5. Beer Sheva: Yad Izhak Ben-Zvi Press, Ben-Gurion Institute, Ben-Gurion University of the Negev. (in Hebrew).

Burawoy, M. 1979. *Manufacturing Consent—Changes in the Labor Process Under Monopoly Capitalism*. Chicago and London: The University of Chicago Press.

De Certeau, M. 1984. *The Practice of Everyday Life*. Berkeley and Los Angeles: University of California Press.

Durrenberger, E.P. 2002. Structure, Thought, and Action: Stewards in Chicago Union Locals. *American Anthropologist* 104 (1): 93–105.

Durrenberger, E.P., and D. Doukas. 2008. Gospel of Wealth, Gospel of Work: Counterhegemony in the U.S. Working Class. *American Anthropologist* 110 (2): 214–224.

Eriksen, T.H. 2014. *Globalization: The Key Concepts*. London and New York: Bloomsbury Academics.

Filc, D. 2006. *Hegemony and Populism in Israel*. Tel Aviv: Resling. (in Hebrew).

Fourcade-Gourinchas, M., and S.L. Babb. 2002. The Rebirth of the Liberal Creed: Paths to Neoliberalism in Four Countries. *American Journal of Sociology* 108 (3): 533–579.

Harvey, D. 2005. *A Brief History of Neoliberalism*. Oxford and New York: Oxford University Press.

Jessop, B. 2002. Liberalism, Neoliberalism, and Urban Governance: A State Theoretical Perspective. *Antipode* 34 (3): 452–472.

Khenin, D. 2000. Freedom from Welfare: Hegemony and Resistance at the End of the Twentieth Century. In *Distributive Justice in Israel*, ed. M. Mautner, 69–76. Tel Aviv: Ramot. (in Hebrew).

Khenin, D. 2004. From Working Class Israel to the Second Israel: Discourse and Social Policy in 1950's Mapai. In *The Power of Property: Israeli Society in the Global Age*, ed. D. Filc and U. Ram, 131–163. Jerusalem and Tel Aviv: Van Leer Jerusalem Institute and Hakibbutz Hameuchad Publishing House. (in Hebrew).

Nissim, G., and D. De Vries. 2017. Rhetoric of Decline in a Neo-liberal Context: Workers' Committees and the Decline of Labor in Contemporary Israel. *Israel Studies* 22 (1): 165–188. https://doi.org/10.2979/israelstudies.22.1.07.

Peck, J., and A. Tickell. 2002. Neoliberalizing Space. *Antipode* 34 (3): 380–404.

Peleg, E. 2005. *Privatization as Publicization: Privatized Bodies in Public Law.* Tel Aviv: Ramot. (in Hebrew).

Scott, J.C. 1976. *The Moral Economy of the Peasant: Rebellion and Subsistence in Southeast Asia.* New Haven and London: Yale University Press.

Scott, J.C. 1985. *Weapons of the Weak: Everyday Forms of Peasant Resistance.* New Haven and London: Yale University Press.

Scott, J.C. 1990. *Domination and the Art of Resistance: Hidden Transcripts.* New Haven and London: Yale University Press.

Shalev, M. 1996. The Labor Movement in Isreal: Ideology and Political Economy. In *The Social History of Labor in the Middle East*, ed. E.J. Goldberg, 131–161. Boulder, CO: Westview.

Sklair, L. 2009. The Transnational Capitalist Class: Theory and Empirical Research. In *European Economic Elites: Between a New Spirit of Capitalism and the Erosion of State Socialism*, ed. F. Sattler and C. Boyer, 497–522. Berlin: Duncker & Humblot.

Spyridakis, M. 2017. Labor Struggles in the Shipbuilding Industry of Piraeus. In *Uncertain Times: Anthropological Approaches to Labor in a Neoliberal World*, ed. P. Durrenberger, 161–183. Boulder: University of Colorado Press.

Standing, G. 2011. *The Precariat: The New Dangerous Class.* London and New York: Bloomsbury Academics.

Swidler, A. 1986. Culture in Action: Symbols and Strategies. *American Sociological Review* 51 (2): 273–286.

Thompson, E.P. 1971. The Moral Economy of the English Crowd in the Eighteenth Century. *Past and Present* 50: 76–136.

CHAPTER 11

Sport, the Market and Society: Contrasting the Rhetoric and Reality of Sport as a Growth Catalyst

Iain Lindsay

Hosting Sports mega events promises intensive urban regeneration, transformation of space and the importation of catalytic market growth. For aspiring hosts willing to play the games required for selection this is a powerful and attractive proposition. If successfully harnessed, the diverse benefits sporting events deliver can be articulated across a diversity of socio-economic indicators that can be used to demonstrate the vitality and image of the host. Consequently, sport has long been used to underpin and enhance diverse and significant social and economic development strategy. However, sport-driven development must be defined, isolated, and contextualised appropriately to enable any meaningful projections, extrapolations, or evaluations of its impact to occur.

After a mega-event host is selected, the conceptual framework of sport-driven growth, or legacy, inevitably evolves and transforms from conceptualisation to delivery, to the post-event legacy milieu, with each concomitant transition eroding the original idealisation. Well-constructed sport brings unparalleled socio-economic growth;

I. Lindsay (✉)
ICSS Enterprise, International Centre for Sport Security, London, UK

© The Author(s) 2018
M. Spyridakis (ed.), *Market Versus Society*, Palgrave Studies in Urban Anthropology, https://doi.org/10.1007/978-3-319-74189-5_11

however, when delivered poorly, the sport-driven growth model articulates, creates, defines and unifies during the bidding phase but prohibits, marginalises and cleanses during the delivery phase; and ultimately damages both confidence and trust whilst draining resources during the after-event legacy period. In recent times the much-heralded notion of sport-event legacies has become increasingly questionable, particularly in relation to perceptions of return on investment and the wider socio-economic benefits. Drawing upon extensive ethnographic research, this chapter unravels this complex milieu.

SPORTING LEGACY: THE IMMACULATE CONCEPTION

This chapter will use arguably the greatest prize in all of sports—the 'Olympic legacy'—as a proxy to contextualise the constructs and contestations that underpin sports' catalytic role within socio-economic development. It will begin by establishing why hosting the Olympic Games in the contemporary climate is inseparable from socio-economic growth—therein defined as the 'Olympic legacy'. Focus will then be placed upon the transitions various stakeholders, processes, and articulations that the Olympic legacy undergoes during the distinct phases of the Olympic paradigm. It will then consider the rhetoric and reality of the Olympic Games as a catalytic primer for post-event growth and offer conclusions.

OLYMPIC LEGACY

When one crystallises conceptualisations of the Olympic legacy prior to its implementation it can be defined as the beneficial outcomes that are projected to occur as a direct result of hosting the Olympic Games. These after-effects are synonymous with allegory, hope, anticipation, meaning, and symbolism. The Olympic legacy implements a systematic, four-phased growth implementation process that evolves from bid, to delivery, to event hosting to legacy implementation. Each phase has its own key stakeholders and the transition from one to another can often modify what came before.

The one constant in this process is that the final goal is always ostensibly and deferentially branded 'Olympic legacy' with critical evaluation and tangible causation analyses often offset by the positivistic lens of the associated sporting event. The opportunity to attain an Olympic legacy is awarded to the victors of an International Olympic Committee (IOC)-governed bidding contest that plays out between prospective host cities. This is the most significant of all Olympic events wherein each city is required to describe how the event will be used to deliver a diversity of socio-economic benefits through their direct involvement—thus articulating a city-specific edition of a larger Olympic legacy paradigm.

This contest of competing legacy conceptualisations ensures a game of brinkmanship with focus placed upon both sports and non-sports—related outcomes that are framed as achievable only through Olympic hosting. This association has led to the term legacy becoming both self-evident and a means of justifying and legitimising the costs of bidding for and hosting the Olympic Games. Accordingly, sporting legacy evolved over recent years to be commonly portrayed as a panacea to address any and all shortfalls of a host city.

The IOC, which is positioned as legacy gatekeepers, is singularly responsible for making the ultimate decision regarding who will host the Olympic Games, with candidates being evaluated exclusively against their own bespoke criteria. To be considered a viable nominee, all potential hosts must present a detailed plan of why they would create the most appropriate next chapter of the on-going Olympic narrative. To enable a coherent plan that theoretically fulfils these criteria, each host is permitted by the IOC to spend up to $25 million on their Olympic campaign (Hill 1996). According to the director of communications and public affairs for London's 2012 bid Mike Lee (2006) the figure stood at approximately £30 million ($48 million) some ten years later. As such, grand conceptualisations of Olympic legacies that attribute their source to the Games and the IOC have become prerequisites for successful Olympic bids.

This raises an important question: how does a sporting organisation evolve to attain such a sociopolitically impactful role whereby governments, world leaders, globally renowned figures, and vast swathes of the populous compete for the rights to pay to host a sporting event and dedicate the glory back to the overarching entity for their benevolence?

THE INTERNATIONAL OLYMPIC COMMITTEE (IOC)

The IOC, founded in 1894, is the organisational body for not just a sporting event but for an entire Olympic Movement. Its foundation is attributable to French nobleman Baron Pierre de Coubertin, whose philosophical ideals were the basis for a set of guidelines that led to its creation, embodied in something known as the Olympic Charter. The

Olympic Charter is a set of rules and guidelines for the organisation of the Olympic Games and Olympic governance. It is a codification of the fundamental principles, rules, and laws of the Olympic Movement. These guidelines, whilst well intentioned were extremely vague, very poorly defined, and lacked the rigid identity commonly associated with such a significant global organisation. Yet, as Nigel Crowther (2001), director of the international centre for Olympic studies, states, what was clear from its outset was that the IOC had aspirations that extended far beyond sport:

> The goal of the Olympic Movement is to contribute to building a peaceful and better world by educating youth through sport practiced without discrimination of any kind, in a spirit of friendship, solidarity and fair play. (Olympic Charter, Rule 1)

The Olympic Movement was and is defined by its fundamental goals, which are:

- Promoting sport and competitions through the intermediary of national and international sports institutions worldwide.
- Co-operating with public and private organisations to place sport at the service of mankind.
- Assisting to develop 'Sport for All'.
- Seeking to advance women in sport at all levels and in all structures, with a view to achieving equality between men and women.
- Opposing all forms of commercial exploitation of sport and athletes.
- Pursuing the fight against doping.
- Promoting sports ethics and fair play.
- Raising awareness of environmental problems.
- Facilitating financial and educational support for developing countries through the IOC institution Olympic Solidarity. (The IOC)

The ostensible use of this altruistic dissemination of a peaceful, inclusive message ensured that the IOC differed from other global sporting organisations. This is because they use their sporting event to promote principles that are applicable not only to the sporting context but also more broadly, as a moral ideology for life. These are collectively referred to as the Olympic Ideals, or Olympism (Muller 2000; Schaffer and Smith 2000; Bale and Christensen 2004; Parry 2006; Girginov 2010).

The IOC have no geographical ties and have always been free to select whichever city/nation they deem to be the most favourable 'political, financial and social regime' (Forster and Pope 2004) to further their movement.

Interestingly, Wamsley (2004) has described Olympism as a 'metaphoric empty flask'; able to merge seamlessly with whichever orientation is advantageous for its prosperity ranging from Nazism (Berlin 1936) to Green issues (Sydney 2000) to wholesale urban renewal (London 2012). This orientation bears credence to the statement made by Olympic critic Lenskyj (1996), who suggested that 'it appears the rhetoric about keeping politics out of sport has been replaced by the explicit politicising of the bid process'. Intuitively it appears that historical ties to fascism, corruption, politicisation, and commercialisation would be significant threats to the legitimacy of the IOC as an organisation and Olympism as an ideology, but this is rarely questioned.

One can surmise that this chameleon-esque *modus operandi* has served the IOC and its partners extremely well. A plethora of evidence suggests that the combination of advantageously selected hosts and the careful cultivation of powerful commercial partners has ensured that the growth and influence of the IOC increased exponentially from a relatively minor organisation to the globally significant incarnation we see today (Real 1996; Whitson 1998; Smith and Schaffer 2000; Barney et al. 2002; Ritchie 2002). The quest for global significance remains an ongoing pursuit, which has seen the IOC use and extend the outreach and impact of the Olympic Games and their legacy as a means of promoting itself as an organisation, their sponsors, and, concomitantly, enhancing the allegory of Olympism. Indeed, this was clearly evident with the selection of London as host of the 2012 edition.

The London 2012 Bid

As we have seen, Olympic legacy is intrinsic to any Olympic bid. Consequently, Olympic bidding must involve myriad stakeholders because of the size, significance, and complexity of the legacy milieu. The decision for London to bid for the 2012 games ultimately rested with the United Kingdom's then-Prime Minister, Tony Blair, and certain key members of his Cabinet. That said, all Olympic bids must be backed and fully supported by national and local governments, who will—in theory—be held accountable for their decisions through the electoral system.

Trepidation around the decision to invest significant resources into a speculative Olympic bid is entirely understandable; the Olympic bidding process requires decisions to be made far in advance of the event. These projections will then be subject to all manner of unpredictable increases, in recent times this has been particularly evident in the field of the Games' security. Additionally, the imposing Olympic timeframe for bids to be constructed, evaluated, and submitted ensures the decision-making process is somewhat fluid.

The Olympic Games offer the potential to supercharge socio-political agendas. Thus, an otherwise unpalatable and unaffordable super-sized regenerative process becomes intertwined with Olympic euphoria and Games-related acceptance of change. This climate ensures that those deciding whether to bid for an Olympics must do so whilst negotiating a concomitant fear of missing out on a once-in-a-political lifetime opportunity for their political reign to be empowered and illuminated by the Olympic Torch. These contested narratives provide a crucial underpinning to a potential Olympic hosts' decision-making process.

That said, numbers must always be available to justify decision-making; however, in relation to Olympic bidding, projections of hosting costs are a highly contentious domain. It has been argued that traditional mechanisms used to project mega-event costs are flawed, with estimates lacking realism, habitually underestimating financial contingencies, and significantly undervaluing safety and environmental costs (Merrow 1988; Flyvbjerg et al. 2003). Other more unforgiving interpretations of the commonality of underestimates include allegations that estimates often systematically and deceptively hide the real costs of construction until the project has begun (Fussey et al. 2011).

This scepticism was validated in relation to the predicted costs of the London 2012 Games, where cost projections rapidly escalated from £1.8 billion to eventually reaching £9.3 billion. After each incremental rise was scrutinised it was systematically revealed that previous incarnations failed to consider basic key items such as costs of purchasing land, upgrading transport facilities, security, project risks, and inflation. As a point of note, in 2013, following the Olympic and Paralympic Games the combined final budget was publicly announced to £8.77 billion, although anecdotal accounts suggest even this was a great underestimate when all security costs are factored in.

As we know the British politicians ultimately decided that the London 2012 Olympics would be strategically beneficial for their political aspirations and went ahead with the bid. Thus began the transition from the London 2012 concept to definition, engagement, and ultimately delivery. At each stage the baton is passed to various newly created, short-term bodies to navigate a compartmentalised part of the Olympic hosting process—Olympic delivery, hosting and legacy implementation—before ceasing to exist. Despite an Olympic bid reaching the inertia point as an almost entirely political decision, once a bid is officially underway politicians inevitably begin distancing themselves from it until the event itself. Problematically, notions of public accountability and democratic process habitually disappear with them.

This transition saw London's legacy evolve in an attempt to win over the IOC. As Mike Lee outlined the London 2012 framework for the bidding campaign:

> It was essentially like an international political campaign. We needed to understand our audiences and develop a global election manifesto. Building domestic support was important but it was just one part of the game. At times this made us unpopular with the wider group of stakeholders who felt we should have been paying closer attention to their demands. But we were clearly focused on the objective and that was to win in Singapore ... We also set about developing key themes that we could reinforce through presentations and communications events. The core elements were regeneration of the East End of London, the diversity of London, the legacy of the Games, use of London's landmark iconic sites and what the Olympics could offer British and world sport. Finally, and this was just as vital to our success, we had to get the best use of the star personalities connected to the bid ... For us that was always the question we came back to – how can we develop a campaign that will attract votes and give us a chance of winning. (Lee 2006)

As can be intimated from the above quote, the focus of those charged with constructing and selling the London 2012 bid was to create an offering that would resonate with the IOC with the priority to win the bid by any means necessary, which they eventually achieved. This brings to the fore the question of whether London's Olympic *legacy* was simply a means to win votes and influence delegates to win the bidding contest rather than being a maximal fit-for-purpose growth generator. Moreover, from the perspective of post-event evaluation, what precisely had London's legacy become as a result of this new strategic direction?

Legacy: London 2012

London's bid was built on a special Olympic vision. That vision of an Olympic Games that would not only be a celebration of sport but a force for regeneration. The Games will transform one of the poorest and most deprived areas of London. They will create thousands of jobs and homes. They will offer new opportunities for business in the immediate area and throughout London. (Straw 2005)

Ostensible, tangible, and demonstrable public support for London 2012—integral to any Olympic bid—was secured through assurances of legacy outcomes that would directly benefit the community. In essence, it was a simple exchange: public support for post-Games benefit. These legacy commitments made to Londoners were:

- Increasing opportunities for Londoners to become involved in sport.
- Ensuring Londoners benefit from new jobs, business and volunteering opportunities.
- Transforming the heart of East London
- Delivering a sustainable Games and developing sustainable communities.
- Showcasing London as a diverse, inclusive, creative and welcoming city.

London's hosting of the 2012 Olympic Games would deliver an intensive process of Olympic-related urban regeneration. This would see extensive visions of ordered and cleansed space being articulated during its delivery. The urban cleansing would transform long-standing area of diversity and deprivation into a utopian 'Olympic city'. All would be winners; housing would improve, accessibility to this locale would be enhanced, the various medical and social malaise that typified the East of the Metropolis would be addressed and the sporting chances afforded the multicultural youth that made up the borough's population would be without parallel in the UK.

Legacy was portrayed as a panacea to address the significant economic, social, and political issues of the most impoverished parts of the host city. This outcome revolved around the consideration that the Olympic Games facilitate a regenerative juncture based upon an assumption that all shared the same opinion of what constituted a 'better life'. Furthermore, one had to assume that all living in the area under consideration had the ability to take advantage of the opportunities presented therein. Paradoxically, Fussey et al., purport that regional and economic 'legacy' benefits can often be seen to exacerbate social disadvantage and inequality rather than remedy it; however, this would not be measurable until long after the event and was not a view that entered the public consciousness at this time (Fussey et al. 2011).

The application of this articulation of legacy fortified the 2012 Games with purpose. It transformed them from a sporting event into a special-purpose vehicle ostensibly capable of delivering not only votes but also myriad beneficial outcomes that extended far beyond the sporting domain. This association is by no means particular to London 2012 and it is variously repackaged and reimagined to enable legacy to become a means of justifying and legitimising the costs of bidding for, and hosting, sporting events the world over.

Post-Olympic London: Utopia or Bust?

The London 2012 Olympic Games have been widely considered as a great success and we are now entering the era of post-Olympic legacy evaluation. Through hindsight the nature of 2012 Olympic delivery followed an easy-to-understand narrative of reclamation. It has been argued that during the post-Games period the less affluent and/or minority multi-ethnic communities who bordered the space of the Olympic Park became subject to increased regulation, surveillance, policing techniques, and displacement to ensure the was area suitable for the habitation of the future populace (Gibbons and Wolff 2012; Paton et al. 2012). However, the reality was that this process began much earlier—during Olympic delivery. This was perhaps best exemplified by their vilification by then head of the Olympic Park Legacy Company (OPLC), Andrew Altman, who dubbed East London's pre-Olympic landscape a 'gash' that required 'Olympic healing' (Armstrong et al. 2011).

It was difficult to argue against the fact that the location surrounding the Olympic Park required regeneration (Newham). Government figures revealed that approximately 30% of the London borough of Newham would move internally or externally each year.[1] Such movement translated to a hugely 'root-less' population that saw the borough as a place of transit and transience, little more than a stop on a journey elsewhere. If, as some argue, place-related identities, relations and histories are formed and asserted via uniformity (Korpela 1989; Johnston et al. 1994), the absence of such identity-affirming uniformity leads to the consideration that the application of Auge's conceptualisation of the 'non-place' to Newham was pertinent. Auge argued that if a 'place' can be defined as relational, historical, and concerned with identity, then a space that cannot be defined as such must be a 'non-place' (Augé 1995).

The tactics adopted for Newham's rebranding provides insight into the nature of how a long-established neighbourhood, synonymous with poverty and deprivation, can be re-packaged and re-branded on a global scale through the use of the mega-event. Interestingly, attempts to sell this diverse, deprived area literally and metaphorically have arisen at a precarious political juncture wherein the UK housing market was suffering turbulence and the fiscal policy of the UK government was increasingly intolerant of those citizens who are dependent on state benefits for their housing costs.

In the post-2012 transitional landscape, the microlevel outcomes of larger delivery processes facilitate a re-negotiation of place-identity and place-ownership. This fosters an environment oriented toward attracting a future affluent population whilst vilifying the pre-Games community. It can be concluded that attempts to re-imagine a deprived location as a post-Olympic utopia that concomitantly empowers pre-Olympic locals and enables prosperous and educated families may be intrinsically flawed, or at the very least requires a significant maturation period.

Problems with Measurement

The nature of relatively short Olympic delivery windows (7 years) and the hyperbolic legacy narratives that permeate legacy discourse ensures unreasonable expectations. Olympic regeneration is both narrative and momentum and ensures a variety of collateral investments (Gratton 2008). Inevitably, this increases property desirability and accompanies

[1] https://www.gov.uk/government/uploads/system/uploads/attachment_data/file/6331/5231109.pdf.

a process of gentrification. The 2012 bidding process saw London's Olympic legacy sold to the UK in general and Londoners in particular as a two-fold stimulus. Short-term gains during the delivery process and long-term gains as a result of a post-Games inheritance.

It is within the post-Games milieu that such presumptive trajectories must be quantified in both social and economic senses, that is to say, its impact must (or at least should) be empirically measured, contextualised by comparative analyses underpinned by established city regeneration market logic and then contrasted against bidding promises and budgets to adequately measure its impact and inform future Games' impact analyses. It can be argued that evaluating the impact of hosting the Olympic Games can be measured in terms of redressing the rent gap of a deprived but potentially valuable location—this was certainly the case in London, with the Games located in a deprived location that lay within an easy commute of The City. The term rent gap refers to the shortfall between the actual economic return taken from an area of land given its present land use (capitalised ground rent) and the potential return it would yield if it were put to its optimal, highest, and best use (potential ground rent). As a rent gap increases, it creates lucrative opportunities for developers, investors, homebuyers, and local governments to orchestrate a shift in land use—for instance, from working-class residential to middle- or upper-class residential or high-end commercial (Smith 1979; Lees et al. 2008).

The 2012 Olympics ensured that the geographies within the proximities of the Olympic regeneration would yield higher returns from its land in the form of rents and property values and as result it has, and will continue to, attract new, more affluent residents to the area. This benefit was intended to help alleviate the plethora of social issues that signified this borough as one of the most deprived in Britain. This consideration rested upon the assumption that benefits would trickle-down to the lower and working-classes in a manner similar to the housing market; however, there is a body of research that indicates these anticipated benefits are often completely captured only by the middle and upper-classes (Holcomb and Beauregard 1981).

That being said, sport in general and the Olympics in particular deliver a nuanced, complex regenerative juncture that ideally requires an as yet to be defined mechanism to adequately quantify. Accounts of sport as a sector should delineate the GDP generated by every type of sports-related activity to enable a base line that could then be monitored against specific events, interventions, or catalysts to extrapolate value and impact. This could then be expanded by isolating each component of legacy and attaching a universally agreed value to fluctuations from the previously defined baseline. Unfortunately, there is no consensus as to what precisely constitutes 'sport-related activity' and not all countries even track these types of data to begin with. Moreover, within nations that do attempt to define and measure the sports sector there are often significant differences in the industry classification used, which significantly limit comparability studies between Olympic Games. It should therefore be no surprise that academics such as Kuper and Szymanski suggest the true impact of mega-events might be entirely intangible. The most apparent measurement issue lies in the fact that as a global society we cannot adequately define or measure what sport actually is, so how can we ever truly aspire to quantify the impact of a sporting event?

The most common means of analysing cross-national economic data within the European Union (EU) is through NACE (Nomenclature statistique des activites economiques dans la Communaute europeenne) data, which provides an interesting diversion. NACE data evaluates economic activity using evidence that comes from statistical classification of economic activities within key sectors of the economy. Problematically, NACE data currently fails to provide enough granularity to appropriately quantify, measure, or evaluate sport as a sector. This limits any meaningful analyses of the sports sector and consequently limits our understanding of not only hosting sporting events but beyond this to wider understanding of the relationships between sport and the rest of the economy.

Ultimately, at the current juncture impacts of legacy are difficult to define, troublesome to measure, and almost impossible to isolate. This issue is made all the more complex because of the fact that there is more to hosting than economic gains. Indeed, to reflect upon the London 2012 legacy, focus was placed upon economic growth, regeneration, sport engagement, and community engagement. This multilayering of legacies did much to assist London in its objective to win the bid, but ensured that quantifying the impact of the Games and evaluating the realism of the claims is enormously difficult to execute.

This is clearly problematic because the design and marketing of ambitious, multi-dimensional, expensive, and significant growth strategies that resonate on multiple levels of socio-economic growth are extremely risky and provide little likelihood that they will ever be able to be sufficiently quantified in relation to impact or expenditure. As a society we must become better at designing and implementing mechanisms capable of justifying hosting expenses for sporting events, offsetting security costs, and ultimately understanding the size, composition, and impact of an Olympic Games in relation to socio-economic growth.

Until we can achieve this understanding, the limited insights we gain from one mega-event may simply not be comparable to another. This inevitably leads to the widespread absence of meaningful cross-comparable reliable and standardised data to permit in-depth projections, justifications, or analysis that is meaningful for policy makers, transparent for stakeholders, or fit for research purposes. Most notably, it appears that in the contemporary climate this lack of good data is having a direct impact upon the bidding inclinations and processes around potential sporting mega-event hosts.

Aborted Olympic Bids

A recent example of this hard data lacuna can be found in the aborted Boston Olympic bid for the 2024 Olympic Games. The narratives on this aborted bid show how deeply embedded the absence of good data is and how this has caused the perception of the value and impact of sport-driven growth to diminish in recent years. This in turn becomes manifest by significant and vocal opposition to sports-driven growth strategies, which ultimately causes bids to fail.

In 2015 the United States Olympic Committee (USOC) named Boston as their candidate city for the 2024 Summer Olympic Games. Newly elected Massachusetts Governor Charlie Baker hailed the selection of Boston as 'an exciting opportunity to promote Massachusetts on the world stage'. The nature of a newly elected political regime looking to the Olympic Games to attain credibility, traction, and investment resonates with the political climate in the UK during the London 2012 bid. Olympic hosting and newly elected politicians are likely bedfellows by virtue of supercharged catalytic potential that comes with the Games.

Problematically, Olympic bidding can also be highly problematic for politicians if there is a lack of sufficient support to bolster an embryonic bid or justify projected costs. In the case of Boston 2024, there was a distinct inability to convince the populous that their Olympic bid would not adversely impact upon perceptibly more important priorities like health care, education, and infrastructure.

Opposition to the Boston Olympic bid was swift, vocal, and significant. Arguably the most notable of the organised opposition was the volunteer-led No Boston Olympics campaign. Despite Boston 2024 purporting a previously powerful Olympic legacy cocktail of jobs, housing, and community development, it could not reassure the public that investing the initial costs of hosting the games in anticipation of future returns was a risk worth taking. Though small, and by no means unique, No Boston Olympics had a significant effect on the public debate around the Boston Olympics—largely a result of an effective social media strategy, something that previous anti-Olympic movements did not have access to and perhaps a testament of what is to come.

Ultimately, the Boston bid formally ended on July 27, 2015, when the USOC withdrew its support based on flagging public and political support. The USOC cited low poll numbers as the primary cause of the breakup with Boston 2024. However, concerns around budget, roles, and responsibilities were also cited with Boston 2024, proposing an Olympic operating budget of $4.6 billion and depending upon projections of circa $4 billion from private developers, not to mention the US federal government being expected to invest $1 billion or more for security. Arguably, a final standoff between the Boston mayor and the USOC over a refusal to sign a host city guarantee—a promise that Boston would cover any cost overruns—ended the bid.

To contextualise this within the existing literature on sports mega-events, there is a body of work that suggests Boston made the right choice to abort due to a lack of sufficient measurement methodologies to isolate 'the specific impact of sport'; there are relatively few positive economic benefits of mega-event hosting. Moreover, if mega-events are hosted within an isolated Olympic Park, as was the case with London, the precise breakdown of who accrues residual benefit is further brought into question. Other economists are concerned with the impacts and re-usability of the expensive and highly specialised sports infrastructure required to be a viable host. Velodromes and Olympic stadiums are filled during the Summer Olympics, but these then require expensive conversions or risk becoming white elephants, as is the case in Athens amongst others.

LIFE THROUGH AN OLYMPIC LENS

It is abundantly clear that measuring an Olympic legacy is a complex, difficult, and multi-faceted affair but nonetheless, attempts must be made to isolate, assess, and evaluate deliverables As each Olympic Games can be considered an episode of a larger Olympic narrative, a Games can easily be amalgamated into shared history that is heavily punctuated with sport and competition. But each occurrence of the Olympic Games is also an isolated, stand-alone event with outcomes directly contrasted against all earlier conceptualisations of legacy that were articulated throughout the entire bidding and delivery process. Only once this process becomes the norm can accurate and dependable analyses and projections of future Olympic legacies be formed.

As we have already established, in the contemporary climate defining and projecting grand visions of diverse Olympic legacies is integral to winning the rights to host; however, quantifying precisely how these are to be measured, quantified, evaluated, and ensured leaves much to be desired. The selection process needs to prioritise the after-Games steak as much as the pre-Games sizzle. By constructing the best mechanisms for evaluation inclusive of a means to ensure accountability for legacy implementation, global faith in the efficacy of sports-driven growth can be renewed.

It can be argued that the key issues that threaten the perceptions of sport as a meaningful growth catalyst revolve around the lack of accountability and the differentiation between the rhetoric of pre-Olympic promises and the reality of after-Games legacy. At present the Olympic Games are awarded to those who can conceptualise the grandest vision, then design and convey the most engaging media strategy and stakeholder engagement campaign at the public, practitioner, and IOC levels. With the explosion of social media we have clearly entered an era where perception management has never been more fluid, accessible, or crucial in macro-level sociological terms. It is no different in the Olympic realm. Arguably, the most significant impact of social media is the ever-growing dependence upon, and faith in, minimally defined headline news, available 24/7. This evolution has seen the capacity and capability of the individual and the collective expand exponentially to enable them to influence narratives, debate, and policy in previously unforeseen ways.

Abridged information is now available through 24-hour news television and radio stations, the internet, Twitter and other forms of social media, permitting instantaneous access to a plethora of extremely current but depth-limited information, which is relied upon as a valuable source of truth. Integral to the above societal evolution are the notions of knowledge and power. Bourdieu's (1998) work *On Television and Journalism* highlights the follies of this means of knowledge processing.

The main theme of his work is the means with which television constructs and produces news, information, and debate in abridged forms. Condensing the news into bite-sized snippets has, he argues, made it impossible for journalists to conduct any meaningful analysis; they are constrained by issues of time and effect. Because of this Bourdieu elucidates news as pared back and less concerned with factual depth and more concerned with catching a viewer's attention. This is achieved through the use of buzzwords that disseminate a specific narrative without any substance, raising the key question that underpins this chapter: is one such buzzword Olympic 'legacy'? Problematically, until new evaluator mechanisms are defined and implemented throughout Olympic delivery and legacy implementation this question will remain almost impossible to answer.

Conclusion

Any study of Olympic legacy is, at its heart, an examination of the transition of multi-faceted complex and evolving environments. The discussions speak to deep-rooted significance and dichotomies of sport-led urban regeneration, the symbolism of identity, the diverse implications of hyper-speed urban renewal and the almost impossible attempt to isolate one agent of change from another. Olympic delivery profoundly augments communities, urban change, identity, time, place, space, and the way in which these inter-relate, which has significant wider applicability for future regeneration processes.

The fact that so much modification is condensed into a relatively short seven-year Olympic delivery window ensures a period of hyper-regeneration. This is the key factor that differentiates sports-led regeneration from other forms. In addition, the sheer scope, magnitude and range of factors that permeate Olympic legacy makes this tremendously multi-faceted and complex. That said, commonalities permeate all regenerative process and within all urban regeneration.

The application of sporting legacy fortifies any societal change paradigm with arguably the greatest catalytic impetus of the contemporary era. The capability to empower and embolden large-scale regeneration and social change projects with the term legacy enables support, self-evident justification, faith, and fervour in varying degrees. This conceptualisation of post-Games reward places focus upon both sports and non sports-related outcomes that are perceived as achievable only through investment in a large-scale sporting event, most notably the Olympic Games, but the paradigm is also applicable to a diversity of other sporting examples.

This perception-based narrative provides the backdrop for the contestation that underpins the entire Olympic process. This worldwide contest is one of resources between global cities, which facilitate an unrelenting frenzy of urban regeneration. The commercialisation of a city ensures 'city space and architectural forms become consumer items or packaged environments that support and promote the circulation of goods' (Boyer 1988). Hosting the Olympic Games can provide an unambiguous boost to any city that aspires to win the global commercialisation contest; yet it must also be acknowledged that bidding to do so also delivers risk.

Legacy is expected to offset the cost and upheaval of delivery, and complimentary narratives permeate wider society, particularly the media, whenever hosting Games is debated. This chapter has demonstrated that the complex, inconsistent interplay between ideology, rhetoric, and evidence is causing Olympic evangelists to pause for thought. In a Durkheimian sense, the processes involved in Olympic hosting appear to hold functionality that augments the position of those imposing change, rather than the publicly articulated beneficiaries of legacy. Positivistic perception is often expected but it is only through repeated articulation that it resonates and eventually becomes reinforced. Failure to adequately do this results in bids that are aborted, as was the case with Boston. It can, therefore, be concluded that the Games will go on, but those articulating the legacy benefits may need to work harder to sell their grand visions beyond the IOC.

References

Armstrong, G., R. Hobbs, and I. Lindsay. 2011. Calling the Shots: The Pre-2012 London Olympic Contest. *Urban Studies* 48 (15): 3169–3184.

Augé, M. 1995. *Non-places: An Introduction to Supermodernity*. London: Verso.

Bale, J., and M. Christensen (eds.). 2004. *Post-Olympism? Questioning Sport in the Twenty-First Century*. Oxford: Berg.

Barney, R.K., S. Wenn, and S. Martyn. 2002. *Selling the Five Rings: The International Olympic Committee and the Rise of Olympic Commercialism*. Salt Lake City: The University of Utah Press.

Bourdieu, P. 1998. *On Television and Journalism*, trans. P.P. Ferguson. London: Pluto.

Boyer, M.C. 1988. The Return of Aesthetics to City Planning. *Society* 25 (4): 49–56.

Crowther, N.B. 2001. The Salt Lake City Games and the Ancient Olympics. *The International Journal of the History of Sport* 19: 169–178.

Flyvbjerg, B., N. Bruzelius, and W. Rotherngatter. 2003. *Megaprojects and Risk: An Anatomy of Ambition*. Cambridge: Cambridge University Press.

Forster, J., and N. Pope. 2004. *The Political Economy of Global Sporting Organisations*. London: Routledge.

Fussey, P., J. Coafee, G. Armstrong, and D. Hobbs. 2011. *Securing and Sustaining the Olympic City: Reconfiguring London for 2012 and Beyond*. Aldershot: Ashgate.

Gibbons, A. and N. Wolff. 2012. Games Monitor, Undermining the Hype of the London Olympics. *City: Analysis of Urban Trends, Culture, Theory, Policy, Action* 16 (4): 468–473.

Girginov, V. (ed.). 2010. *The Olympics: A Critical Reader*. London: Routledge.

Hill, C. 1996. *Olympic Politics: Athens to Atlanta 1896–1996*. Manchester: Manchester University Press.

Holcomb, H.B., and R.A. Beauregard. 1981. *Revitalizing Cities*. Washington, DC: Association of American Geographers.

Johnston, R.J., D. Gregory, and D.M. Smith (eds.). 1994. *The Dictionary of Human Geography*, 3rd ed. Oxford: Blackwell.

Korpela, K.M. 1989. Place-Identity as a Product of Environmental Self-regulation. *Journal of Environmental Psychology* 9: 241–256.

Lee, M. 2006. *The Race for the 2012 Olympics: The Inside Story of How London Won the Bid*. London: Virgin Books Ltd.

Lees, L., T. Slater, and E. Wyly (eds.). 2008. *The Gentrification Reader*. Oxon: Routledge.

Lenskyj, H.J. 1996. When Winners Are Losers: Toronto and Sydney Bids for the Summer Olympics. *Journal of Sport and Social Issues* 20 (4): 392–410.

Merrow, E.W. 1988. *Understanding the Outcomes of Megaprojects: A Quantitative Analysis of Very Large Civilian Projects*. Santa Monica, CA: The Rand Corporation.

Muller, N. (ed.). 2000. *Pierre de Coubertin, 1893–1937: Olympism, Selected Writings*. Lausanne: International Olympic Committee.

Parry, J. 2006. Sport and Olympism: Universals and Multiculturalism. *Journal of the Philosophy of Sport* 33: 188–204.

Paton, K., G. Mooney, and K. McKee. 2012. Class, Citizenship and Regeneration: Glasgow and the Commonwealth Games 2014. *Antipode* 44 (4): 1470–1489.

Real, M.R. 1996. The Post-modern Olympics: Technology and the Commodification of the Olympic Movement. *Quest* 48: 9–24.

Ritchie, I. 2002. Cool Rings: Olympic Ideology and the Symbolic Consumption of Global Sport. In *The Global Nexus Engaged: Sixth International Symposium for Olympic Research*, ed. K.B. Wamsley, R.K. Barney, and S.G. Marts, 61–70. London: University of Western Ontario.

Schaffer, K., and S. Smith. 2000. *The Olympics at the Millennium. Power, Politics, and the Games*. New Brunswick, NJ: Rutgers University Press.

Smith, N. 1979. Toward a Theory of Gentrification. In *The Gentrification Reader*, ed. L. Lees, T. Slater, and E. Wyly. Oxon: Routledge.

Smith, S., and K. Schaffer. 2000. *The Olympics at the Millennium: Performance, Politics and the Games*. New Brunswick, NJ: Rutgers University Press.

Straw in Hansard. 2005. *House of Commons Debates: London 2012 Olympic Bid*. Retrieved May 8, 2012, from http://www.theyworkforyou.com/debates/?id=2005-07-06a.404.0.

Wamsley, K.B. 2004. Laying Olympism to Rest. In *Post Olympism: Questioning Sport in the Twenty-First Century*, ed. J. Bale and M.K. Christiansen, 367–384. Oxford: Berg.

Whitson, D. 1998. Olympic Sport, Global Media and Cultural Diversity. In *Fourth International Symposium for Olympic Research*, ed. R.K. Barney, K.B. Wamsley, S.G. Martyn, and G.H. MacDonald, 1–9. London: University of Western Ontario.

CHAPTER 12

Autonomy and Adaptivity: Farmer's Work in France

Martin Büdel

It is an evening near the end of July when I stop by to see Catherine and Alain. Entering their house, in a small mountain hamlet, I find the young farm couple sitting together for an aperitif with friends from Lyon, who are visiting the Northern Cantal for holidays, as they do every year. After offering me a drink, Alain backs out in a neighbouring room to make a phone call to arrange the sale of a few calves as a new sales market has opened for cattle breeders this year. There is an emerging demand from Turkey, in addition to the existing export markets to countries like Italy or Spain, where most calves had been transported for fattening so far (Rabhi 2015).

The Turkish market demands relatively young calves weighing not more than 300 kilos at the point of disposal. As a consequence, they can be sold earlier than usual, allowing farmers to generate some income during a period of the year when their savings begin to get rather scarce and they are waiting for much-needed state subsidies.

Catherine goes on to explain that along with the new market in Turkey, the demand from Italy was already in decline, as farms there had

M. Büdel (✉)
Institut für Ethnologie, University of Freiburg,
Freiburg im Breisgau, Germany

© The Author(s) 2018
M. Spyridakis (ed.), *Market Versus Society*, Palgrave Studies in Urban
Anthropology, https://doi.org/10.1007/978-3-319-74189-5_12

generally been reducing the fattening of cattle, turning partly to the production of biogas and other activities. With these market changes, she sees emerging new opportunities but also certain risks for their farming work. 'But', Catherine said, 'these are the market conditions and as producers we need to adapt to it, taking sales possibilities where they are'. Right in time for dinner, Alain returned to the table, smiling, as he had succeeded in selling nine calves to a merchant who would export them to Turkey the week after.

FARMER'S WORK AND GLOBALIZED FOOD MARKETS

In this chapter, I illustrate some of the challenges that dairy and cattle farmers in the French uplands of the Auvergne region face within globalized food markets. My findings are based on 12 months of fieldwork in Northern Cantal. During two periods of about 6 months in 2014 and 2015, I lived and worked with farmers and craftsmen in the building trade, sharing their everyday lives and getting to know their attitudes and concerns towards the recent developments within their working fields.[1] I will deal with this subject less by analysing agricultural policy or production chains. Instead I will focus on the daily working experiences of farmers themselves.

Although one of the largest exporters of agricultural produce, France has also always been known as favouring a comparatively small-scale, family-based agricultural system, with the advantage of a relatively sound use of land and other natural resources. An observation by sociologist Douglas Harper, who intended to ignite a debate to re-think the overall conditions of a more industrialized agricultural production in the United States is worth noting. He said: 'Only now [...] have non-farmers begun to enter the dialogue about the design of an agriculture which will serve the needs of farmers, the environment, rural communities and non-farmers. [...] It is startling to look at another System in France, nominally like ours, and see prosperous farms with herds of forty milkers, a gorgeous landscape, and the most exquisite dairy food in the world' (Harper 2001: 278).

[1] I am grateful to the collaborative research centre 1015 (SFB 1015) at the University of Freiburg/Germany, that funded my research. I also thank my supervisor Gregor Dobler and my colleagues Maike Meurer and Pia Masurczak for critical comments on early drafts of this chapter.

As will be made clear with the following descriptions of farmer's work in Auvergne, the substance of Harper's observation no longer holds entirely. Instead, the agricultural system in France, as in the European Union (EU) in general, seems to develop in a quite similar direction that Harper worriedly criticized in case of the United States. In France, it is not only farmers themselves who express concern about the changes in agricultural production, integrated into globalized food markets, and a political system that demands constant adaptation to changing conditions. While some of the farms have given up entirely, others try to adapt to the changing conditions, either by increasing in size and production output, or by developing alternative and more diverse forms of agricultural production, resembling other rural areas elsewhere in Europe (Spyridakis and Dima 2017: 269).

To provide an overview, I will first describe some general aspects of agriculture in France and then turn to some insights from anthropological theories of work that will guide my ethnographic accounts of farmers' daily working experiences. While the agricultural system undoubtedly influences farmers' working conditions, many other aspects that determine daily work come to the fore when looking at actual experiences. After describing some aspects of livestock farming in Auvergne in detail, I will conclude by working out some connections of daily work and overall economic conditions.

The Context of a Changing Agriculture

Agriculture in France, as in Europe in general, is passing through constant changes, and together with its overall socioeconomic context, the modalities of farmers' daily work are being transformed. Especially since World War II, French agriculture has changed massively. While during the 1930s and 1940s almost half of the French population was living in the countryside, with about 35% of the country's active population working in agriculture, these numbers fell to 30 and 12% by 1970 and 20 and 3.3%, respectively by 2010 (Madeline and Moriceau 2013: 371).

In a reciprocal process of a purposely promoted modernization of agricultural production and the necessity of meeting the demands of a growing urban population, French farmers were further integrated into capitalist market-oriented production. Young farmers especially often organized in syndicates such as the *Jeunesse Agricole Catholique* (*JAC*) (*Catholic Association of Young Farmers*), and were one of the main moving forces within the modernization project of French agriculture (Bluche 2012; Madeline and Moriceau 2013: 299–308; Muller 1984: 61–85). The movement favoured the shift to a motorization of farms, the introduction of other technology and chemistry in agricultural production, an extended recourse to loans, while at the same time opening up the possibility of more freedom and leisure for farmers and farm workers, as was occurring in other areas like the manufacturing or service industries (Madeline and Moriceau 2013: 231, 300).

This emphasis on modernization and progress has been in a constant state of crisis—at least since the 1980s—in line with an enhanced European integration process and the growing importance of the EU's Common Agricultural Policy (CAP). The latter started off as a kind of welfare system for a largely family-based agriculture. But the CAP is nowadays often seen as one-sidedly promoting industrial agricultural production (Salzer 2014: 27–31). Further, EU subsidies are mainly distributed according to the amount of land and production volume of farms, a system that obviously favours increased production and land purchase (Knudsen 2009). Not least due to ongoing difficulties of its reform, the CAP and its central instrument, the subsidies, were often described as, at least partly, causing problems including a growing oversupply and an aggravated competition among farmers in the context of European and global markets. The EU's agricultural system is thus often blamed as promoting an intensified agriculture with negative effects on the environment, animals, and humans themselves (Lémery 2003: 11).

The overall development of European agriculture and food production is not only causing a certain discomfort and insecurity among consumers, but, even more significantly, complaints and sorrows of those who work in the sector. A growing influence of the so-called agrobusiness and even financial firms without much substantial interest in agriculture, leaves less and less space for a diversity of the organization of agricultural production. French rural sociology is quite concerned with the fact that family-based or individual farms embedded into local communities might disappear more rapidly (Hervieu and Purseigle 2011: 68). In part, this is seen in connection to a political and societal ignorance regarding the future of French agriculture within the European Union and the wider context of globalized food markets (Hervieu and Purseigle 2008: 681).

Nevertheless, public discourse in France has a long history of concern about the loss of peasantry and a certain hesitation towards a solely market-driven agricultural production. Worries relate especially to the social function attributed to farmers' work: to preserve territory and landscape and to obtain rural life in general. This is reflected in sociological as well as in more popular publications (Mendras 1970; Bourguignon 2015; Nicolino 2015). Against the fact that France is one of the world's biggest producers and exporters in agriculture, there might be some ambiguity in these lines of argumentation (Rogers 2000: 51–53). But, it is also reflecting the conflict between different actors in the field of agricultural production and politics. Simply put, the main line of conflict divides those concerned with the problems and working conditions of smaller producers and the ecological problems caused by intensive agricultural production, in contrast to those supporting the latter. The ongoing changes also encourage debates on food quality as well as about alternative ways of agricultural production and a novel transition to a sound and sustainable, so-called 'post-industrial agriculture' (Heller 2006: 320–321). Besides political action syndicates, such as the *Confédération Paysanne (CP)*, to promote a small-scale, family-based agriculture that Heller refers to, there also exist grass-root movements, sometimes affiliated with CP, with the aim of overcoming a growing dependence on global food markets. Some of them try to develop different forms of direct marketing or even active involvement of the consumers, such as community supported agriculture (CSA), in France called *Associations pour le maintien de l'agriculture paysanne (AMAP)* (Mundler 2007). Most farmers in Northern Cantal observe these changes reservedly, with only few of them having converted to certified ecological agriculture, in France known as *Agriculture Biologique (AB)*.

Beside the systemic challenges sketched above, the actual working conditions of farmers and the question of their identity within a globalized and market-driven agricultural production come to the fore. When discussing recent developments in global food markets and the role of agriculture within it, I argue that there is a need to literally bring production back into social analysis, to paraphrase a concern of Don Robotham for anthropological theory in general (Robotham 2005). As part of this, a thorough investigation into daily working realities would complement assessments that explore agricultural transformations from a more general perspective. On these grounds, I will take the daily struggles of farmers and the production relations they are situated in as a starting point.

By drawing on ethnographic accounts of the work and daily lives of cattle farmers in Northern Cantal, a part of the French mountainous upland region *Massif Central*, I will illustrate some examples of working conditions in agriculture. These conditions need to be seen within the context of a market-oriented production and repeatedly changing demands from politics or consumers. Before turning to the special case of cattle farming in the Auvergne region, I will refer to anthropological literature concerned with work as a central part of an analysis of economic structures.

LESSONS FROM THE ANTHROPOLOGY OF WORK

What has been said earlier about European agriculture strengthens central concerns in anthropology in understanding the contradictions and shortcomings of a globalized economy. Taking people's actions and strategies in confrontation with larger circumstances into consideration, Keith Hart and others developed the idea of a human economy that places efforts of satisfying human needs first, instead of prioritizing economic profit (Hart et al. 2010; Hann and Hart 2011: 165). Based on classic sources in anthropology and beyond, these authors map out a framework that puts economic processes and a dialectic of human action in the centre of social theory. One of the main aspects that can be drawn from this is that human action, especially with regard to economic reason, is always directed at both: an aspiration for individual profit on one side and communal commitment on the other side (Hann and Hart 2011: 51). Framed in this way, the human economy gives the possibility of understanding economic action as embedded in social relations. Human actors seek for personal advantage and the fulfilment of common goals coincidently (Hann and Hart 2011: 173).

In this light, work and its element of production as an economic activity cannot be understood entirely without considering aspects that go beyond a model of work as an income-generating activity. Rather, other attributes such as 'reciprocity, competition, joy of work, and social approbation' should be considered as well (Polanyi 2001: 277). Gerd Spittler (2009: 160) emphasizes the need to integrate an analysis of such different aspects of work to come to a better understanding of the development of social and economic relations in capitalism. Rereading early anthropological writings on work and the economy, Spittler highlights aspects that were largely pushed to the background of anthropological and ethnographic concerns: the integration of work, production, and economic behaviour into other aspects of daily life; the possibility of individual freedom in organizing working tasks; the relevance of the actual performance of work; or other elements such as the interaction with animals and machines, to name just a few (Spittler 2009: 162). To understand work relations and processes in their encompassing socioeconomic context, it is therefore necessary to involve exemplary descriptions of actual working experiences, in addition to institutional or structural perspectives on production and work, as only then we can get a more coherent picture of people's agency in confrontation with changing political or economic structures (Spittler 2016: 283; Spyridakis 2013: 3, 8). Such an ethnographic perspective also allows a view of different spheres of life connected to work beyond a simplifying angle that only takes work's economic utility into account (Wallman 1979: 7).

Looking at farmers' work, it is particularly important to be aware of the influence of rhythms of time. Working tasks in farming are integrated into daily structures, overlapping with other activities that are not necessarily regarded as work. This is true especially on individual or family-based farms, where labour power is to a great part recruited within the family. There, working tasks can be done whenever they need to be done or whenever there is time to do them. So, even under conditions of industrialization and the conditions of a mechanized agriculture, task-orientation is an important aspect of farmers' work (Ingold 1995: 8–10; Dobler 2014: 59).

There are obviously influences like the frame of agricultural policy or overall economic developments that give some aspects of farming work a heteronomous character. But the lived reality of task-oriented working activities that are mutually integrated into daily structures of individual and family life outside of work indicates that within these formerly mentioned conditions there are possibilities to experience a certain freedom or autonomy. Gregor Dobler (2014: 67–68), among others, highlighted as a general aspect of working tasks the inherent possibility of structuring one's working activities by oneself and according to one's own preferences and temporal or bodily rhythms. Even if structural conditions might be a kind of converse force to this, working activities themselves can still entail a kind of freedom under certain circumstances. Autonomous work in this sense, standing in contrast to alienated work, entails the potential of experiencing work and its product as one's own, even though it might be part of hard and arduous labour, as it is the case in farming.

Coming back to the situation of cattle farmers in Cantal, this leads to the question of the possibility of experiencing autonomy against the backdrop of an almost exclusively market-oriented production. The relation of autonomous and heteronomous aspects of work, conceptualized dialectically, can reveal certain aspects of freedom in work, that might, for example, be visible in an affective attitude towards certain elements of one's work objects. Still, even if most farmers work independently and profit from a certain freedom in their daily work, they remain in dependency of overall structures. It is not uncommon that farmers deny themselves a certain comfort, take high risks with making loans and work hard to meet the demands of the economic system they are integrated in. Pierre Bourdieu (2001: 261–262) referred to this ambivalence as the two-sided character of work, with the risk of self-exploitation at one of the extreme ends of this spectrum, which can be observed quite frequently among farmers in the region.

STRUCTURES AND WORKING ATTITUDES IN CATTLE FARMING

Temporally determined rhythms in agriculture are also in place when looking at the influence of seasons or those of animals and their needs. Studies on human–animal relations in farming highlight the central role of close relationships between farmers and their livestock that is working in two ways and improving both, animals' well-being 'in terms of health and productivity' and farmers' pleasure and joy for their occupation (Bock et al. 2007: 109). Even if animal husbandry on farms serves almost exclusively economic ends and a large part of a herd is bred for later slaughtering and meat production, the wellbeing of their animals is part of many farmers' understanding of good work (Bock et al. 2007: 121).

At the same time farmers' relations to livestock entails a certain ambivalence. Farmers often develop a sort of pragmatic-emotional tie to animals, which is especially true for cattle breeding that also has a physical and sensual dimension. Farmers' everyday work is for the most part determined by the necessities to look after their cattle, it is often arduous or even troublesome and painful. But as many characterize work with their livestock as a passion, quite some time is also spent to observe the characteristics, qualities, and behaviour of individual animals out of interest and pleasure (Jürgens 2009: 227–228).

Elaborating the de facto working conditions of those who work in agriculture and juxtaposing these to the debate about changes in agriculture or agrofood systems in a global perspective can thus contribute to a better understanding of such processes. French sociologist Bruno Lémery is drawing on such an approach that is integrating farmers' own concerns in a study on cattle breeders in Burgundy. The categories he developed can help to correlate actual working conditions or individual circumstances and the wider context of the European agricultural system. In his analyses of interviews and visits on farms, Lémery (2003: 13–14) identified three main groups, which he categorized along different lines of argumentation. The first group contains the more traditional farmers, who question the changes that have come about, especially with the Common European Agriculture (CAP). They look quite critically upon the ongoing intensification of agricultural production in general and many of them think about giving up their farms, or do not bother to find a successor. Another group argues in a quite similar way when speaking about their own position within the agricultural sector. But unlike the first group, this second group of farmers are looking for ways to renew what they regard as traditional values and more sustainable ways of farming in comparison to an intensified industrial food production. A last group, contrarily, sees the constant modernization of agricultural production as a chance. Even if they might have difficulties as average individuals or family-based farms to adapt and to grow in line with the outside demands, they regard these changes as a field of opportunities, to which they need to respond strategically as business-like farmer-entrepreneurs (Lémery 2003: 15–21).

In conversations during my fieldwork farmers often moved between different arguments that correspond to more than one of these groups. Lémery's scheme nevertheless shows that the question of farmers' own views of their role corresponds to the indecision on the problem of agricultural production in public discourse and political action in France that other authors have studied. The controversially discussed development of European agriculture is heavily criticized for static concepts of economic efficiency and its preference for practices of capital accumulation by corporations. At the same time, political framing of the system seems to ignore the tolerability of those working in the sector. Therefore, I need to stress again that when thinking about the development of agriculture in Europe and beyond, it is crucial to consider actual working conditions more than has been done so far.

LIVESTOCK FARMING IN NORTHERN CANTAL

Even if many farmers in Northern Cantal define their region as rather backward and remote, especially in technical terms compared to farming in other French regions, they are nevertheless noticing some of the consequences of recent general political and economic developments in European agriculture. Due to regional specialization and the specific geographical conditions of an upland area, large parts of agricultural production in the region are either based on milk and cheese production or cattle breeding at a comparatively small size. Dairy farms, cattle farms and mixed dairy and cattle farms make up about 80% of all farms in Cantal district (Chambre d'agriculture du Cantal 2014). Thus, quite a few producers were directly affected by the changes in the EU's milk quota system in March 2015 and of some other consequences in the wake of this change. Given the increasing production of milk in France and other European countries on larger farms with lower production costs altogether, relatively small producers in the region with only 30–40 cows were then driven out of the market. As an economic consultant of the chamber of agriculture told me, small milk-producing farms only had two possibilities to deal with this situation. Either they began to refine their milk directly on the farm or they needed to transform to cattle breeding for meat production entirely if they were interested in continuing their farms. Some of those dairy farmers who have not refined their product directly on the farm so far, already spoke of difficulties in maintaining and keeping up their working morale. They felt that their working efforts were no longer reasonable, as remuneration for their product was decreasing and no longer profitable.

Cattle farms in Northern Cantal differ in size, shape, and working patterns, depending on their organizational form, the number of individuals involved, the size of the farm land, and the number of livestock. While individual farms still make up the majority, their number has been decreasing during the last years, with a growing number of associated farms in the legal forms of *Groupement agricole d'exploitation en commun (GAEC)* or *Exploitation agricole à responsabilité limitée (EARL)*. Though not directly involved in changes in the dairy market, cattle farmers faced a difficult year in 2015 as well. Some articulated fears of becoming touched indirectly by falling milk prices through a possible transformation of a growing number of farmers from dairy to cattle farming, as the latter is economically profitable with a lower number of animals than the first. This would increase the supply of cattle and thus also affect prices on the regional and export cattle markets. The worries about possible negative developments in overall economic conditions set apart, French farmers were already troubled with what they viewed as disadvantages against production conditions in other European countries.

Many farmers in Northern Cantal are concerned about the overall development of their profession and their own possibilities within these changing conditions. They face an ongoing specialization in cattle farming as well as a decline in the diversity of farming and in the number of farms in their region. Rural life in Cantal is very much connected to its agriculture and land characterized by its use as pastures or meadows for cattle and dairy farming. With the decline in the number of farms and individual farmers, people already talk about some mountainous areas as resembling a 'desert', with almost nobody left who is working the land. This reflects a fear of a disappearance of agriculture and thus the region's central identifying feature and economic factor, but also shows farmers' commitment not only for their own professional future, but also the communal development of their region.

Working with Cattle

For the daily organization of working tasks, family habits and individual preferences towards work play a major role. It can be said that the diversity in organizational forms is also reflected in this regard by the different attitudes farmers take towards their work. As it has been recorded elsewhere with a focus on alternative agriculture in Cantal (Macombe 2007), there is a wide range of work attitudes among farmers. This corresponds with my own observations as well as with farmers' own reflections in conversations on the topic. On one side of the spectrum are farmers with a strong work ethic, leading their farms with idealism and sometimes accepting relatively low technical standards, *à l'ancienne* (ancient working practices). At the other extreme, there are farmers who regard their work not as a vocation but consider their farm more like a business that could be sold as well if no longer profitable. As I met farmers who were especially compassionate about their work with cattle, the strong work ethic was reflected, thus also highlight some aspects of the desire for autonomy in farmer's work.

The selling of calves that I referred to in the beginning is quite an important period for cattle farmers in Cantal, economically as well as with respect to their daily working efforts. Up to then, they spend several months of hard and time-consuming work, taking care of breeding and birthing their animals. Salers, the region's traditional cattle, is nowadays predominantly used as meat breed. Their milk yield is significantly lower than that of today's specialized dairy cattle and there is only a small number of farmers who still milk their Salers cows, and if so, almost exclusively for cheese production on the farm (Roque and Marsilhac 2006; Samson and Raymond 2015).

Taking care of cattle requires a lot of daily routine work. During winter, which usually lasts from November to April in the uplands of Northern Cantal, the animals are kept in cowsheds. Many farms currently invest or have already invested in larger sheds where cattle can move in several parks of about ten to twelve animals on a straw loft. They can also be attached for feeding, mulching, or clearing away the dung. But many farms keep parts of their livestock in tethered housing as well. Work there differs from larger stables, as dung needs to be cleared by hand. And while in the large stable hay is simply unrolled or unpacked in front of the feed lots, in the older sheds it needs to be distributed with a pitchfork, which is a quite physical task.

To facilitate the process of calving and to concentrate it mainly from December to February, farmers organize mating and insemination of their cows around the same period, usually a few weeks after the cow's last delivery. The farmers spend most of their working time in the sheds to monitor the animals. Some even make use of a navigable camera that allows monitoring them on a TV screen from the house, also during the night. Even if Salers cows are considered to bear quite easily, they usually need assistance to prevent accidents or even the death of a newborn. It is quite an intense period during a year's cycle and work is focused and organized around care for the animals. Due to an altitude of almost one thousand meters above sea level with snowy and raw winters there is not a lot of outdoor work to do anyway, beside some repair of tools, machines or pasture fences after days get a bit less cold, usually beginning in March. Sometimes this routine is interrupted by unforeseen events as when calves get sick and need to be treated or when one of the cows dies of a disease, leaving a small calf behind that needs to be brought up by other means.

There are some fairly warm and sunny days during March and April, but winter season in this part of the *Massif Central* only comes to an end in May. By the end of April, farmers lead most of their animals to the mountain pastures. To let their animals slowly adapt to staying outside, they usually take three or four days to let them outside in front of the shed, moving them back in before night. Calves born inside the shed and have not stayed outside so far especially need some time to get used to this new situation before being driven to the mountain pastures.

CHANGES WITH SUMMER SEASON

Work with cattle changes with summer season. Many farmers talk about the day when their herds are driven to the pastures as a relief. Folkloristic festivals such as the *fête de l'estive*, the festival of the pastures in the village Allanche give an idea of the historic meaning of this seasonal event and its ongoing relevance to farmers today. Even if the amount of work might not actually diminish for the coming months, most of it will take place outside and under more pleasant weather conditions. Besides regularly observing their animals out on the pastures, cattle farmers continue to fix fences and clean the sheds, besides tending to other work such as cutting firewood for the next winter season or preparing their hay meadows. The latter is mainly done by driving a drag over the meadows— many farmers in the region use old tractor tires attached with a chain as a drag substitute—and carting out dung and liquid manure. Depending on weather conditions and other factors, some farmers use artificial fertilizers such as aluminium nitrate sometimes as well.

The time spent observing and caring for the herds on pasture differs widely among farmers. Some keep their herds on pastures that are more than an hour's drive away and therefore cannot afford to go and see their cattle more than once a week. As for Catherine and Alain, parts of their pastures lie on a mountain close to their farm and they visit their herd twice a day. Alain even continues to drive the herd into a small park in the evenings, as it had been done by his grandfather some decades ago. This was necessary to keep the herd together for milking the next morning, but also allowed him to closely observe the animals in case one of them was sick or other problems developed. As Salers today are seldom held as dairy cattle, this practice is usually seen as abundant.

While it is very time-consuming, Alain sets store on continuing to bring the cows together in the evenings and to change the electric fence of the park every morning, leading the herd to a certain grazing area for the coming day. As the animals leave their dung on the spot where they spent the night, Alain uses this practice as a natural fertilizer that helps to maintain the quality of the pastures. He often says that at the end of summer days, he enjoys heading to the mountain, observing his herd for a while and driving them together into the park. For him, this is no longer part of the day's work, but a pleasurable activity where he can take some time to see his animals, calmly completing his day. Occasionally, he is also passing some time at a neighbor's place who is spending the summer making cheese in a mountain hut nearby, discussing work or some of the latest news with his fellow farmers.

Therefore, depending on one's commitment, but also on distances and the layout of one's pastures and meadows, during the summer period, work in connection to cattle remains often as intense and time consuming as in winter. This intensity is also notable in the time spent in organizing and conducting the rotation of several herds of livestock on different pastures. Some farmers keep their cattle on the same pasture throughout the summer season if it is big enough and if they are not able to visit and change their herd to another pasture on a regular basis. Others have several smaller parcels of pasture land and need to rotate their cattle on those on a regular basis. What is more, herds are usually divided into at least two groups: one group of mother cows with their calves and another group of young females that are kept with the purpose of replacing cows as soon as reaching their prolific age in their third year of life. Thus, many farmers have several groups of animals to monitor and to change from one pasture to another once or twice a week. Rotating the animals serves an optimal use of pastures and contributes to the fattening of calves. As they continue to be fed by their mothers' milk in addition to grazing, a regular pasture needs to be ensured.

The work of cattle farmers in Cantal is much more diverse than what I could describe here. Nevertheless, to provide for their animals is a central aspect of their daily occupation and daily structures are shaped by the demands of livestock. It is not least for this that Alain often stresses: 'If you don't love cattle, you wouldn't be able to do this job'. A close and attentive relationship to their animals is what many farmers describe as pivotal for doing good work, sometimes even laying more weight on it than on concern for a profitable business.

DAILY WORK AND THE ECONOMY

This leads me back to economic aspects of the events that become apparent in the introductory anecdote and the descriptions of farmers' work. The ethnographic accounts show that economic or financial considerations play a significant role in daily work even if this is not always articulated or directly apparent. While there is obviously an emotional and even sensual side in farmers' work with cattle, it is at the same time a pragmatic production process. Caring for the animals and all other work connected to it also implies thinking ahead to the revenue produced when selling cattle on the market. Losing one of them due to disease or other incidents always directly affects farmers' income, which is only partly backed up by state subsidies.

To be able to make a living out of livestock farming, farmers need to calculate carefully the size of their farm, especially when it comes to the number of animals kept, among many other aspects. Still, while being relatively free in choosing their own way to organize their work, it is especially due to wider economic and political influences that they need to adapt. It might become clear with some of the examples I described here that it is a fragile venture full of risks, to breed cattle and obtain a constant number of calves every year for selling. To produce enough revenue, farms often keep about 40 or 50 cows per associate. Farms in Cantal and elsewhere were forced to constantly grow during the last decades, to be able to meet the demands of markets and society and produce enough revenue for themselves simultaneously. Seen from a perspective that stresses a thorough human–animal relation, this development might have reached a climax a while ago, and farmers' central concern for taking good care of their animals is an indication of the need for reconsidering the general conditions of agricultural production in the region.

Due to these risks and economic challenges—and the obstacles to continue farm work on a rather small scale in comparison to industrial farming—there is a constant number of farmers in Cantal giving up their farms or advising their children to do so. The general debate on agriculture in France and the farmers' endeavours to do good work and to keep some autonomy in what they—often passionately—do for their living, reflects the need for a thoughtful revision of working conditions in agriculture. Seen from a perspective that understands work and economic relations in general as being integrated into and shaped by historical processes of social reproduction (Narotzky 1997: 158, 167), these cases show that an individual's or family farmer's decision to withdraw from farming and to give up their family tradition comes about mainly due to socioeconomic developments and political decisions. Against the backdrop of the human economy approach cited earlier, the current French and EU agricultural regime seems to a large extent not to serve the needs of the producers. Instead, it even forces individuals or families to give up their original livelihood.

Farming in Northern Cantal is one of the main factors contributing to rural life in general and it connects several individual and communal interests at the same time, such as the breeding of cattle for economic profit and the tending of land connected to this type of agricultural production. Agricultural work is thus serving not only the farmer's own profit or the production of food for society, but goes beyond this. While the EU's system of subsidies does not leave farmers in a sole dependency on market demand, it is not built in favour of small producers that are integrated into rural communities, which is regarded as an important factor for a sound agricultural production. To be able to perform good work, cattle farmers in Cantal often stress the importance of a reasonable size for their farms, to be able to care for their animals in as good a manner as possible. As they can individually decide on the actual performance of their work, they gain from this a certain autonomy in their work and thus a necessary freedom to perform what they regard as good work.

REFERENCES

Bluche, L. 2012. *Von Bauern zu Europäern? Der agraristische Diskurs in Frankreich, 1944–1962*. Frankfurt am Main: Lang.

Bock, B.B., M.M. van Huik, M. Prutzer, F. Kling-Eveillard, and A. Dockés. 2007. Farmers' Relationship with Different Animals. *International Journal of Sociology of Agriculture and Food* 15: 108–125.

Bourdieu, P. 2001. *Meditationen: Zur Kritik der scholastischen Vernunft*. Frankfurt am Main: Suhrkamp.

Bourguignon, C. 2015. *Le sol, la terre et les champs - Pour retrouver une agriculture saine*. Paris: Sang de la Terre.

Chambre d'agriculture du Cantal. 2014. *Le Cantal et son agriculture*. (Unpublished presentation)

Dobler, G. 2014. Muße und Arbeit. In *Muße im kulturellen Wandel: Semantisierungen, Ähnlichkeiten, Umbesetzunge*, ed. B. Hasebrink and P. Riedl, 53–67. Berlin: De Gruyter.

Hann, C., and K. Hart. 2011. *Economic Anthropology: History, Ethnography, Critique*. Cambridge: Polity Press.

Harper, D. 2001. *Changing Works: Visions of a Lost Agriculture*. Chicago: University of Chicago Press.

Hart, K., J.-L. Laville, and A.D. Cattani. 2010. *The Human Economy*. New York: Wiley.

Heller, C. 2006. Post-industrial 'Quality Agricultural Discourse': Techniques of Governance and Resistance in The French Debate over GM Crops. *Social Anthropology* 14: 319–334.

Hervieu, B., and F. Purseigle. 2008. Troubled Pastures, Troubled Pictures: French Agriculture and Contemporary Rural Sociology. *Rural Sociology* 73: 660–683.

Hervieu, B., and F. Purseigle. 2011. Des agricultures avec des agriculteurs, une nécessité pour l'Europe. *Revue Projet* 321: 60–69.

Ingold, T. 1995. Work, Time and Industry. *Time and Society* 4: 5–28.

Jürgens, K. 2009. Die Mensch-Nutztier-Beziehung in der heutigen Landwirtschaft - Agrarsoziologische Perspektiven. In *Gefährten - Konkurrenten - Verwandte: Die Mensch-Tier-Beziehung im wissenschaftlichen Diskurs*, ed. C. Otterstedt and M. Rosenberger, 215–235. Göttingen: Vandenhoeck & Ruprecht.

Knudsen, A. 2009. *Farmers on Welfare: The Making of Europe's Common Agricultural Policy*. Ithaca: Cornell University Press.

Lémery, B. 2003. Les agriculteurs dans la fabrique d'une nouvelle agriculture. *Sociologie du Travail* 45: 9–25.

Macombe, C. 2007. Work: A Necessary Sacrifice or a Suffered Chore? Labor and Farm Continuity in Alternative Agriculture in France. *Renewable Agriculture and Food Systems* 22: 282–289.

Madeline, P., and J.-M. Moriceau. 2013. *Les paysans (1870-1970): Récits, témoignages et archives de la France agricole*. Paris: Les Arènes.

Mendras, H. 1970. *La fin des paysans: changement et innovations dans les sociétés rurales Françaises*. Paris: Colin.

Muller, P. 1984. *Le technocrate et le paysan*. Paris: Les éditions ouvrières.

Mundler, P. 2007. Les Associations pour le maintien de l'agriculture paysanne (AMAP) en Rhône-Alpes, entre marché et solidarité. *Ruralia* 20: 2–20.

Narotzky, S. 1997. *New Directions in Economic Anthropology*. London: Pluto Press.

Nicolino, F. 2015. *Lettre à un paysan sur le vaste merdier qu'est devenue l'agriculture*. Paris: Éditions les echappés.

Polanyi, K. 2001. *The Great Transformation: The Political and Economic Origins of Our Time*. Boston: Beacon Press.

Rabhi, C. 2015. L'ambassadeur de Turquie à la rencontre des éleveurs cantaliens. *La Montagne*, viewed 22 August 2017, from http://www.lamontagne. fr/auvergne/actualite/departement/cantal/2015/06/20/lambassadeur-de-turquie-a-la-rencontre-des-eleveurs-cantaliens_11488806.html.

Robotham, D. 2005. *Culture, Economy and Society: Bringing Production Back In*. London: Sage.

Rogers, S. 2000. Farming Visions. Agriculture in French Culture. *French Politics, Culture & Society* 18: 50–70.

Roques, M., and T. Marsilhac. 2006. *La Salers par monts et par veaux*. Aurillac: Glob.

Salzer, I. 2014. TTIP, GAP und die Macht der Konzerne. *Widerspruch* 64: 23–32.

Samson, C., and J. Raymond. 2015. *Salers La vache*. Lascelle: Éditions de la Flandonnière.

Spittler, G. 2009. Contesting the Great Transformation: Work in Comparative Perspective. In *Market and Society: The Great Transformation Today*, ed. C. Hann and K. Hart, 160–174. Cambridge: Cambridge University Press.

Spittler, G. 2016. *Anthropologie der Arbeit. Ein ethnographischer Vergleich*. Wiesbaden: VS Verlag für Sozialwissenschaften.

Spyridakis, M. 2013. *The Liminal Worker: An Ethnography of Work, Unemployment and Precariousness in Contemporary Greece*. Burlington: Ashgate.

Spyridakis, M., and F. Dima. 2017. Reinventing Traditions: Socially Produced Goods in Eastern Crete During Economic Crisis. *Journal of Rural Studies* 35: 269–277.

Wallman, S. (ed.). 1979. *Social Anthropology of Work*. Academic Press.

CHAPTER 13

Economic Rationality and Human Experience: Global Agrifood Chains from the Perspective of Social Anthropology

Alicia Reigada

Introduction

In his study on peasant conflicts in the twentieth century, Wolf (1973) drew a clear relationship between their struggles and the global expansion of a particular cultural system, that of North Atlantic capitalism. Taking regional differences into account, Wolf studied cultural and social formations that came about due to these conflicts, and in so doing he articulated the local from an increasingly global perspective. He viewed change as a constant aspect of social life and understood the relationship between continuity and cultural transformation as being enmeshed in contradictory processes. Such transformative processes can appear incoherent, senseless, and distressing to the social groups affected, forcing them to take a stand against new dilemmas.

A. Reigada (✉)
Department of Social Anthropology, University of Seville, Seville, Spain

© The Author(s) 2018
M. Spyridakis (ed.), *Market Versus Society*, Palgrave Studies in Urban Anthropology, https://doi.org/10.1007/978-3-319-74189-5_13

Based on an analysis of the intensive cultivation of strawberries in the province of Huelva (Andalusia, Southern Spain), this chapter[1] discusses some of the contradictions and dilemmas that affect the lives of small family farmers that supply global agrifood chains.[2] By examining the changing human experience of these subjects in the context of transformations in work, production, and distribution practices, the research examines how the identity of these strawberry growers is grounded in their sense of pride at being self-made. Taking this starting point, the text explores the moral economy of these agricultural producers and the role that feelings of pride play in their sense of grievance, injustice, and vulnerability.

Taking inspiration from Wolf's approach and by situating these smallholders' experiences in the local history of farming and the social formation of the productive model, the analysis identifies key factors for understanding how their lived reality and cultural system give meaning to their values and economic behaviour. In taking this approach, this chapter shows that it is not possible to reduce the concept of economy to monetary value. Rather, monetary value should be articulated in conjunction with the cultural and moral values that guide economic practice. This is to say, it is from a moral economy (vision, conviction, belief, practice) that these strawberry growers define how the global agrifood markets should behave, and where the limits should lie between the tolerable and intolerable (Thompson 1971, 1991; Scott 1976).

[1] This contribution has been developed within the framework of the Contrato Postdoctoral de Acceso del V Plan Propio de la Universidad de Sevilla and was developed during a postdoctoral research stay at FLASCO-Ecuador (2016).

[2] It is based on a qualitative research project (financed by the government of Andalusia) that employed in-depth interviews (83 in total) and participant observation. The researchers spent one year and nine months (2006–2007) living in the strawberry producing area of Southern Spain. Observation was carried out in two of the main strawberry production areas (Moguer and Palos de la Frontera) in the Province of Huelva. All informants' names have been changed to protect their identity. The research was continued under the auspices of a second collective project: "Migration, global agrifood chains and rural development: A comparative analysis between Spain, Mexico, Argentina and Uruguay" (2011–2012), financed by Fundación Carolina.

THE PRIDE OF THE SELF-MADE

In the modern history of agricultural production in the areas of Moguer and Palos de la Frontera, a number of distinct phases are evident, which extend from traditional agricultural production and isolationist economic policy through to the introduction of intensive agriculture and subsequently globalization. A brief overview of this history helps to illustrate not only the profound change that has occurred in the area, but also how it informs contemporary social values. From 1870 up until the late 1930s the area was dominated by traditional agriculture, most notably the cultivation of grapes and wheat. With changes in political autonomy and isolationist economic policies during the dictatorship of General Franco, production changed to the cultivation of local subsistence crops such as cereals, potatoes, and legumes (Márquez 1986), as well as a smaller sector dedicated to strawberry production. However, low earnings from agriculture forced the majority of smallholders to supplement their income by multi-jobbing in other sectors, such as fishing and construction, or by diversifying activity within agriculture, such as cultivating as well as hiring out their workforce. During the 1960s there were two important changes in the area under the National Stabilization Plan (1959): an industrial production complex was developed in an area close to Moguer and Palos de la Frontera, and measures were also introduced to capitalise production and introduce new intensive agricultural techniques.

The introduction of the most advanced technology from California meant that production could take advantage of the province's climate (temperate-warm and dry), soil type (sandy) and subterranean aquifers. With this expansion, many parts of the province that had previously been used for forestry and charcoal production were converted to strawberry cultivation, which now covers almost 7000 hectares of land in the province. An important aspect of land development in the province came about because more than 50% of the terrain was publicly owned, which meant that planning policies were defined by social, rather than commercial, criteria. This saw the local authority cede land to residents that could prove that they were agricultural labourers who only worked small parcels of one or two hectares (Martín 1995).

It is also important to highlight the structural changes in the agricultural labour force that came about due to social changes and the need to find labour for the expanding industry. As traditional domestic sources of agricultural labour, such as women and, to a degree children, gave up working in the fields, there was a progressive introduction of a paid workforce, sourced from neighbouring provinces. Subsequently, from the mid-1990s onwards, labour needs were met by employing immigrants from North Africa, and then later on from Sub-Saharan Africa. These workers gradually supplanted local unskilled labour and were themselves substituted, in part, by workers from Eastern Europe and Morocco; hired directly in their home countries to work for the agricultural season on temporary contracts.

These investments in agriculture and the introduction of intensive farming methods meant that the province of Huelva became the number one strawberry exporting area in Europe, and, at a global level, only second behind California. The success was so sudden that the metaphor red gold was coined to describe the wealth generated by strawberry cultivation. This notion of wealth was configured in monetary terms (productivity-growth-profitability) and a cultural belief in technological progress. This localised framework of cultural values makes sense as a symbolic imaginary adopted from global level and the Californian model, which was thought of as a paradigm of modernity, technological innovation, and economic growth. The slogan, Andalusia, the California of Europe, coined by the regional government in the 1980s, further encapsulated this social imaginary. It illustrated the local pride in the success of the model, particularly when the social origins of the strawberry growers are taken into account.

As such, the work and life trajectories of these smallholders underwent a rapid and unexpected transformation. In a relatively short period of time, people who had previously subsisted by multi-jobbing became full-time, modern agricultural cultivators exporting produce. It is precisely this underlying social structure of strawberry production, the way that the land was acquired, the class origins, and economic orientation of production that distinguishes it from the old bourgeois estate owner model and the large holdings characteristic of the modern capitalist model. Despite some consolidation of holdings, this smallholder structure (≤ 7 ha) remains largely true today. Consequently, as opposed to the lack of connection that the owners of large farms have with the land, these smallholders place great value on making a success of their farms through their own labour. As such, their sense of cultural identity is very much formed out of their pride for being self-made.

In contrast to the 'archaic and poverty stricken' (Fourneau 1983) forms of agriculture that were characteristic of the region, these developments also brought with them new cultural meanings and values. There was a feeling of pride in their newfound spirit of entrepreneurship, as well as the capacity to be flexible and to change, openness to innovation, and ability to adapt to market demands. Additionally, these small family farmers increasingly saw themselves as export leaders to global markets, capable of taking risks and investing in the professionalisation of their sector. In some cases, they also consolidated and expanded their holdings and increased their workforce. The scope and scale of these changes and the meanings that they came to acquire helps to explain how many of these strawberry growers have come to identify themselves, at least in certain contexts, as agricultural entrepreneurs, as opposed to subsistence farmers:

> I was studying, but at 17 I didn't like it much, so I left. I went to work in the companies on the industrial complex that they were setting up. I worked there until I went to do my military service, when I was 20. And, when I came back my girlfriend had a parcel of land that had belonged to her parents, and I, well, I was starting out, the strawberries weren't like today, but there were lots of people starting with the strawberries, not as farm labourers [like before] but as companies [...]. When I started we were already using the plastic [plasticulture] and all that. (Antonio Pérez, grower)

This historic formation of the strawberry producing sector helps us to understand the coexistence of paradoxical cultural values and behaviour constituted in the tensions between the rationality of agricultural smallholders and that of capitalism. Integration to the capitalist processes of the global agrifood industry brings with it a business dynamic that comes from the intense professionalisation and commodification of the sector (Friedland 2004). These dynamics include: productivity as a continuous goal; the commodification of labour, land, and natural resources as the basis of the model; a system based on private property and competitiveness that promotes individualism and, in many, cases mistrust between producers; and a production model based on total flexibility and the need to adapt and respond to the instability of global consumer markets. The values, cultural meanings, and ways of thinking that come with these dynamics play an important role in the feelings of pride amongst producers who have professionalised and achieved the requirements necessary to survive and flourish in such a competitive environment. From this interpretative framework, we can understand the nature of these farmers' grievances toward the Common Agricultural Policy (CAP), and their demand that it should support 'professional and productive farmers', instead of protecting large holdings run by absentee landowners.

However, the main objective that guides the socio-economic strategies of these strawberry growers is not the accumulation of capital, but sustaining the farm holding and, in the sense defined by Narotzky (1997) and Narotzky and Besnier (2014), the social reproduction of the household unit. In this respect, although there are clear differences in the way that such objectives are achieved, research amongst other similar social groups in Andalusia, such as day labourers (Palenzuela 1996), flower growers and small vineyard owners (Cruces 1994), or fishing families (Florido 2004) identifies that they are, in general, occupied with the same goals and socio-economic strategies.

Even in the red gold era the expectations and practices of these agricultural families were focused on what was culturally understood as a way to improve their social position and quality of life. This included not only the purchase of consumer goods (expensive cars, holiday homes), but also the possibility of guaranteeing third-level education for their children. It also meant that the women in the family could give up labouring in the fields, which should be understood in the context of a cultural framework that viewed farm labouring as slavery at the same time that there was a clear gender-division in the organisation of work. Along with these economic investments in quality of life, income was also re-invested in the farms, such as upgrading greenhouses and improving the facilities in cooperatives, or converting fallow land to agriculture, and in some cases the purchase of additional property for cultivation. However, and importantly, the boom of the red gold era didn't result in any social aspiration toward the formation of large companies. In general, these farmers lived within the dual margins of an identity and values associated with modern, prosperous agriculture and the maintenance of the family unit. However, we shouldn't ignore analysis that questions whether this is a true domestic model of agriculture, especially in light of the development of a paid workforce of agricultural labourers (Camarero 2017).

The beginning of the twenty-first century saw the red gold metaphor change to a discourse centred on a sector in crisis, which was principally associated with an imbalance between costs and income that set in around the second part of the 1990s. This situation came about with other changes and instability in the global agrifood chains, which brought with them a new dynamic of social tensions in the strawberry fields. Along with growing competition and rising costs of production inputs, the large distribution chains exerted ever more pressure to lower prices and increase quality, along with demands to adapt to new ordering systems and packaging formats. To illustrate, strawberry prices at the beginning of the twenty-first century were 3.8% lower than in 1989 (Verdier 2006). An analysis of the strawberry value chain in Huelva, at the start of the 2000s, shows that the large supermarket chains took three quarters (73%) of the final sale value. Of the balance, 20% went to paying production inputs. A progressive reduction in margins was also accompanied by increased levels of indebtedness (Delgado and Aragón 2006: 463). Another side effect of these downward pressures was the implementation of cost-oriented labour force strategies that saw producers replace Moroccan and Sub-Saharan immigrant workers with a temporary female workforce contracted directly in their home country. Subsequently, this led to protests and strike actions at the beginning of the century.

These transformations have moulded the life and work experiences of these producers and analysing them helps us to understand the role played by feelings of injustice, grievance, vulnerability, and being at risk in their moral economy. Appadurai (1984) maintains that there is no reason to choose between 'moral economy' and 'political economy' approaches to peasant rationality or rural revolts. He argues that an exclusive emphasis on one or the other is likely to lead to distortion. In particular, he emphasises the ideas of enfranchisement and entitlement in specific historical and social contexts to keep morality and economy distinct and yet dialectically related.

In this sense, current concerns with monetary value and business profitability in the context of the economic recession should be understood as part of more deeply felt and broader experiences of losing a certain, culturally defined, quality of life. And, as we will see in the next section, through these experiences, their feelings of pride are being renewed, although in a context of new social actors and new social conflicts.

REVITALIZATION OF PRIDE THROUGH VALUES
OF JUSTICE, LOYALTY, AND LEGITIMACY

Thus, producers' demands for a fair price, originating in a general feeling of grievance with the dynamics of the value chain and relations with the large supermarkets, have become a central concern, much the same as in other regions and agricultural sectors. At the same time, it has become a key factor in the revitalization of these farmers' sense of pride. As such, the progressive concentration of power by the main players in the distribution chains (Burch and Lawrence 2009), so that they can impose lower prices, has become a decisive factor in the new configuration of the sector. However, the growers' sense of grievance cannot be limited only to the decreased monetary value of their fruit, but rather it embodies a range of meanings associated with their perception of the value of their work and their lived experiences. For these farmers, toiling day after day on their farms corresponds to a shared idea that their presence on the land and dedication to their holdings is key to the sustainability of the model.

The distinction that these producers draw between the just and unjust reflects how moral values impregnate economic behaviour. They place great value on work, effort and the recognition of a job well done. They feel that their overriding goal, which is to provide for their families, is a legitimate and dignified one, which contrasts to the abusive behaviour of the large supermarket chains who are 'playing with the livelihoods of a million families'. In this sense, their principal demand is that the supermarkets 'stop devaluing our work by agreeing low pricing pacts that only do one thing: destroy our income!' (Both quotations from the General Secretary of the Coordination of Farmers and Livestock Organisations [COAG], during a protest march in 2001 entitled 'The supermarket chains are destroying us'). For the farmers, the unfair prices offered by the supermarkets represent a manipulation of the market that devalues their work and misappropriates money from the value chain. In this context, speculation is considered to be a morally illegitimate practice. This normative view of how the agrifood markets should operate serves to remind us that the moral economy is localised and politically contingent (Hossain and Kalita 2014). By taking this localising factor into account we can explain the growers' grievances with the large supermarkets, such as Carrefour, Lidl, or Mercadona, for misappropriating the value that the growers add to the product:

There are times when they say, "no, the added-value of the fruit...". But, hang on, the only one who adds value to the fruit is the farmer, because, it's what I'm telling you, I take the fruit to my co-op, that's where the pallets end up, [...] it gets done properly [the packaging], it gets strapped, packed, ready [for shipping] and it's put in the cooler until the truck comes and then it's loaded. If the strawberry is for export, there are a group of women that operate the machinery, they get them ready, they take them out of the plastic boxes that they are transported from the fields in, and they put them in a cardboard box, which is then covered in plastic [the same packaging they are sold in]. So, who's adding value to the strawberry? (Secretary of the agricultural organization 1)

In 2006, an awareness campaign, entitled 'Who gets what *you* pay for?', was launched by a coalition of groups that included COAG, the Union of Spanish Consumers [*Unión de Consumidores de España (UCE)*] and the Spanish Confederation of Homeworkers, Consumers and Users [*Confederación Española de Amas de Casa, Consumidores y Usuarios (CEACCU)*]. The campaign's purpose was to raise awareness about the huge difference between the prices paid to farmers and retail prices. The organisers undertook, amongst other actions, to hand out information leaflets at the entrances to supermarkets (Antentas and Vivas 2007). In 2017, the Andalusian Interprofessional Strawberry Association (Interfresa) took legal action against the supermarket chain Aldi for advertising strawberries from Huelva at below-cost prices. These actions are inscribed within a moral framework that articulates the values of fairness and legitimacy with the value of loyalty: 'there just isn't any loyalty, they are discrediting the image of our products across the whole sector' (Diario *Huelva Información*, 01/02/2017).

Thus, we can see how the perception of the supermarket chains changes from something abstract and impersonal to a more specific and localised configuration. The aim of the protests and the awareness and information campaigns was to make visible the growers' feelings of injustice as well as the illegitimate practices by the supermarkets. While in other regions of the world the presence of brokers helps to conceal the degree of control exercised by the supermarket chains (Bonanno and Cavalcanti 2012), in Spain, the confrontation is direct and personalised. Although in the negotiation processes with the supermarkets the strawberry growers in Huelva tend to determine a fair return in terms of a minimum price that guarantees the viability of their farms, it seems appropriate to consider Luetchford's proposal in relation to moral economy and equivalence. The author proposes that inevitably something gets lost when the value of an object is translated to monetary value; a fair price is relative and the integral values (social and moral) exceed notions of equivalent value in another context (Luetchford 2014).

However, the lack of equality between the different agents in the value chain isn't the only factor that contributes to the tension between production and distribution. The convergence of beliefs and practices from two distinct economic rationalities is also a source of conflict. If the concept of economic rationality permits us to understand the principles, strategies, and objectives of the growers, it also helps to explain the way in which their cultural identity influences their relation to production, distribution, and public administration. In this sense, the substantial mismatch between the producers' worldview and the principles and economic objectives of the supermarket chains to maximise profit and accumulate capital, stands out. However, as we saw in the previous section, we shouldn't forget that the practices and objectives of the producers are driven by distinct and complex logics. Although identification with the traditional farmer has moved closer to one of an agricultural entrepreneur, and particularly so in the case of medium and large landowners, the importance of the conflict with the large supermarkets has seen the emergence of an ever greater sense of pride and cultural identity as strawberry growers.

Paradoxically, this identification and the emphasis placed on the conflictive relationship between production and distribution serves to illuminate other conflicts in the value chain that are often made invisible, such as the tendency for the local imaginary to diminish the contradictions that exist between the growers and the workers they employ. Labour-related tensions have long played an important part in the social dynamic of agricultural production in the area, which at times has erupted into open conflict. In the 1970s and 1980s it was autochthonous Andalusian day labourers who sought improvements in working conditions, while at the beginning of this century north African and Sub-Saharan labourers held work stoppages and sit-ins (Reigada 2017). As the workers' day-to-day relationship is with the landowner—in this case the strawberry growers—they see the multinational companies and supermarket chains as distant agents and hold the farmer responsible for the injustices that they suffer. In this sense, diminished rights, lack of equality, and abuses experienced by the growers are passed on to the working class. However, in acknowledging this we should also recognise that the growers' configuration of their moral economy may also be a political strategy that provides them with an ideological justification for their demands and protests (Scott 1976; Hossain and Kalita 2014), poor working conditions, and labour conflicts (Reigada 2017).

The moral norms that the growers employ to define legitimate and illegitimate practices in their relations with the supermarkets are also used to evaluate the behaviour of other social actors. They accused the large producers of being disloyal for investing in strawberry production in Morocco, Huelva's main competitor in the European markets. At the same time, they criticise other growers that, in recent years, have left the large co-operatives to set up small independent family enterprises, which they view as fragmenting and weakening their negotiating position with the supermarkets.

On the other hand, they also use this frame of reference to evaluate government institutions.[3] As in other areas of the economic market where protectionist policies coexist with the free market system, the growers maintain that the government should intervene to guarantee their rights. Indeed, the very conceptualisation of grievances into *rights* makes evident the impossibility of understanding economic phenomenon through the restrictive optic of monetary value. Martínez (2014) proposes that the very notion of a fair price reveals a certain contradiction between the dependence that the producers have on market value and the way that social value is employed to establish a fair and equitable price (the reproduction of the domestic unit and the dignity of work). Following Polanyi's line of thinking, Martínez observed that the producers' conceptualisation of a fair price was one based on a regulated or controlled market and not a free one (Martínez 2014); demands that make sense within a regulated economic framework inherited from the Keynesian state, which was designed to control market excesses. In this sense, a large section of farmers and agricultural associations believe that public administrations—specifically the state—should ensure a fair price that guarantees the

---

[3] Speculation, linked to corruption, and the responsibilities assigned to the government authorities also constitute two central elements of the moral economy that influenced the protests related to the food crisis in 2007–2008 (Hossain and Kalita 2014). For an analysis of these protests and the grievances that they address in relation to the degradation of social reproduction implied by the neo-liberal food regime, see Patel and McMichael (2009).

profitability of agriculture as an economic sector. Without questioning the fundamentals of a model that is strongly competitive and commercialised, they hope that the government will take on the task of stopping the abuses perpetrated by the large supermarket chains:

> Our problem is with the market, the market is free and everyone does whatever they like. That's where the government needs to get involved, and at least do a bit of research on the free market, and enforce reasonable prices. (Javier Moreno, grower)

> The problem that agriculture has in general, not just with the strawberry, is the difference between those that produce and those that consume, an intermediary that takes all the profits for the market, do you not see that it's a free market? They set the prices at whatever they like. And that's what we talk about a lot, that the government should intervene in some way. The market has to earn what the market has to earn, but not 300%. That's where it's just crazy [...]. I think that it should be the government, the state should take measures and establish a pricing structure, a scale, and regulate the price that we sell in relation to the retail sale price. (Antonio Pérez, grower)

However, what creates more indignation amongst the growers than the lack of protection they receive is their belief that public administrations actively promote deregulation of the market. In particular, they view the CAP reforms as a way of putting the sector at the mercy of market speculation: 'We want a CAP for producers and not for speculators', said one of the slogans during the COAG protests in 2013. Along with the pricing problem, they hope that public institutions will support them and implement measures to protect them in emergency situations, and provide a more equitable distribution of government assistance. In this sense, they regard the European Commission's Direct Payments Regulation as unfair because it is based on a system of support calculated according to number of hectares of eligible land. As far as the growers are concerned, this bears no relationship to productivity and therefore favours large holdings, often owned by absentee landowners. This vision of institutional responsibility stands in opposition to the concept of a 'fair market' as defined by the World Bank and the Organisation for Economic Co-operation and Development (OECD), which is one that is not dependent on CAP subsidies, as competition and profitability should make it self-sustaining.

Feelings of abandonment are most palpable when they evaluate the role of public administrators, particularly the state and the EU, in the agreements with third countries, such as Morocco. The growers accuse them of using Andalusian horticulture as a bargaining chip in the agreements with Morocco to gain more favourable deals for other sectors of the economy. They believe them to be complicit and responsible for the advantages that Morocco enjoys, such as reduced production costs, the volume of produce they can sell to European countries, and less stringent quality control. These advantages are considered to represent an unequal treatment of their sector that creates unfair competition. This sense of a lack of protection is accentuated and acquires meaning when it is related to feelings of risk and insecurity that pervades the agricultural system in the context of present day globalization; a feeling that has a profound influence on the modes of work and living of these agricultural families.

FROM FEELINGS OF LACK OF PROTECTION TO ONES OF RISK AND INSECURITY

Embarking on a project of modernisation, intensification, and globalisation has brought a significant increase in feelings of being exposed to risk and lack of security. Although the growers try to maintain a certain degree of control and balance that guarantees the social reproduction of their holdings, the language of insecurity is increasingly prevalent in their mentality and behaviour: 'right now farming is a lottery, you have to do everything perfectly if you want to survive' (Javier Moreno, strawberry grower). Once inserted into this model there is little margin to avoid the risks that come with the dynamics of the global agrifood industry, such as price fluctuations, intense competition, free market economics, and demands for highly flexible production. The dynamics of the chain mean that the producers have little freedom to take decisions and have become greatly dependent on agents that are better positioned on both sides of the value chain. For example, multinational suppliers and Californian laboratories control the costs of inputs, such as fertilisers, seeds, and technology, while on the output side, the large supermarket chains enforce the sale price, the packaging, and quality certification (Konefal et al. 2005).

Some of the strategies employed by the producers to deal with the instability of the market reflect these circumstances. In response to segmented consumer trends and the supermarkets' demands, growers have adopted a product diversification strategy, which mostly consists of developing new formats based on variations in weight, size, strawberry type, and packaging:

> Each market and retailer asks for a specific format, they insist on that format and we adapt to it. If a different supermarket wants a different format, well that's what we do. At the moment, we're doing first national [first class and for the national market], which are the wooden boxes, and, for example, this morning we changed format twice, and when we get to the next parcel [of land] we'll have to change to another format. (Pedro Moreno, farm manager)

> Sometimes you are doing one thing and they phone all of a sudden and say, 'hey, I need this'. (Daniel Sánchez, grower)

The trend toward increasingly diverse products is illustrated particularly well by the special formats that are being developed. Alluding to customisation, differentiation, and innovation as brand values, the slogan for a new type of packaging designed by one of the co-ops in Huelva that specialises in artisanal berries states: 'Berrybowl, the only packaging for the jewels of the countryside'. Another example is the St. Valentine's Day packaging used by many growers, which contains relatively few, homogeneously sized and smaller than normal, strawberries all carefully arranged in a heart-shaped container. When deciding whether or not to prepare special formats, the producers take into account the quantity of extra work involved and whether or not increases in production costs are compensated by the superior prices in niche consumer segments:

> Here, we've done a special presentation, for example, we leave some of the stem on and lay out the strawberries in a row on a cushion so that all of one side is visible, in F60 format, it also has a lid and two stickers. There's more packaging than fruit and we've even lost money on it. There are more requirements than what the fruit is worth. Then in England they multiply it [the price] ten times, but we don't see any of it. (Francisco López, grower)

Another strategy they adopt is to experiment with the relationship between varieties, climate, productivity, and price. Industrial agriculture, based on technological advances and biogenetic research, makes it possible to alter the natural cycle of growth and experiment with different strawberry varieties. Focusing on the production of an early maturing variety can mean a reduction in productivity but better prices due to low supply in the marketplace. On the other hand, betting on a late maturing variety means greater productivity due to better climatic conditions but lower prices as a result of oversupply, as competing countries such as France and Morocco enter the market. However, there is considerable risk inherent in this approach, both in terms of the market and the climate. For example, in the case of opting for late rather than early maturing fruit the high summer temperatures may come earlier than usual, which can cause an acceleration in growth and an oversupply of fruit and a drop in prices so drastic that the growers may choose to discard part of the harvest. Late spring frosts can have a similar effect on early season harvests. On other occasions instability comes from the lack of predictability of the market and sudden falls in the expected average price for the corresponding time of the season:

> Depending on the strawberry variety, the business owners [strawberry growers] employ one of two strategies: bet on the early strawberry and get good prices in the market, but lower production, or go for the late one and get more kilos, more production, but lower prices. The problem is, this year people have bet on the early strawberry and the prices weren't good and, well, what do they do now? Because now, in this part of the season [end], they have a bad strawberry and they can't compete. (Manager in agricultural organization 2)

On top of these adversities, other emergency situations also add to tensions and have repercussions on the volume of export and/or prices. One such example was the 2011 veto by Russia on the importation of European products as a tit-for-tat response to EU sanctions over the crisis in the Ukraine and Crimea. Another example was the *E.coli* outbreak that resulted in the deaths of dozens of people in Germany during the same year. The Andalusian producers lived through the indignation of being falsely accused of being the origin of the epidemic (associated with Almerian cucumbers). They also expressed their grievances at the fact being excluded from the indemnity paid by the EU to farmers affected by the Russia veto; they valued their losses at some €6 million. Paradoxically, the feeling of safety provided by technologically advanced quality control systems is juxtaposed with the growing apprehension of social (and global) fears related to health risks and environmental sustainability. The increase of this type of crisis in industrial agriculture has lead some authors to argue that the industry only creates an 'illusion of control' through technological innovation (Stuart 2008).

As such, the consequences of the global agrifood model on the economy of the growers can't be measured exclusively in terms of income. It needs to be considered in conjunction with the implications of living and working under conditions of great uncertainty and anxiety:

> This is fairly problematic. The growers, whether it's now, yesterday or a month ago, or next week, we're always the same. We get paid a very low price and then we see that our products are being sold abroad at exorbitant prices, well, you know, anyone would be angry. Nowadays having a hectare of strawberries in production costs a lot of money. By the time a grower has laid down plastic and all that, well they don't sleep at night, because they have a lot of money tied up in it. I always call it 'uninvested' money, well, it's invested, but I always say it's just thrown there on the ground, because it's in the ground, in the field, and it's thrown there, and until the season is over well it's impossible to sleep, because they're thinking, 'will the campaign be ok, will it be ok?'. (Secretary of the provincial farmers association 1)

Severe frosts across Europe during the 2016/2017 campaign saw a drop in competition and strong demand for fruit and vegetables, which led to a significant increase in prices. However, as a producer, interviewed on television, stated, 'The prices are exorbitant, but, as growers, we don't want this any more than we want the [low] prices from the previous campaigns'. Growers' demand for balance, including when circumstances are good, reflects their desire for stability as a principal on which to organise agricultural economies in the face of the incoherence that seems to reign in the logic of the market. In this sense, along with their demands for better state intervention (regulation, support plans, protection), the co-ops and agricultural associations are important instruments in growers' attempts to assert some degree of balance and stability, although they are often beset by their own internal conflicts. Although growers emphasise unity within the sector, we shouldn't forget the lack of trust and cooperation that has been present since the beginning of the period of intensive agriculture in Andalusia (Camarero et al. 2002).

As Spyridakis and Dima (2017) have succinctly observed in other agricultural regions of the Mediterranean, most specifically Greece, a lack of social cohesion and cooperative culture at the local level has undermined the sustainability and success of cooperatives, both historically and in the present day.[4]

As well as being self-made, and having to deal with the problems and challenges of operating in global supply chains, the changing experiences of these strawberry growers reveals how a sense of pride is reborn out of feelings of abandonment, risk, and lack of security. However, as opposed to the feelings of pride that emerged in the red gold era, in the present day these feelings have gained strength from a generalized feeling of being victims (of price fluctuations, pressure from the large supermarket chains, the measures taken by the state and EU that are viewed as creating unfair competition). This self-identification as victims is born out of and acquires meaning in the framework of a sector in crisis, and therefore constitutes a key element of the moral economy of the agricultural producer.

Conclusions

In the context of global agrifood markets, this chapter has shown how strawberry growers in Moguer and Palos de la Frontera, in the province of Huelva, think, feel and act. By taking this local and historic viewpoint, we can better understand how value, conviction, and behaviour is given meaning in the framework of the life experiences and work of these strawberry growers as they operate within global agrifood chains. The feelings of pride of these self-made producers is configured by cultural beliefs and practices associated with notions of productivity, professionalism, innovation, and progress, which contrasts sharply with previous models, such as the bourgeois large estate owners and the labouring peasant. In the present day, this pride is redefined through values of justice, legitimacy, and loyalty, along with insecurity and risk, which is now contrasted with the large supermarket chains and free market economy. The pride of people who went from a subsistence living and poverty to

---

[4] Furthermore, the authors have explored how, in response to local and family needs in a crisis hit Greece, a break with this logic has emerged in new agricultural initiatives that are based on trust, local networks and the quality of social relations (Spyridakis and Dima 2017).

become the number one European exporter of strawberries is continued in the pride of those that face up to the injustices and adversities of the market in order to reclaim what belongs to them. By demanding a fair price for their produce, they seek to reclaim the quality of life of the domestic unit, the profitability of their farms, and recognition for the value of their work and effort.

The moral economy of the strawberry growers of Huelva is inscribed in the framework of this changing experience and their feelings of being victims of the illegitimate behaviour of the market and government institutions. They come from a cultural logic that contrasts such behaviour with what they see as legitimate objectives such as supporting the family, improving their quality of life, and being rewarded for a job well done. However, although they are still faced with the problem of illegitimate speculation and the logic of capital accumulation, these producers haven't contemplated alternatives to the current model. In a context of crisis they are attempting to maintain their position within the production chains of globalised agrifood, demanding what cannot be given to them.

REFERENCES

Antentas, J.M., and E. Vivas. 2007. Las resistencias a las cadenas de la gran distribución comercial. In *Supermercados, no gracias. Grandes cadenas de distribución: impactos y alternativas*, ed. E. Vivas and X. Montagut, 135–148. Barcelona: Icaria.

Appadurai, A. 1984. How Moral Is South Asia's Economy? A Review Article. *Journal of Asian Studies* 43 (3): 481–497.

Bonanno, A., and J.S. Cavalcanti. 2012. Globalization, Food Quality and Labor: The Case of Grape Production in North-Eastern Brazil. *International Journal of Sociology of Agriculture and Food* 19 (1): 37–55.

Burch, D., and G. Lawrence. 2009. Towards a Third Food Regime: Behind the Transformation. *Agriculture and Human Values* 26: 267–279.

Camarero, L. 2017. Territorios encadenados, tránsitos migratorios y ruralidades adaptativas. *Mundo Agrario* 18 (37): 1–18.

Camarero, L., R. Sanpedro, and J.L. Vicente-Mazariegos. 2002. Los horticultores: una identidad en transición (1988). *AREAS. Revista de Ciencias Sociales* 22: 43–69.

Cruces, C. 1994. *Navaceros, nuevos agricultores y viñistas: las estrategias cambiantes de la agricultura familiar en Sanlúcar de Barrameda*. Sevilla: Blas Infante.

Delgado, M., and M.A. Aragón. 2006. Los campos andaluces en la globalización. Almería y Huelva, fábricas de hortalizas. In *La agricultura española en la era de la globalización*, ed. M. Etxezarreta, 423–474. Madrid: Ministerio de Agricultura, Pesca y Alimentación.

Florido, D. 2004. *La Pesca en Andalucía. Factores Globales y Locales de un Proceso de Crisis*. Sevilla: Fundación José Manuel Lara.

Fourneau, F. 1983. *La provincia de Huelva y los problemas del desarrollo regional*. Huelva: Diputación de Huelva.

Friedland, W. 2004. Agrifood Globalization and Commodity Systems. *International Journal of Sociology of Agriculture and Food* 12: 1–12.

Hossain, N., and D. Kalita. 2014. Moral Economy in a Global Era: The Politics of Provisions During Contemporary Food Price Spikes. *The Journal of Peasant Studies* 41 (5): 815–831.

Konefal, J., M. Mascarenhas, and M. Hatanaka. 2005. Governance in the Global Agro-Food System: Backlighting the Role of Transnational Supermarket Chains. *Agriculture and Human Values* 22: 291–302.

Luetchford, P. 2014. (Re)valuing the Local: Moral Economies of Food in Andalusia. Paper presented at the *Value and Values in Agro-Food Processes* workshop, June 10–12, EHESS, Marseille.

Márquez, J.A. 1986. *La nueva agricultura onubense*. Sevilla: Instituto de Desarrollo Regional.

Martín, E. 1995. El cultivo del fresón en la zona de Palos y Moguer: Cambios socioeconómicos y sectores sociales implicados. *Aestutaria Revista de Investigación* 3: 31–55.

Martínez, B. 2014. About Moral Economy: Fair Price, Quality and Sustainability in Galician Farming Exploitations. Paper presented at the *Value and Values in Agro-Food Processes* workshop, June 10–12, EHESS, Marseille.

Narotzky, S. 1997. *New Directions in Economic Anthropology*. London: Pluto Press.

Narotzky, S., and N. Besnier. 2014. Crisis, Value, and Hope: Rethinking the Economy. An Introduction to Supplement 9. *Current Anthropology* 55 (S9): 4–16.

Palenzuela, P. 1996. *Buscarse la vida. Economía jornalera en las marismas de Sevilla*. Sevilla: Ayuntamiento de Sevilla.

Patel, R., and P. McMichael. 2009. A Political Economy of the Food Riot. *Review, A Journal of the Fernand Braudel Center* 12 (1): 9–35.

Reigada, A. 2017. Policies, Economic Forces, Class Relations, and Unions in Spain's Strawberry Fields. In *Uncertain Times: Anthropological Approaches to Labor in a Neoliberal World*, ed. E.P. Durrenberger, 286–320. Colorado: Colorado University Press.

Scott, J.C. 1976. *The Moral Economy of the Peasant: Rebellion and Subsistence in Southeast Asia*. New Haven: Yale University Press.

Spyridakis, M., and F. Dima. 2017. Reinventing Traditions: Socially Produced Goods in Eastern Crete During Economic Crisis. *Journal of Rural Studies* 53: 269–277.

Stuart, D. 2008. The Illusion of Control: Industrialized Agriculture, Nature, and Food Safety. *Agriculture and Human Values* 25: 177–181.

Thompson, E.P. 1971. The Moral Economy of the English Crowd in the Eighteenth Century. *Past & Present* 50: 76–136.

Thompson, E.P. 1991. *Customs in Common*. London: Penguin.

Verdier, M. 2006. *Reflexiones en torno a la situación actual del sector fresero de Huelva*. Huelva: Freshuelva (Unpublished).

Wolf, E. 1973. *Las luchas campesinas del siglo XX*. Madrid: Siglo XXI.

CHAPTER 14

Neoliberal Agrarian Policies and Its Effects: Labour Flexibility and Regimentation in Mexico's Export Agricultural Industry

Christian Zlolniski

INTRODUCTION

Common conceptualisations of neoliberal economic policies focus on deregulatory measures that minimize the role of the state and advocate for free markets. In the global arena, deregulation is used as a policy tool to tear down barriers and tariffs that interfere with international trade and the free flow of capital and commodities. Domestically, national governments use deregulation policies to lift labour protection for workers as a tool to foster full employment and enhance flexibility in the labour markets. Flexibility to hire and dismiss workers, the use of temporal employment agencies to reduce labour costs, and a concerted attack on labour unions portrayed as hindering economic growth and free labour markets are among the many effects that neoliberal policies have had in both industrialised and developing countries in all employment sectors (Durrenberger 2017; Lazar 2017).

C. Zlolniski (✉)
University of Texas at Arlington, Arlington, TX, USA

© The Author(s) 2018
M. Spyridakis (ed.), *Market Versus Society*, Palgrave Studies in Urban Anthropology, https://doi.org/10.1007/978-3-319-74189-5_14

But while the effects of neoliberal labour policies in flexibilising work and the labour markets have been extensively documented, their impact on the work process has received comparatively lesser attention. What is the effect of neoliberal labour policies on the production process in different industries and occupations? How is the workplace transformed by these policies? And how are workers' tasks affected by these changes? Examining the rules and norms set up by transnational corporations and domestic employers in the workplace is an important analytical task to develop a full and nuanced understanding of the multilayered effects of neoliberal labour policies on the environment in which labourers around the world perform their everyday tasks.

In this chapter, I examine the production of fresh produce in northern Mexico for consumer markets in the United States and its impact on the working conditions of farm labourers in the San Quintin Valley in Baja California. While labour flexibility is at the heart of the global fresh-produce industry, at the same time, work has become more standardised and regimented than ever before under rules that seek to control, measure, and enhance workers' productivity. The result is a new labour regime characterized by heightening discipline and labour control. I focus on five elements that have transformed the work process in the fresh-produce industry in the region: production in sheltered environments, piece-rate system, the merging of harvest and packing tasks in the field, the use of good agricultural practices (GAP) to meet export-certification requirements, and the use of time as a mechanism for labour control. Together, I contend, these components sustain a production ecosystem that has led to the quantitative and qualitative intensification of the work process for farm labourers. I refer to this regime as 'regimented flexibility', a system that has enhanced labour flexibility regarding the employment of farmworkers to reduce labour costs while, at the same time, it has created new regulations in the workplace to extract surplus value from workers and enhance productivity.

First, I provide a brief history of the development of export agriculture in the San Quintin Valley. The next sections dissect the five main pillars of the agricultural production system; I describe each of these features, discussing their effects on the labour conditions for farmworkers. By using an ethnographic perspective to view the workplace regime of export agriculture, a better understanding of how the structural forces of the global fresh-produce industry permeate the conditions in which farm labourers perform their everyday jobs is gained.

THE GROWTH OF EXPORT AGRICULTURE
IN NORTHERN MEXICO

Favored by neoliberal policies, export agriculture has become a global strategy for economic development in many developing countries, including in Latin America (Alvarez 2006; Echánove 2001; Lara Flores 1996; Llambi 1994; Reynolds 1994). In Mexico, the fresh-produce industry has dramatically expanded since the late 1990s because of demand by US consumers for fresh vegetables and fruits for healthier diets, and government agrarian policies promoting export agriculture as a vehicle to generate jobs, reduce poverty, and curtail labour migration to the United States. The approval of the North America Free Trade Agreement (NAFTA) in 1994 facilitated US agribusinesses moving south of the border attracted by that country's land, labour, and soft environmental regulations (Echánove 2001; Gonzalez 2014; Weaver 2001; Zabin 1997). As a result, a system of transnational agriculture has consolidated in which large US agribusinesses outsource production south of the border to ensure a continuous supply of fresh crops.

Located about 300 kilometers south of the Mexico–US border in Baja California, the San Quintin Valley is one of the most technologically advanced and economically dynamic agro-export regions in Mexico. Export agriculture in the region started in the mid-1970s with the completion of the Transpeninsular Highway, which connected it with San Diego on the US–Mexico border. At that time the region shifted from growing potatoes for local and domestic markets to producing tomatoes for export to the United States. Since the late 1990s, the diversity of export crops produced has increased, providing increasing job opportunities for farmworkers. While tomato production—the leading commercial crop that has fueled the growth of San Quintin's horticultural industry since the early 1980s—accounted for more than 70% of all horticultural production in 1995, by 2008 tomato production had declined to 40% while other export crops such as berries, cucumbers, broccoli, and celery gained currency. By 2015, San Quintin ranked first in the export of cucumbers from Mexico to the United States, second in tomatoes (after Sinaloa), and is a growing powerhouse in the production of strawberries and blueberries, including organic berries exported to the United States.

The growth of export agriculture led to a rapid population growth of farmworkers from southern Mexico. Between 1990 and 2000, the population almost doubled from 38,151 to 74,427, and by 2010 it had reached almost 94,000 inhabitants. The region also experienced a shift from seasonal temporal workers to a more permanent labour force composed of indigenous workers from some of the poorest states in southern Mexico. These include Mixtec, Zapotec, and Triquis from the states of Oaxaca and Guerrero with a history of labour migration to the region that goes back to the mid-1980s (Velasco et al. 2014). Since the early 1990s, when employment in agriculture became more stable, former migrant workers began to settle in San Quintin, often bringing their families with them. They were attracted by the opportunity to work in agriculture for longer periods of time, the availability of land lots to settle on and build their homes (even though at first these were often shacks), and the lack of employment opportunities in their home communities in southern Mexico. Despite settling down and having access to more stable job opportunities, indigenous workers occupy the lowest-paid and more labour-intensive occupations in the horticultural industry. Local agricultural employment is segmented along ethnic and gender lines, with indigenous workers, many of them women, employed in the most labour-intensive jobs of harvesting, land preparation, cultivation, and pruning.

Surprisingly, few ethnographic studies have examined the impact of export agriculture on the workers that specialise in the production of fresh crops for consumers in the United States. Yet the production and labour regime of the fresh-produce industry raises some important questions: How has the production regime of export agriculture affected the conditions under which farm labourers perform their jobs? How do workers assess changes in the workplace associated with this production regime? Based on an ethnographic study conducted in a rural region in northern Mexico, I address these questions, analyzing the workplace regime that prevails in this industry and its impact on farmworkers.

FROM OPEN FIELD TO INDOOR AGRICULTURE

Growing fresh produce in green- and shade-houses constitutes a key dimension of modern industrial agriculture. Generally known as controlled environment agriculture, or simply indoor agriculture, horticultural production in sheltered facilities is a system that involves the combination of engineering, plant science, and computer-managed systems to optimize plant growing and productivity. In Mexico, the expansion of cultivation of water-intense export crops in greenhouse facilities is the most important factor behind the intensification of horticultural production (Gonzalez 2014). Between 1999 and 2005, for example, the extension of production in greenhouses of export crops such as tomatoes, green peppers, and cucumbers increased from 721 to 3200 hectares (1781–7907 acres) in the main export regions of northern Mexico (Sinaloa, Jalisco, Baja California, Baja California Sur, and Sonora) (Gonzalez 2014: 298–299). Productivity in protected environments is considerably higher than in open-air cultivation, with estimated per-hectare productivity 300–600 higher (Gonzalez 2014: 299).

In San Quintin, indoor agriculture began in the late 1990s after the collapse of the former capitalist model of extensive production in open fields that precipitated a water shortage crisis. After two decades of over-exploitation of the underground water table, many water wells went either dry or had a high salinity content that made water unfit for crop irrigation; in response, large companies started to produce in protected environments to reduce water use and have higher crop yields (Zlolniski 2011). Companies that invested in this technology reaped good benefits as productivity sharply increased. According to data gathered from the local office of the Secretariat of Agriculture, tomato production in protected environments, for example, went from 72 hectares in 2004 to 1400 hectares in 2011. And while open field cultivation in 2011 during the spring–summer season yielded 60 tons per hectare, in greenhouses it reached 92 tones. Moreover, production in protected environments requires less land and labour, as well as lower costs for herbicides and pesticides, allowing the production of more homogenous and standardized crops to meet the preferences of US consumption markets.

But, while contributing productivity, production in sheltered environments has also had a major impact on the working conditions for farm labourers. As anthropologists Paciulan and Preibisch point out, indoor agriculture fosters a 'fast-paced and high-pressure work environment' in which workers' schedules are highly variable and instable depending on crop cycles and market demands (2013: 179–180). During fieldwork, I often heard farmworkers complain about the hardships and endurance it takes to labour long hours inside hot and humid shade-houses. They also experienced a significant increase on their workload as well as intense pressure from supervisors and managers to perform a high 'quality job'. Anayeli Fernandez, a Zapotec field worker employed by Agricola San Simon illustrates this experience. Born in 1988 in a rural village in the southern state of Oaxaca, Anayeli first arrived in San Quintin in 2003 along with her parents and siblings. She soon began working for Agrícola San Simón in diverse tasks such as weeding, pruning, and harvesting, earning about 1500 pesos a week (about $140 dollars). In 2005, however, the company began producing in shadehouses. With the change, her work became more challenging because the high temperature and humidity and the stricter requirements and expectations placed on her. As she said:

> Shadehouses get very hot which slows you down and you're less productive. [Moreover] they [company supervisors] are stricter regarding how you treat the plants; it wasn't like that in the open field, so there you could be a bit more productive. …Moreover in the shadehouses the plants are more fragile and you've to be very careful, if you break them you don't get paid for the whole work task.

Anayeli's comments point out two important dimensions of work performed in the artificial environments of indoor agriculture. First, the climatic conditions: with average temperatures of 90° and 95° Fahrenheit in green- and shade-houses in the late spring and summer, high humidity, and lack of natural air breeze, farm labourers' work is more taxing and physically demanding than performing the same tasks in open fields. A second aspect refers to the surveillance and control under which workers perform their jobs. Because green- and shade-houses require high capital investments by growers, the requirements on workers to increase productivity are racketed up. As a result, labour control in the workplace is intensified with several layers of supervisors monitoring their work, including the *mayordomos* (crew supervisors), the company's field supervisor, and occasionally field agronomists. Workers complain about a ubiquitous surveillance regime that slows them down and penalizes them for any errors made at work. Luis Flores, a farmworker employed by Monsanto to grow seeds as well as a variety of fruits and flowers, complained about the hot temperature that made his work more difficult and physically taxing:

> You can't work at ease inside because of the heat, there is no breeze coming in. In the open field it's hot but sooner or later there's always a breeze and you cool down a bit. In the shadehouse you are enclosed and you feel like burning.

In addition, Luis also noticed an augmentation of the work load since he began working in the shadehouses.

> Before [open field] they gave us six furrows per task and we worked in the field with the breeze. Now they give us seven furrows and you are enclosed inside, you cannot work "a gusto' [at ease], it's very hot inside, no, no, it's very difficult to bear it!

Health hazards associated with working in green and shade-houses is also a common theme that emerged when talking to farmworkers. While there are no official statistics on job accidents in San Quintin's horticultural sector, I found considerable information in the field about work accidents and health problems farm labourers face. Field workers complained about feeling dizzy, having episodes of high blood pressure, fainting, as well as accidents at work, revealing a new set of occupational hazards in the workplace. While some of the risks and hazards farmworkers face are not restricted to sheltered environments, they are exacerbated when working in this environment where they have to work faster and harder than before. This shows that, as medical anthropologists have argued, biopolitics are deeply embedded in the production technologies of the fresh-produce industry, shaping power relations and affecting the health of farmworkers in the workplace (Holmes 2013; Bronwen Horton 2016).

From Day Wages to Piece Rates

In modern industrial agriculture, piece-rate rather than hourly or day wages is the predominant system for workers' remuneration. In this system, the unit of product instead of unit of time is used to calculate the payment (Hernández-Romero 2012: 74). Discussing the incentives for piece rate in agriculture, economic anthropologist Sutti Ortiz points out that this system keeps the costs of specific work tasks constant while stimulating productivity (2002: 404). Interestingly, labourers also prefer the piece rate because it allows them to increase their earnings and gives them more freedom to decide when to come and leave. A downside of piecework, Ortiz indicates, is that it enhances absenteeism and promotes speed at the expense of quality (2002: 405). Piece rate has become a key tool to increase productivity and a major management strategy used by horticultural companies around the world (Ortiz et al. 2013). In this context some scholars contend that piece rate 'promote(s) individual competition among workers' pitting workers against each other (Paciulan and Preibisch 2013: 181), and serves as a mechanism for the intensification of labour for tasks formerly paid at a time rate (Rogaly 2008: 504–505).

The fresh-produce industry in San Quintin did not escape this trend. Until the late 1990s, most companies and growers paid their field workers *'jornales'* or daily wages, a fixed amount for labouring a day shift of eight hours a day. Since the early 2000s, however, daily wages began to be replaced by piece rate as a means to increase productivity and reduce labour costs. It was also a strategy by growers to compete for scarce labour during the harvest at a time when many farmworkers had moved out of labour camps owned by their employers and settled in colonias in their own homes, providing them more freedom to choose the growers for whom to work. Rather than a single piece rate type, however, there is a large variety of piece rate forms companies use. Some tasks are paid by individual piece rate, while others are team-based on tasks performed by a labour crew. Moreover, some other work activities are still paid by day wages. Planting and harvesting, for example, are often paid piece-rate, while other 'culture tasks' such as pruning and preparing the soil for the next cycle are frequently paid by daily wage. A worker employed by the same company may be remunerated by each of these systems depending on the work task at hand, crop, season, and whether work is performed in an open field or a greenhouse.

The flexibility of remuneration forms used by agricultural companies in San Quintin is illustrated by the case of Ramón Suarez. Born in 1972 in Tetujín, a small Mixtec village in Oaxaca, since 2006 Ramón has worked for several years for Rancho *Vigor*, one of the oldest ranches in the region that grows strawberries and tomatoes for a US distributing company. As an employee of this company, from January to February 2013, he worked pruning strawberry plants, an activity for which he was paid a day wage of 110 Mexican pesos (about $8 a day). During the harvest, from February to June, he was switched to piece rate, earning about $19 a day, and in July he was sent to a different field, for which he was paid piece rate, barely making between $6 and $8 a day, less than the day wage. In September, he began preparing the soil and furrows for the next production cycle and was switched back to $8-a-day wage. Finally, from October to December when work slows down, Ramón was only employed three to four days a week by day wage, supplementing his meager income with earnings from a temporary job as a *peon* in construction. In my conversations with him, his frustration and resignation about how the company treated him and other workers often came to the surface. Conveying a sense of power inequality in which growers have the upper hand, leaving workers little room to maneuver, he commented:

> Wages always fell short. I think that growers take advantage of us because they know that all the people who live here cannot go to work somewhere else and that we can only work in the field, especially if we are not schooled. The *patrones* know that sooner or later we will end up working in the field, even if we don't want to, that's why they don't raise our wages.

Ramón's predicament reflects the decline of work opportunities in San Quintin's agriculture since production in open fields has diminished. Production in green- and shade-houses employs fewer workers, increasing competition for jobs among farm labourers and pushing them to accept higher workloads under piece rate. The intensification of labour also means that farm labourers have to work harder to earn the equivalent of a day wage. The flexibility to constantly change the form of remuneration is used by growers as a vehicle to reduce labour costs and increase workers' productivity by racketing up the workload.

From Harvest to Packing

A third vector in the re-organization of production in the fresh-produce industry consists in the integration of sorting and packing tasks as part of the regular workload of farm labourers. Describing the work process with strawberries, table grapes, and lettuce in California's Central Valley, anthropologist Manuel Hernández-Romero points out that the harvest of these crops 'is immediately integrated with packing, and the products leave the fields with the same presentation with which they will reach the consumers' (2012: 75). As William Friedland—a leading scholar in the globalisation of the fresh produce industry—indicates, this practice demonstrates the tendency in this industry 'to increase profit margins at retail through value-adding' (cited by Hernández-Romero 2012: 79).

In San Quintin, the introduction of packing as part of the labour process among strawberry workers gained momentum in the early 2000s, when transnational US companies began to produce in the region. Companies growing strawberries added sorting and packing to the work tasks assigned to workers in the field. Farmworkers harvesting strawberries were required to sort and package the delicate fruits according to specific instructions of size, color, and degree of ripeness. These tasks were folded into part of the harvest, in what amounts to an unpaid component of the work process given that workers are paid by piece-rate based on the volume of berries harvested.

The labour intensification that resulted from incorporating packaging to the harvest did not go unnoticed by farmworkers. One day while observing strawberry workers employed at a middle-sized company growing raspberries for Driscoll, I had the opportunity to notice the ramifications of this dimension of the labour process. It was mid-morning on a summer day when a group of about eighteen field workers, mostly women, were in the last days of the picking season. As they explained, they were paid 14 Mexican pesos (about $1 at the time) for each box of fruits, each containing six baskets of 12 ounces, amounting to 2.3 pesos [17 cents] per basket. Experienced workers made an average of 25–30 boxes at the pick of the harvest season when the plants are full of fruits, but when the harvest is coming to an end, they only make about 10 boxes a day. Completing eight boxes a day, they explained, was the equivalent to a day's wage; going above that threshold was considered good and an incentive to work hard. Yet to be paid, the fruits each worker harvests has to pass a quality check, which has several steps. As I observed in the field, every time a worker filled two boxes, he/she had to bring them to a checking station where a *checadora* or inspector counted and checked them to make sure they met the instructions for type, size, color, and degree of ripeness specified for the day. Afterwards, a truck takes the boxes to Driscoll's cooling and packing plant to minimize the time between when they are picked and when they arrive at its cooling facility.

That morning, shortly before I was about to leave this field, a pickup truck arrived from Driscoll's cooling plant bringing back about dozen raspberry boxes. When I asked the driver why he was bringing them back, he replied that these fruits had not passed a second quality checkpoint at Driscoll's cooling plant. Whenever berries arrive to this facility, he explained, they are inspected for quality purposes and if there are boxes that fail the test, they are sent back to the field where they were harvested. A tracking number in the boxes allows identification of the field and work-crew that harvested and packaged the boxes. Once back in the field, the workers who picked, sorted, and packed the berries, have to replace them with good fruits and repack the boxes to pass the inspection in order to get paid.

As this brief episode reveals, by integrating packing as part of the harvest, workers contribute to the value-add of the produce in the consumer market but are not remunerated for this component of the labour process. This system is based on negative reinforcement that penalizes labourers when the fruits do not meet the company's quality standards. Modern digital traceability technologies are used as a tool of labour control, allowing companies to closely track and monitor the performance of their workers. Thus in today's fresh-produce industry, companies maintain better internal records of who picks and when and where the produce was picked than administrative records to officially register them in the social security system to receive labour, health, and pension benefits to which they are entitled.

ENFORCING 'FOOD SAFETY AND QUALITY'

The fourth element that characterizes the production regime of export agriculture in Baja is the result of certification rules for food safety and quality in the horticultural industry. A renewed emphasis on food safety began in 1997, when the United States launched the Produce and Imported Food Safety Initiative under the US Department of Agriculture (USDA) with new technical regulations to enhance food hygiene and phytosanitary conditions to prevent food contamination. These included norms for sanitation, toxic pesticide residues as well as packing, labelling, storage, and transportation of perishable produce (De Grammont and Lara Flores 2010: 235). After September 11, 2001, new regulations went into effect when the US Congress approved the Bioterrorism Act, which sought to further raise the levels of protection for food safety by requiring growers exporting produce to the United States to register with this government agency and obtain laboratory analyses for phytosanitary control (De Grammont and Lara Flores 2010). The new rules required Mexican growers to make significant capital investments in adjusting their produce infrastructure, pushing many small companies out the market, which some authors interpret as a form of 'protectionism' based on technical barriers to trade (Avendaño et al. 2007).[1]

The agribusiness sector also developed new commercial standards regarding the quality of fresh fruits and vegetables for US consumer markets. These norms mostly consist in the standardization of size, shape, texture and color of fresh produce, a trend imposed by shippers and large supermarkets in the United States. Unlike food safety norms, such 'quality' standards are market-driven and aimed at shaping consumers' preferences for aesthetic traits on the appearance of freshness (Fischer and Benson 2006). British anthropologist Ben Rogaly calls this trend 'commodity fetishism', whereby working conditions in modern industrial agriculture are rendered invisible to the consumers of fresh produce (Rogaly 2008: 507). The standardisation of fresh-produce production, he argues, has increased the speed, care, and effort required from farm labourers in the workplace.

In San Quintin, the renewed emphasis on fresh-produce quality began in the late 1990s. While in the past growers emphasized quantity or volume, in response to new certification requirements and market trends, quality became the new mantra. In the process, a new corporate culture of food safety and quality was set in place affecting the organization of production. Horticultural companies began implementing a set of so-called GAP, aimed at ensuring produce meets the standards required for export crops. These norms are usually carried out by the supervisors and crew-leaders through talks for workers, elsewhere known as escuela or school, informal workshops to train workers in the norms of food safety and quality. This type of workshop serves as informal social institutions 'for converting technical knowledge—embedded in the definitions of each commodity—to workers' daily practice' (Hernández-Romero 2012: 79). They also help in socializing workers to the new efficiency and quality requirements of the agribusiness sector, reducing the use of coercion as a tool of labour control (Lara Flores and Sánchez Saldaña 2015: 81).

The way in which the set of GAP are instilled in workers' minds is illustrated by Esther Chávez, a forty-four-year-old worker employed by Monsanto in San Quintin. When Monsanto arrived in the region in

[1]The most important costs were those resulting from the installation of new sanitary infrastructure for workers, agricultural machinery, storage facilities for chemical products, water treatment plants, post-harvest handling and cold rooms (Avendaño 2004; cited in De Grammont and Lara Flores 2010: 237).

2005 after acquiring the multinational Seminis, it reorganized its work-force, lying off former in-house workers and replacing them with tempo-rary workers hired by Global Source, a third-party company specialising in managing temporary workers. It also implemented a new managerial culture that included workshops on GAP to enhance productivity as well as food safety and quality. To improve safety and reduce job accidents in the workplace, it provided new personal equipment, such as gloves, safety glasses, overall, and boots, to workers. It also developed new and higher expectations regarding the personal hygiene of workers, most of them women, and the appearance of their working clothes. Norms about personal appearance do not allow women to wear makeup, bracelets, rings, trinkets or any personal jewelry, and require them to keep their hair tightened and their nails short. Talking with Esther, a worker who had been employed for several years by Seminis and later by Monsanto, she expressed her ambivalence about these rules. On the one hand, she was glad about feeling safer at work.

> I am happy because they give us protective gear to wear at work which is called 'protective personal equipment' which is given to each worker and isn't transferable. Gloves, safety glasses, overall, boots, and if you don't bring your equipment to work they don't let you in.

At the same time, she commented on the intense control and surveil-lance she and her co-workers were subjected to in the workplace with respect to their personal appearance:

> We have to bath at home and come clean; sometimes workers look dirty and they get reprimanded...The "*mayordoma*" check us when we arrive and if our overall isn't clean she calls our attention saying 'why didn't you wash your overall?'

GAPs sessions not only referred to instructions on how to carry out their jobs, but also included a new protocol stating workers should refer to their supervisors as their 'clients'. Describing the change experienced when this company took over Seminis, Esther explained,

> The supervisors aren't called supervisors anymore but now we call them our 'clients', I have to refer to them as my client. My duty is to satisfy my client with my work; all this is contained in the quality policy the company

teaches us when we are hired. The policy has several goals. The first goal is to deliver our products on-time; if we satisfy our client, then they in turn satisfy their boss. The second goal is to increase our efficiency or productivity; we need to increase the quality of our work every day we work. Every day when we arrive in the morning they give us a *'plática'* [talk] and they ask us "hey Berta, what is the first objective of the company's philosophy?" Sometimes they caught us in blank and we don't know what to answer… Every third day they keep repeating, repeating, and repeating these principles and we have to memorize them because sometimes the company's inspectors come to our work areas and ask you point blank "Do you know what is the first principle in the company's quality policy?" So they keep us training and orienting us all the time.

Esther's comments convey the mixed feelings I often found among farmworkers regarding the effects of the implementation of GAP. On the one hand, she was happy to have a work uniform to wear at work instead of her own clothes, which in the past got dirty and worn down. She particularly appreciated talks about how to handle pesticides, and having access to drinking water in the workplace as well as clean (portable) restrooms. On the other hand, her experience reveals the intensification of labour implicated in the new regime of food safety and quality where workers are required to meet high norms of personal hygiene and appearance. The new managerial approach brings the neoliberal language of 'customer satisfaction' from the supermarket into the workplace. In so doing it naturalizes the expectations on productivity and food quality, an important component of the commodity fetishism identified by Rogaly (2008).

THE CONTROL OF THE WORKING DAY

The fifth pillar of the production regime in the fresh-produce industry refers to the implementation of new norms about the length of the working day. The struggle over the working day is a classic theme in the Marxist tradition of work studies. As David Harvey reminds us, this struggle is linked to the social construction of time and temporality in the capitalistic mode of production, representing an important feature of class struggle (2010: 135). In a study of indigenous rural peasants in Ecuador turned into farmworkers in modern horticultural production, anthropologist David Syring (2009) argues that they resent capitalist notions about the proper ways to organize time and labour and relationships between work and everyday life. This is because the workplace regime in industrial agriculture submits them to a more exacting labour discipline, illustrating what he calls 'transnational encounters with global capitalist temporality' (Syring 2009: 119).

Beginning in 2000, large companies in San Quintin, along with norms about food safety and quality, began implementing new rules about the length of the working day. These rules included punctuality, lunch breaks, and workers' shifts aimed at improving the coordination and synchronisation of labourers' activities in the workplace to enhance efficiency and productivity. Employers also instituted new policies to lay off workers for several days when they missed work, economic incentives to encourage workers to stay working for them, as well as homogeneous time shifts for all workers. Piece-rate workers who in the past had some leeway to go home after completing their work-tasks were now required to wait until the end of the working day before they could leave.

But while the control of time has become another tool for labour disciplining, it is also an arena for resistance and labour struggle. The new rules were often met with resistance by farmworkers who felt they had lost flexibility to control and organize their own time. Luis Flores, for instance, an employee of Monsanto, noticed the imposition of new and more rigid rules about the work shifts when this company took over Seminis. In the past when working in the fields, he explained, he could leave after completing his task around 1 pm, but after the change he had to wait until 3:30 pm to leave along with all workers.

> Before you could leave after finishing your work task. ... Now you have to stay until 3:30 pm or the time the company says. Sometimes they give us additional tasks... Moreover, if you don't want to continue working, they tell us not to come the next day because there won't be any work for us; ... It's different than before because ... you have to wait until everybody finishes and then and only then they let us leave.

For women who have to carefully balance wage work with household chores and community responsibilities, the new time-control policies are especially troublesome. Anayeli Fernandez, the worker employed by Agrícola San Simón, told me that the single most important factor that led her to quit her job at this company was the new policy with a longer and more rigid work schedule. Losing the flexibility to leave work before 3:30 to attend her children was the final stroke that broke the deal for her as a single mother. Indeed, many women prefer working for what in the region are known as 'rancheros', farmers running small-sized companies rather than for large transnational companies because of the greater flexibility to control their time. As in the case of norms regulating workers' physical appearance, norms about the length of the working day reveal the conflict between the logics of production and social reproduction in the labour regime of export agriculture in which workers are reduced to a mere labour-cost input that is stripped from the reality and constrains of their local lives.

CONCLUSION

Deregulation and labour policies aimed at increasing flexible practices in the labour market are at the heart of neoliberal economic policies that have dominated the global economy since the early 1980s. In addition to undermining workers' labour protections and benefits, these policies have also had an important impact on the workplace transforming the conditions in which workers carry out their everyday tasks. Examining the transformation of the workplace, I argue, is an important analytical task to fully understand the multidimensional and complex effects such policies and their micro effects have on labourers across different industries and occupations.

In this chapter, I have discussed five changes in the fresh-produce industry that have transformed the lives of farmworkers in Mexico who grow fruits and vegetables exported to consumer markets in the United States. The shifts from cultivation in open fields to production in sheltered environments, day-wages to piece-rate, the integration of harvest and packing into a single work-task, codes and regulations about GAP, and the use of time as a tool of labour control and discipline have transformed the workplace in which farm labourers perform their work. Farmworkers labouring in greenhouses in Baja face additional workloads under a heightened system of surveillance and control, while new norms about produce safety and quality have placed additional burdens and responsibilities on their shoulders. In the workplace they are subjected to a tight control of time that seeks to optimize each of their activities and movements from the time of arrival to their time of departure from work. The combination of these five elements form the production eco-system of the modern fresh-produce industry, fostering a labour regime I call regimented flexibility. Regimented flexibility combines two apparently opposite traits, namely labour flexibility and a rigid code of norms regu-lating work in the workplace. Labour flexibility—a cornerstone of neo-liberal agrarian policies—involves the ability of companies in Mexico to contract workers as temporary labourers with limited labour benefits and protections, often through subcontracting arrangements to reduce labour costs and externalize legal responsibilities to labour contractors and other labour intermediaries (i.e., temp agencies). Labour flexibility also has an internal component that provides employers great latitude to change and rotate workers through different tasks and assignments, and use different payment systems such as day wages and piece rates as tools to reduce labour costs and foster productivity. This labour flexibility stands in sharp contrast to the internal code of rules and regulations these companies have implemented, which have made farmwork a highly scripted and monitored occupation. Codified in a technical language of 'product safety and quality,' a new corporate culture has taken hold, one which fosters the intensification of labour (Lara Flores 2006; Velasco et al. 2014). Labour flexibility and work regimentation, I contend, are thus two sides of the same production regime in the global fresh-produce industry.

The production regime of transnational agriculture embodies the neoliberal governance system that prevails in the horticultural industry. At the turn of the twenty-first century, the control over the production and distribution of food gradually shifted from the state and national actors to the international system and large agribusiness corporations. In this system of transnational agriculture, the United States has gained increasing power to regulate the terms for the production, export, and commercialisation of fresh produce from Mexico, including imposing certification for food safety and quality, a central ingredient of the neo-liberal regime. Norms of GAP are also an integral part of the new gov-ernmentality, one that has created a highly regimented labour regime with heightened discipline and labour control. Requirements about workers' personal hygiene, dress codes, and personal appearance also lay bare the gap between employers' expectations and the living condi-tions of farmworkers in San Quintin. Most houses where they live are made of cardboard, they have latrines rather than bathrooms, their colo-nias have no sewage systems, and their homes often do not have run-ning water. I was always amazed that workers managed to stay healthy, maintain personal hygiene by washing themselves with hoses or buckets, and kept their homes clean in such circumstances. The gap that separates the strict corporate culture requirements and the reality of workers outside the realm of employment reveals the tensions between the spheres of production and social reproduction generated by the production regime of transnational agriculture.

But the new labour regime of regimented flexibility has not gone uncontested. In today's global fresh-produce industry, workers have developed forms of resistance, from work stoppages and minor and localized strikes—so-called everyday forms of resistance—to more structured 'offensive strategies' such as judicial litigation to challenge companies' unfair and illegal labour practices (Alonso-Fradejas 2015). The San Quintin Valley has not been immune to these forms of labour protests. Instead, the intensification of labour brought by the new production regime has opened new spaces for resistance by indigenous workers. Thus, in spring 2015, a massive labour strike exploded, bringing to a complete halt the production of fresh produce for several weeks in the region. Workers took over the highway companies use to send the produce by trucks to the Mexico–US border and refused to return to work until their demands—for higher wages, a stop to the sexual harassment of women workers by their supervisors, and the creation of an independent labour union to represent their voice—were heard. Relying on the support of binational indigenous organizations that span the US–Mexico border, this collective labour mobilisation is an open expression of the class and ethnic inequalities the modern labour regime of the fresh-producing industry has engendered and the political fractures it has created (Zlolniski 2017).

REFERENCES

Alonso-Fradejas, A. 2015. Anything but a Story Foretold: Multiple Politics of Resistance to the Agrarian Extractivist Project in Guatemala. *The Journal of Peasant Studies* 42 (3–4): 489–515.

Alvarez, R. 2006. The Transnational State and Empire: U.S. Certification in the Mexican Mango and Persian Lime Industries. *Human Organization* 65 (1): 35–45.

Avendaño, Belem. 2004. *El impacto de la iniciativa de inocuidad alimentaria de EEUU en las exportaciones de hortalizas frescas de México*. Doctoral thesis. Mexico City: CIESTAAM-Universidad Autónoma Chapingo.

Avendaño, B.R., R. Schwentesius, and S. Lugo Morones. 2007. La inocuidad alimentaria en la exportación de hortalizas mexicanas a Estados Unidos. *Comercio Exterior* 57 (1): 6–18.

Bronwen Horton, S. 2016. *They Leave Their Kidneys in the Fields: Illness, Injury, and Illegality Among U.S. Farmworkers*. Berkeley: University of California Press.

De Grammont, H., and S. Lara Flores. 2010. Productive Restructuring and 'Standarization' in Mexican Horticulture: Consequences for Labour. *Journal of Agrarian Change* 10 (2): 228–250.

Durrenberger, P. 2017. *Uncertain Times: Anthropological Approaches to Labor in a Neoliberal World*. Boulder: University Press of Colorado.

Echánove, H.F. 2001. Working Under Contract for the Vegetable Agroindustry in Mexico: A Means of Survival. *Culture and Agriculture* 23 (3): 13–23.

Fischer, E., and P. Benson. 2006. *Broccoli & Desire: Global Connections and Maya Struggles in Postwar Guatemala*. Stanford: Stanford University Press.

Gonzalez, H. 2014. Specialization on a Global Scale and Agrifood Vulnerability: 30 Years of Export Agriculture in Mexico. *Development Studies Research* 1 (1): 295–310.

Harvey, D. 2010. *A Brief History of Neoliberalism*. Oxford: Oxford University Press.

Hernández-Romero, M. 2012. Nothing to Learn? Labor Learning in California's Farmwork. *Anthropology of Work Review* XXXIII (2): 73–88.

Holmes, Seth M. 2013. *Fresh Fruits, Broken Bodies*. Berkeley: University of California Press.

Lara Flores, S.M. 1996. Mercado de Trabajo Rural y Organización Laboral en el Campo Mexicano. In *Neoliberalismo y Organización Social en el Campo Mexicano*, ed. H.C. de Grammont. Mexico City: Plaza y Valdes.

Lara Flores, S. 2006. El trabajo en la agricultura: un recuento sobre América Latina. In *Teorias sociales y estudios del trabajo: nuevos enfoques*, ed. E. de la Garza Toledo, 323–343. Barcelona: Anthropos.

Lara Flores, S.M., and K. Sánchez Saldaña. 2015. En búsqueda del control: enganche e industria de la migración en una zona productora de uva de mesa en México. In *Asalariados Rurales en América Latina*, ed. A. Riella and P. Mascheroni, 73–94. Uruguay: CLACSO.

Lazar, S. (ed.). 2017. *Where Are the Unions? Workers and Social Movements in Latin America, the Middle East and Europe*. London: Zed Books.

Llambi, L. 1994. Comparative Advantages and Disadvantages in Latin American Nontraditional Fruit and Vegetable Exports. In *The Global Restructuring of Agro-Food Systems*, ed. P. McMichael, 190–213. Ithaca: Cornell University Press.

Ortiz, S. 2002. Laboring in the Factories and in the Fields. *Annual Review of Anthropology* 31: 395–417.

Ortiz, S., S. Aparicio, and N. Tadeo. 2013. Dynamics of Harvest Subcontracting: The Roles Played by Labour Contractors. *Journal of Agrarian Change* 13 (4): 488–519.

Paciulan, M., and K. Preibisch. 2013. Navigating the Productive/Reproductive Split: Latin American Transnational Mothers and Fathers in Canada's Temporary Migration Programs. *Transnational Social Review* 3 (2): 173–192.

Raynolds, L. 1994. Institutionalizing Flexibility: A Comparative Analysis of Fordist and Post-fordist Models of Third-World Agro-Export Production. In *Commodity Chains and Global Capitalism*, ed. G. Gereffi and M. Korzeniewicz, 143–162. Westport: Grenwood Press.

Rogaly, B. 2008. Intensification of Workplace Regimes in British Horticulture: The Role of Migrant Workers. *Population, Space, and Place* 14: 497–510.

Syring, D. 2009. *La Vida Matizada*: Time Sense, Everyday Rhythms, and Globalized Ideas of Work. *Anthropology and Humanism* 43 (2): 119–142.

Velasco, L., C. Zlolniski, and M.L. Coubes. 2014. *De Jornaleros a Colonos: Residencia, Trabajo e Identidad en el Valle de San Quintín*. México: El Colegio de la Frontera Norte.

Weaver, T. 2001. Time, Space, and Articulation in the Economic Development of the U.S.-Mexico Border Region from 1940 to 2000. *Human Organization* 60 (2): 105–120.

Zabin, C. 1997. U.S.-Mexico Economic Integration: Labor Relations and the Organization of Work in California and Baja California Agriculture. *Economic Geography* 73 (3): 337–355.

Zlolniski, C. 2011. Water Flowing North of the Border: Export Agriculture and Water Politics in a Rural Community in Baja California. *Cultural Anthropology* 26 (4): 565–588.

———. 2017. Growers, Unions, and Farm Laborers in Mexico's Baja California. In *Uncertain Time: Anthropological Approaches to Labor in a Neoliberal World*, ed. P. Durrenberger, 209–232. Boulder: University Press of Colorado.

CHAPTER 15

The Renegotiation of Identity and Alterity in an Economically and Spatially Changing Context: The Case of a Former Industrial and Mining District of Saint-Etienne (France)

Corine Vedrine

In the French post-industrial context, using Le Soleil as a case study, I attempt to show how the connection between economy and society is manifested in urban spaces, urban practices, urban imaginations, and therefore in the representations about both local identity and alterity. Le Soleil, a former metallurgic and mining district of Saint-Etienne, is in the northeastern part of the city. The industrial development, primarily coal mining, metallurgy, textiles, ribbon and weapon manufactures, was foisted on Saint-Etienne through economic, demographic, and spatial development. The city grew from nearly 20,000 inhabitants in

C. Vedrine (✉)
Cnrs LAURE-EVS (Environnement-ville-société) and
ENSAL (Ecole Nationale Supérieure d'Architecture de Lyon),
Vaulx-en-Velin, France

© The Author(s) 2018
M. Spyridakis (ed.), *Market Versus Society*, Palgrave Studies in Urban Anthropology, https://doi.org/10.1007/978-3-319-74189-5_15

1792 to 146,600 in 1901,[1] becoming the largest French industrial town, which was an incentive for a rural exodus, as well as foreign immigration, from Italy, Spain, Poland, Algeria, Morocco, and other places.

In this context, Le Soleil became the main place of exploitation of the incorporated company, 'Société Anonyme des Houillères de Saint-Etienne', with about twenty winding towers. The activities of the innovators, the weapons manufacturers, the ribbon makers and the metallurgists, also participated in the change of the rural landscape as supporting industries and trades led to an increase in the population.

Thus, the transformations of Saint-Etienne in general, and of Le Soleil in particular, took place within the discourse of industrial capitalism, which produced particular spaces and landscapes, particular times or rhythms linked to work, particular social groups, and values and myths (linked to progress, the work force, the miners, etc.). From this period on, a stereotyped identity still survives to this day: inhabitants of Le Soleil have been dubbed, variously, 'proletarian', 'united' and 'cosmopolitan'. Social inequalities, which existed between different corporate associations, erases the possible suspicion of racism because, as one can hear in all mining cities, 'deep down the mine, everyone was black'.

This discourse tries to re-appropriate the past and to interpret a present that is no longer industrialised; but is trying to re-identify itself as undergoing renewal. Indeed, from the 1970s, the transformations of capitalism—from Fordism to neo-liberalization (Brenner and Theodor 2002)—along with transformations in modes of production and the evolution of the energy industry—led to the end of both mining and the golden age of industry. Of course, this economic decline had important consequences on both the spatial level (closing down of the mines—the last one in 1982—closing down of numerous factories and shops, empty homes) and the social level of Le Soleil. Though the area is still populated by workers and employees [80.7% versus 67.9% in Saint-Etienne according to the INSEE (Institut National des Statistiques et des Études Économiques) in 2006], it became an aging neighborhood, both depopulated, as almost half of the inhabitants have left the district since 1990, and impoverished. According to INSEE and the urbanism agency of Saint-Etienne, Le Soleil was one of the poorest districts of Saint-Etienne in 2006, and remained so in in 2013.

[1] In the beginning of the twentieth century, Saint-Etienne was still a growing city hosting new industrial sectors such as bicycle manufacture.

In this chapter, I will show how the contemporary policy of economic and spatial renewal in a precarious market context is differently interpreted according to two imagined generational communities: the industrial one and the post-industrial one. With their different discourses, they produce two opposing stereotypical figures, 'the unbearable youngster' and 'the nostalgic oldie'. This dichotomy, if you will, helps to illustrate the difficulty of understanding how the fear ofinsecurity remains within the context of the 'renewal' (as this takes place in an insecure post-industrial society) and, finally, the difficulty of both sides understanding each other.

My research is based on participant observation and 29 interviews between 2009 and 2011, with various inhabitants, shopkeepers, members of urban and housing services from the Municipality, EPASE (Etablissement Public d'Aménagement de Saint-Etienne), local schools, the 'Maison de quartier' and 'Amicale laïque' (association structures). Methodologically, the district was approached as a place of residence, activity, and work (Hannerz 1983). The research was also enriched by an analysis of documents (from press, Internet, Municipality, Maison de quartier and private resources).

BEING WITNESS TO THE TRANSFORMATIONS WITHOUT BEING INVOLVED IN THEM

In this post-industrial context, the municipality tries to rewrite its discourse, the new capitalist one, which presupposes that one takes part in a generalized economic and urban competition through neoliberal urbanism and urban marketing, which have been extensively described by many authors, such as Harvey, Sassen, Holm, etc. The municipality's aim is to introduce policies to improve the negative image of Saint-Etienne, a symbol not only of France's industrial past, but also the difficulty of inscribing oneself in the new global economy. The improvement is supposed to attract new investors, and to reflect a positive image to the inhabitants, widely seen as victims of unemployment (19.8% locally versus 9.4% at the national level, according to 2013, INSEE data), of precarious living conditions (21.6% according to 2013, INSEE data) and of depopulation.

Indeed, since 1990, the shrinking city of Saint-Etienne has lost nearly 22,000 inhabitants. This situation has resulted in many regeneration projects by public institutions. The state agency Agence Nationale de la Rénovation Urbaine (ANRU), created in 2003, finances both the demolition and rehabilitation of housing estates as well as wider urban renewal in the inner city. In 2007, Etablissement Public d'Aménagement de Saint-Etienne (EPASE), a public body financed by the French government and local authorities, was created in order to restore Saint-Etienne's attractiveness for the middle and upper classes.

Its promise, "le Grand projet stephanois[2]" is nothing less than a new city. First, it intends to offer more mobility with the development of the tramway. Second, it will provide an aesthetic dimension to its new buildings and its former industrial sites, transforming them into cultural assets thanks to the promotion of new values carried by artists and people in charge of heritage (beauty, memory, respect for the past, solidarity of the inhabitants from the former mining city, etc.). Lastly, the symbolic re-appropriation of the city also takes place through marketing it as the 'City of Art, History and Design'. For example, 'La Cité du Design', designed to help with the reinvention of a local economic and cultural identity, was built in the former *Manufacture d'Armes* in 2009. This urban project is part of the now-classic 'creative' city's projects, which includes, in addition to the urban renewal realised by ANRU, four main urban projects: (1) The regeneration of a former industrial part of the city into a 'creative district', called 'Manufacture–Plaine Achille', situated close to Le Soleil, where 'La Cité du Design' is located; (2) the regeneration of the main railway station area into a business district (higher services sector, Châteaucreux, or, as the slogans say, a 'business district' to attract companies and newcomers). Le Soleil is situated just behind this station; (3) The economic and urban renewal of the city centre; and (4) the regeneration of a former mining site ("Le Couriot") into a park, where a Museum of the Mine was created in 1991.

Aesthetic pleasure through architecture and art, industrial heritage through culture and memory, and access to nature through development of the landscape are the assets put forward in the construction of a new identity for Saint-Etienne, the 'capital of design' according to Biennal of design 2017. It is an attempt to produce a new economic dynamic thanks to new spaces, new values and new urban myths linked to urban renewal as expressed in the 'Grand Projet Stéphanois'.

[2] 'Stephanois' means coming from Saint-Etienne.

The urban projects of Saint-Etienne illustrate the new narratives produced by urban policies about 'renewal'. They promise a better quality of life with a green and sustainable city, built through a participatory democracy and a new social cohesion made up of inhabitants and other involved users as well as actors of shared life spaces.

How is Le Soleil involved in this political project of urban transformation? Even though it adjoins two of the main urban projects (Plaine Achille and Chateaucreux), it is nonetheless outside the areas affected by projects the ANRU and EPASE projects and ignored by the urban local policies. Actually, none of the local regeneration policies involve Le Soleil, which is isolated behind the railway station where the tramway stops. And even though Le Soleil is considered by its inhabitants as the ideal 'miner and working class, popular district' of Saint-Etienne, the urban marketing by the municipality refers to it as Le Couriot, or the 'mining' site. One such example of the industrial heritage of Le Soleil is the former publicbaths. Once a common type of public space in the industrial period, today this historic building is occupied by a boxing club, and will probably be destroyed, because the municipality does not know what to do with it.

THE EXPERIENCE OF LE SOLEIL INHABITANTS

My research on how the inhabitants of Le Soleil view the urban renewal is that there are clear lines drawn with regards to the age of the residents and how they view the current re-invention of their town. As I said before, the period of de-industrialization is inscribed in different periods, discourses, and images. As Augé wrote, 'what is [...] a generation if not the sharing of a few images?' (Quoted in Belting 2004: 109). My assumption is that the collective modes of imagining the social (Baczko 1984) nourishes various generational identities. Common images, representations, and the memory of a generation participate in the construction of a particular, imagined generational identity.

In Le Soleil, the shared knowledge about the district differs between those whose childhood was lived *before* and those whose childhood occurred *after* the definitive closure of the factories and mines of Saint-Etienne. Members of the older generation broadly share a common imaginary with their parents and their children who grew up during the industrial period (45 years old or older at the time of research). But because the younger people (less than 45 years old at the time of research) did not live through this period, they do not share the same temporal, spatial, and discursive points of reference and therefore do not share the same images about the district. Thus, it is not the memory of their social group which is linked to the mines or factories but those of their grandparents and parents whose childhood was marked by the local working history. Therefore, I suggest calling these two communities, corresponding to the 'imagined communities' described by Benedict Anderson (2002), as the imagined generational communities, which have different connections with the local economy and history as well as with familial and social memories. I support the view that they form two communities of knowledge, of practices, of ways of inhabiting, of ways of living former and contemporary economic and social contexts, and of ways of representing their identity and their alterity. Indeed, the most invoked figures of the 'Other' are, according to their community of affiliation, 'the unbearable youngster' or 'the nostalgic oldie'.

Of course, the imagined generational communities are mobilized here as a model of analysis. This means, on the one hand, that these two communities are not completely compartmentalized. On the other hand, there is an intermediary generation (between 35 and 45 years old at the time of research), witnessing the global and local changes, often children of the first community and parents of the second one. It is this intermediary generation that tries to maintain a link and to ease the tensions between the two generational communities, who have such different connections with the industrial memory and the post-industrial present.

Resisting the Local Changes Through Heritage and Memory

Those who belong to the first imagined generational community have the feeling of not being worthy of rehabilitation, of not being of interest, of being abandoned, neglected, and isolated: '*they don't care for us because we don't have any social value*', says an inhabitant (a 54-year-old woman). Moreover, they suspect the municipality is practising an 'erasing policy' of their working past and their proletarian identity, which, as they say, they should not have to be ashamed of. Even though they agree that it is necessary to improve the image of Saint-Etienne in order to attract new activities, they are not convinced by the 'Cité du Design', which for them is very elitist. They are aware of dealing with a 'look' or 'façade', as they say, and do not want to take part in it. Therefore, because they are not included in the construction of the new identity of Saint-Etienne and do not believe in the new economic and urban narratives, they invent their own way of re-appropriating their story and identity.

The link they have with the district is inscribed in a nostalgic discourse, expressed in an associative group called *Soleil Autrefois*, which re-experiences the places known only to them since they do not exist anymore. The creation of this association was the result of an individual initiative that led to an exhibition of the school pictures of residents of the old district. A former inhabitant of Le Soleil solicited a local association, the '*Maison de quartier*', in 2005 to help him find the alumni of his school. The appeal in the local newspaper was a huge success. This prompted the director of La *Maison de quartier* to suggest organizing an exhibition of all the classes between the 1930s and the 1960s. It attracted a lot of people who came to find themselves in the pictures, which turned to be the supportive data for the relevant accounts and the ground for memories exchanging. Led by this enthusiasm, a few inhabitants suggested prolonging the adventure with the constitution of a 'memory group', the *Soleil Autrefois*. There are now over twenty members, between 54 and 83 years old (at the time of research). They met each other in *La Maison de quartier* once a week to report on the progress of their work organized into workshop groups. The first one conducted interviews with the 'ancients' of the district, and the second one did archival research, while a third one wrote a book (*Le Soleil, histoires et mémoires d'un quartier*, Éditions Ville de Saint-Étienne, 2011) and a fourth prepared exhibitions around the following topics: the bombardment of the area during the war, the associations of the area between the 1930s and the 1950s, and the 'shops of yesteryear'.

However, this memory is the reality of a small group, half of whom no longer live in Le Soleil and are mainly French and Spanish. It must be noted that these projects were done without the participation of North Africans, for instance, essentially because they are absent from the public sphere due to feelings of illegitimacy. Yet, they have been present in the district for many decades. Nevertheless, the strong success of the edited and exhibited works of *Soleil Autrefois* regarding the first generational community of the district, garnered a lot of attention and may one day include all former residents.

The main preoccupation of the members of this association is less with the transmission of a memory and more with the passing of time. The pleasure of participating in this group is also regularly evoked: a collective pleasure which is essentially enjoyment of both the talking and the images of the past, which often triggers strong emotions. Moreover, the group sings at the end of each meeting, accompanied by the guitar played by the youngest member. The aim of this group is mainly the desire to be together, to talk about their history, to look after and find again what its members used to experience and what they were before— that is, before the end of the industrial period and and their industrial identity. Moreover, the imaginary of the district is combined here with the reactivated and idealized imaginary of their childhoods.

Soleil Autrefois was born when these older residents needed to make sense of the new economic and social context they found themselves in. Faced with the insecurity of the renewal, they invented new forms of appropriation of their history and identity. The success of the exhibitions regarding the first generational community underlines the need for this work of re-appropriation of both local memory and the emblems of the industrial period forgotten by the municipality. In fact, the new building of the *Maison de quartier* integrates in its architecture some wooden poles, thus paying tribute to the mine's galleries, as requested by the older people who go often there. *Soleil Autrefois* is being institutionalized with the support of local institutions such as the municipal archives, which took part in an exhibition in March 2011, and Saint-Étienne as 'Ville d'Art et d'Histoire', a title given by the Ministry of Culture, which was included in a book published by that Ministry. Though the members of *Soleil Autrefois* are glad to see the institutions interested in their work, they criticise what they call a dispossession: on the part of the municipality. On the one hand, the municipality must sustain the entrepreneurial logic of the economic and urban development that attempts to erase a part of the local history;on the other hand, it must show it can protect the older inhabitants and pay attention to the their memories and local history.

With *Soleil Autrefois*, the inhabitants are able to re-invent new narratives that convey other legitimized value s in the construction of a stereotypical identity, together with the values that are linked to the mine, which promote a particular 'savoir être'. The values linked to solidarity, mutual aid, fraternity, friendship, and commitment, are justified by the common conditions of both workers and miners. The values of open-mindedness and a welcoming attitude are justified by the presence of foreign communities, evoked in an idealized discourse about diversity and cultural exchange. Incidentally, the figures of the foreigner, the miner, and the worker all work together, and because they all used to work together, they are supposed to have nourished a culture of respect and mutual aid, which theoretically explains the success (as they say) of the ethnic diversity of the district. These values are opposed to those of the young people, who are representative of the new economic, social, and cultural world. As such, they are suspected of being selfish and are accused of being noisy.

THE PRODUCTION OF THE 'UNBEARABLE YOUNGSTER' FIGURE

Indeed, in this context, for the first generational community, the figure of alterity that incarnates its stereotypes, is changing. The figure of the foreigner is no longer that of a miner, but of the youngster who is a stranger to local history, memory and, more generally, to industrial discourse. He is inscribed in a contemporary world with its new economic rules and urban renewal, both of which are strange entities for the first generational community.

Who are these youngsters? They are teenagers and young adults. Some differentiations can be made. First, there is the student or the young professional who appreciates the village life of the district, which often has been the setting of his childhood. Second, there is the case of the precarious, who is in pain, or 'en galère' (Dubet 1987), who considers the district and, more generally, Saint-Etienne, as an enclave in geographic, social, and economic terms. He is the one who is angry with the older people who leave him with nostalgia but without future employment opportunities or projects. That is why he hijacks the miner's values to transform them into negative characteristics: '*yes, sure they have the miner mentality here, with a chickpea in the head*' (Anis, 32 years old). Their common experience with their peers is not the working or the miner condition, but the "pain" of unemployment and precariousness. Lastly, there are newcomers who are: (1) middle class families, between 35 and 40 years old. They came from other areas in Saint-Etienne or other cities taking advantage of the quality of life and the low rents; (2) displaced persons, beneficiaries of the ANRU program, often in a precarious situation; and (3) foreign newcomers.

These three figures are grouped by the first imagined generation into a generalized one, the youngsters, who seem not to be interested in local industrial history and identity, as many younger people did not attend the exhibitions organized by the *Soleil Autrefois*. This group is accused of participating in the disappearance of local identity and of bringing negative values, opposed to those of the miner, that is: individualism, selfishness, diffidence, and disrespect. In addition, it is accused of being 'noisy' and of disturbing the social peace of the district. This stereotyped figure of the 'youngster' mobilised as reference to disorder, often specifically implies a 'young man from North Africa', serving as symbol of alterity in cultural, spatial, and geographical terms. Indeed, the 'young Arab', *'probably coming from other areas of Saint-Etienne'* (which makes the issue exogenous) is invoked to represent the foreign disturuptive element and the 'Arabification' of the district, in demographic and spatial ways along with the presence of numerous North African shops and the building of a mosque, which opened in 2012. Bencharif (2002) has shown that North African commercial ventures had became widespread in Saint-Etienne by 1945, so these shops and bars are not really new. What is new, however, is their increasing proportion at the expense of other ethnic shops, such as the Spanish groceries, which were once abundant in the district before its deindustrialisation. Indeed, the old people who complain about the youngsters are neither Kabylians nor Moroccans but those who see the points of reference of their ancient world disappearing.

To be more specific, what do these youngsters in the public spaces of Le Soleil actually do? Some of them sit on the benches and the gate of the main park of the district and hang around a small square surrounded by bars, kebab and grocery shops, etc. They talk, drink some beer, and smoke (probably some cannabis) and leave empty beer cans and bottles in these public spaces, creating the perception of incivility. Moreover, the presence of these young people and the masculine way they occupy the public space, is experienced as a dispossession of the territory by the older residents, who no longer dare to sit down in these places, while the youngsters are often indifferent to their presence. This dispossession of public spaces is at the heart of the objections expressed by the first generational community during the neighbourhood council meetings, created in 2002, to promote the democratic participation of inhabitants in municipal management. When the councillors suggested adding new furniture to these public areas to allow for intergenerational cohabitation. The older residents reacted aggressively, accusing the councillors of not understanding them. They said they prefered to see an increase in the height of the gates surrounding the place in order to prevent the young people from sitting on them. Some of them even suggested razing the place and transforming it into a roundabout, a suggestion applauded by many older inhabitants. Others suggested the installation of cameras to ensure police surveillance. A few weeks before, these same inhabitants organized a petition for driving the young people out of the place, but as no crime was committed, this petition was not followed up.

As we can see, with the closing down of the mines and the loss of the professional identity of the district, the foreigner, who is here represented by the youngster, classically stirs up fears. The youngster also represents the disturber for the industrial generation. He represents a new world with rules and codes the oldie does not understand. Moreover, the youngster is the object and beneficiary of the renewal and the new global world. He doesn't share the same history and memory, neither the same practices nor representations of the neighbourhood in particular, and of the city in general of the older generation.

The older generation, because it is not involved in the global thinking about the economic and urban renewal of the city, can cannot make sense of the younger generation. Therefore it digs itself deeper into resurrecting a fantasized past which, in the final analysis, it is not really interested in handing it down. As for the younger people, their way of being noisy in the public space is a manner of asking to be acknowledged by the older people, of being visible and having a voice.

What Does It Mean to Belong to a Post-industrial Generation?

The post-industrial generation as inscribed in a global world discourse is seduced by the transformation of Saint-Etienne because it takes part in it as a user of new public space and because it needs to take part in it in order to participate in economic and urban regeneration. Hence, we should understand what it means to live in a post-industrial context. What does it mean to grow up in a 'post' discourse? What does it mean not to have known the period which gives meaning to the 'post'? The generation of de-industrialization has to build, to carry on, and to defend its own values, in the context of the renewal of what the industrial generational community has known: namely, its relations with the labour market, with training, with local and global scales, and with ways of thinking how the city can create both economic and symbolic wealth. This necessary renewal of a city with economic difficulties is inscribed in the context of global capitalism, with a new spirit justifying its inherent values (Boltanski and Chiapello 1999), with an international labour market and with urban competition. It is in this context that the second generational community has to read again, appropriate, and sometimes put aside, the industrial past in order to move on to something else, something which is presupposed by the post and by both the difficult economic and urban renewal. Finally, in this context, the notion of urban renewal[3] has almost become an emblem, like 'Industry' or 'Progress', thus generating social imaginaries and legitimizing certain practices.

As De Certeau wrote, 'the language of power is urbanizing itself' (op. cit: 144–145). As industry (or mining) is no longer a unified entity, the municipalities are trying to generate social cohesion through the promotion of an urban identity; that is why the impact of the urban project is political. In this respect, urban marketing around these projects, opposed to the functionalism linked to the industrial period, are evocative: posters, bulletins, models, and discourses are vectors of the production of architectural, aesthetic, cultural, and heritage images supposed to be linked to the local identity. 'The planning of the urban spaces has to be carried on by a vision of the city—and the society- [...] The project has to carry on urban values, it has to express the identity of the local places or of the territory', writes Gilles Pinson (2009: 12). He adds, 'the city is no longer a straightforward, developed space but all at the same time, a collective actor, a society to be mobilized, a unique social equation expressed as architectural legacy, a local identity which has to be valorised in a context of greater territorial competition', in order to attract investors and newcomers.

Saint-Etienne is part of what Max Rousseau calls 'losing cities' (Rousseau 2008). According to him, these cities have two main problems in attracting new inhabitants. The first is objective and corresponds to economic and social problems. The second is subjective and is linked to the image of the city. As it happens, the image of Saint-Etienne is not only that of a black city because of the mine, it is also that of a city precisely 'in renewal', where *we have the feeling that we have to break our*

---

[3] In France, the notion of "Renouvellement urbain" refers to specific urban policies which I cannot develop here. In this contribution, I use this notion to refer to urban regeneration in general.

backs [...] We aren't duped. The golden age will not come back [...] We will not return to what contributed to the building of this city' Khallil (34 years old) says. The second imagined generational community thus has to consider its future in this particular context. This invites it in its turn to create a stereotyped figure of alterity, represented by the generation that has known another world, the industrial one. This figure, incarnated by the old people, is that of the 'nostalgic oldie', an element in the decor of the village life offered by Le Soleil.

THE PRODUCTION OF THE 'NOSTALGIC OLDIE', AN ELEMENT OF VILLAGE LIFE

As I said above, the aim of *Soleil Autrefois* is more the pleasure of meeting and remembering the shared past than the transmission of an industrial memory to the young generation. As regards the second generational community, only the children of the local school come to the exhibitions organised by the group. What seems most efficiently transmitted is regret, nostalgia, and melancholia: '*I like the melancholic aspect, it's a thing... I like it*', confesses Mr. Blanc. The object of regret concerns a period in which the young no longer take part, from which they are excluded—yet included as subjects of the transmission. As regards the young inhabitants from immigrant communities, it is a nostalgic legacy that reminds them of their nostalgia for their country of origin. The feeling of not belonging is inherent to both the country of origin of the parents and to the vanished industrial city in which the latter came to work and which gave meaning to their arrival in Saint-Etienne, in other words, both to a geographic and an historical, distant place. Faced with this difficult transmission of memory, the members of the second generation turn to the present and future, to projects and what promotes hope, inscribed in geographic scales which go beyond those of the district. They effectively stay away from the exhibitions of *Soleil Autrefois*, sensing that it is not really addressed to them. Moreover, they need a discourse which is turned towards the future and takes into account their own aspirations, desires and fears, expressed in a contemporary discourse. At the same time, this new discourse must seriously consider the story they are writing in turn. As Ahmed (19 years old), grandson of a miner, said, '*the old people, they like the story of the district, while we, we are less touched by this, we weren't born yet. We, we are living our history, now*'. The figure of the oldies is then mobilized to refer to elderly persons who shut themselves away in a nostalgic discourse that describes a mythological previous age. The reproach of the post-industrial generational community to them is not taking into account both the present and its own economic and social conditions. As far as the increasing difficulties of the oldies in reading the contemporary context is concerned, it prevents them from giving their support to the youngsters vis-à-vis knowledge, networks, and transmission of competences that they think are now without value in a world where their former workplace sometimes also both their former job and know-how have disappeared. What is more, the new young migrant adults are complaining about the absence of help from the *'old who don't talk, don't tell us anything, don't transmit anything. They send the money home and that's all they are interested in, to send the money home'* (Anis). The nostalgic oldies thus incarnate those who are both grumpy and out of their depth. They have two discourses toward the youngsters. The first one is that of irritation: young people are unbearable. The second one is of compassion, tinged with pity (*'it's not easy for the youngsters nowadays, with unemployment and so on'*), which in turn sends them back to the nostalgic discourse of their glorified past (*'we, in our time'*...). But this discourse also refers to their powerlessness in helping this generation in a world where old people (themselves), do not matter. This powerlessness is interpreted as uselessness by some of the youngsters.

When members of the second generational community describe Le Soleil, the vocabulary used is then linked to the life of the district, described as a network of social connections, the presence of little shops and the events that give rhythm to the weeks and the years (markets, carnival, and neighbourhood party). This life of the local area, described as pleasant and tranquil, is assimilated to what they imagine to be the village life. This imaginary, linked to the phantasm of village life, is justified by these young people by the isolation of Le Soleil from the rest of the city, through both its spatial organization (the place with the church, surrounded by bars and the school) and what for them stand for the typical figures of the village appropriation of the public space: the 'old lady sat on a bench', the 'old man playing bowls' and, more generally, 'oldie' strolling in the marketplace.

For the second generational community, the values linked to the inhabitants of Le Soleil—fraternity and solidarity—are no longer justified by the industrial and mining past, but are linked to the characteristics of contemporary village life of the district. And Le Soleil, formerly organized around factories and mining, gave way to an area lived as a network, together with the other areas of the city. Whereas the oldest people regret the end of a working class and autarkic district, the younger people appreciate the quality of life offered by its peacefulness, thought of as an element of a mobile city. As users of the renewed spaces of the inner city, they are equipped with a greater mastery of the territory at the scale of the whole city. As Galland and Stellinger state, 'in the final analysis, these urban young people are "modern" young people, privileging both individual initiative and mobility; and these values are in tune with the urban way of life. Moreover, they attach great importance to sociability and encounters, which corresponds again to what the urban setting can offer' (2008: 116).

Nevertheless, the tranquillity of the residential district appreciated by the second generational community is interpreted by the first generational community as a symbol of the death of industrial activities. But it is the death of its district (the industrial one) that it complains about. We can observe here the ambiguity of the situation: while the first generational community is complaining about the death of the district, it cannot bear the signs of the life emitted by the young men in the public space. This reaction is nourished by a certain bad faith, since, during the interviews, the oldies ascribed the great number of bars in Le Soleil during the industrial period, which produced in public spaces a lot of noise and scenes of violence linked to alcohol.

Conclusion: Sharing the Same Spaces but Living in Two Different Districts

In conclusion, one could say that the members of the industrial generation continue to produce meaning by means of identification to the phantasized district from which the younger people are excluded. This seems the best way to protect the group from a new economic and urban world with different rules that do not mean anything to them, a world where they sometimes feel themselves useless, because they feel they cannot be of help to the younger people, who are more experienced in the contemporary world.

Actually, it seems that the two generational communities do not live in the same district: in 'the former industrial district', now *dead* for the one, in a pleasant dormitory district that offers 'village' life for the others (and for them, the mining area of Saint-Etienne is not Le Soleil but Le Couriot...). This division is one of the reasons they sometimes fail to understand each other and produce classical stereotypes linked to 'youngster' and 'oldie'. Of course, as we know, and as Bourdieu said, youth and old age are socially constructed and 'in the logical division between young people and old people, what is at stake is power' (1984: 144). Further on, the author adds, 'a lot of conflicts between generations are conflicts between systems of aspirations constituted in different ages' (op.cit: 151) producing an anti-youth racism from old people in social decline who '...are against everything that is changing, everything that is going forward, etc. Precisely because their future is behind them' (op.cit.).

We can see here how, in a complicated post-industrial context, the inhabitants pinpoint their identity using both social imaginaries for 'elaborating a self-representation' (Baczko 1984) and representations of the other. The contemporary representative inhabitants are no longer the miner, the metallurgist, or the worker but the youngster and the oldie, clichés used by the inhabitants to express their values and opposing relations to the history, space and local identity in a new global world. That is why they translate social relations less in terms of social classes than in terms of generational classes, in the form of imagined communities. And one can see here the danger of widening the gap between these two generations. It can be expressed through radical discourse for the one who damaged the so-called solidarity values, and through disrespect for the others. These are, in fact, two very similar ways of expressing the tensions we have to bear in the difficult context of renewal.

References

Anderson, B. 2002. *L'imaginaire national. Réflexion sur l'origine et l'essor du nationalisme*. Paris: Editions La Découverte et Syros.

Baczko, B. 1984. *Les imaginaires sociaux. Mémoires et espoirs collectifs*. Paris: Payot.

Belting, H. 2004. *Pour une anthropologie des images*. Paris: Editions Gallimard.

Bencharif, L. 2002. *Pour une géohistoire de l'immigration maghrébine à Saint-Étienne: entre espace encadré et espace approprié*, thèse de doctorat de géographie 'Villes et sociétés'. Université Jean Monnet.

Boltanski, L., and E. Chiapello. 1999. *Le nouvel esprit du capitalisme*. Paris: Editions Gallimard.

Bourdieu, P. 1984. La jeunesse n'est qu'un mot. *Question de sociologie*, 143–153. Paris: Editions de Minuit.

Brenner, N., and N. Theodore. 2002. *Spaces of Neoliberalism. Urban Restructuring in North America and Western Europe.* Oxford: Blackwell Publishing.

Dubet, F. 1987. *La galère, jeunes en survie.* Paris: Fayard.

Galland, O., and A. Stellinger. 2008. Les jeunes et la ville. In *Vivre en ville, observatoire des modes de vie urbains,* ed. J. Darmon, 183–207. Paris: PUF.

Hannerz, U. 1983. *Explorer la ville.* Paris: Editions de Minuit.

Pinson, G. 2009. *Gouverner la ville par projet. Urbanisme et gouvernance des villes européennes.* Paris: Presses de la fondation nationale des sciences politiques.

Rousseau, M. 2008. Bringing politics back in: la gentrification comme politique de développement urbain? Autour des villes perdantes. *Espaces et sociétés* 132, 75–80. Paris: Eres éditions.

CHAPTER 16

'Weak Heritage' and Neighbourhood in Contemporary Cities: Capitalism and Memories of Urban Utopias

Michel Rautenberg

INTRODUCTION: THE NOSTALGIC MEMORY OF THE FORMER INDUSTRIAL CAPITALISM

In the introduction of his book *The Culture of the New Capitalism*, Richard Sennett, quoting Max Weber, defends that industrial capitalism helped form the founding politics of so-called social capitalism. Predictable time was one key concept of the culture that supported capitalism in factories. 'Time lay at the center of this military, social capitalism: long-term and incremental and above all predictable time. This bureaucratic imposition affected individuals as much as institutional regulations. Rationalized time enabled people to think about their lives as narratives—narratives not so much of what necessarily will happen as of how things should happen' (Sennett 2006: 23). For example, it became possible for many workers to consider their career, or to dwell in a fixed place. Whatever our opinion of

M. Rautenberg (✉)
Univ-Lyon, UJM-Saint-Etienne, CNRS,
Centre Max Weber UMR 5283, Saint-Étienne, France

© The Author(s) 2018
M. Spyridakis (ed.), *Market Versus Society*, Palgrave Studies in Urban Anthropology, https://doi.org/10.1007/978-3-319-74189-5_16

this heavily critiqued book may be, it is a view worth debating today, at least in regard to recent developments in the study of heritage and its uses to protect from and to adapt to changes in the new capitalism.

Since the deep mutation of capitalism that emerged in the 1970s, a new ideal self emerged in the cutting edge institutions that became a model—often contested—for a whole society: an individual constantly learning new skills, whose potential ability to move from one task to another is more valuable than his skills and experiences in doing his job. But 'these qualities of the ideal self are a source of anxiety because they are disem-powering to the mass of workers' (Sennett 2006: 127). Craftsmanship and professional experience, which were the basis of the workers' values and identity, are depreciated by the culture of the new capitalism. 'Skills extinction is a durable feature of technological advance. Automation is indifferent to experience. Market forces continue to make it cheaper to buy skills fresh rather than to pay for retraining' (Sennett 2006: 98). Workmen and workwomen, who constituted not only the workforce, but also a main part of citizenry and inhabitants, have lost their pivotal place in production. The standard of life of a large part of middle class people is stagnating while capitalists get richer and richer. The former social capitalism became a 'nostalgic memory' (Sennett 2006: 37), the memory of a time when people kept the control of time and when personal skills were a richness. Society was supposed to be more protective and reassuring.

This is the guiding argument of this chapter: this nostalgic memory contributes to shape some practices and forms of heritage—I will call them 'weak heritage'—that people claim in order to preserve themselves from the hardiest effects of the new capitalism. In the following pages I successively discuss what I call new capitalism and how it impacts heritage, particularly by extending it to social practices and believes; then I explain how neighbourhood and the memory of the basic utopias of a French new town can be considered as 'weak heritage'. A little team of three persons carried out the fieldwork between 2002 and 2006 with interviews, direct observations, participants' comments and documentary research. The main results have been published in 2010 (Lefebvre and Rautenberg 2010).

Heritage and Its Extension in the New Capitalism

Besides the public stream that associates heritage to different identities, we observe an economic trend to bring cities' heritage into an international competition. Following David Harvey (1990), many authors have pointed out that the last third of the twentieth century was characterised by a big shake up in culture as well as in economics. The late capitalism, which arose after the decrease of the Ford-Keynesian capitalism of the post-war boom, implied more flexible labour, more competition, a quasi-religion of the market, more mobility, and more consumption practices that involved more and more sectors of human activity.

A substantial number of sectors of human activity—like education and culture—which were more or less set apart from the free market, became henceforth important issues economically. This process produced new conceptions of time and space (Harvey 1990), which affected our practices of heritage because they were "accompanied by other social and economic shifts, which have reconfigured heritage (…) including process of deindustrialisation, reconfiguration of the 'tourist gaze' and the emergence of heritage as an element of a new 'experience' economy" (Harrison 2013: 79). At the end of the twentieth century, the heritage industry that emerged during the Seventies (Hewison 1987) shifted away from the preservation of collective benefit to neoliberal policies focused on the economically driven desire of heritage dedicated to tourism and consumption. Quite a lot of old buildings and former factories have been transformed into malls and supermarkets since 1976, the year of the opening of the Quincy Market in place of the old Faneuil Hall Market, which had been erected in early 1740 in Boston (USA) (Harrison 2013: 83).

This extension of heritage is concomitant with contemporary forms of capitalism—which defined themselves as post-industrial—and the arising of a new World Economy (Cohen 2006). Daniel Cohen explains that the cost of the conceptualisation of a pair of sneakers—or anything else—and of marketing to sell them equals the cost of their manufacture. 'The conceptualisation of goods (…) and the prescription of goods (…) dominate over the cost of their production' (Harrison 2013: 80). According to Cohen, a second feature of this second globalisation is that it encourages every image to be on display for everybody.

This is especially true for urban heritage. Since the 1980s, heritage has been largely included in urban regeneration policies when it started being used as a political background in debates between city dwellers and local government (Rautenberg 2012) and contributed to societal entertainment. Many cities have opened historical festivals, they put on display their traditions, they transformed their vernacular memories into tourist events, they invented new storytelling by mingling history, legends, and their most famous local figures, they renewed and promoted pilgrimages and they opened tourist tours of their old districts. In a nutshell, they shifted the social value of heritage into economic value.

This conversion of cultural heritage into goods sheds light on an odd paradox that is inherent to the heritage of modern capitalism: heritage is supposed (in the social imagination) to be sustainable, but as a commodity it is supposed to be used and destroyed. In other words, adding to the value of its consumption would be the best argument for valuing tangible or intangible pieces of culture as a part of heritage. This paradox highlights the singular place of culture in producing goods in contemporary capitalism, as emphasised by Nigel Thrift (2005). According to him, 'three particular routes as the be all and end all of a contemporary capitalism (have been taken). One is to lay an undue emphasis on money and finance (…). The second is to lay an undue emphasis on information technology (…). The third is to argue that there has been a major shift in the regulation of the rules of possession (…). (Consequently) new prescriptive and normative frameworks have been coming on apace arising out of new legal orthodoxies, the proliferation of global actors and the assembly of different kinds of commodity' (Thrift 2005: 5). Within this new context of capitalism, three elements can be identified: 'the discursive power of what I call the 'cultural circuit' of capital, the changing from the commodity, and the pivotal role of space and time' (Thrift 2005: 6). The 'capital circuit of capitalism' is probably the 'chief creation' of contemporary capitalism. It has been constituted by business schools, management consultants, manager gurus, and the media. Its strength comes from its capacity to produce 'a feedback loop which is intended to keep capitalism surfing along the edge of its own contradictions' (ibid.). It emphasises emotions and game, which are at the core of new sets of markets, the power of virtuality over materiality, and the appropriation of any private exchange which is put on the media. This new capitalism is based on what Boltanski and Chiapello named the 'cité par projet' (Boltanski and Chiapello 1999: 154–238). Social life is no more thought of as being based on a social organisation where individuals belong to social groups and organisations that share interests or are in opposition to each other. Social life is regarded as being made up of networks of individuals who are supposed to make up projects. Then, the new capitalism develops a deep redefinition of the public/private spheres, singularly by the extraordinary increase of the spread of the internet. Our private life becomes more transparent, private exchanges have more visibility, and limits between the familiar circle and the public sphere are more porous (Cardon 2010).

Consequently, we may say that the emergence of 'new forms of commodity and commodity relation' (Thrift 2005: 7) also involved heritage and heritagisation. Heritage exists in the economic sphere as goods to manage and as immaterial value as well. Its material form is bound up with the mediatisation of everyday life that makes it ubiquitous, 'always present, always on'. It is a new world where materiality is at the same time self-evident and evanescent, located and virtual, past and present (and future). Heritage, as one of many consumer products, is 'becoming part of an animate surface that is capable of conducting thought; thought is increasingly packaged in things' (id). We must then consider that heritage can be present in monuments as well as in the triviality of everyday life and in the name of the memory of former social local linkages that people can mobilize.

Tourism, Luxury, and Sustainability: Heritage in Economics and to Guard Against Economics

A report about the inputs of culture in the French economy considered that heritage (museums and monuments) represented €8.1 billion of added value to the national economy in 2011 (Kancel et al. 2013). Though, if we have a larger conception of heritage that takes into account all the cultural resources people use 'to light on their choices to build the future' (Greffe 2011: 936), heritage is involved in many sectors of the economy. Three areas are particularly lightened: heritage in tourism, in luxury, and in sustainable development. The relationships between heritage and tourism got tied up at the outset in many cases. For example, in Quebec (Canada), heritage protections were engaged during the 1920s alongside the roads followed by the American visitors (Morisset 2009). Closer to our time, during the 1980s in Great Britain heritage became synonymous with neoliberal policies and entrepreneurship (Smith 2006: 39), leading sometimes to its Disneyfication. At the same time and until today, the United Nations Educational, Scientific and Cultural Organization (UNESCO) launched several programs aiming to facilitate the management of heritage and the development of tourism at World Heritage properties[1] while trying to preserve local

---

[1] http://whc.unesco.org/en/tourism/.

community interests (Labadi 2013), but with contested results. The tourism boom of the past 20 years has strongly contributed to the heritagisation of many places, landscapes, and cultural practices. They take new values and have a new life. Luc Boltanski and Renaud Esquerre (2014) connect this considerable extension of heritagisation to another phenomenon they put on display: in our world, which is both less industrial and more commodified, heritagisation is used as an instrument to put new values on objects. The former capitalist economy was centred on industrial production; nowadays it is more commodification-centred. As industrial capitalism has migrated to emerged economy countries, in the developed ones the enrichment process moved to other ways of enhancing. Thanks to heritagisation they are introduced into a 'collection' in which they become valuable by themselves; independently of their owners and their production process (Boltanski and Esquerre 2014: 69). It can be a collection of old cars, a collection of paintings, a collection of traditional regional products, or a collection of places recognized by UNESCO. We can say that heritagisation is henceforth directly associated with new capitalism by its ability to recycle every remainder and ruins of the industrial society.

However, there are several gaps in this deep transformation of heritage by the new capitalism. UNESCO and European institutions contributed to balance the capitalistic pressure on heritage resources by providing several international conventions. It is also worth highlighting that heritage can go hand-in-hand with alternative models of development and strengthening participatory democracy, broadening the concepts of heritage and developing people-centred approaches. Therefore, heritage is 'ultimately [being] about intergenerational transfer and about the present-day as a bridge from past to future' (Auclair and Fairclough 2015: 9). Heritage is particularly active through places and landscapes whose everyday aspects and uses are also components of social and cultural sustainability. It helps to interact between people, and between people and the materiality of the world.

Indeed, we can draw a parallel between the decline of Weberian bureaucracy caused by the new capitalism and the transformation of the institution of heritage. On the one hand, the new rules of international capitalism and the financialisation of the economy have shaken bureaucracy. On the other hand, the 'authorised heritage discourse' (Smith 2006), i.e. the national narratives and the cultural institutions that framed the national imagined communities, have been harshly competing with local actors. In the making of heritage, 'communities of practice' are now playing a growing part (Adell et al. 2015). From a wider point of view, those policies are based on the emphasis on proximity in heritage practices, resulting in a revived interest in neighborhoods (Morell and Franquesa 2011). Henceforth the 'authorized heritage discourse' held by states and cultural institutions faces competition from ordinary citizens who view their everyday practices and habits as legitimate as monuments or collections of museums (Smith 2006).

Another point to be stressed is that heritage supports feelings of continuity while expressing physically these feelings, as pointed out a long time ago by David Lowenthal (1985). Heritage conveys the idea of timeless values and makes sense of the scattered events of life. Heritage witnesses this fundamental, obvious, but often forgotten property of life as it unfolds in time (Micoud 1996). It is a main component of individual and collective identity (Graham and Howard 2008). Heritage is now determined by the commitment of communities rather than by academics and experts, it expresses the diversity of cultures, of influences and identities (Internationale de l'imaginaire 2012; Graham and Howard 2008). It takes part in the creolisation of the world (Boswell 2011), in the renewal of local identities (Anheier and Raj Isar 2011) and in the new modes of dialogical democracy (Harrison 2013). In short, on the one side heritage contributes to the commodification of the world; on the other side, it is mobilized to challenge the social and cultural consequences of the market.

In the same way, I assume that people try to institute the heritagisation of social practices as a symbolic place where economic inputs do not rule our life and where capitalism is not able to disrupt the social. I draw here on ethnographic research we conducted in the town of Villeneuve d'Ascq, in the North of France, where some inhabitants were engaged in safeguarding local political devices and neighbourhoods. Those practices, considered as a legacy from the first inhabitants, who call themselves the 'pioneers', belong to what I defined as a 'weak heritage', i.e. everything that people wish to preserve because it is supposed to stabilise the environment where they live. It is made up of everything that people wish to save for the future because they are attached to it (Rautenberg 2015).

NEIGHBORHOOD AS HERITAGE

Culture cannot be reduced to its apparatus and the identifiable circulation of its meanings: cultural flows 'only make sense through local mediations and filters' (Assayag 2005: 277). Most people think and act locally. Social actors always experience the world and imagine the future *'en contexte'*, they are not 'insular individuals, mobile and without memory' (Assayag 2005: 277). In Hannerz' *Cultural Complexity* (1992), this is seen in terms of the notion of 'form of life': 'it involves the everyday practicalities of production and reproduction, activities going on in work places, domestic settings, neighbourhoods, and some variety of other places' (Hannerz 1992: 47). Cultures usually need places and forms of life in which to be externalized, and cultural flow is not a continuous current that never stops. It takes shape in any place, in the village of Kafachan, Nigeria, or in the urban swirl of Calcutta, and 'rather than a flow of meanings divided into a multitude of separate currents, (it) is an inclusive cultural swirl' (Hannerz 1992: 204). Neighbourhoods may be considered as main places in cities where culture and form of life develop themselves. They also are objects of interest for public policies. As shown by David Harvey almost thirty years ago, the general movement is to move power in cities from local government to local governance by incorporating business agents of the 'third sector': that's what he called the 'Entrepreneurial turn' in urban policies (Harvey 1990). Following these policies coming from the top, neighbourhood is better taken into account and dwellers seem to have more weight in the decision making they are supposed to be concerned in. Marc Morel, following other similar expressions of thought, described the consequence of this new topic of urban planning as an emphasis made on place rather than on territory. It also favoured the adoption of 'neighbourhood scale' which 'goes hand in hand with a new political discourse that stresses cultural questions and the idea of participation and citizen involvement' (Morell and Franquesa 2011: 197). Then neighbourhood becomes a very prolific 'raw material' for reshaping cities by localizing memory, a 'frontier field of frictions between domination and appropriation' because of its unevenness and the potential role it can take in the idealisation of place. Emphasised by the European Union and UNESCO because it is supposed to help the promotion of local democracy and the associated commitment of inhabitants, neighbourhood can be understood as a form of 'community of practice' that we saw above. Revaluating local debate is supposed to help in the revaluation of the inhabitants and their responsibility in the management of the place where they live. To achieve this objective, local memory and heritage could provide cultural content. This is typically weak heritage. In Villeneuve d'Ascq, I try to show that neighbourhood constitutes a 'weak heritage', which is made of narratives and collective memories that people tell while drinking a cup of coffee. It is also made of the mundane landscapes of everyday life that people wish to preserve because they retain the essential traces of their personal and collective stories and their common will to perpetuate some collective practices that favour local sociality.

Villeneuve d'Ascq: A "New Town" Looking for Its Identity

The 'New town' of Villeneuve d'Ascq is located on the site of three former communes, very close to Lille, a large city in the North of France. A special public agency, EPALE,[2] was created to manage expropriation, public institutions, and the birth of the new town. When the works began in 1969, there were nearly 20,000 inhabitants. The first new dwellers settled in 1973, when the city was still a big mess: very few pavements, no lights along the streets: 'it was like after the American bombing in 1944' a man we interviewed told us. Moreover, many houses have building problems: cracks in the walls, damp, very bad sound proofing, an so forth.

In 1977 a new mayor was elected with a very simple program: to stop the development of the town. 'We stay as we are; we decide on our own what we want to be'. The city's population was around 55,000 inhabitants, but the government subsequently expected 100,000. After several years of conflict, the government decided to dissolve the public agencies and Villeneuve d'Ascq became a fully legal municipality. Nowadays, its population is around 62,000.

The public authorities and professionals who worked on Villeneuve d'Ascq were very concerned that it have a proper identity. Villeneuve d'Ascq was supposed to be clearly different from its surroundings and also different from the other 'Villes nouvelles' that were built at the same period. The French government was pursuing two main objectives: balance the urban development of the country from different regions while Paris was growing very fast by applying a very French 'colbertist'

---

[2] "Etablissement Public d'Aménagement de Lille Est".

(centralised) policy[3] and creating a new model of urban planning to propose to other local authorities. This model was supposed to give local governments more power than previously in the decision-making process as well as to adapt the national rules to their contemporary social milieu.

On the one hand, the history of Villeneuve d'Ascq illustrates well this national framework. On the other hand, it also denotes a peculiar situation since its local authorities succeeded in excluding the national government from local affairs. However, the main interest for us is that Villeneuve d'Ascq has experimented with the grandeur nature of some urban utopias of the 1960s and 1970s. It is a place where we could observe practical utopias thirty years later. Based on interviews that we arranged with the architects, some people of the staff who built the town, and the local government, we have identified three main issues that can explain how those practical utopias have been implemented.

- The implementation of the project follows more or less Thomas More's thought in his famous chef d'oeuvre, *Utopia*. It is a criticism of what existed before (here, the functionalism which was considered as responsible for a 'dehumanisation' of cities); the project of a friendly and harmonious city where local democracy was supposed to be reinvented; a city which blended the advantages of urban facilities and the quietness and leisure of nature (Choay 1965).
- The city was first planned in the middle of the 1960s, but the project plan began to be drawn up in the early 1970s, that is to say a few years after 1968, which is a very symbolic date for the French: new ways of life and, above all, new ways to deal with politics were popularised. A generation of young people discovered that changing their life was possible; collective dreams could transform into concrete projects. Villeneuve d'Ascq appeared then as a place where it was possible to experiment with new ways of life and new ways to make a city.[4]

---

[3] Under the responsibility of the "Ingenieurs des Ponts et Chaussée", a typical French corporation of "hauts fonctionnaires" (high civil servants).

[4] 'Changer la vie' (Change the life!) was the slogan of the socialist party between 1977 and 1981, as they access to the power when François Mitterand became *président de la république*. It has been also the hymn of the party, with a music by MikisTheodorakis'.... Il nous faudra reprendre nos villes/qui ne sont plus que des ghettos géants/où le printemps n'a plus le droit d'asile/où meurent les vieux, les arbres, les enfants/c'est dans nos propres murs qu'on nous exile/changeons la vie ici et maintenant...' http://www.youtube.com/watch?v=YDEgNp62jGk.

- A third point rarely mentioned must be recognized: the interconnection between the utopias of the public engineers, architects and settlers of whom many have been political and trade union militants. Several places existed where these utopias were able to interconnect.

I identified two groups of utopias. Probably the most common one concerns the merging of natural and urban landscapes. More exactly, Villeneuve d'Ascq is a very characteristic example of this popular issue: 'bring the countryside into the cities' in order to oppose the harmony of nature with the brutality of the 'cités dortoirs' (dormitory cities) constructed during the 1960s. The place of nature is clearly expressed by the several lakes that have been created (most people think they are natural), the large number of public meadows, the preservation of few farms on the territory, and the creation of an eco-museum of mills and rural life. I noticed a several associations involved in environmental issues, the success of organic food in external markets and the frequent broaching of all these issues in the local newspapers. When we interviewed inhabitants, this feature of Villeneuve d'Ascq was largely mentioned in order to characterize the city. For many, it was one of the principal reasons to move there.

Another group of utopias relates to the apologia for local democracy. It was inaugurated as soon as the beginning of the construction site when the EPASE invited the population of the three former villages to public presentations of the project. A few years later the local government created different arrangements to associate the inhabitants with public policy. For example, the *Commission extra municipales de quartier* were created in 1977, where elected representatives of the municipality and inhabitants debated environmental problems, the relationship with the university that had moved from Lille, and the defence of local interests. The municipality also used some public means that were provided by law, as the *Locaux Collectifs Residentiels (collective rooms for the inhabitants)*. The law provided any settlement over 2000 or 3000 people to have a place where people could meet for collective activities: association meetings, trade union meetings, but also any non-formal cluster purposing to debate any subject. More than in many other cities, those *Locaux Collectifs Residentiels* have been a real success.

PRACTICAL UTOPIAS

These elements are intermingled in the narratives that I have collected from the first inhabitants, and they cross through the written material I have consulted. These inhabitants have to be interpreted in terms of the social conditions they shared. Most of them were couples with young children. Parents met at school waiting for their children, or during extracurricular activities; they shared common concerns about school, but also the housing, the neighbourhood and the development of public space. They began to help each other looking after children, then joined school association to organise a school feast. During summertime, they met for barbecues in their gardens.

At that time, there was a very favourable ideological backdrop, a political atmosphere that sustained social innovation and urban utopias. Following the architects, the role of the specific urbanism and architecture can be assumed in the quality of the neighbourhood sociality. Some inhabitants highlighted the layout of their house or their apartment that preserved intimacy while fostering social exchange with the neighbour, the private gardens that gave opportunity for discussion, the large number of pedestrian paths that favoured walking and bicycle riding. The free urban configuration is considered by many as the main factor of the quality of local relationships: 'So, we don't meet very often, because people move a lot, but there are many little places and spaces, between houses, here and there, where the children can play, and open to interaction between inside and outside, with large windows and the prohibition of the planting of hedges around the gardens and the houses' told us a man we interviewed. For many, Villeneuve d'Ascq was a place to experiment with dreams of a more convivial life in a town similar to a village. However, its social configuration and the urban design are not enough to explain why Villeneuve d'Ascq was supposed to be a little bit different. People evoke something like a common view shared by the majority of the neighbourhood, a common will to promote friendly relationships and local exchanges. There was a special spirit that had stamped its mark on the people's consciousness of this generation.

Let's take the example of François, a pioneer who became interested in the project while he was a university student. He does not hesitate to compare this period with the American frontier.

'There was a very common view about what we expected there. This had been going on fifteen or twenty years. Everybody moved in more or less at the same time, and I can say that everybody made a real choice to live here, and they came with a real pioneer spirit, as those people who left home to discover a new world, to build a new world, with a new way of life. It was a very exciting thing, very fascinating'.

Thanks to this pioneer spirit, to this neighbourly friendliness, thanks also to the subdivision by-law that forbade the building of walls or the planting of tall sheltering hedgerows between each property, nobody was isolated and nevertheless everybody's intimacy was preserved.

In those neighbourhoods and subdivisions of neighbourhoods that had been planned in order to favour social exchange, people were encouraged to practice local democracy, initiate dialogue among themselves, and to participate in collective activities and solidarity. That generation, who had more or less participated ten years prior to the May 1968 events, was still full of dreams of a better world and hoped to put them into practice in this new town.

In one borough I have researched, architects built a lot of circular lots that were not common in France at that time. Property management associations had been created by the EPALE in each settlement in order to manage local problems and to be the point of contact for public authorities. However, several of them became lobbying groups not only for defending inhabitants' interests against promoters, but also against the government agencies and the city's politicians. Rapidly, they also assured the welcoming of new people and became supports for local exchanges. Their members invited each other for each other for a drink, some of them joined together to buy a collective lawn-mower, one could ask neighbours to watch one's children or grandparents. Gardens and children were two great subjects of mutual aid. People also organized regularly local parties: barbecue parties, 'moules-frites' parties (Mussels-French potatoes parties) and jumble sales. The most famous has been the 'feux de la St-Jean' (St. John's fires) that were organised on the 24th of June every year. Created by the parents of pupils of the neighbourhood, this feast attracted the inhabitants both of the neighbourhood and beyond.

One element is important for a utopia to be practical: it has to be shared, and it was in Villeneuve d'Ascq. A shared feature, which connects dreams and reality, is quoted by the pioneers and many of the stakeholders to the social networks we met. Professionals, architects who built the city, activists or ordinary householders use the same formula to characterize the city: the word ouverture or openness. Villeneuve d'Ascq would be the city of openness. It would be home to openness to new ideas, to new technologies, to new people. The development boasted of its gardens, public areas, its architecture, and of the relationships between neighbours. Nevertheless, that part of this storytelling has more to do with mythology than with reality.

Conclusion: Memories and Heritage in Villeneuve d'Ascq: 'Weak Exchanges' Make 'Weak Heritages' for Preserving Local Attachments

The story of Villeneuve d'Ascq can be seen or read as a modern epopee. It is the way it is usually reported in some books and articles (Percq and Stievenard 1980); it is the way it was told by several of the people who have been involved in the project. It is also the story reported by the pioneers.

However, in 2010, the official website of Villeneuve d'Ascq exposed another story: a town rooted in the most ancient past of the country after archaeologists found a Roman villa. Every cross along the roads, every farm, and every chapel had been carefully investigated and were exposed on the web site; the dramatic story of the 40 people executed in 1944 by the Nazis in the village of Ascq was largely told. Everything seemed to be made in order to forget the singular history of the town.[5]

Actually, I can say that several memories of the town cohabitate with several heritages. The utopias we are talking about took their place, even if they were not asserted in the official history. They were claimed by the candidates in the electoral period in order to mobilize old and young militants; they were claimed by local associations in order to create a better balance of strength with the local government. All those who defended the idea that Villeneuve d'Ascq must not grow up claimed them, as did the opponents to the construction of a new football stadium in 2010. May we qualify 'heritage' as the re-iteration of those narratives and practices?

The narratives we collected have a common point: they refer to the presence of the people in the place, they say that Villeneuve d'Ascq is not a city of politicians, architects, and technicians of urban management,

---

[5] It is to be said that the new web site is very different: the new town seems not to reject anymore its history.

but a city appropriated by its dwellers who recognise themselves above all by the ward where they live. That is heritage because it is determined by the commitment of local communities dwelling in the place; it is expressed in the diversity of neighbourhoods, and the memory of those utopias gives people the feeling of getting closer to both the past and their contemporary environment. This heritage does not make any distinction between material and immaterial, between tangible and intangible goods, between social and economic resources for the local social network. Its specificity is to be particularly sensitive to the mixture of social and material exchanges. These take shape by the blending of individuals and collective stories that are considered worthy of perpetuation for the common good. It belongs to social practices that are barely visible from outside the place where people usually live.

I call them 'weak heritages' because they are micro-local heritages that are not supposed to be known by the local authorities and which are not supposed to be shared by or shown to strangers. This is not really new, it has been the usual functioning of local groups of inhabitants as described by sociologists and ethnographers for decades. But henceforth those appropriations of the environment inscribe themselves in larger frameworks. Discourses on locality, symbols, and values are not strictly identical as they used to be twenty or thirty years before because they are irrigated by the mainstream of the heritagization process that emerges at every level of the public sphere. The newness is not the expression of local solidarities but the articulations that people make with the past of their community, in their wish to preserve their living environment in the name of a major value that we call heritage. Heritage is supposed to be able to manage the different levels of what one works to save. Through this weak and local heritage, inhabitants do not oppose the 'system'; they create something beside it that they have the ability to keep under control.

People find opportunities in their history and culture in order to defend themselves against 'the spiral of individualization (which) destroys the given foundations of social coexistence' (Beck and Beck 2002: XXI). Weak heritage is not a weapon to fight against capitalism, but a value that allows adaptation to different levels of social life. In Villeneuve d'Ascq, the heritagisation of utopias recall previous practices that allow the taking of time for social relationships in the neighbourhood. To recall the founding utopias of the town is a manner of instituting the time of the neighbourhood community as an alternative to the stresses and demands of the modern life. One main advantage of heritage is its supposed predictability. It shows that social skills are still useful. The memory of the old time is evoked for preserving the intimacy of the intermediary space that has been patiently shaped by householders between the private and the public spheres. An intermediary space that lays at the front of the home's door and inside the lot, and that is a main stake of the dwellers. In a world characterized by instability of work and the risk of social anomy, housing and its social surroundings can appear as a good investment, far from that of commodification. Better than an analysis in terms of domination, as well as in terms of a dialectic process between top/down and bottom/up movements, as usually undertaken in heritage studies, I observed that it rises when local linkages (i.e., neighbourhood) seem to decrease. It is an adaptation to the merging patterns of capitalism and modernity.

REFERENCES

Adell, N., R.F. Bendix, C. Bortolotto, and M. Tauschek (eds.). 2015. *Between Imagined Communities and Communities of Practice: Participation, Territory and the Making of Heritage*. Göttingen: Universitätsverlag Göttingen.

Anheier, H., and Y. Raj Isar (eds.). 2011. *Heritage, Memory and Identity*. London: Sage.

Assayag, J. 2005. *La mondialisation vue d'ailleurs. L'Inde désorientée*. Paris: Editions du Seuil.

Auclair, E., and G. Fairclough (eds.). 2015. *Theory and Practice in Heritage and Sustainability. Between Past and Future*. London and New York: Routledge.

Beck, U., and G.E. Beck. 2002. *Individualization. Institutionalized Individualism and Its Social and Political Consequences*. London: Sage.

Boltanski, L., and E. Chiapello. 1999. *Le Nouvel esprit du capitalisme*. Paris: Editions du Seuil.

Boltanski, L., and R. Esquerre. 2014. La collection, une forme neuve du capitalisme. La mise en valeur du passé et ses effets. *Les Temps modernes*, 679, 5–72.

Boswell, R. 2011. Multiple Heritages, Multiple Identities: The Southwest Indian Ocean. In *Heritage, Memory and Identity*, ed. H. Anheier and Y. Raj Isar, 169–176. Los Angeles, London, New Dehli, Singapore, and Washington, DC: Sage.

Cardon, D. 2010. *La démocratie internet. Promesses et limites*. Paris: La république des idées.

Choay, F. 1965. *L'Urbanisme, utopies et réalités: Une anthologie*. Paris: Editions du Seuil.

Cohen, D. 2006. *Trois leçons sur la société post-industrielle*. Paris: Éditions du Seuil.

Graham, B., and P. Howard (eds.). 2008. *Heritage and Identity*. Aldershot, Burlington: The Ashgate Research Companion.

Greffe, X. 2011. L'économie politique du patrimoine culturel. De la médaille au rhizome. Openarchive.icomos.org/1307/1/IV-3-Article6_Greffe.pdf.

Hannerz, U. 1992. *Cultural Complexity. Studies in the Social Organisation of Meaning*. New York: Columbia University Press.

Harrison, R. 2013. *Heritage. Critical Approaches*. London and New York: Routledge.

Harvey, D. 1990. *The Condition of Post Modernity. An Enquiry into the Origins of Cultural Change*. Cambridge and Oxford: Blackwell.

Hewison, R. 1987. *The Heritage Industry*. London: Methuen.

Internationale de l'imaginaire. 2012. *Le patrimoine, oui, mais quel patrimoine?* Paris: Babel.

Kancel, S., J. Itty, M. Weill, and B. Durieux. 2013. *L'apport de la culture à l'économie en France*. Paris: Inspection générale des finances.

Labadi, S. 2013. *UNESCO, Cultural Heritage, and Outstanding Universal Value-Based Analyses of the World Heritage and Intangible Cultural Heritage Conventions*. Lanham: AltaMira Press.

Lefebvre, B., and M. Rautenberg. 2010. *Utopies et mythologies urbaines à Villeneuve d'Ascq*. Villeneuve d'Ascq: Presses du Septentrion.

Lowenthal, D. 1985. *The Past is a Foreign Country*. Cambridge: Cambridge University Press.

Micoud, A. 1996. Musées et patrimoine: deux types de rapport aux choses et au temps. *Hermès, La Revue* 2 (20): 115–123.

Morell, M., and J. Franquesa. 2011. Playing Snakes and Ladders in Ciutat de Mallorca: An Ethnographic Approach to the Production of the Neighbourhood Scale. In *Contested Mediterranean Spaces. Ethnographic Essays in Honour of Charles Tilly*, ed. M. Kousis, T. Selwyn, and D. Clark, 195–220. New York and Oxford: Berghahm Books.

Morisset, L.K. 2009. *Des régimes d'authenticité. Essai sur la mémoire patrimoniale*. Rennes: Presses universitaires de Rennes.

Percq, P., and J.M. Stievenard. 1980. *Villeneuve d'Ascq, une ville est née*. Paris: Cana.

Rautenberg, M. 2012. Le patrimoine dans les projets urbains, entre gentrification et revendications. In *Patrimoine et développement durable*, ed. N. Dris, 35–44. Rennes: PUR.

Rautenberg, M. 2015. L'urbanité comme patrimoine de la ville. In *Diogène. Placing Urban Anthropology*, ed. W. Kaltenbacher, I. Pardo, and G. Prato, Special Issue, 90–102.

Sennett, R. 2006. *The Culture of the New Capitalism*. New Haven, London: Yale University Press.
Smith, L. 2006. *Uses of Heritage*. London and New York: Routledge.
Thrift, N. 2005. *Knowing Capitalism*. London: Sage.

CHAPTER 17

Anthropology in a Neoliberal World

Paul Durrenberger

SOCIETY OR ECONOMY?

Taken together, these studies show that peoples' experience shapes their patterns of thought—culture—and that changing conditions create changing patterns of culture. The solidarity and community of industrial workplaces has been replaced by neoliberal images of individualism in an unrestrained market economy devoid of human or community values. Thus the economy does not serve, sustain, or provision society, but erodes solidarity and community, as Spyridakis points out in his introduction. It becomes a national issue when such significant portions of the population are exposed to the dangers of precarious livelihood, as has happended in Greece.

All of these papers point to the increasing polarization of wealth as a capitalist class transfers value from its producers to itself, and in the process creates the deindustrialized zones of Europe, with attempts made to transform former industrial areas into artistic sites in an illusion of creativity. That may be appropriate in a postmodern neoliberal world based on the fundamental illusion of money as the motivating power of our species, as Hornborg suggests. Illusion begets illusion. Soon we

P. Durrenberger (✉)
University of Iowa, Iowa City, IA, USA

© The Author(s) 2018
M. Spyridakis (ed.), *Market Versus Society*, Palgrave Studies in Urban Anthropology, https://doi.org/10.1007/978-3-319-74189-5_17

are unmoored from any palpable reality, afloat in a sea of postmodern imagery.

For anthropologists this poses the question of whether we want to serve solidarity in a war between classes or perpetuate illusions to serve the capitalist class. I will return to these issues as I see them playing out in the United States, but first, a few words about the ethnographic bases for what I have just said.

The Ethnographic Foundation

Misunderstandings between older industrial and younger post-industrial people of Le Soleil, France are based on the difference between a culture based on labour solidarity and industry on the one hand and the contemporary rhetoric and policies of renewal of the deindustrialized landscape to repurpose arms factories as artistic venues to attract the creative class.

D'Aloisio suggests that our ethnographies that focus on locales cannot detect the causal variables that determine the shapes of those locales., For instance, the official corruption and assistance that accompanied the FIAT factory's opening and subsequent downsizing in a southern Italian community with a weak union structure that was attractive to the auto maker. During a downturn in 2011 and the constriction of incomes with the resultant negative effects on the local economy, former workers dealt with the decline in incomes by engaging their networks of support. The 2014 merger of FIAT with an American firm involved the workers and the community in a global enterprise and new forms of insecurity.

These networks of support, Prato suggests, are the same clientism that many hold responsible for industrial failures in Southern Italy where the Right and Left agreed on the desirability of state control of such networks. Fascists, Socialists, Communists, and Catholics have all, in their various ways, attempted to break the ties of clientism to make room for state policies amid the backward uneducated lingering peasant reactionaries. After the Second Wolrd War, the World Bank offered loans that some argued should be used for agrarian development and others for industrial development; these loans were not articulated with any local systems and resulted in ineffective local opposition, and when completed, environmental health problems that affected agricultural production. As a result, a move to create national parks and increase tourism via a propaganda program promoted by the Chambers of Commerce was initiated.

This historical view shows the importance of policies and politics in regional economies and suggests that even neoliberalism needs the support of political structures and that the Italian political elite is incapable of working in the interests of the people of the region.

A Farmer's Work in France shows us the relationship between the daily work of French livestock farmers and the global market. French policy maintains small production units while EU policies favor larger, more capitalized operations to the detriment of the environment, the animals, and people as well as the continued existence of small farms. The purpose of farmers to preserve landscapes and rural ways of life would be unrecognizable in the thoroughly industrialized agriculture of the United States, as would the concept of work as providing more than income as a reward to workers, or the notion of autonomous work. These factors engender debates between supporters of each perspective. The author describes how such remote factors shape the daily work of livestock farmers.

Zlolniski examines how neoliberal policies and trade agreements favored industrial production of vegetables in Northern Mexico for the market in the United States and how those processes shape the alienating and strictly disciplined conditions of work for the Mexican workers, creating conditions of class and ethnic inequality that have evoked workers' resistance.

Carrier likens neoliberalism to bank robbery because, as Woody Guthrie said in his song about Pretty Boy Floyd, the Outlaw, 'Some men rob with a six gun and some with a fountain pen'. Economy versus society? As Margaret Thatcher famously said, there is no society, only individuals. Thus, no obligation, reciprocity or any of the relationships that make a society and any financial 'punishments' handed down by the state are simply the cost of doing business.

South Africa's Steve Biko said that the most potent weapon of the oppressor is the mind of the oppressed. So, when retail workers in Israel began to believe that the market naturally structured all relationships, they abandoned any political orientation. In Israel we see the global transformation of state-led socialism to neoliberalism in microcosm. Stewards of workers' committees who stand between labour and employers have accepted the inevitability of the eradication of their jobs as the work moves to China. In Israel, prolonged strikes only prove the weakness of labour and the strength of capital, and unions negotiate the terms of their own surrender and then help management run their companies professionally and prudently in terms of the market. They relegate social-ism to anachronistic and useless ideology. Whatever power workers may have comes not from organization but from alliances with business experts and ownership of corporation stock, the antithesis of worker soli-darity. Under these conditions, radical thought, Nissim suggests, arises when anger meets frustration. The acceptance of neoliberalism rests on the denial of its political content and acceptance of its assumptions as ontologically true. While there are organic neoliberal intellectuals to shape workers' committees' responses, there are no organic social-ist intellectuals to create any alternatives and the committees remain enmeshed in the system that oppresses them. Yet, as in Mexico, there are spontaneous organizations that indicate some return to socialist ideas.

Olympic bids promise to bring benefits, though they often exacerbate inequality. The London Olympics of 2012 were an exercise in mass gen-trification. Because there is no consensus on how to quantify contribu-tion of sport to GDP or compare costs and benefits of bids with results, Olympic games go to bidders who have the grandest vision. This vision involves developing the most effective media campaign, which focuses on an undefinable legacy that is supposed to offset the costs of developing an Olympic campaign and delivering an acceptable venue. These mega-pitches join the unreality of neoliberalism.

Media expand the range of imagined communities and graft onto them newly created traditions dubbed heritage. This moniker is used to exploit—economically via tourism that is dependent on the declining dis-posable income of the middle class. Villeneuve d'Ascq is a new French planned town whose inhabitants revolted and took it over. The physi-cal layout was supposed to foster interaction and democracy and in fact has provided an escape from neoliberal chaos and perhaps, with the new organizations in Mexico and Israel, some hope.

Alf Hornborg points to the widespread suffering neoliberalism has wrought. Neoliberalism is based on markets and markets are corollaries of the cultural artifact of money, and as Polanyi pointed out years ago, to regulate markets and money requires a state. There is, additionally, a contradiction between producing commodities for markets and pro-ducing sustenance, so that the spread of markets has been at the cost of human sustenance. Neoliberalism has systemically degraded land, labour, and money around the planet. Money operates according to the logic of magic. Neoliberalism's consequences are universally deleterious, but because it is a cultural construct, it can be changed.

In Argentina after the Second World War, the government helped to expand manufacturing to absorb agricultural workers from the countryside displaced by the industrialization of agriculture. Workers organized unions to protect their rights and, with the government, provide certain reproductive functions such as health care and education. The neoliberalization process fostered by the 1976 dictatorship passed virtually all such functions into the hands of private enterprises, from the provision of water to health care. There followed the loss of the rights of workers and the declines in wages, working conditions, and employment. Thus was labour subjugated to capital. In the steel industry, the process resulted in the creation of a number of small operations to provide specialized services that had been part of the larger firm, thus de-industrializing the production process and making labour precarious and re-defining its relationship with capital. Soul's dynamic ethnography throughout this development shows us how these processes affected working people and their families and resulted in the disorganization of the Argentine working class and the emergence of union activism under these changed conditions, again suggesting some optimism.

Like Soul, Pardo injects a welcomed note of empirical analysis to argue the limits to democracy and legitimacy set by the exercise of power that neoliberalism encourages. This is balanced by the social dimensions of the exercise of individual choice in a situation of deepening inequality, high unemployment, inaccessible credit, and urban decay on the one hand and the privileging of the few on the other, which makes the distinction between the legal and the legitimate problematic and provides the context for the mobilization of individual networks of relationships to provide a living.

Via detailed local ethnographic and historical work, Reigada examines the limits of the tolerable and intolerable that result from contradictions that face small strawberry producers in southern Spain because of their involvement in global agrifood chains and how their identity, rooted in their pride of being self-made, makes them vulnerable to feelings of grievance, injustice, and vulnerability to show the relationships between monetary value and cultural and moral values.

Streinzer shows the invisible hand of the market crushing people in Greece and the role of cooperatives in softening the pain of German extraction of value from Greece in an examination of the dichotomy of market versus society in everyday activities and emotional responses to situations as they arise, creating a political space.

THE REALM OF ILLUSION

If the illusory is manifest in the neoliberalism of these examples, in the United States it is epidemic. Much of the world is trying to understand how Donald Trump could have won the American presidential election of 2016. They haven't been paying attention. It's not a question of ideology or identity, it's a question of class and Americans don't want to admit to being a land divided by class divisions. As Joe Baegent put it in 2007, 'that ain't no underclass; it's 250 million rugged individuals being pissed on'.

It was to them that Donald Trump, himself the son of privilege, appealed with his ignorance and gaucherie that matched their own.

Late in the 1980s, when white collar managerial jobs were being exported along with blue collar manufacturing jobs, Katherine Newman began to investigate the differences in white and blue collar responses to joblessness in the United States. She saw that while the guiding ideology of white collar workers, meritocratic individualism, dictated that success is the natural and just return to demonstrated merit, that they still deserved their income and social positions. With this self-congratulatory smugness came the opposite proposition, that those who did not enjoy success deserved what they got. Poverty, for instance, was the fault of the poor. When unemployed white collar workers were in that position, then, their ideology dictated that they also deserved what they got. Many were depressed or turned to alcohol or other drugs. Meanwhile, Newman argued, working people did not blame themselves for losing their jobs; they knew it was not a consequence of their actions or merit, but simply the operation of corporations that left them without incomes (Newman 1988).

In the mid-1990s when Suzan Erem and I were doing ethnographic work with unions in Chicago and Pennsylvania, I tested that proposition by several approaches to conclude that while Newman's notions made sense, they did not match the ethnography (Durrenberger 2001). In fact, working people subscribed to the ideology of meritocratic individualism. Later, Dimitra Doukas and I (2008), concluded that the ideology was only widespread among the working class because it had been successfully propagated by a thoroughgoing cultural revolution that started toward the end of the nineteenth century when the powerful trusts consolidated and began transforming themselves into corporations. This transformation required a cultural logic to accompany and justify it.

Thus was the discipline of economics created and endowed in universities in the United States and given the mantle of science as a way of proving that corporate rapacity was natural, inevitable, justifiable and even desirable. The invisible hand of the market was the hand of god guiding human affairs. Or the hand of nature. In either case, inevitable. And the discipline of economics could reveal the inner workings of these mysteries by the uses of mathematics to make it appear to be scientific (Doukas 2003).

The discipline of economics is the codification and formalization of the ideology that was invented and propagated to favor the interests of the emerging corporations of the nineteenth century as they evolved legal structures to support their transformation from the earlier trusts to the modern corporate organizations that are the dominant institutions of today's global economic and political systems. This ideology has become hegemonic. Any discussion of economic life is measured against its tenets. It provides the ideological underpinnings of neoliberal political practice.

Yet, as Doukas and I (2008) show, working-class people of America do not universally hold this ideology. Some hold an ideology derived from a pre-corporate agro-industrial economic system. Doukas (2003) calls this the Gospel of Work, the idea that work creates all value. This is in opposition to the ideology of economics, which is based on the Gospel of Wealth articulated by Andrew Carnegie, that wealth naturally creates more wealth and should be managed by the most capable people who prove their abilities by becoming wealthy. Like Donald Trump.

Corporate wealth created organizations such as the National Manufacturers' Association and the Chambers of Commerce to manage a continuous program of culture change. In spite of these efforts, the American cultural revolution was not universally successful. In response, there developed two poles of cultural coherence with a complex topography of mixed allegiances between them. None of these stances map well onto the dichotomies of social or political thought such as left/right or capitalist/non-capitalist (Doukas 2003: 167).

Marshall Sahlins (1972) outlined the basic components of household economies in his *Stone Age Economics*. The Gospel of Work grows organically from the household economies that have been the basis of most economic systems from simple to complex until the period of corporate hegemony. Some deride household economies as static, incapable of growth because their chief aim is simply to produce sufficient means for the support of the household. No more. Such systems cannot imagine, much less support, the idea or the actuality of a virtuous cycle of infinite costless growth imagined by economists who have overseen the near destruction of our planet in their realization of it. Household economies run on what feminist economist Nancy Folbre (2001) calls 'love,' reciprocity, mutuality, and sharing, the antithesis of the rapacity that fuels capitalism. People value property and things to the extent that they are useful, not as distant or abstract investments. Households form communities of mutuality and that mutuality is important to each, whereas community is irrelevant to capitalism, corporations, and the Gospel of Wealth.

World views built on the foundations of these two economic orientations are virtually unintelligible to each other. Proponents of each, if one may call unwitting participants in 'common sense' proponents, speak past one another in incomprehension as surely as members of different cultures do if they can find a common language. Such standing misunderstandings is the stuff of anthropological lore, but in the United States Suzan and I saw this kind of situation repeatedly when union workers negotiated with employers to establish the contracts that govern the terms of their work. The employers tended to argue in terms of economic categories and budgets in which labour is one of many abstract components, whereas workers based their positions on the needs of their households. Each side was incomprehensible to the other. Only relative power can determine the resolution and it's been a long time since American unions had sufficient power to win such a face-off with corporations. Defeat breeds anger.

Journalist Bageant (2007: 89) doesn't hypothesize working class anger; he experiences it, and places its source in the daily insults working people suffer from their powerless positions with respect to their employers, all levels of government, and the managerial middle class, including academics and journalists, all of whom share a middle class educated liberal disdain for them and describe them with terms like 'gaucherie'. Ethnographic evidence suggests that some working people have internalised the ideology of meritocratic individualism (Durrenberger 2001). The contrast between that ideology and the everyday lives of working people, whether or not they've ever known a wage-paying job, may be a source of inner rage as Baegent suggests.

Journalistic accounts suggest a working-class 'them' to a middle-class readership that has the leisure and inclination to contemplate such matters. Such stories assume a cultural continuity across class boundaries that our findings have forced Doukas and me to question. We believe that the ideological spectrum of the United States is more diverse than existing accounts have represented, and that its diversity can be accurately measured with a combination of ethnographic and statistical methods. To this end, in 2009 we recruited a group of colleagues to work on a three-year ethnographic program that we hoped the National Science Foundation would fund. Our application to them was not successful, so that project waits for a more promising time when it makes more sense to funders.

Economists suppose that markets spring from the actions of self-interested individuals. This self-interest they style 'rationality' and anthropologists have long discussed this term and defined rational behavior as that for which the ends are mutually coherent and the means are appropriate to the ends. One of Malinowski's motives in his Trobriand ethnography was to ascertain whether Trobrianders were the rational 'economic men' of economic theory or whether the theory was ethnocentric. He found the theory to be ethnocentric. Whatever their differences, it seems that most anthropologists agree on the premise that what appears to be irrational behavior is either ritual or informed by some system of rationality that is different from the observer's calculus. Doukas and I proposed to investigate whether different systems of rationality are characteristic of different class positions in the United States, and how they are different.

While some observers may see anger and failure, ethnography suggests a different process that incorporates place and history in a distinctive set of class-specific, local values. Doukas, working in an area of high residential stability, found that people remember ancestors and events that have been obscured or obliterated by official histories. In this light, the present-day sense of 'apathy' is constructed on the repeated failure of numerous attempts to remedy injustices—zoning battles lost in city councils dominated by real-estate interests, failed resistance to urban renewal projects promoted by the same interests, failed attempts to block highway routing decisions promoted by developers and non-local traffic and highway experts—the residuals of repeated political actions, including unions, that ended in repeated defeat. In the United States the working class is a defeated class in a long-standing war. In the distinctive set of values that these people maintain, they can be moral superiors, and the 'people who think they're better than us' are just plain wrong. Doukas and I proposed that the critique of dominant values that Doukas observed ethnographically (2003) is a class-based cultural processes, rather than the *sui generis* sense of anger or internalised sense of failure that journalists report.

Kendall Thu and I (1997a, b) observed similar struggles in process in North Carolina as rural residents banded together to resist industrial swine production but faced defeat on every front. We observed the same process in Iowa as small diverse farms were replaced by large industrial ones. After generations of such defeats, people may develop a cynical view of democracy or conclude that voting cannot make a difference. Thus they join the non-voting majority rather than either national political party. Thus can a ruling corporate class extinguish democracy.

Finally the traces of class struggle are obliterated in the re-writing of history to make it consistent with the Gospel of Wealth. So, for instance, Suzan (2008) and I found that the official history of the Port of Charleston, South Carolina had expunged all reference to slaves and to black people. So, for another instance, the farmers' uprising of 1931 in Iowa has been omitted from all history books. Every place can provide its own examples that leave only living memory and local landmarks as fast fading repositories.

In our proposal to the NSF, Doukas and I asked what American voters who vote for Republicans are voting for? Do they ever have a chance to vote for their economic interests? Do national issues ever translate to local concerns? Perhaps they are voting simply to be left alone. Or to lift the increasingly heavy yoke of capitalism from their necks to satisfy the needs of their households as their jobs are deported in a global market. That would be consistent with the oldest popular ideology in the United States: get the people who are 'better than us' (aristocrats, bureaucrats, city people, the middle class) off our backs, let us enjoy the fruits of our own labour and we'll be fine, because *we're willing to work*. Our ethnographic experience suggests that if we asked working-class Republican voters about it, they'd say that they *are* voting for their economic interests.

The Politics of Unreality

Greider (1992) argued that neither American political party is responsive to the electorate. Teixeira and Rogers (2000) agree. Economist John Kenneth Galbraith (1992) argued that it is rational for most Americans not to vote at all because they rightly observe that the outcomes of elections have very little impact on their daily lives. If it doesn't matter who wins or loses, isn't it rational to devote *no* energy to voting, to abstain from the process, as the majority of eligible electors do in the United States?

Another economist, Michael D. Yates (2003) suggested that US policy differences are expressions of the disparity within neoclassical economics between libertarians who advocate a wider role for markets and a narrower role for government versus liberals who promote a wider involvement of government and a constriction of markets. Both share a common understanding of economic processes based on neoclassical assumptions, which Yates argues fail to meet any empirical test of adequacy. His conclusion reinforces Doukas's finding that economics is an ideological construct rather than an empirical enquiry. This becomes especially clear when governments, whose functions are supposedly limited by neoliberal practices and institutions, provide such liberal support for financial institutions—subsidies for the capitalist class—as Spyridakis describes in the introduction, making the states hostages to their economic elites.

Teixeira and Rogers (2000) suggest that neither US party addresses the difficulties that working-class voters experience as a result of the neoliberal economy: health insurance, retirement, education and training, tensions between work and family. 'Competing in a global economy', they say (2000: xi), 'is making it harder, not easier, to ensure one's family a decent standard of living'. Are people who don't have any margin for error in their lives withholding their votes in anger or resentment or resistance toward a system that punishes them, even in a booming economy? Or do they express their experience as a kind of pent-up anger that can be released in local violence, in a racial slur, or in voting for the apotheosis of rage, Donald Trump.

While knowledge of background variables for voters allows us to play endless speculative games with voting data, voting data cannot help us to understand the outlooks or practices of that majority of Americans who never vote. Only ethnography can do that.

In summary, there are converging empirical and theoretical studies as well as ample anecdotal evidence to suggest relationships among class, family structure, and political values in the United States. At the same time, there is the suggestion that everyday concerns do not translate straightforwardly into political alternatives that are meaningful to voters or in the American electoral system. Spyridakis shows in his introduction how massive vulnerability is normalized and made non-political so that there is no political response—at least within the current political structures—and to remove from responsibility those economists and policy makers who are responsible. They have made the choices; they have created the conditions; they are responsible. If current political structures cannot return dignity and security to human life on this planet, then it is obviously time to change them.

Hence the interpretation of voting patterns is not an adequate guide to the cultural constructs of Americans (Teixeira and Rogers 2000).

Doukas and I suggested that the resolution of these issues would require empirical ethnographic work in the United States to ascertain how working-class culture and capitalist-class cultures interact in practice. We are convinced that anthropology can contribute accuracy and insight to this important national conversation, but that opportunity awaits others who can organize such a program of research because it is well beyond the reach of a single person or even a few people working individually.

ANTHROPOLOGY AND CLASS STRUGGLE

My initial critique of Ostrom's theory of collective action (Durrenberger 2009) was that she had not honored the cultural variability that we see ethnographically. There's nothing wrong with that critique; it is what brought some reality to the discussion of the tragedy of the commons and showed that it isn't necessary or universal. But I think that Ostrom's arguments are more deeply flawed than just taking insufficient account of ethnographic facts in the definitions of her categories. Economists Stiglitz (2003) and Galbraith (1992) are among those who have suggested that if economics had a feedback loop between theory and fact in the manner of scientific enquiry, it would have ceased to exist. That it hasn't suggests that it is an ideology akin to religion rather than a science.

The main flaw is in the basic assumption of economics: methodological individualism, the idea that institutions are the totality of individual decisions and their outcomes. Other anthropologists have argued more eloquently than I can that this assumption is a cultural artifact of capitalism, not a fact or even a reasonable assumption. Sahlins (2000) devotes an essay to the cultural matrix and history of the underlying assumptions of the dismal science. Doukas (2003) shows that economics as a discipline is an important component of the corporate-sponsored cultural revolution. It was promoted by the backers of the revolution to achieve scientific status for the doctrine of wealth that would serve their purposes so well. Rappaport (1979: 236) points out that economics defines rationality as competitive activities that pit people against each other and is, by necessity, antisocial.

Thus, economics defines a kind of humanity that is quite different from the social animals that anthropology knows—creatures that evolved over five million years. The evolutionary view of humanity has the strong helping the weak in solidarity. Goldschmidt (2006) argues that what made us human is the selective advantage that flexibility conferred on groups whose members could be more committed to serving group interests than replicating themselves—groups that were more committed to collective action than individual advancement.

Everything human, Goldschmidt argues, takes place in the 'gap between the encoded genetic instruction and behavioral performance' (2006: 18). In that fissure is culture, collective thought. Goldschmidt argues that we learn culture because of an inborn necessity to please those who are trying to teach us—a trait known as 'affect hunger'. The individuals and groups who could not transcend the first competitive evolutionary imperative—the selfish gene—with cooperation—collective action—have long since perished, unable to be sufficiently responsive to changing conditions of time and space.

In this sense, collective action is part of our species' evolutionary history. What needs to be explained is not collective action, but any departures from it. Thus, the questions we should try to answer are not 'Why is there collective action', or 'Why is there solidarity', or 'Why is there Society', but 'Why are there economists?' and other *departures* from collective action.

In the mid-1970s when I began teaching, I used to end my introductory anthropology courses with a lecture warning that if our species did not soon awaken to the dangers it had created, we would face destruction in a nuclear disaster. I grew up in the duck-and-cover drills of the cold war and the Cuban Missile Crisis that had many American seeking the shelter of the nearest bomb shelter. Though the clock of the Bulletin of Atomic Scientists is still dangerously near nuclear midnight, the widespread fear propaganda in the United States has shifted to terrorists and we no longer practice for our demises nor do we fear nuclear war. So that lecture became outdated.

Not only did it become outdated, but my perspective shifted as well. I began to see that from our beginnings in Africa we have had a long history as a species. As a species, often seemingly bent on killing one another, we have continued to prosper and grow. I began to think that nuclear disaster wouldn't destroy the whole species, only the white portions of it, allowing a new evolutionary process. And so with global pollution. Just as British moths could evolve from white to black in the ever-present coal dust of the industrial revolution, so might humans evolve to live with high levels of radiation, agricultural chemicals, and other pollutants. I changed my concluding lecture from a pessimistic one prophesying nuclear disaster to an optimistic one whose message was that where there is life there is hope.

But as I write these lines, I remind myself that it is a dimension of American culture always to look for happy endings and messages of hope to disguise the grim realities of everyday life of working people in the United States.

To be human is to be social. To be human in a neoliberal world, therefore, is to resist neoliberal governments and policies with everything we can bring to the task. That is our role as anthropologists and as people sharing this planet.

REFERENCES

Baegent, Joe. 2007. *Deer Hunting with Jesus: Dispatches from America's Class War*. New York: Random House.

Doukas, Dimitra. 2003. *Worked Over: The Corporate Sabotage of an American Community*. Ithica: Cornell University Press.

Durrenberger, E. Paul. 2001. Explorations of Class and Consciousness in the U.S. *Journal of Anthropological Research* 57 (1): 41–60.

———. 2009. The Last Wall to Fall: The Anthropology of Collective Action and Unions in the Global System. *Journal of Anthropological Research* 65 (1): 9–26.

Durrenberger, E. Paul, and Dimitra Doukas. 2008. Gospel of Wealth, Gospel of Work: Hegemony in the U.S. Working Class. *American Anthropologist* 110 (2): 214–224.

Durrenberger, E. Paul, and Kendall Thu. 1997a. Signals, Systems, and Environment in Industrial Food Systems. *Journal of Political Ecology* 4: 27–38.

———. 1997b. *Pigs, Profits, and Rural Communities*. Albany: State University of New York Press.

Erem, Suzan, and E. Paul Durrenberger. 2008. *On the Global Waterfront: The Fight to Free the Charleston Five*. New York: Monthly Review Press.

Folbre, Nancy. 2001. *The Invisible Heart: Economics and Family Values*. New York: New Press.

Galbraith, John Kenneth. 1992. *The Culture of Contentment*. Boston: Houghton Mifflin.

Goldschmidt, Walter. 2006. *The Bridge to Humanity: How Affect Hunger Trumps the Selfish Gene*. New York: Oxford University Press.

Greider, W. 1992. *Who Will Tell the People: The Betrayal of American Democracy*. New York: Simon and Schuster.

Newman, Katherine. 1988. *Falling from Grace: The Experience of Downward Mobility in the American Middle Class*. New York: Free Press.

Rappaport, Roy. 1979. *Ecology, Meaning, & Religion*. Berkeley: North Atlantic Books.

Sahlins, Marshall. 1972. *Stone Age Economics*. Chicago: Aldine.

———. 2000. *Culture in Practice: Selected Essays*. New York: Zone Books.

Stiglitz, Joseph. 2003. *Globalization and Its Discontents*. New York: Norton.

Teixeira, Ruy, and Joel Rogers. 2000. *America's Forgotten Majority: Why the White Working Class Still Matters*. New York: Basic Books.

Yates, Michael D. 2003. *Naming the System: Inequality and Work in the Global Economy*. New York: Monthly Review Press.

INDEX